IMAGES
of America

BANGOR

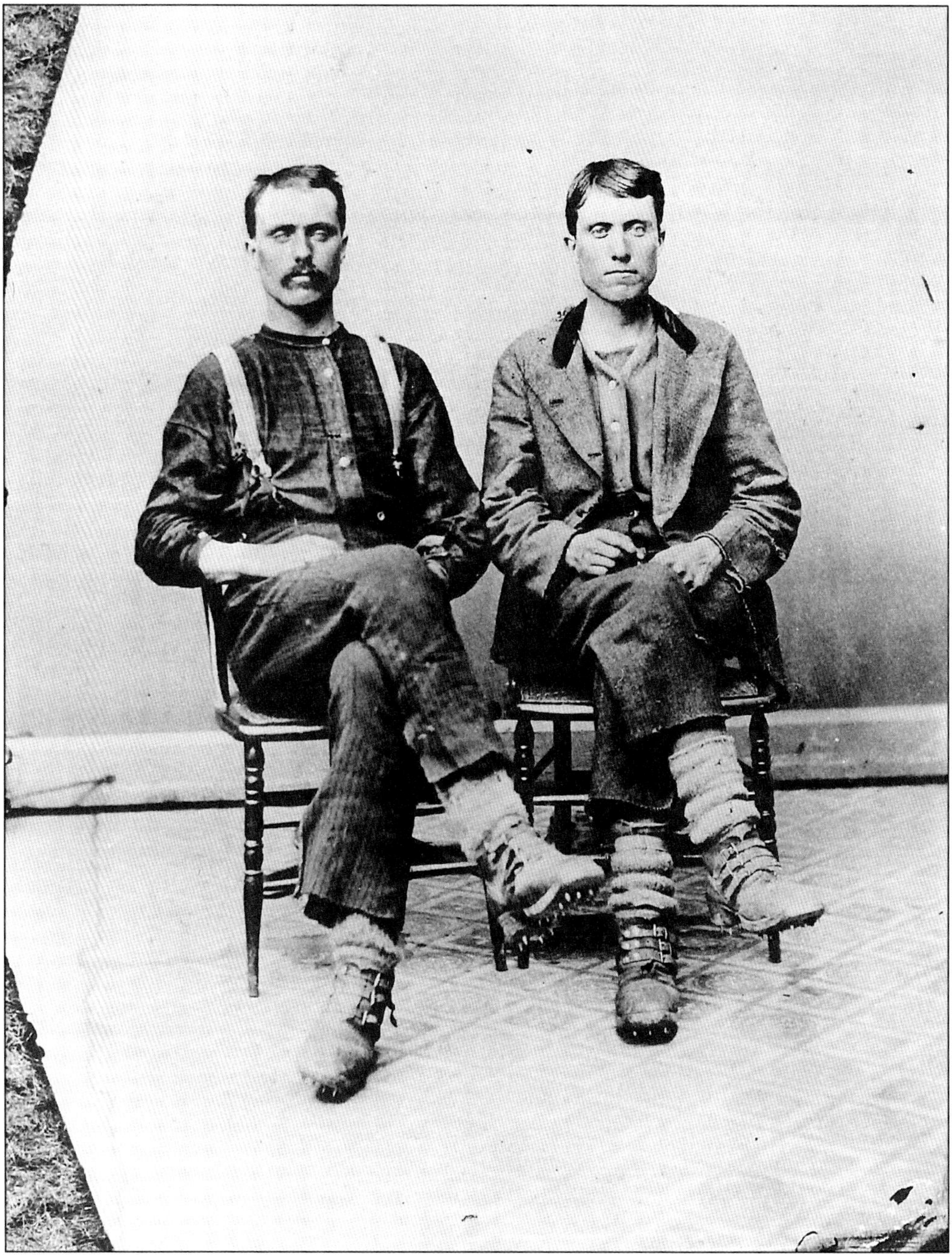

Penobscot river drivers, *c.* 1880s. Well-scrubbed and clean-shaven for the photographer, they proudly display the woolen stockings and spiked shoes of their trade.

IMAGES
of America

BANGOR

Compiled by
Richard R. Shaw

ARCADIA
PUBLISHING

ISBN 978-0-7385-3702-3

Published by Arcadia Publishing
Charleston, South Carolina

Printed in the United States of America

Library of Congress Catalog Card Number: 2004111105

For all general information contact Arcadia Publishing at:
Telephone 843-853-2070
Fax 843-853-0044
E-mail sales@arcadiapublishing.com
For customer service and orders:
Toll-Free 1-888-313-2665

Visit us on the Internet at www.arcadiapublishing.com

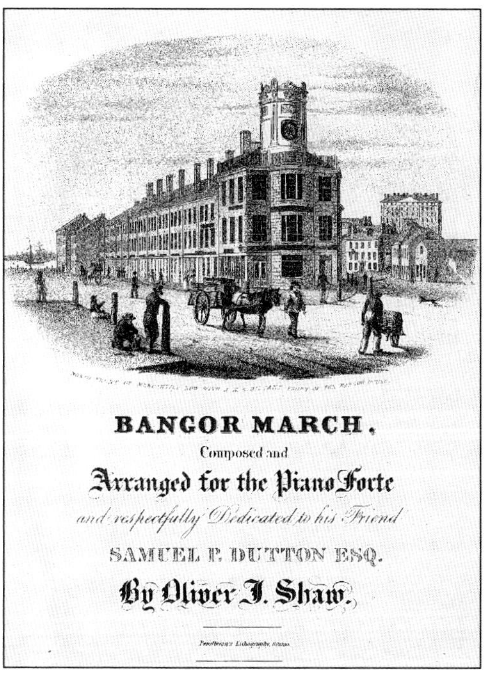

Contents

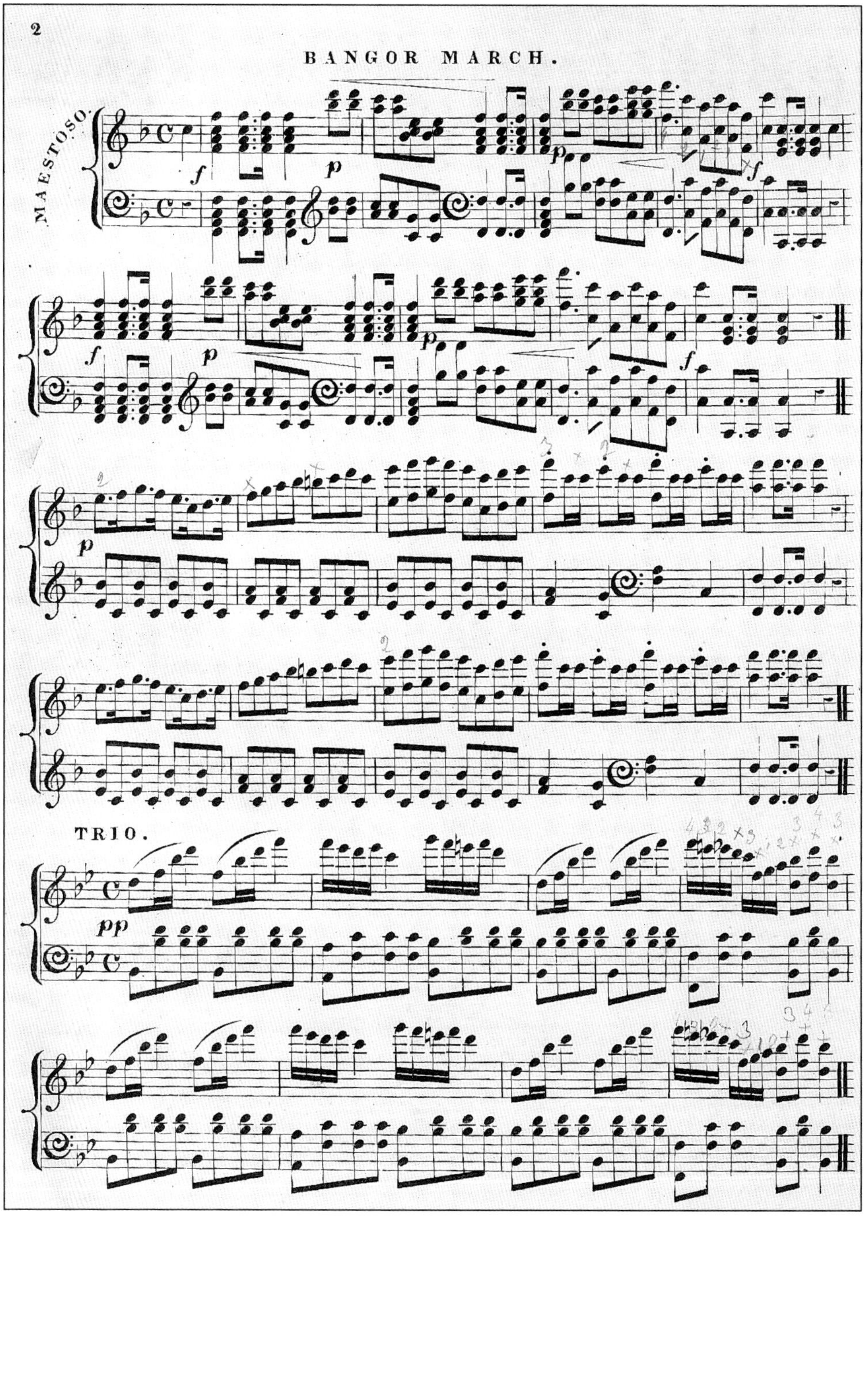
2
BANGOR MARCH.
MAESTOSO.
TRIO.

Introduction

When I began working for the *Bangor Daily News* in 1976 a co-worker turned to me one day and exclaimed, "You're the oldest young man I've ever known." She was dumbfounded at how often I, age twenty-four at the time, delved into the past. Well, after all these years, antiquity still sends shivers up my spine. In fact, it is so important to me that for six months I spent many hours collecting the photographs in this book. My task was easy and tough, all at once: easy because I was comfortable with my subject, having been born to parents from Bangor, Maine and having lived there all of my life, but tough because I had amassed a mountain of old photographs and ephemera that at times defied categorization. Now that the project is complete, however, I am content knowing that this is not intended to be a definitive Bangor book, just a casual look back at what will hopefully strike a chord in anyone who has ever lived or visited there.

The oldest photographs show the "Queen City of the East," as publicists called Bangor as early as the 1840s, with dirt streets, gas lanterns and a resolve that set it apart as a town that cared about itself despite its harsh climate and geographical isolation. "You can't get there from here," the Down Easter mumbles in the old anecdote, but the adventurous got to Bangor in increasing numbers after Jacob Buswell, the first white settler, sailed up the river and settled there in 1769. Photographs show the *Katahdin* and the *City of Bangor*, Boston steamers that linked the frontier town to the outside world. Bangor was also a railroad town. Scenes depict the trains that all met at Union Station, a fine old building so named because of the union of different rail lines in the city.

Later photographs mirror happy and sad moments from the twentieth century. Two of my favorites capture a man and woman soberly guarding their meager belongings plucked from the Great Fire of 1911, which claimed $3 million worth of property and two lives, and President Kennedy striding across Dow Air Force Base a month before Dallas. There are scenes of white and black families having their portraits taken and heartbreaking views of soldiers marching off to war. Some returned in pine boxes.

I hope the faces in this book—the locals such as the log drivers on page 2 and the visitors like Amelia Earhart on page 79—intrigue you as much as they do me. People make a city, and here they are in all their glory, from the bootleggers and lumberjacks to the timber barons and debutantes. They all made Bangor sing, and for that we owe them a debt of gratitude.

Richard R. Shaw

One

River and Stream

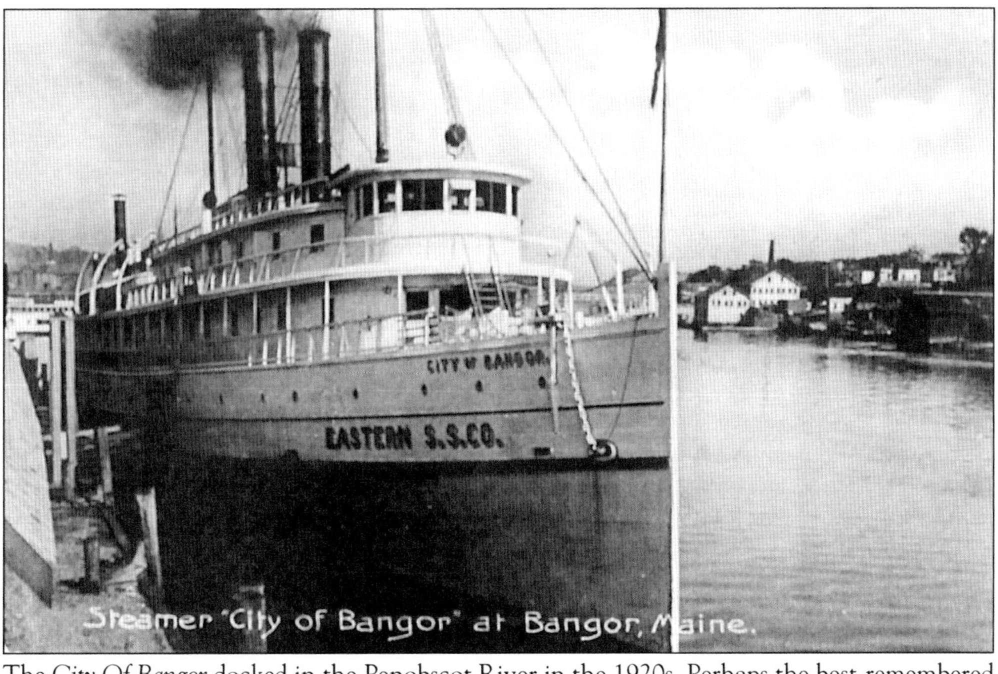

The *City Of Bangor* docked in the Penobscot River in the 1920s. Perhaps the best-remembered of the steamers known collectively as the Boston Boats, the 278.5 -foot-long ship sailed three days a week.

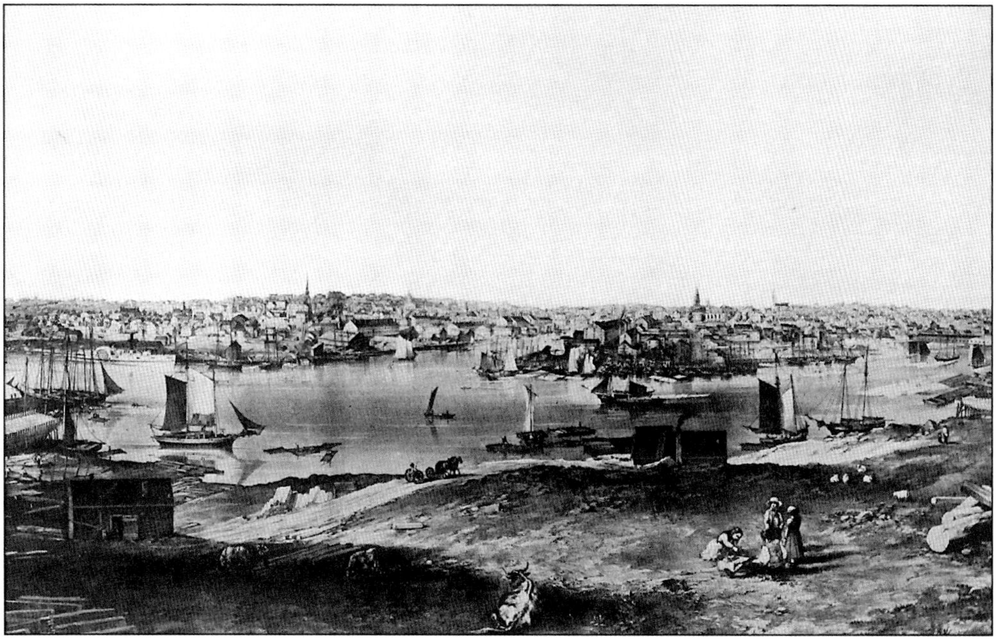

This 1853 lithograph pictures a busy Bangor Harbor dotted with small vessels as well as the steamer *Katahdin* fully visible at the far left. Many fine wooden ships were constructed in the town of Brewer which is laid out in the foreground.

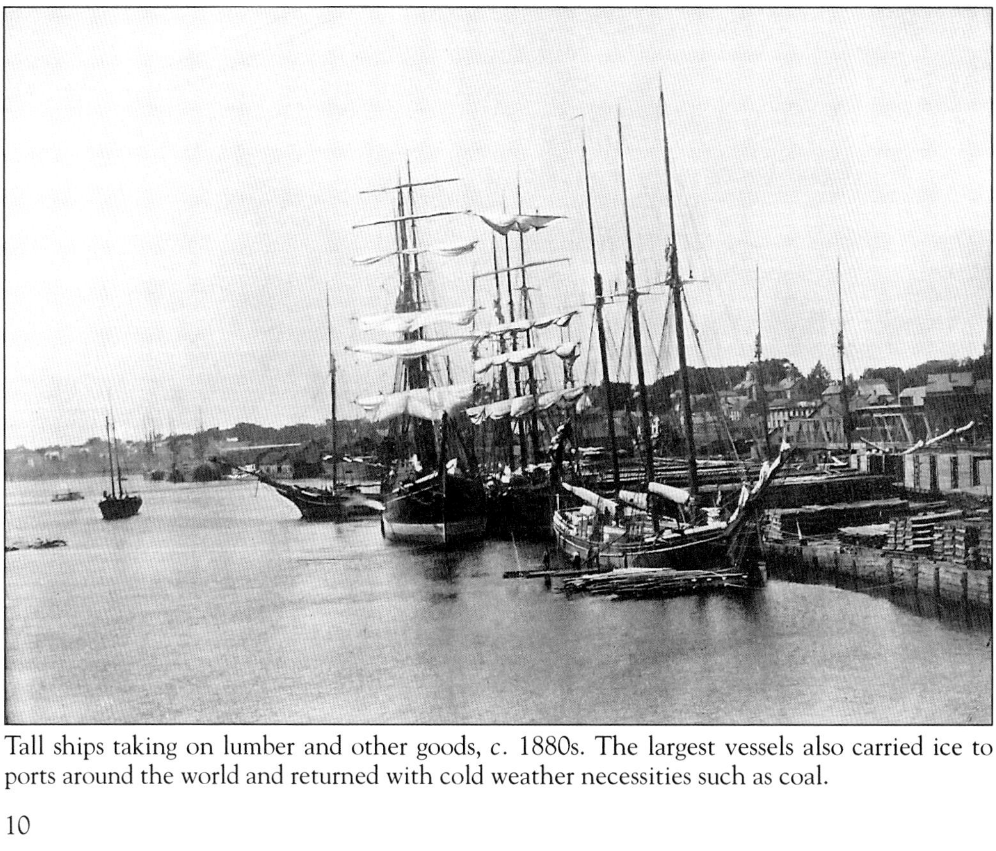

Tall ships taking on lumber and other goods, *c.* 1880s. The largest vessels also carried ice to ports around the world and returned with cold weather necessities such as coal.

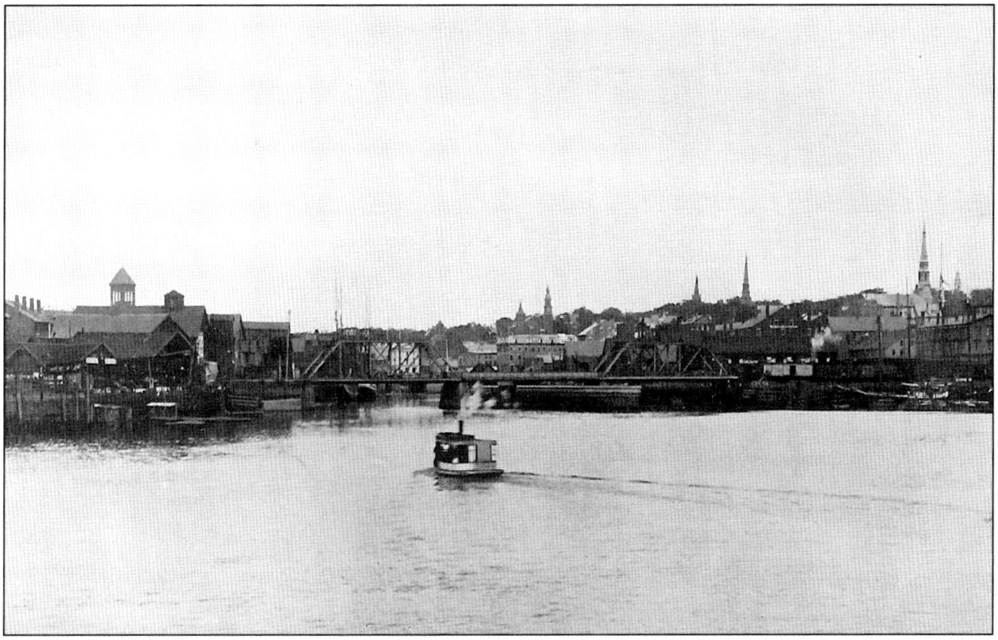

The *Bon Ton I* plies the waters of the Penobscot River between Brewer and Bangor. Workmen and shoppers at first rode for a penny. The fare was hiked to three cents when the *Bon Ton II* and *III* later took over the short run, which was discontinued after a fire in 1939. The toy-like boats were often pressed into service to nudge the Boston steamers on their way.

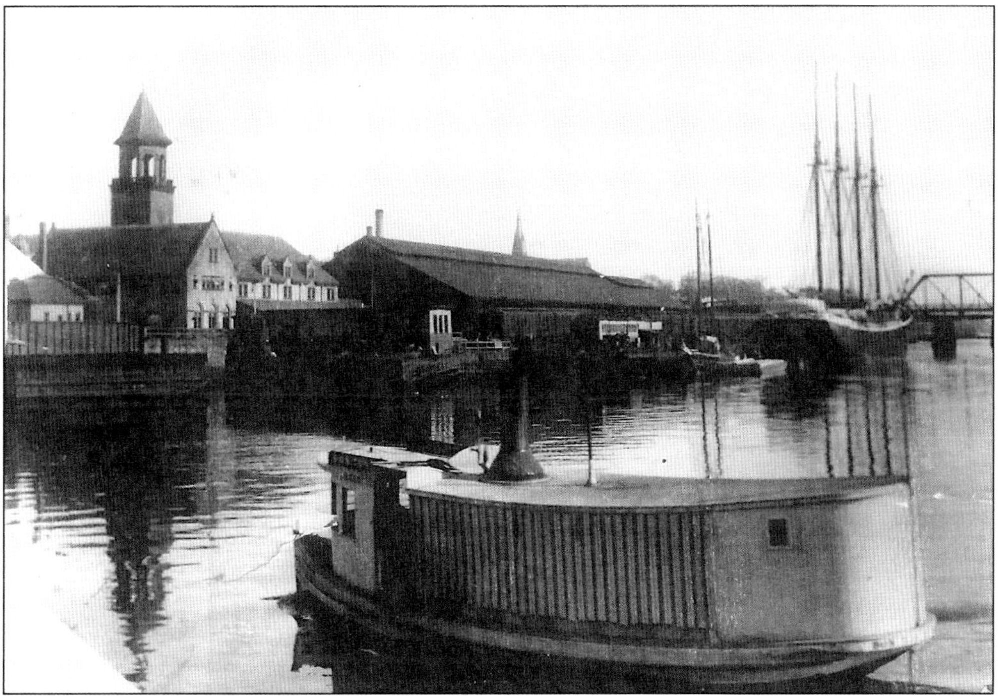

The bell tower of Union Station in Bangor keeps watch over the arrival of the *Bon Ton II*, said to have been the smallest steam-driven commercial boat in the United States. In the distance stands the four-masted schooner the *Erine May*.

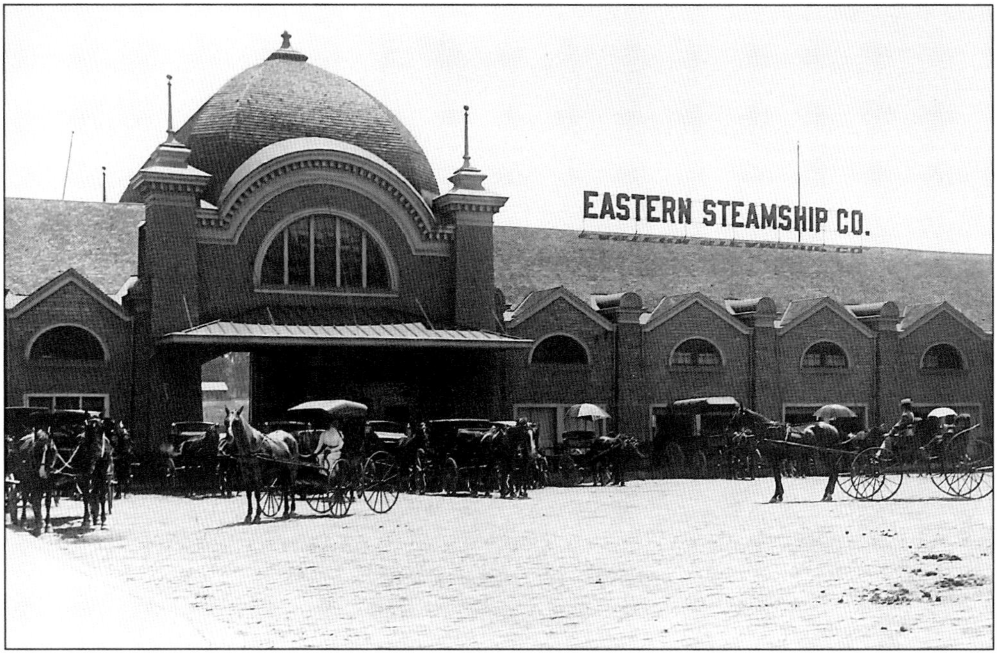

Local hotels provided free carriage rides to the spacious steamboat depot on Front Street. This 1908 view shows the gaudy Gothic-style terminal awaiting passengers from downriver.

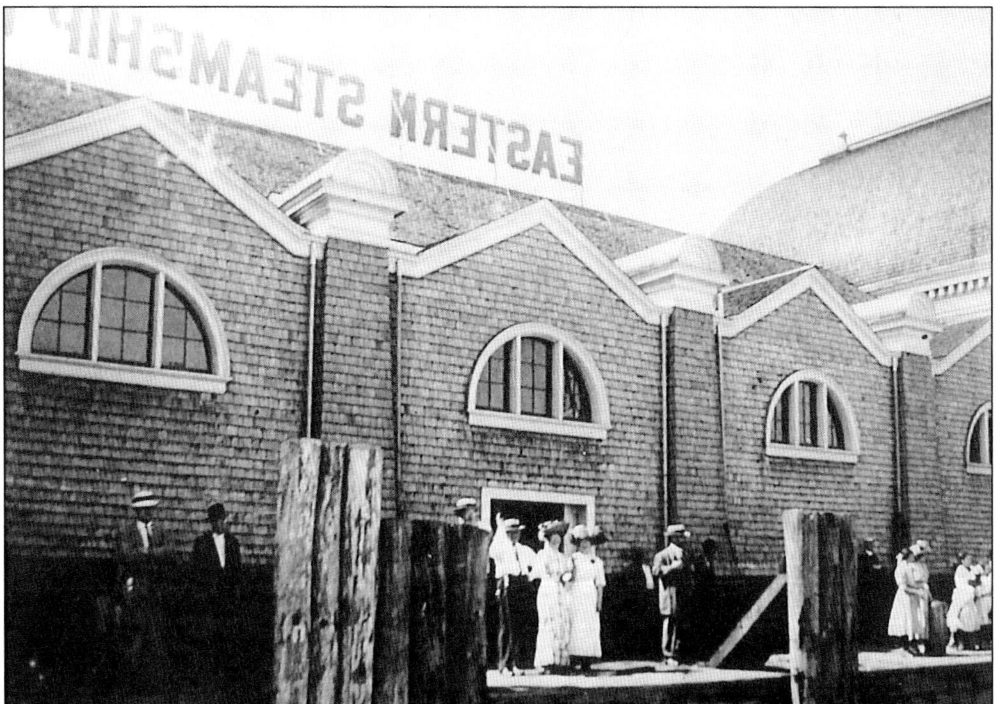

Men and women in full dress stand on the passenger slip of the Eastern Steamship Company c. 1913. The terminal was conveniently located near downtown hotels and businesses that prospered from its proximity. Many people preferred the luxury of steamboat travel to trains.

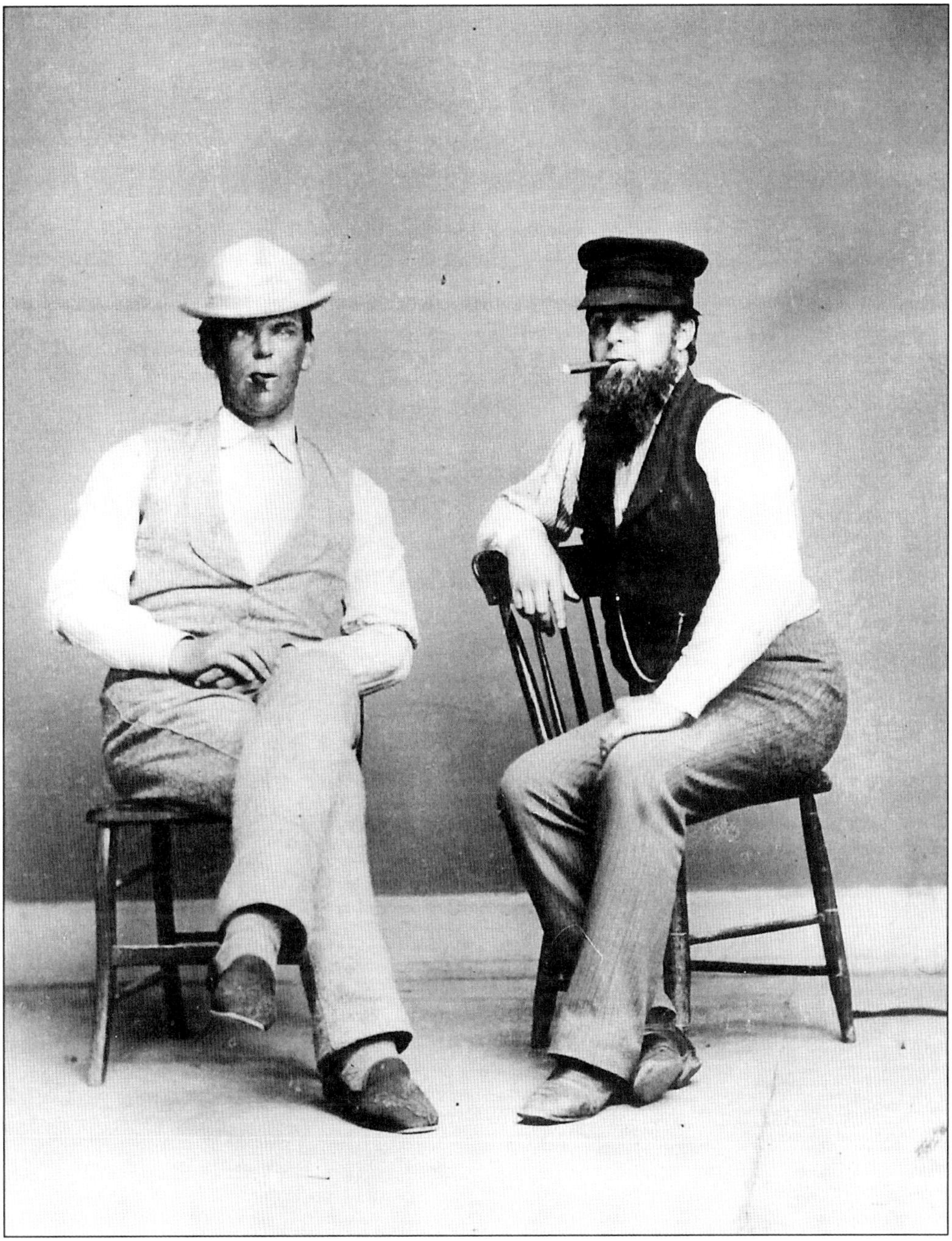

Two of Bangor's best-known bon vivants strike a jaunty pose *c.* 1860. Captain Charles B. Sanford (right) was the aristocratic owner of a steamboat company. He often gave free passage to such honored guests as Civil War soldiers and Molly Molasses, an Indian woman who never tired of riding the boats. Timothy Field (left) had a penchant for fast horses and his native Ireland.

The Great Pleasure Route

—TO—

Mount Desert,

Penobscot River and Bay

AND THE SUMMER RESORTS OF

Picturesque Maine.

Steamers leave Foster's Wharf, Boston, at 5 o'clock daily, (Sundays excepted), from May 31 to October 17, for Rockland, So. West and Bar Harbors, (Mount Desert), Camden, Belfast and Bangor, and all Pleasure Resorts on the Penobscot River and Bay, arriving at Bar Harbor at 11 A. M., and Bangor at 12 M.

About 100 State Rooms on each Steamer, Electric Bell in each room, Capacious Dining Halls, Courteous and Polite Uniformed Officials, Careful and experienced navigators.

Who could resist a summer ride on a Penobscot River steamer, especially if it meant having your own state room and being attended to by "courteous and polite uniformed officials," and knowing that the ship was being navigated by "careful and experienced" personnel?

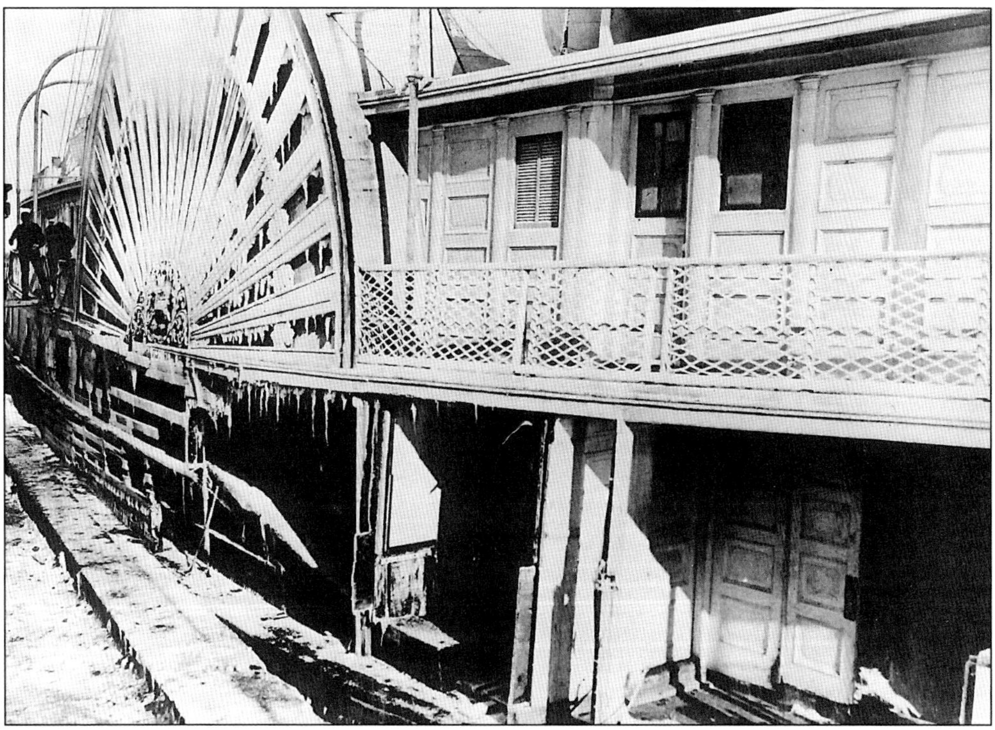

Experienced navigators no doubt helped save the steamer *Katahdin* from oblivion on January 9, 1886, when she ran into a heavy gale off Cape Porpoise, Maine. She eventually made it back to Portsmouth, New Hampshire, where this photograph was taken to show people back in Bangor the damage done to her bulwarks and decks.

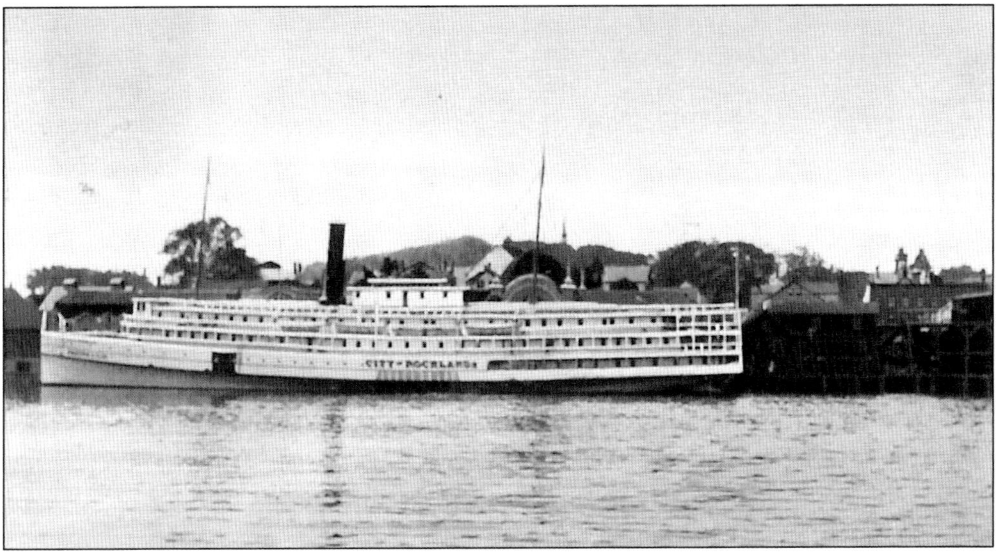

The steamer *City of Rockland* was a sister ship to the *City of Bangor*. The queen of the Boston & Bangor fleet when she was launched in September 1900, she was famous for her grand staircase from the main saloon and for her four hundred state rooms and berths.

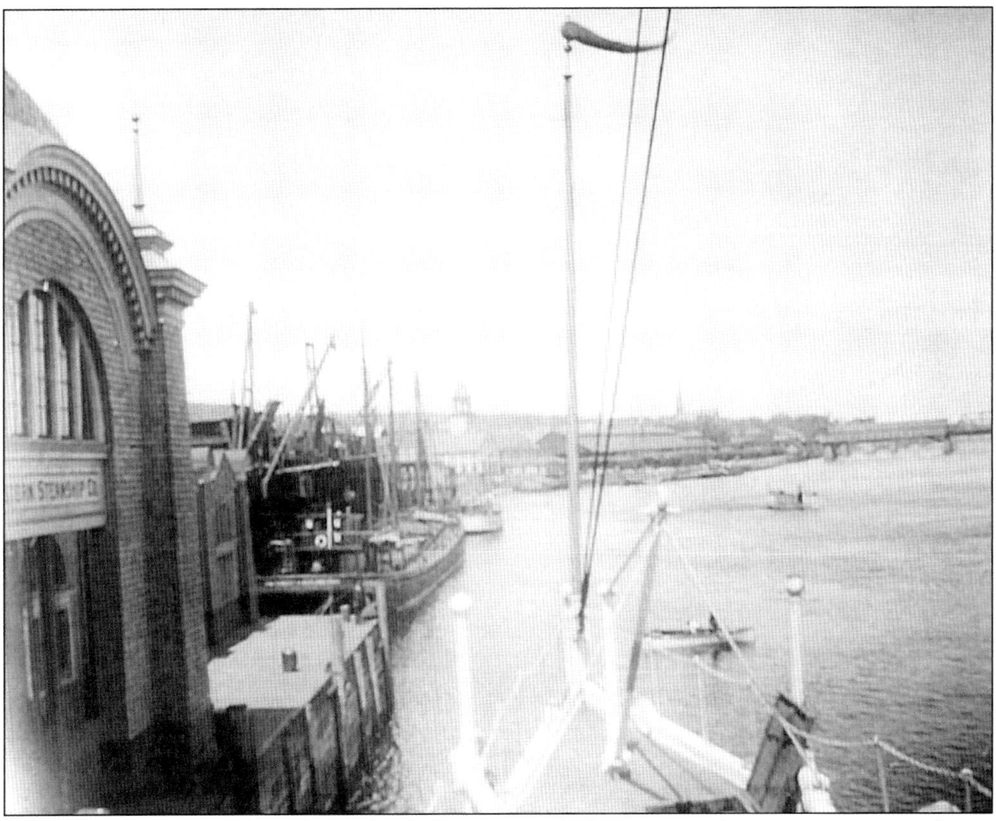

Bangor Harbor as seen from the deck of a boat, *c*. 1913. Contrasting this view are stories of river life in the 1800s, when ships were packed so closely together that seamen could dance across the Penobscot on their decks without getting wet.

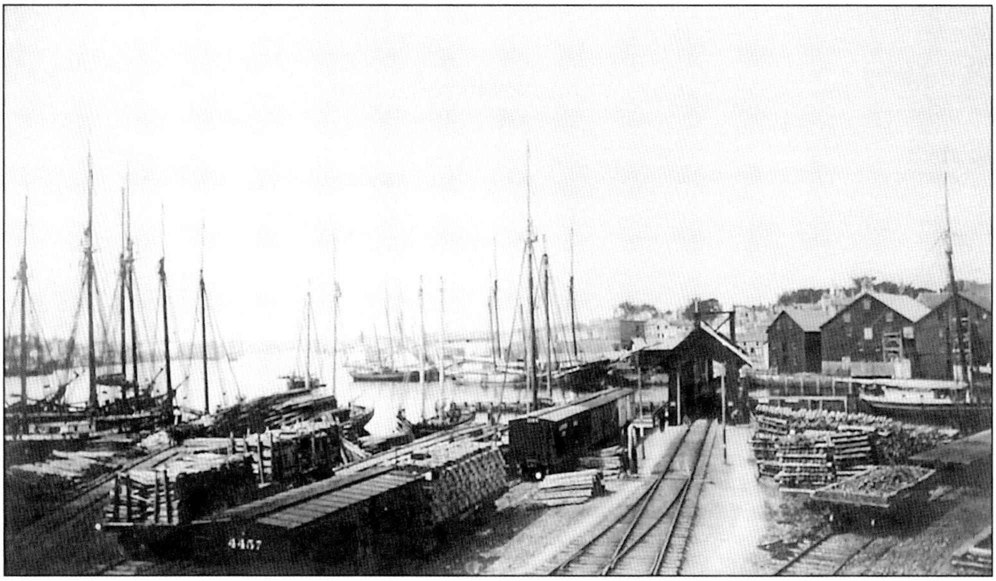

The late 1800s saw brisk activity on the river. This scene shows lumber stacked on a railroad siding, waiting to be loaded onto a schooner. The covered railroad bridge at the center had a draw span that allowed ships to sail up the Kenduskeag Stream as far as State Street Bridge.

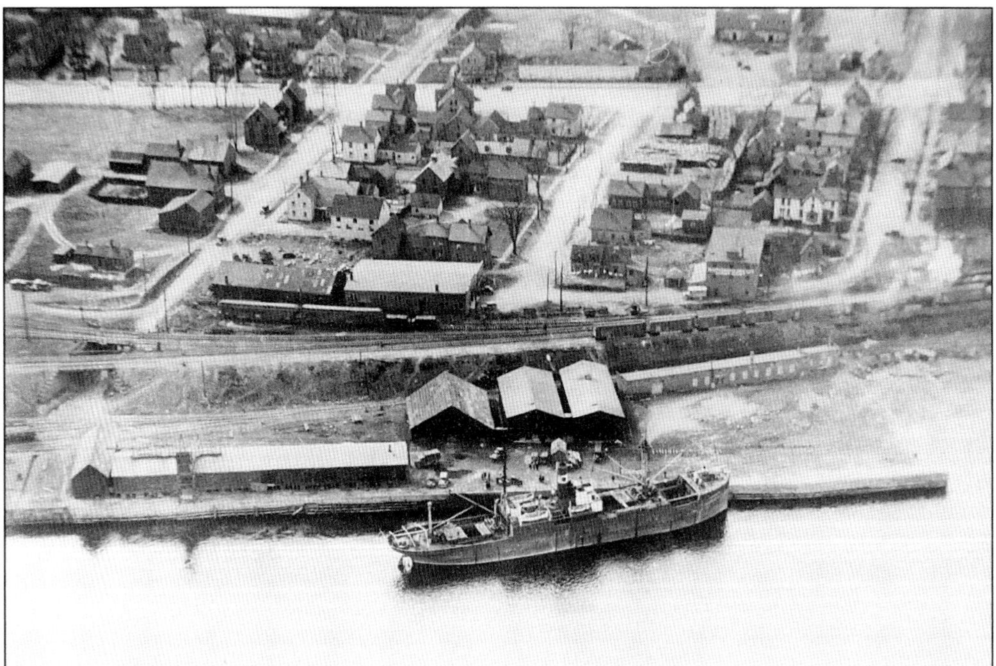

Lower Main Street, *c.* 1920. A steel-hulled vessel, probably loaded with coal, is docked by the Maine Central Railroad tracks. Sailors once knew this part of Bangor as High Head because of the tall gravel embankment that was visible downriver.

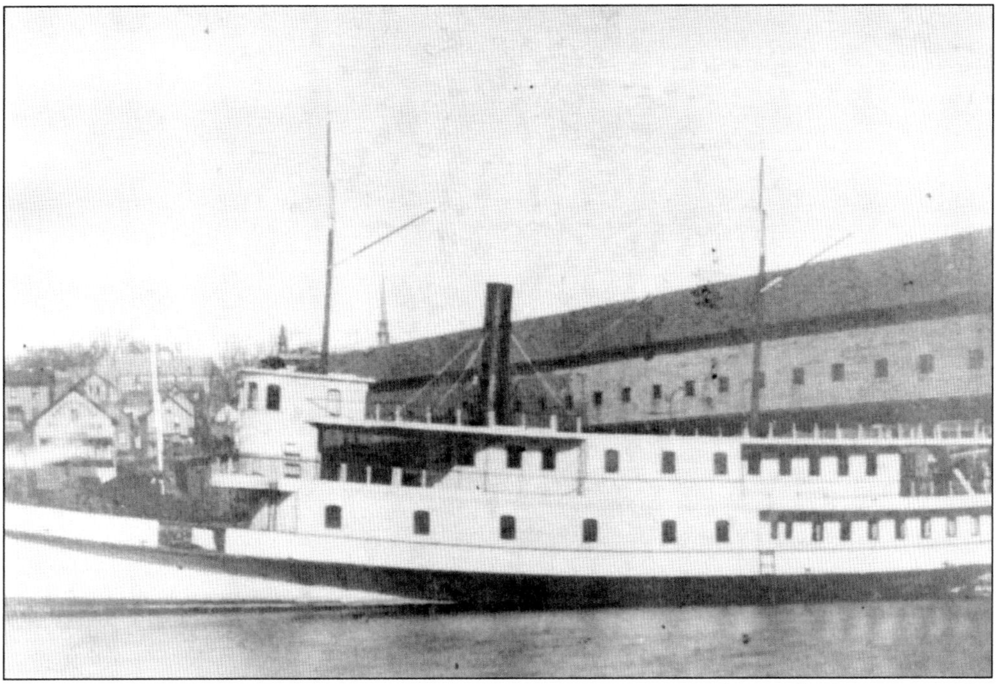

The steamer *Cimbria* photographed near the old Bangor-Brewer Bridge in the late 1800s. The *Cimbria*, thought to have been named for a Russian ship that ran onto Mount Desert Rock many years before, was considered the finest of the ships built at the famous Barbour shipyard in Brewer. It ran excursions from Bangor to Bar Harbor.

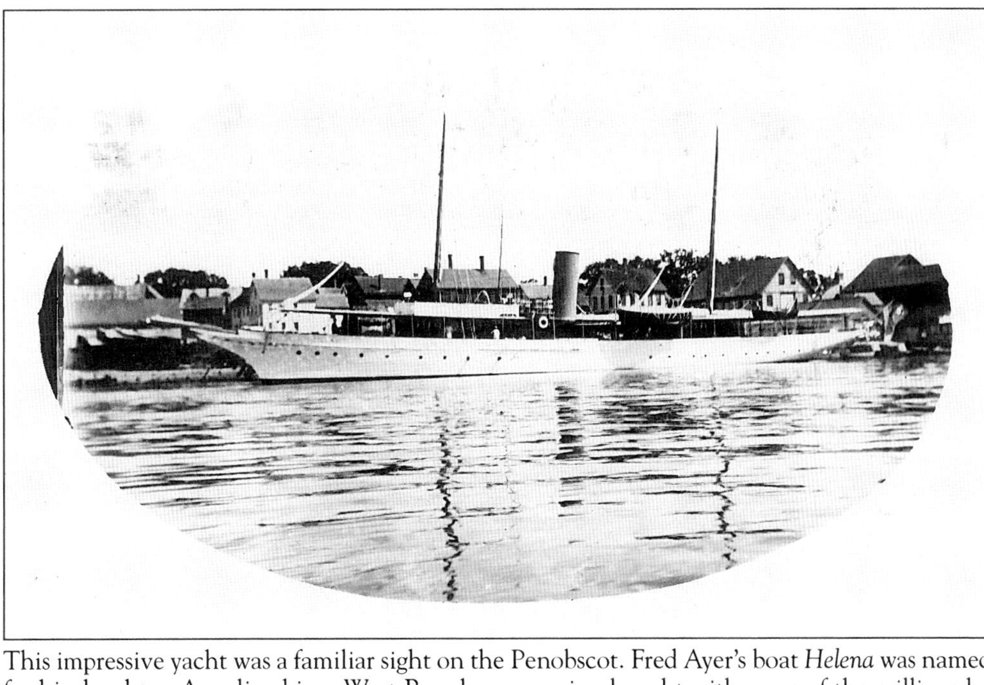

This impressive yacht was a familiar sight on the Penobscot. Fred Ayer's boat *Helena* was named for his daughter. Ayer lived in a West Broadway mansion bought with some of the millions he earned in the lumber trade.

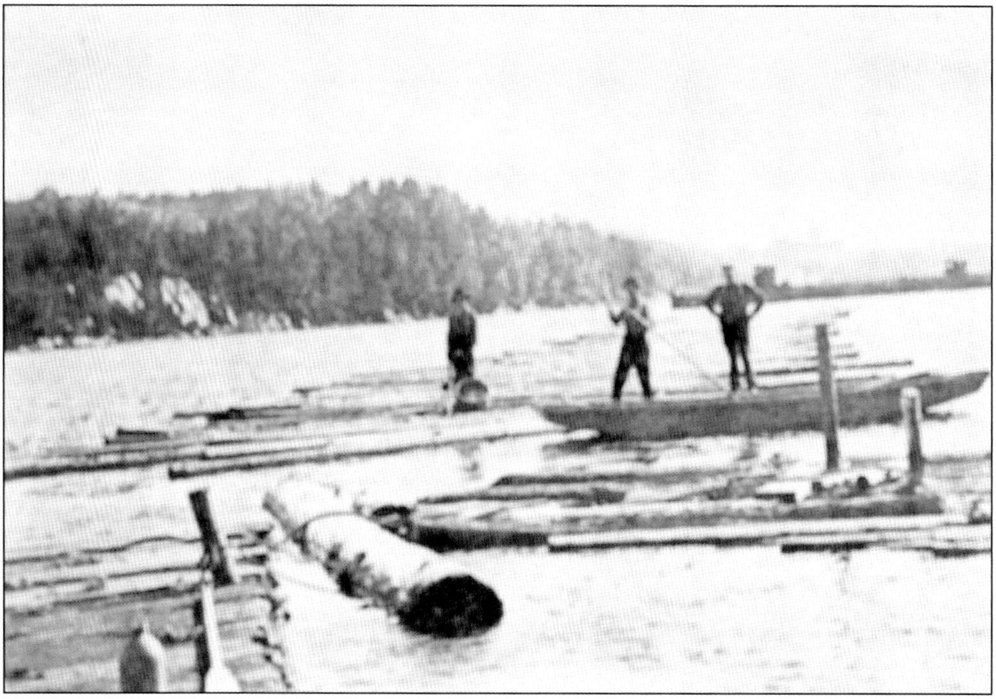

River drivers, or Bangor Tigers, had nimble feet and nerves of steel. Rafting logs involved separating timber from large booms and marking it for delivery to its rightful owners in the city. Branding cattle followed the same technique.

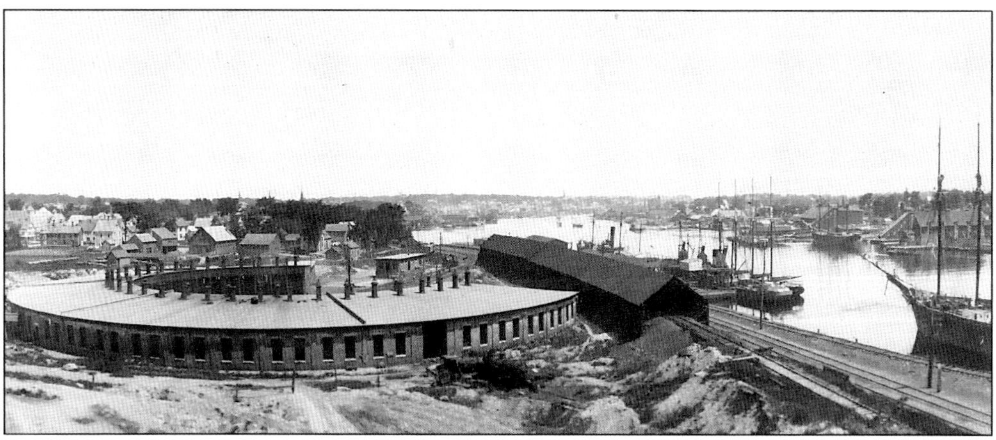

Sailing ships tied up at High Head represent one mode of transportation, while the Maine Central Railroad roundhouse, seen in the lower left corner, represents another. For many years trains were spun around inside this building. It has since fallen victim to the wrecker's ball.

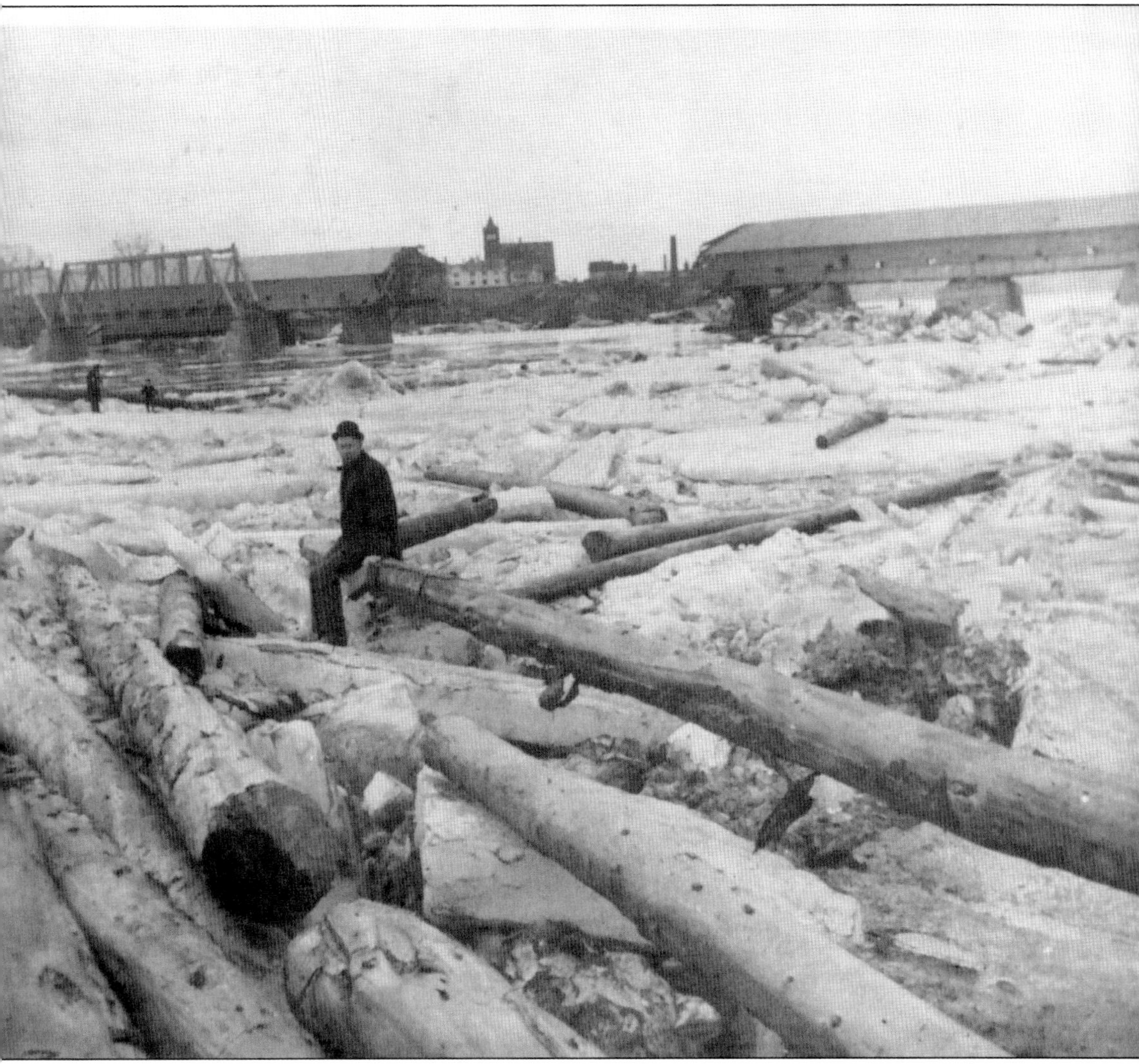

Massive logs were tossed around like matchsticks in the Bangor Flood of 1902. In March, just prior to the great spring log drives of April and May, a mighty wall of ice swept down the Penobscot River and slammed into the Bangor-Brewer Bridge, ripping out its middle span and part of the railroad bridge beside it. Nobody died in the disaster, but spectators standing on the bridge and on railroad cars along the riverbank ran for their lives when the ice floes shifted violently. To many it seemed like a replay of the Great Flood of 1846, although without the damage to public and personal property.

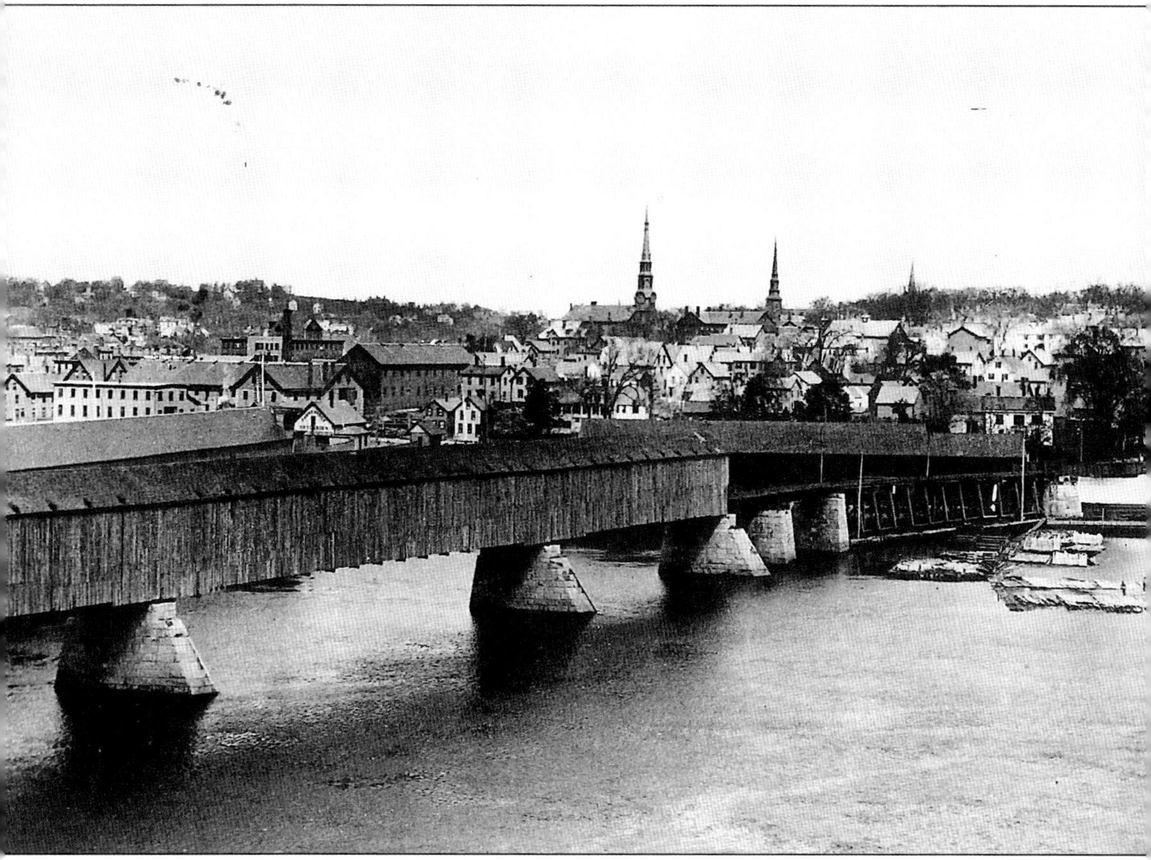

A tranquil river scene from the late 1800s. A raft of logs lies in the Penobscot just upstream from the covered railroad and toll bridges. The colorful neighborhood near the bridges was long remembered for its grog shops and brothels. Standing tall over these landmarks are church spires, just blocks away. Until the 1950s, when the Joshua Chamberlain Bridge added a second link between Bangor and Brewer, the "Old Bridge" was the only way vehicles could pass from one city to the other. Today a third link, the Veterans Remembrance Bridge, ties the Twin Cities together in yet another location.

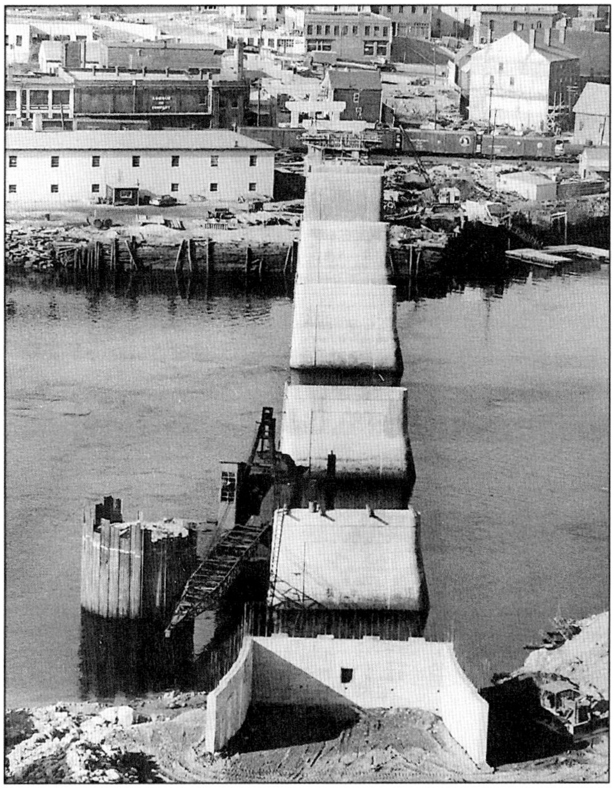

Joshua Lawrence Chamberlain, the Brewer native who fought heroically at the Battle of Little Round Top, lent his name to the second bridge to span the Penobscot River. Completed in 1959, the bridge traces the route of the *Bon Ton* ferries.

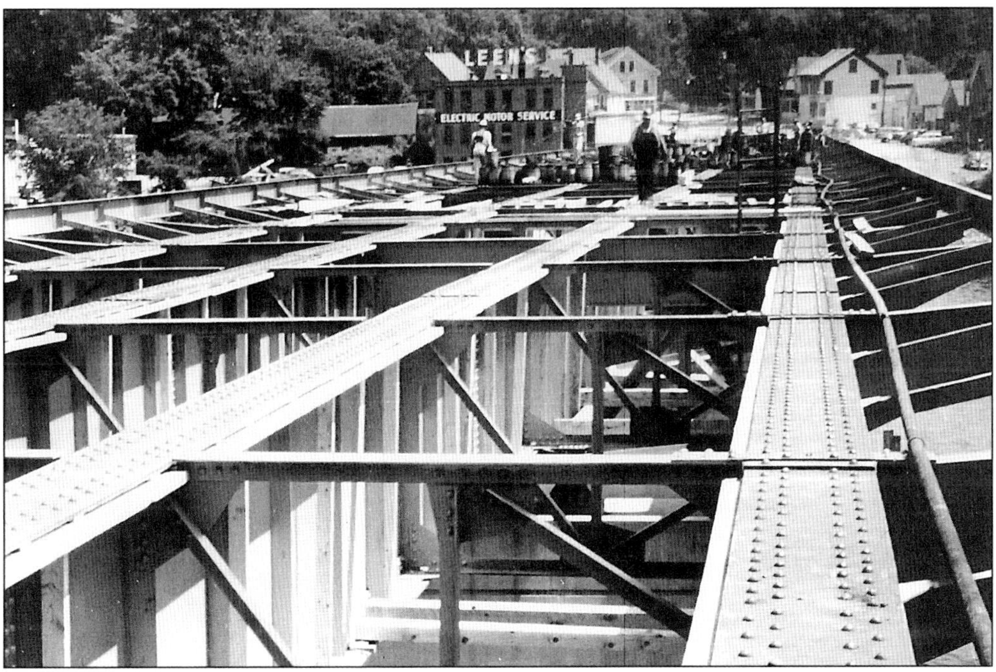

The Joshua Chamberlain Bridge under construction, looking toward the Brewer side. For the first time, drivers and pedestrians could travel from the downtown districts of Bangor and Brewer without boarding a boat or bothering to go upstream to the Old Bridge.

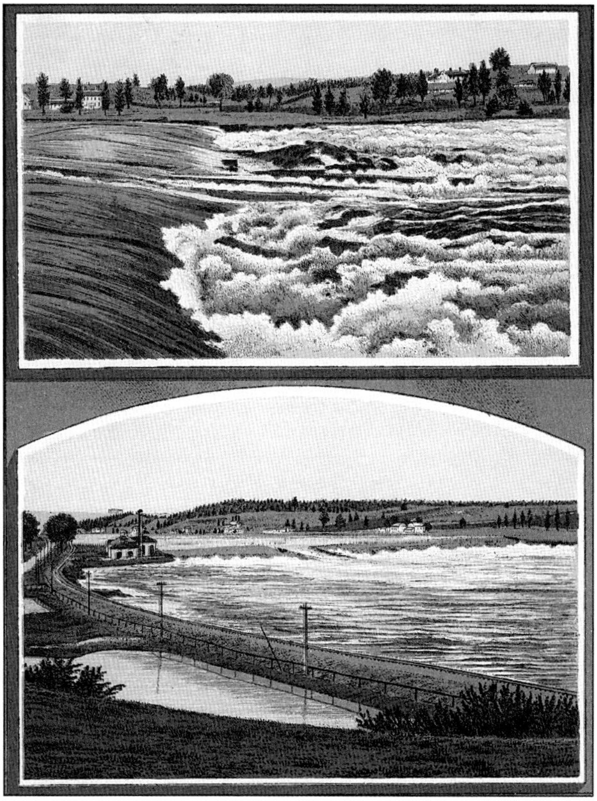

The Bangor Water Works and Dam were built at Treats Falls in the 1870s to provide electrical power for the city. Visitors to the picturesque place could sometimes almost smell salt in the air, so reminiscent is the area of the ocean, complete with the rising and falling of tides. Penobscot salmon have long been sought by fishermen in the springtime.

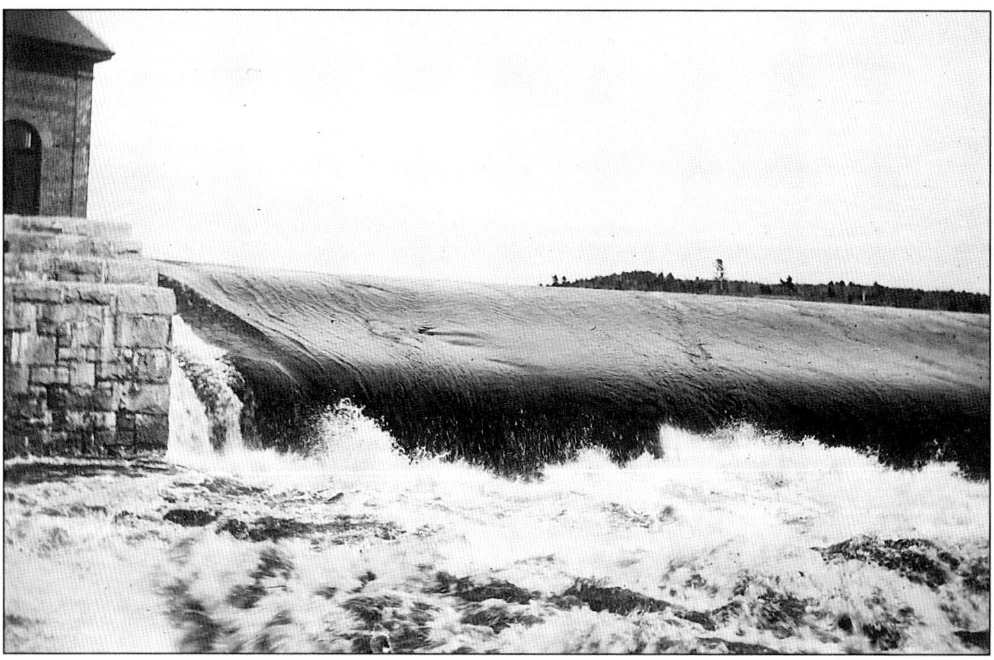

The fast water of the Penobscot River resembles silk in this old postcard view taken at the water works. The dam has been destroyed and no longer generates electricity.

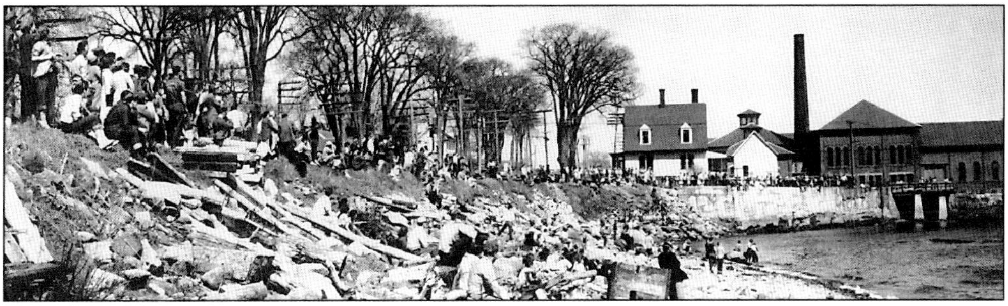

Hundreds of spectators line both sides of the river in April 1954 to have a look at the mysterious marine mammals that made their way inland from the ocean to the Salmon Pool. Were they whales? Sharks? Porpoises? Initial reports at the Bangor Police Station reported a body floating in the river, but closer inspection revealed mammals of some sort. Experts soon discovered that the visitors were White Beluga whales that had pursued smelts up the Penobscot. The spectacle has never been repeated (neither have the traffic jams), but readers can relive the incident in Gerald Hausman's children's book, *The Day the White Whales Came to Bangor*.

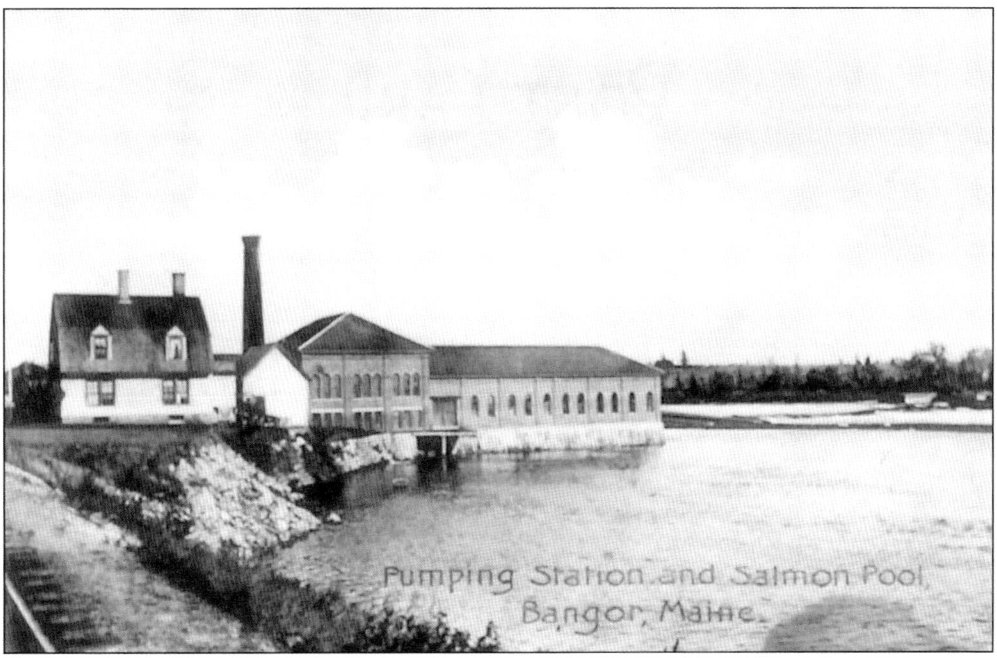

A scene from another era shows the Bangor Water Works and Dam in the 1920s. Martin Burke, chief engineer with the Bangor Water District, and his wife, Mary, lived in the keeper's house next to the dam.

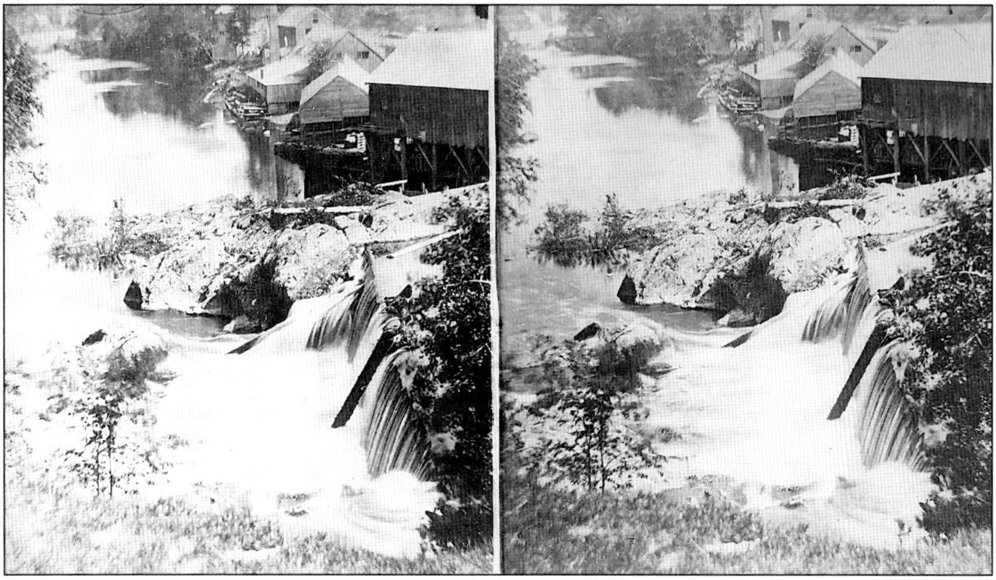

The S.A. Maxfield Company, dealers in tallows and hides, operated this factory on Valley Avenue. This bucolic scene was actually just a short walk from downtown.

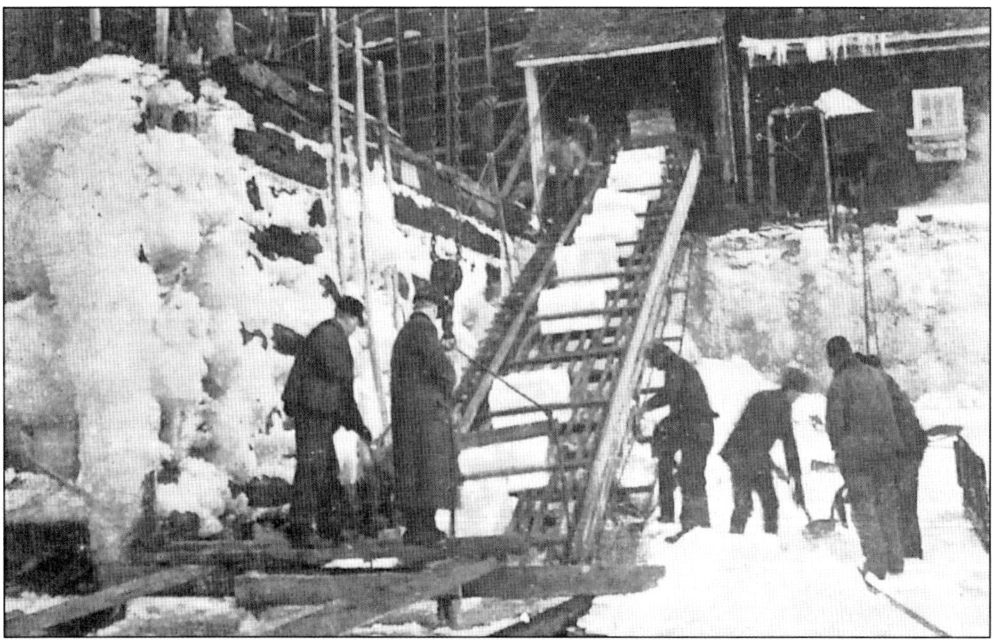

Harvesting ice was a cold, miserable job, but someone had to supply the kitchens of Rio De Janeiro and Buenos Aires. Ice from the Kenduskeag Stream and Penobscot River, packed in sawdust and shipped around the world, was long sought until modern refrigeration and water pollution made the frozen stuff unneeded and undesirable.

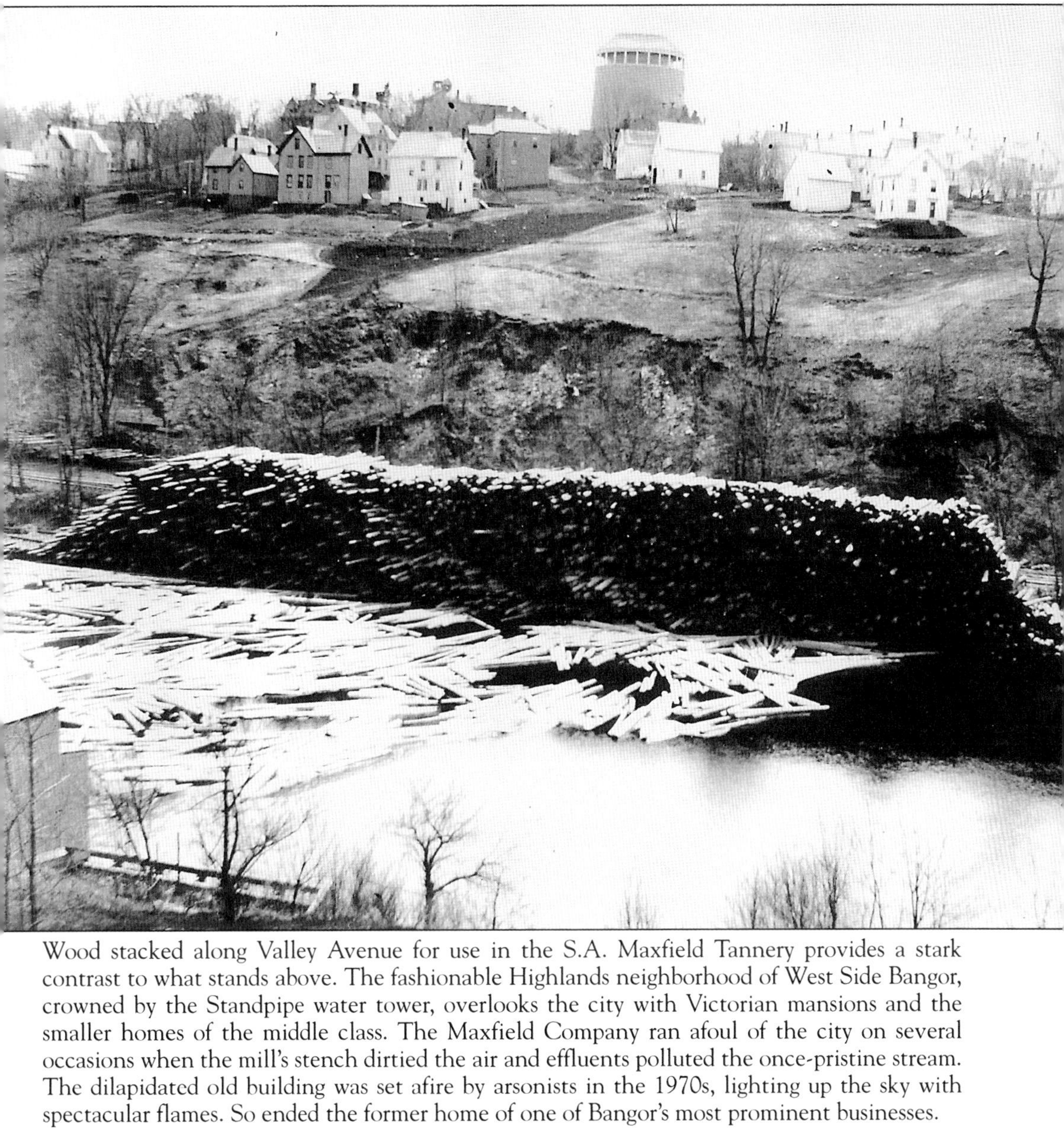

Wood stacked along Valley Avenue for use in the S.A. Maxfield Tannery provides a stark contrast to what stands above. The fashionable Highlands neighborhood of West Side Bangor, crowned by the Standpipe water tower, overlooks the city with Victorian mansions and the smaller homes of the middle class. The Maxfield Company ran afoul of the city on several occasions when the mill's stench dirtied the air and effluents polluted the once-pristine stream. The dilapidated old building was set afire by arsonists in the 1970s, lighting up the sky with spectacular flames. So ended the former home of one of Bangor's most prominent businesses.

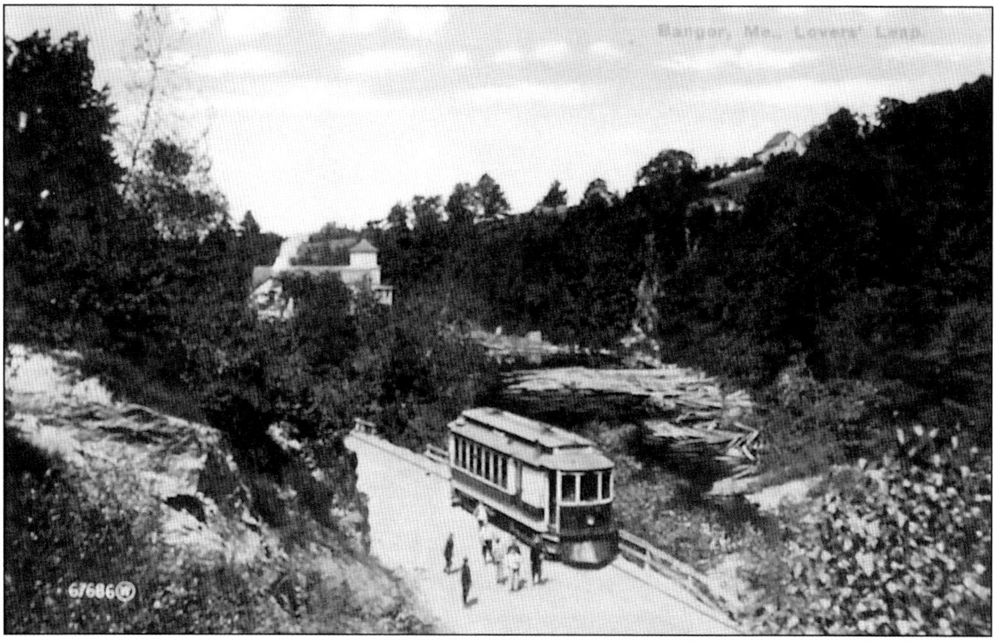

This 1911 postcard view shows wood in the stream near the Maxfield Tannery building, as well as a streetcar from the Penobscot Central Railway which provided service as far as Charleston, 26 miles to the north.

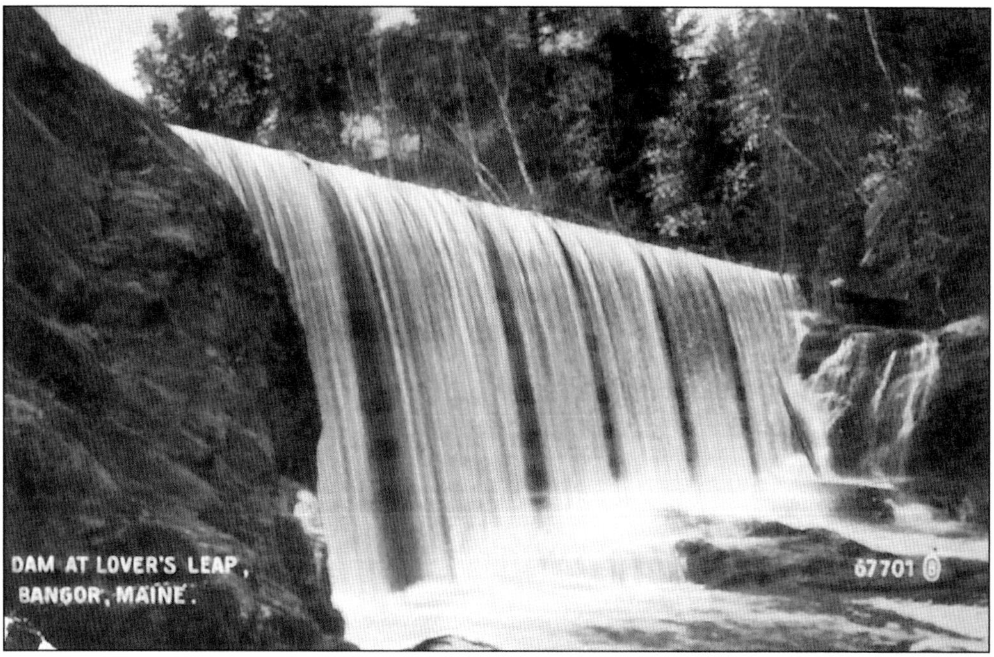

The falls near the Maxfield building were a desirable picnic spot on a warm summer day. The craggy cliff known as Lover's Leap took its name from several nineteenth-century poems that concocted a story of star-crossed Penobscot Indian lovers who joined hands and jumped to their deaths.

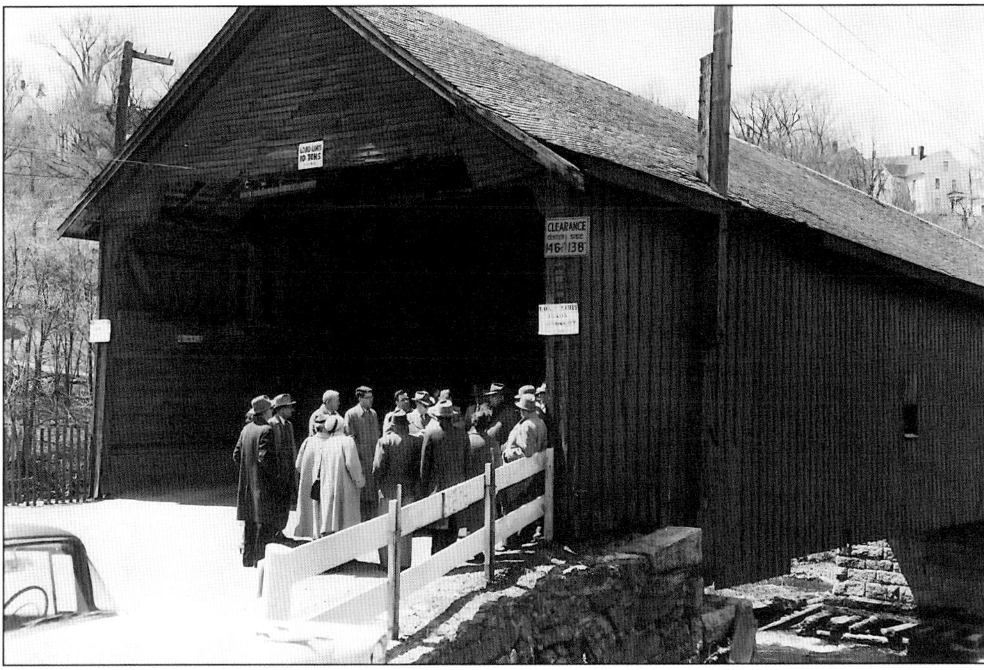

Galen Cole, president of Cole's Express, meets with local citizens at the old Morse's Bridge on Valley Avenue. By the mid-1950s the bridge, which spanned the Kenduskeag Stream next to Llewellyn J. Morse's Lumber Mill, had been posted at 10 tons and despite the pleas of such civic-minded citizens as Mr. Cole to keep the landmark at its original site, the bridge was dismantled and later reassembled downstream. In 1983 it was burned by an arsonist.

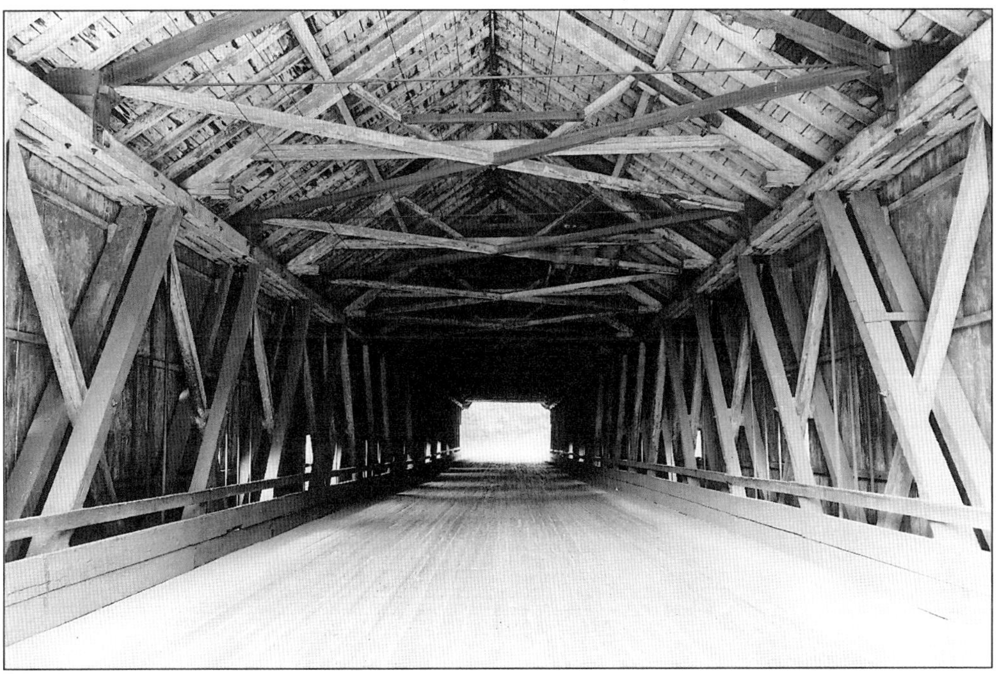

The intricate pattern of design and construction is displayed in this interior view of Morse's Bridge. The City of Bangor had the 212-foot-long bridge structure built in 1884 for $8,300.

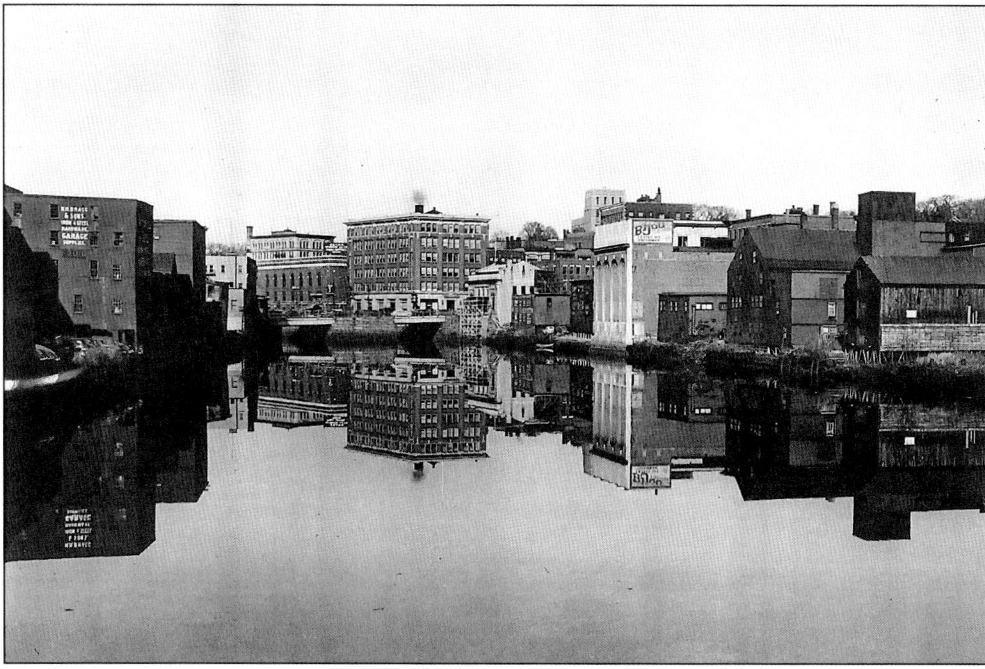

Downtown buildings are mirrored in the Kenduskeag Stream as it used to look before the Urban Renewal project of the 1960s filled much of the area in with concrete.

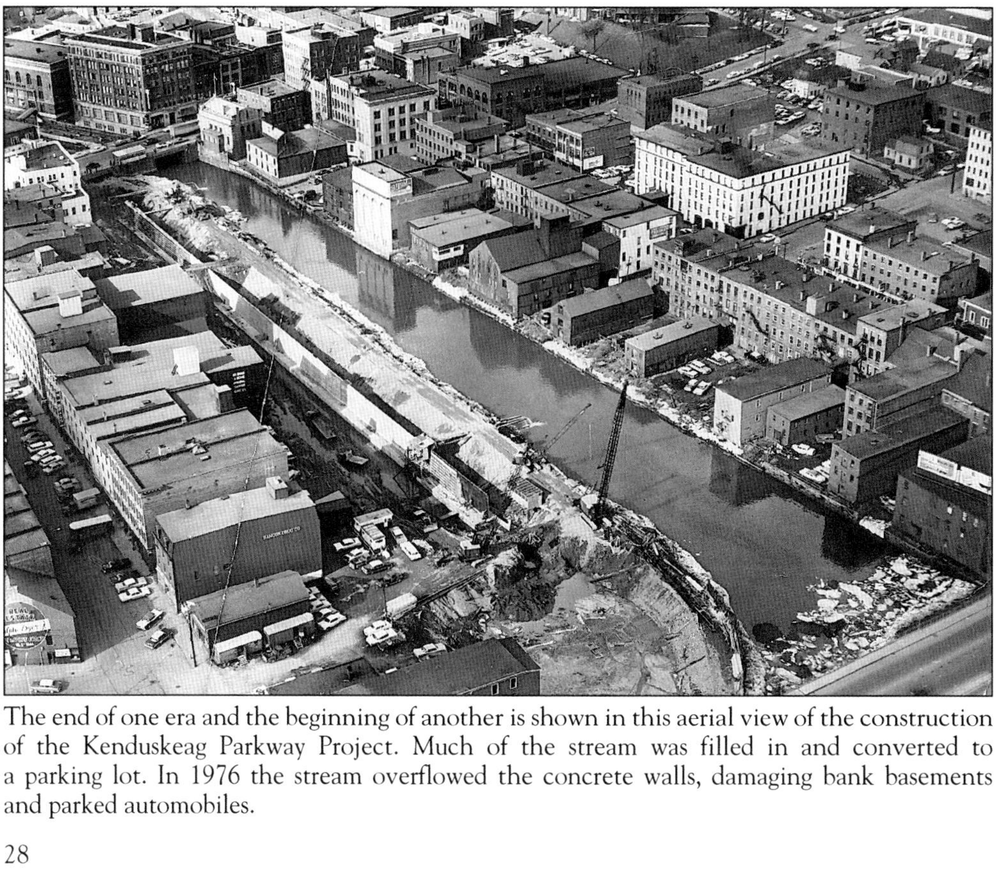

The end of one era and the beginning of another is shown in this aerial view of the construction of the Kenduskeag Parkway Project. Much of the stream was filled in and converted to a parking lot. In 1976 the stream overflowed the concrete walls, damaging bank basements and parked automobiles.

Two

Saints and Sinners

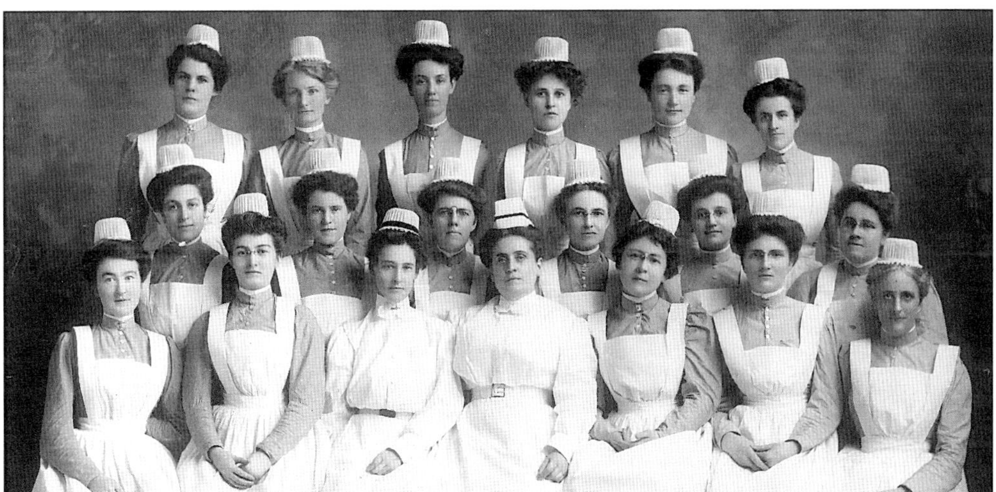

Young nurses could be identified by hospital and level of training by studying the style of their caps. Two registered nurses dressed completely in white are in the front row. Opened in 1892, the Bangor General Hospital was later renamed Eastern Maine General. It now operates as Eastern Maine Medical Center.

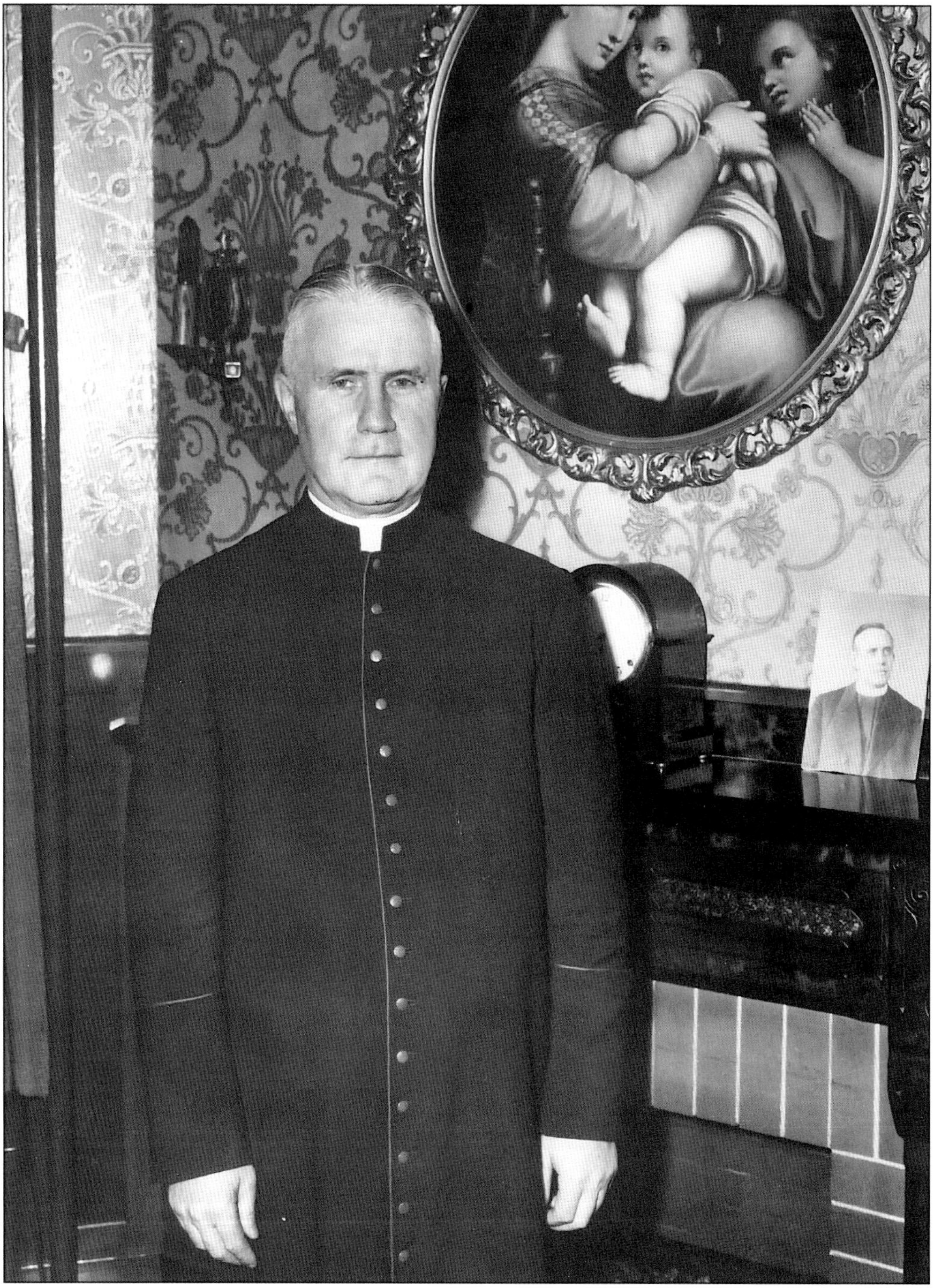

Monsignor Edward F. Ward of St. Mary's Catholic Church inside the church rectory near a copy of Raphael's classic painting *Madonna of the Chair*. Monsignor Ward came to St. Mary's in 1950 and retired in 1971, and is one of the most popular figures in the church's long history. During his pastorate he oversaw the implementation of Vatican II, including the extraordinary transition from a Mass recited in Latin to that in English. Ordained in 1928 when Pius XI was the Pontiff, Monsignor Ward moved on to Portland where he taught at Cheverus High School.

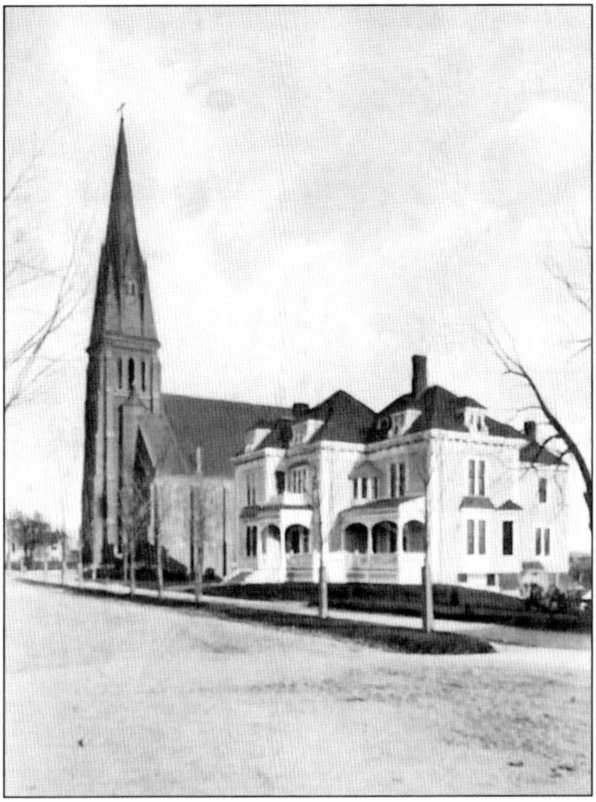

St. John's Catholic Church has served the east side of Bangor since Mass was first celebrated in its basement on Christmas morning, 1855. Many Irish immigrants who settled here in the 1840s worshipped at St. John's. Jacob Buswell, Bangor's first white settler, built his log cabin near this site after moving here in 1769.

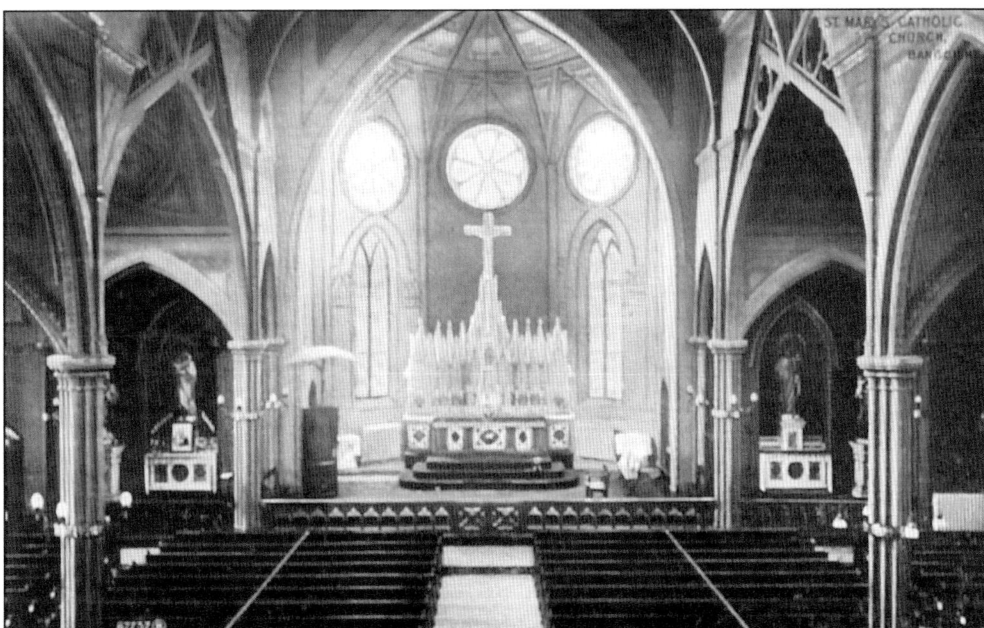

This splendid interior was laid to waste in 1978 when an arsonist sneaked into St. Mary's Catholic Church on Cedar Street and set the building ablaze. Spectators standing in the chill night air wept and recalled happy and sad occasions inside the 104-year-old landmark.

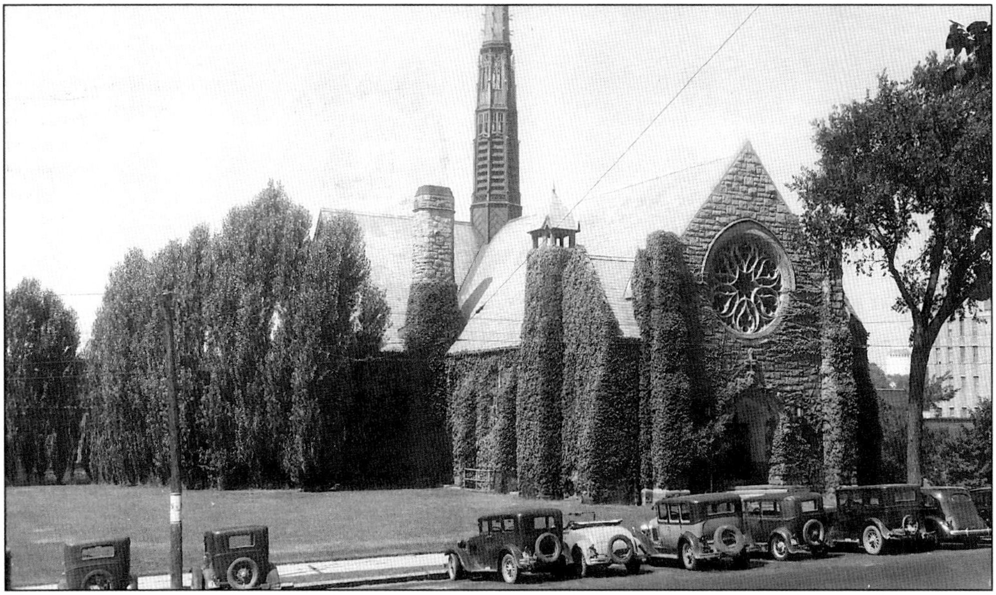

The All Souls Congregational Church was covered in vine when this postcard view was made in the 1920s. When the church was built after the Great Fire of 1911, granite of different shades was used in its outer wall to symbolize the melding of the First and Central Congregational Churches, both destroyed in the inferno.

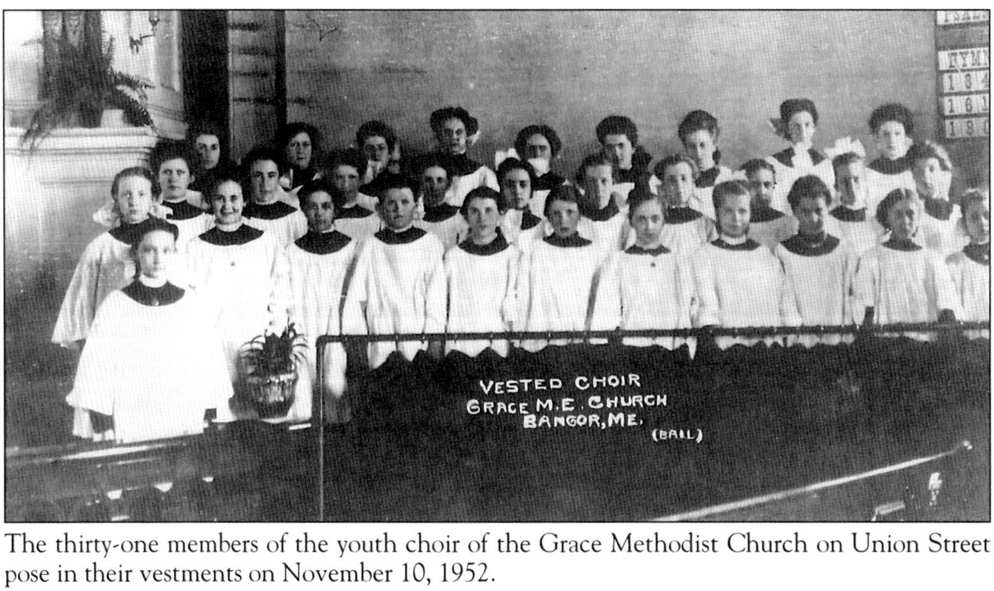

The thirty-one members of the youth choir of the Grace Methodist Church on Union Street pose in their vestments on November 10, 1952.

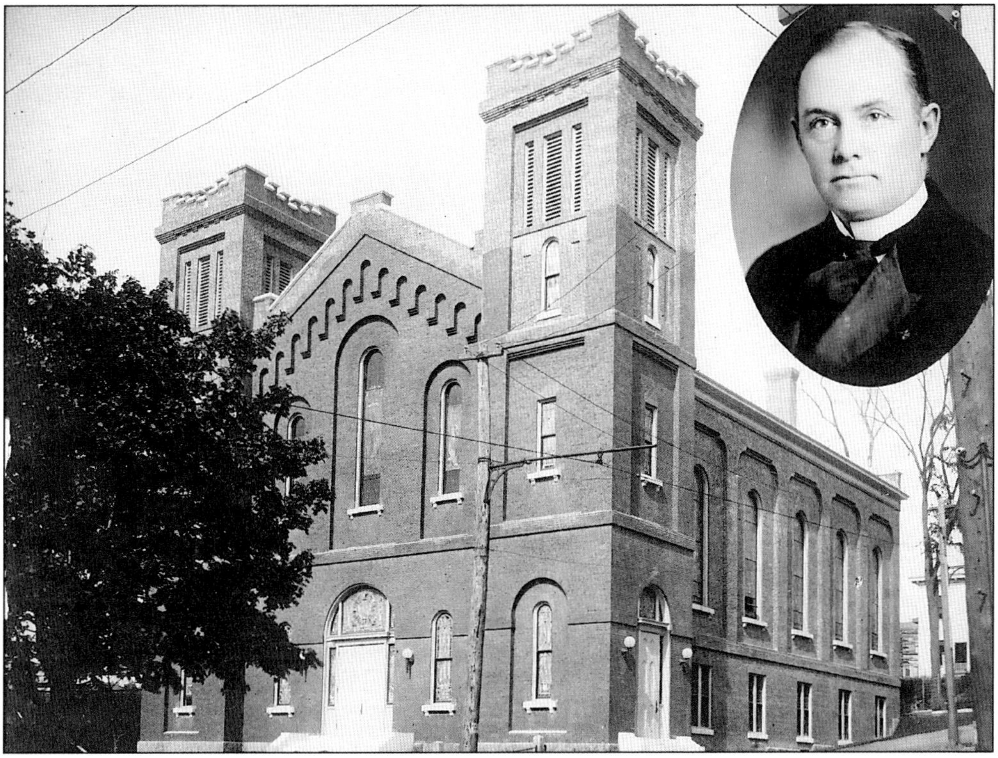

The Reverend Ashley A. Smith was the minister at the First Universalist Church from 1911 until 1936, the longest pastorate in the church's history. Reverend Smith was installed only five weeks before the Great Bangor Fire and oversaw the rebuilding of the church, which was gutted in the disaster.

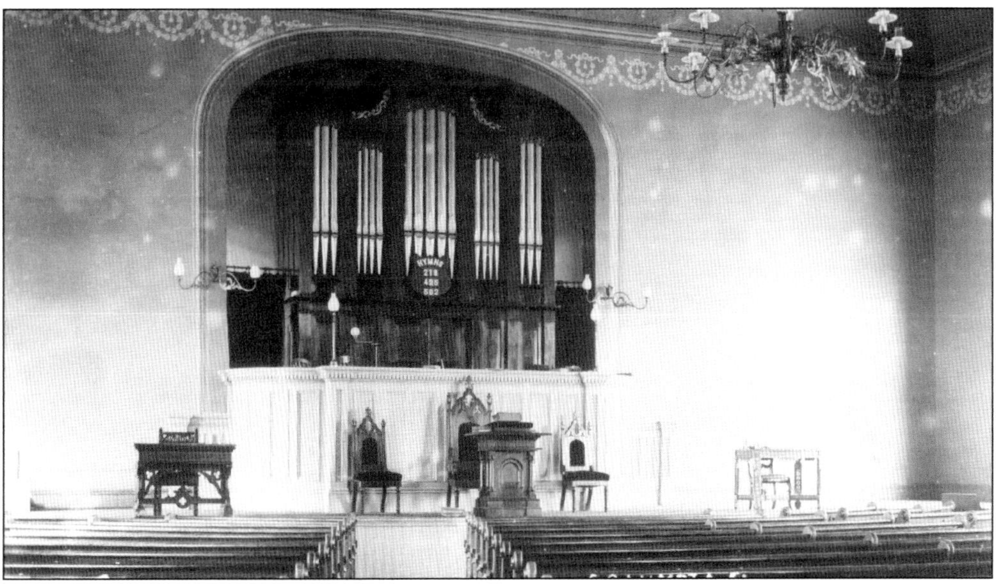

The main auditorium of the Columbia Street Baptist Church, *c.* 1910. The church's origins date back to a seaman's mission near the waterfront, started in 1845. Originally it was called Second Baptist.

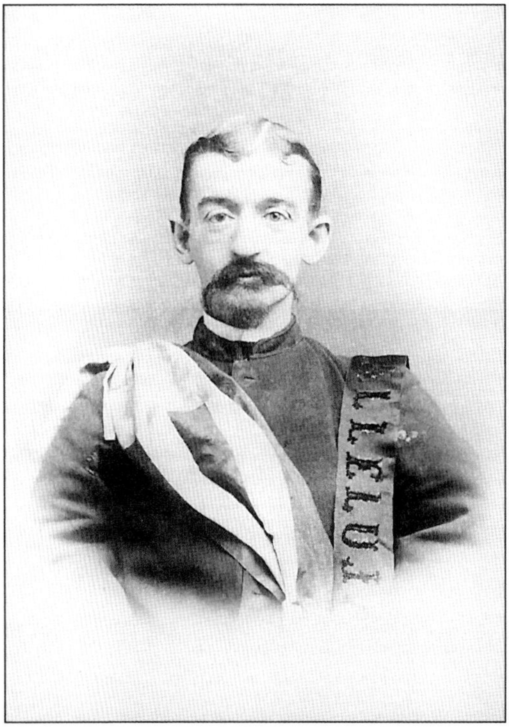

Captain James Stephen O'Brien headed the Salvation Army in Bangor in the 1930s. His nickname, "The Converted Showman," suggested a former life not up to the army's standards.

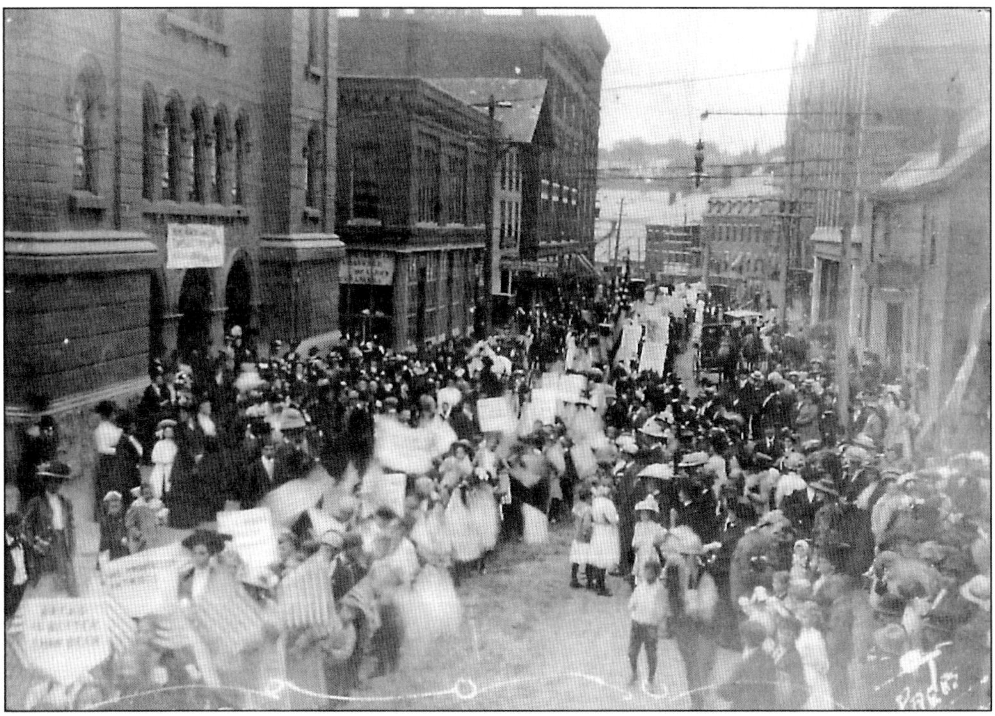

The Women's Christian Temperance Union, dubbed the "Cold Water Army" by friends and foes alike, parades up Columbia Street on September 15, 1909. Public drunkenness was commonplace in Bangor during the years of Prohibition.

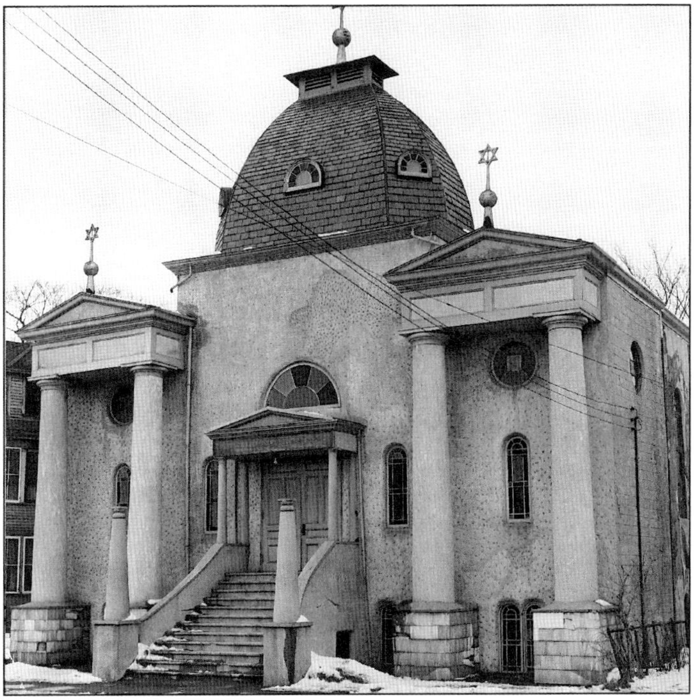

The oldest Jewish congregation in Maine has met in this synagogue on York Street since it was built in 1913. It met in other places around the city before that. The Beth Israel Synagogue's three Stars of David are visible for some distance.

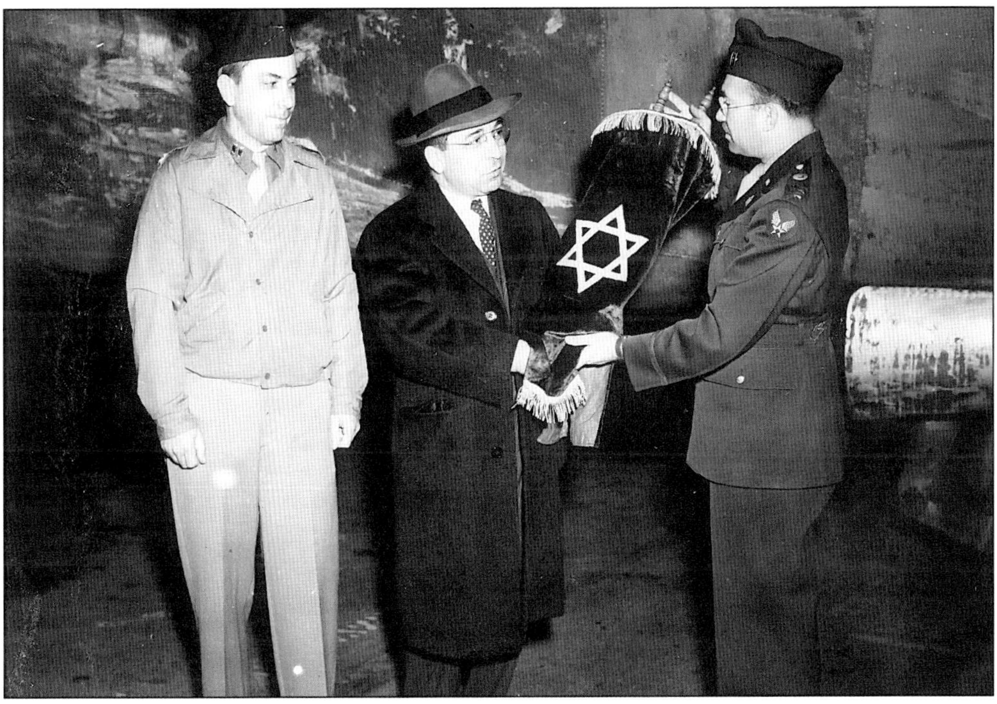

During World War II Captain Harold H. Gordon (right), Jewish chaplain for the North Atlantic Division of the Air Transport Command, carried a holy scroll more than 75,000 miles to Jewish soldiers stationed along the North Atlantic route. Here Captain Gordon is shown in March 1945 with the "Flying Torah," presented by Congregation Beth Israel at Dow Air Force Base in Bangor.

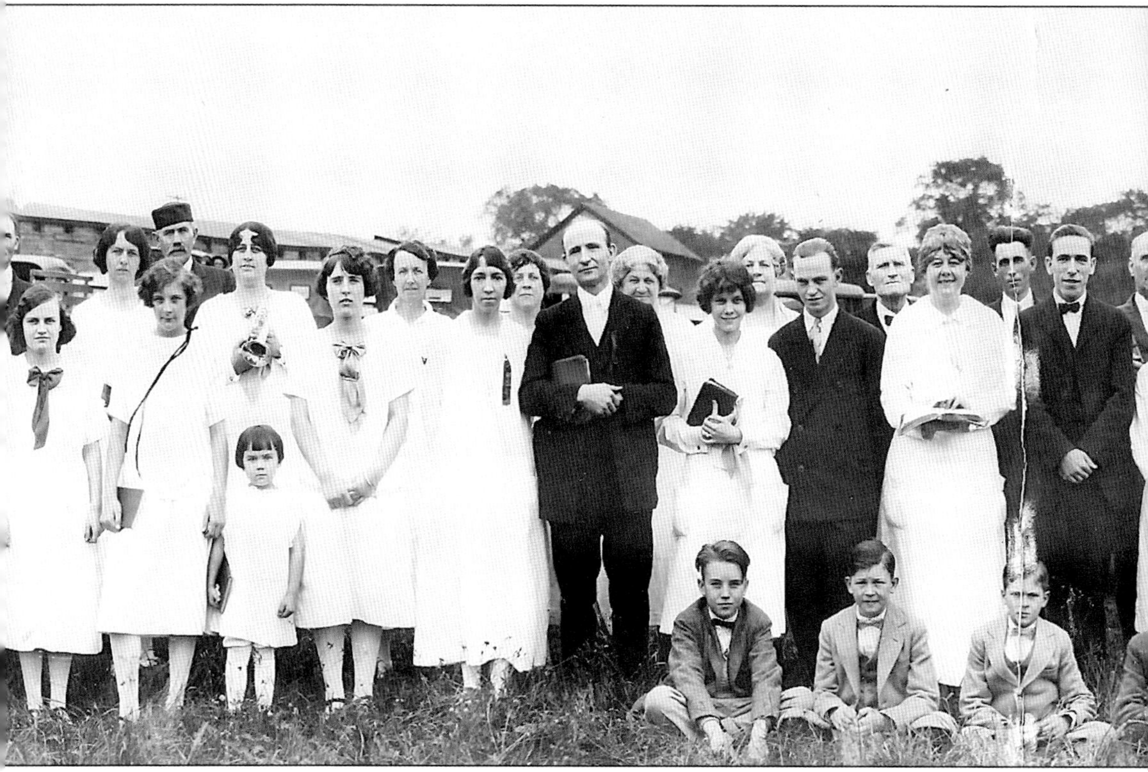

Mattie Crawford, a traveling faith healer, conducted services at the Old Bangor Auditorium (in the background) during a visit in 1925. Standing with area church members are two of Sister Crawford's family: her daughter and son-in-law, Alma and Phineas, at her immediate right (Mrs. Crawford is near the center, dressed in white, holding an open Bible.)

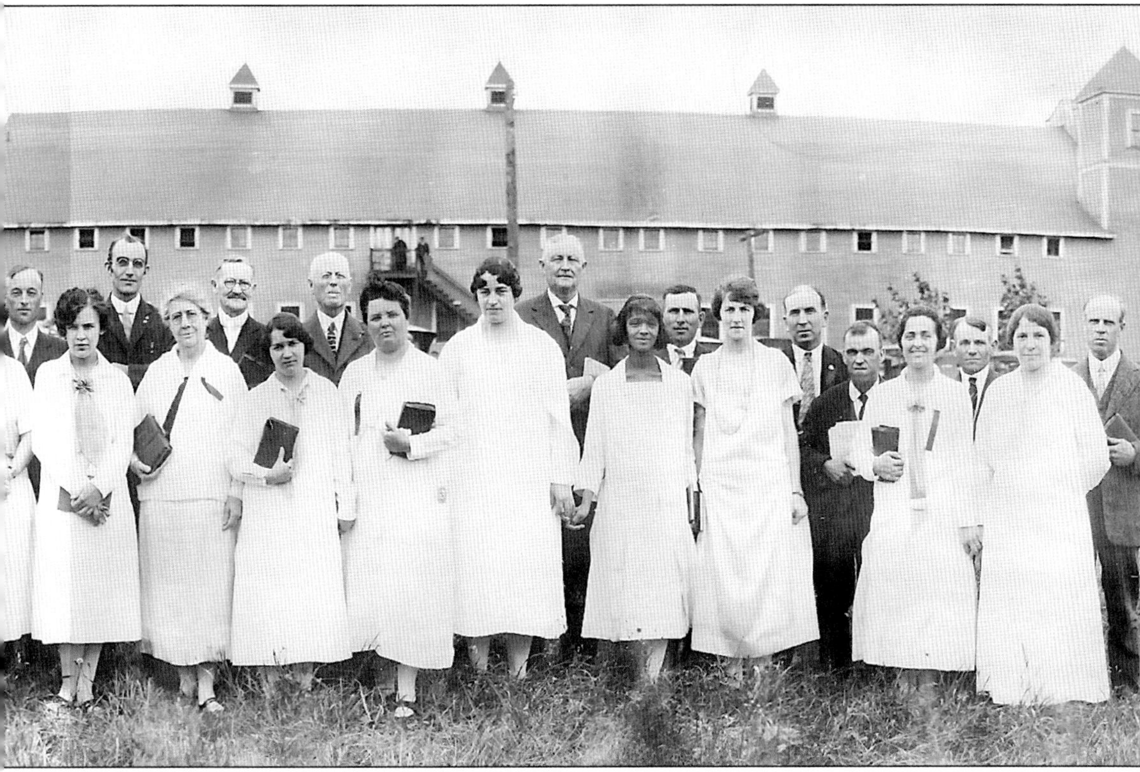

Seated are Gerald Howard, Floyd Bartlett, Maynard Bartlett and Charlie Cook. Mrs. Crawford's claims of miracle cures were discounted by the Bangor Ministerial Association, which investigated the evangelist. Undaunted, she returned to Bangor later that year for a "vindication meeting."

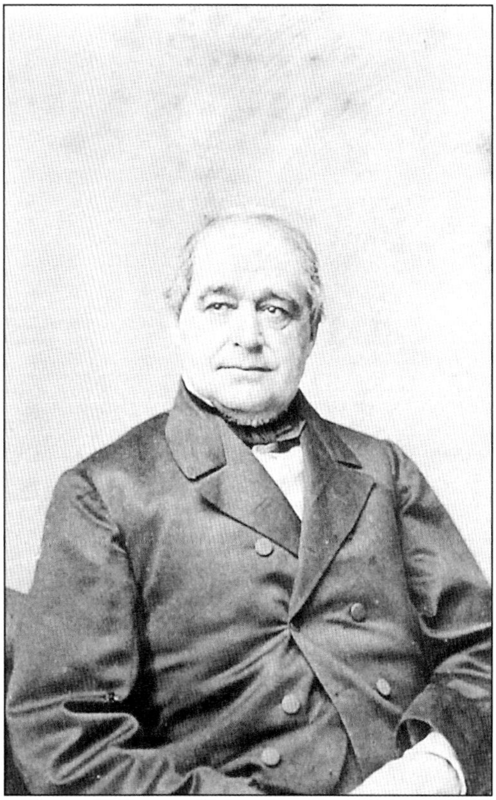

Hannibal Hamlin, Abraham Lincoln's first vice president (1861–1865), lived for many years at a mansion on Fifth Street. He was much loved by local residents, who respected his good humor and kindly manner.

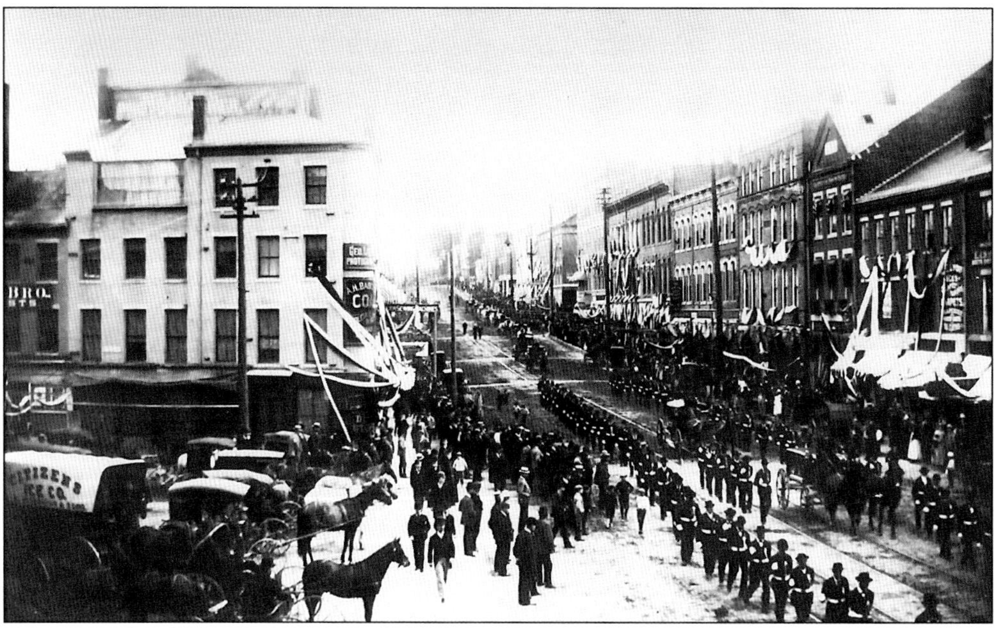

When Hamlin died unexpectedly at the Tarratine Club while playing cards on July 4, 1891, all of Bangor wept. The old statesman's remains were carried down Main Street in an impressive funeral ceremony witnessed by thousands. The procession ended at Mount Hope Cemetery, where he lies in the Hamlin family plot.

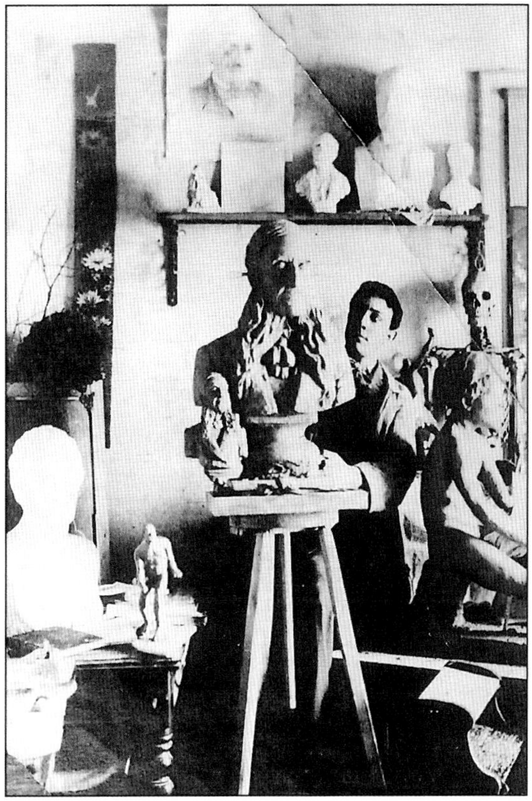

Charles Tefft, a Brewer sculptor, creates a bust of Hannibal Hamlin. The former senator, governor and vice president peers down from a high shelf in a portrait taken in his later years. Tefft later sculpted the full-size bronze statue of Hamlin located in a downtown mall.

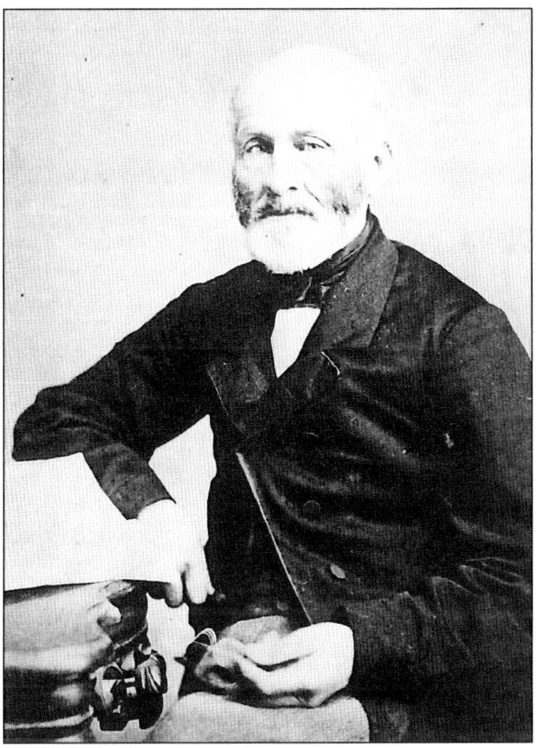

For many years Dr. William Mason healed the sick. The wealthy surgeon enjoyed the distinction of being one of five generations of Harvard graduates, all doctors, which was quite an accomplishment in his day.

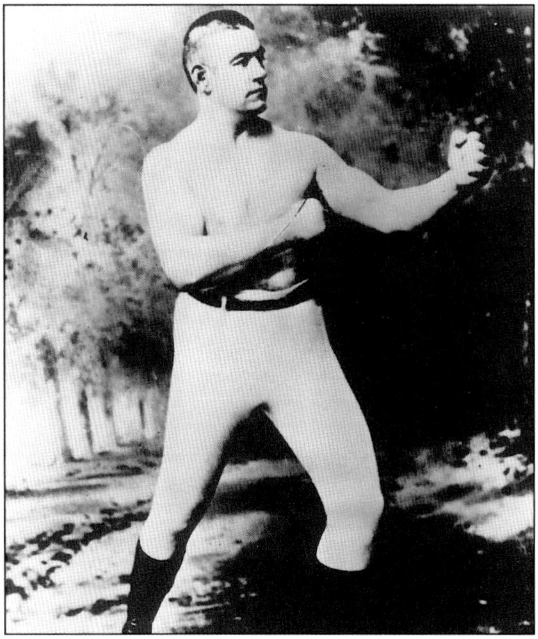

John L. Sullivan, the bare-knuckle heavyweight boxing champion of the world, was famous for his drinking and womanizing. He once spent a night in the Bangor Jail for rowdy behavior. The Boston Strong Boy's other promotional visits to the city were less newsworthy.

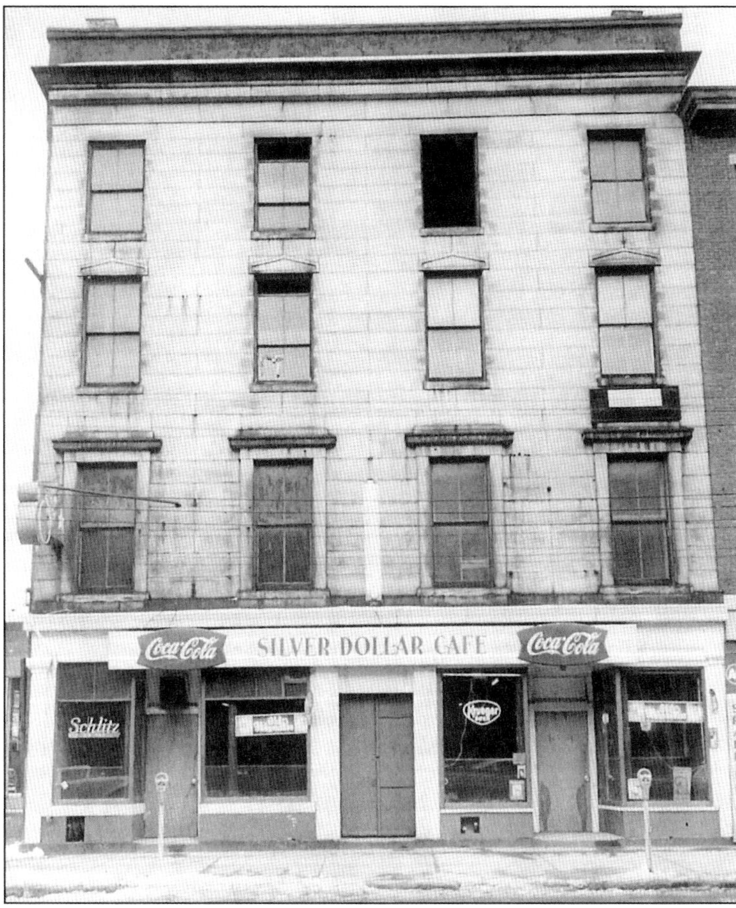

The Silver Dollar Cafe on Exchange Street was notorious for its free-flowing liquor and high-decibel country and western music. Bill Cyr, who opened the bar in the 1950s, advertised his business with an electric sign of a winking moon.

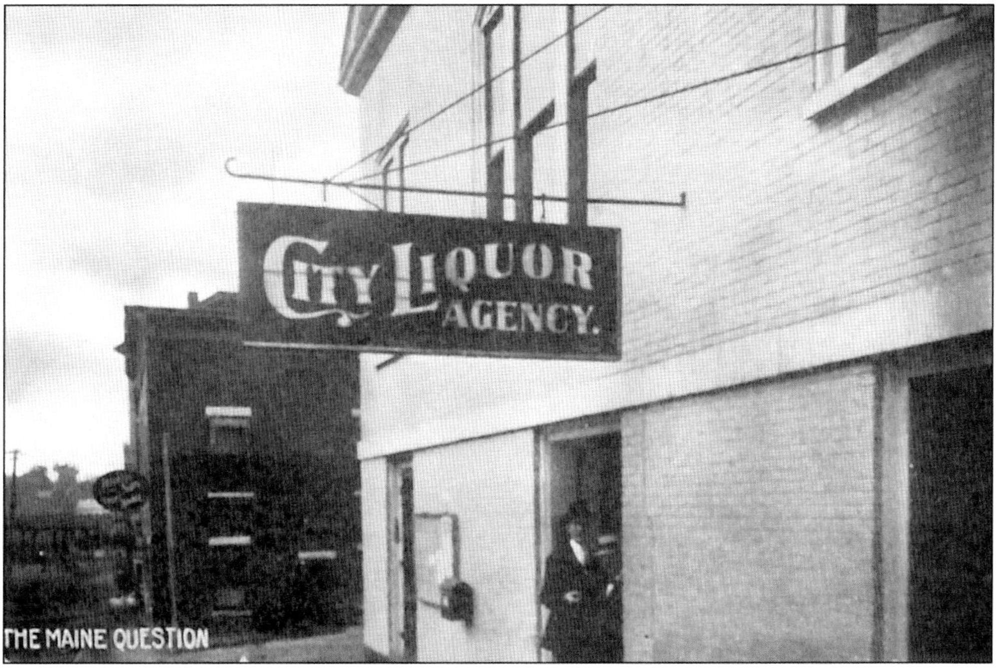

The "Maine Question" posed on this Prohibition-era propaganda card was whether to reverse the law and allow the legal sale of alcoholic beverages. City Liquor Agencies such as this were only fronts for corrupt activity.

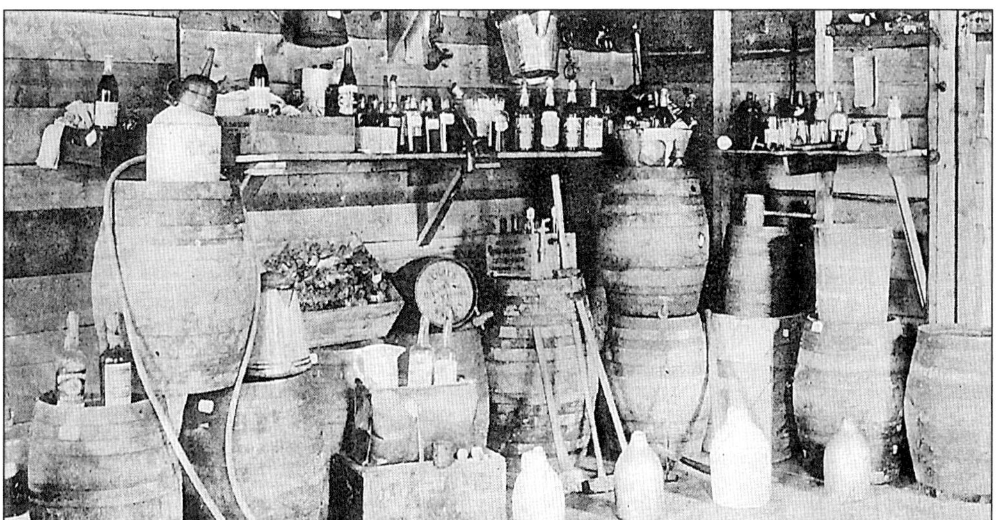

Caught in the act in a room on Franklin Street. This 1909 postcard shows whiskey barrels and paraphernalia seized during a raid on one of Bangor's many bootlegging operations. No wonder the Salvation Army was located at 57 Franklin Street at this time.

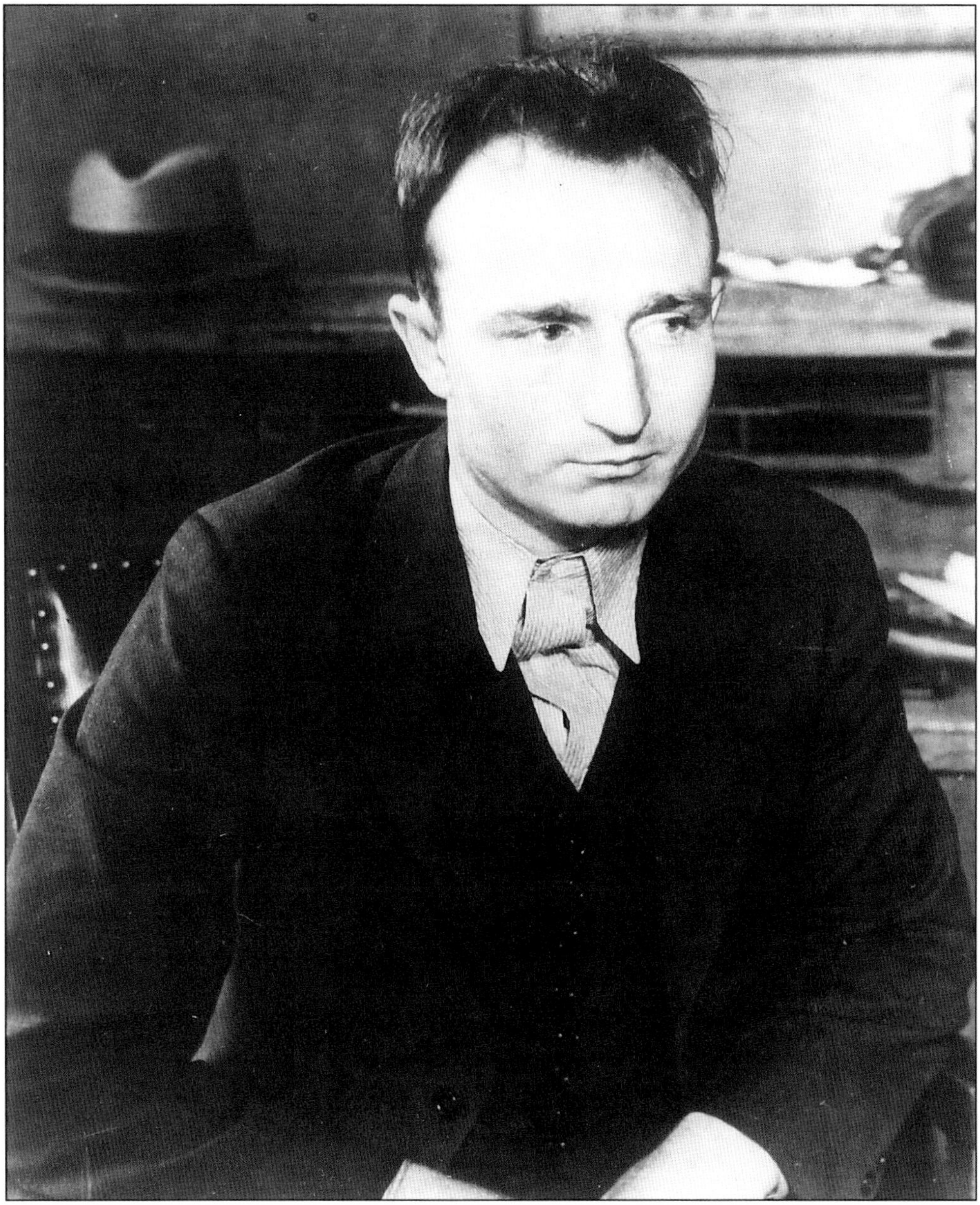

Alfred James Brady looks like the cat that ate the canary in this 1936 photograph taken at the Cook County Jail in Chicago. Brady was well on his way to becoming Public Enemy Number One after he and his gang were arrested for the murder of an Indianapolis police officer. The Hoosier and his cronies would gun down one more lawman before being cornered by FBI agents on a downtown Bangor street in 1937.

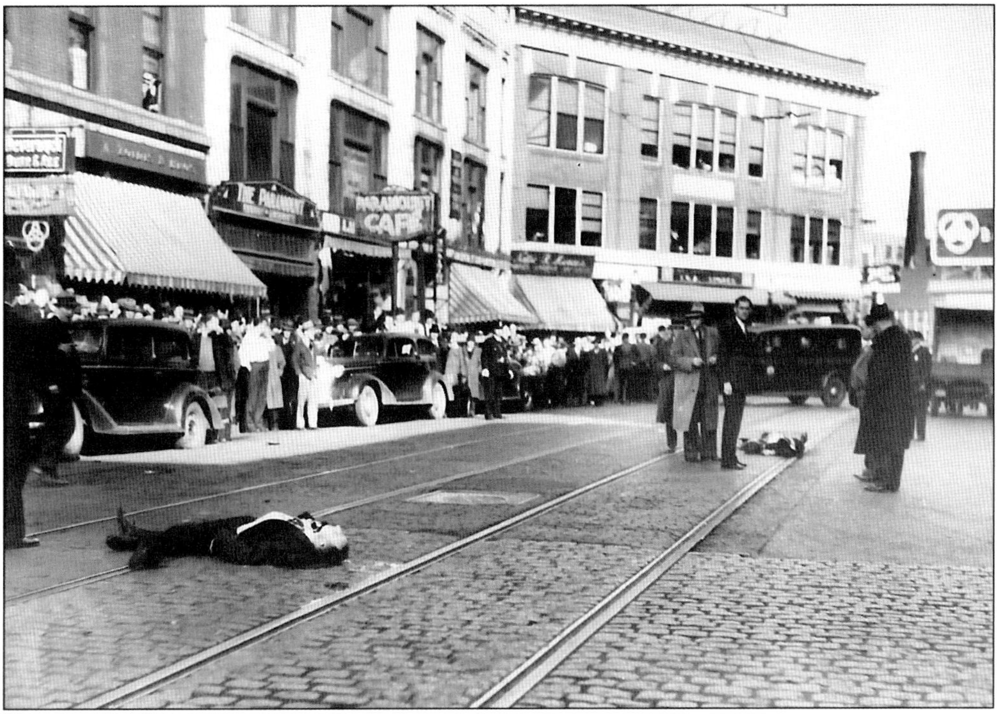

The blood of gangsters Al Brady and Clarence Lee Shaffer, Jr., runs onto Central Street on October 12, 1937, after they were shot with more than fifty bullets from the weapons of FBI special agents. Brady (foreground) was only twenty-six years old, Shaffer, twenty-one. A third member, James Dalhover, was captured inside Dakin's Sporting Goods when he tried to purchase a machine gun.

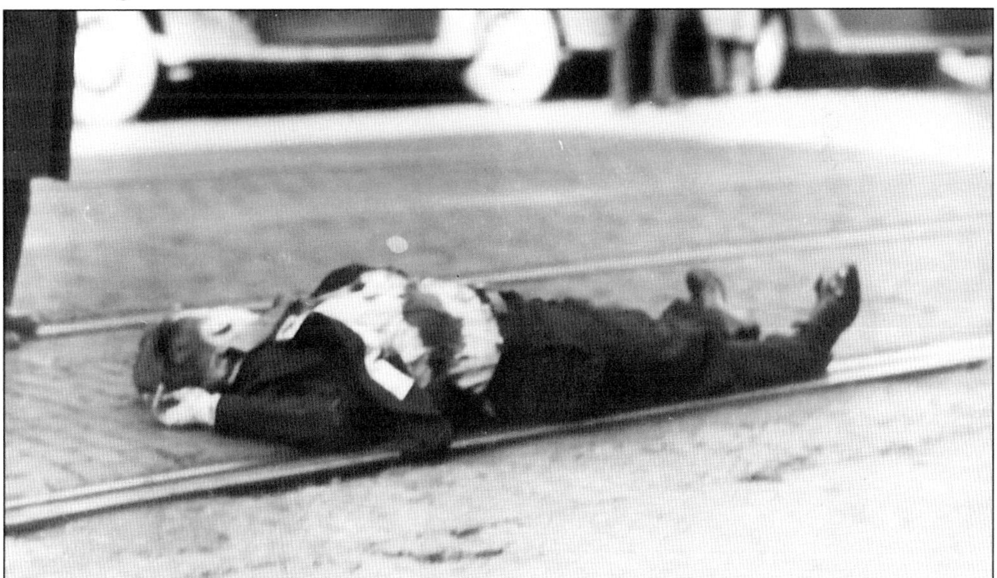

Clarence Lee Shaffer, Jr., drove the getaway car during the Brady Gang's numerous armed robberies, but he had to leave the gang's stolen Buick behind during the "Columbus Day Massacre." Shaffer's body was nearly cut in half by the force of the lead.

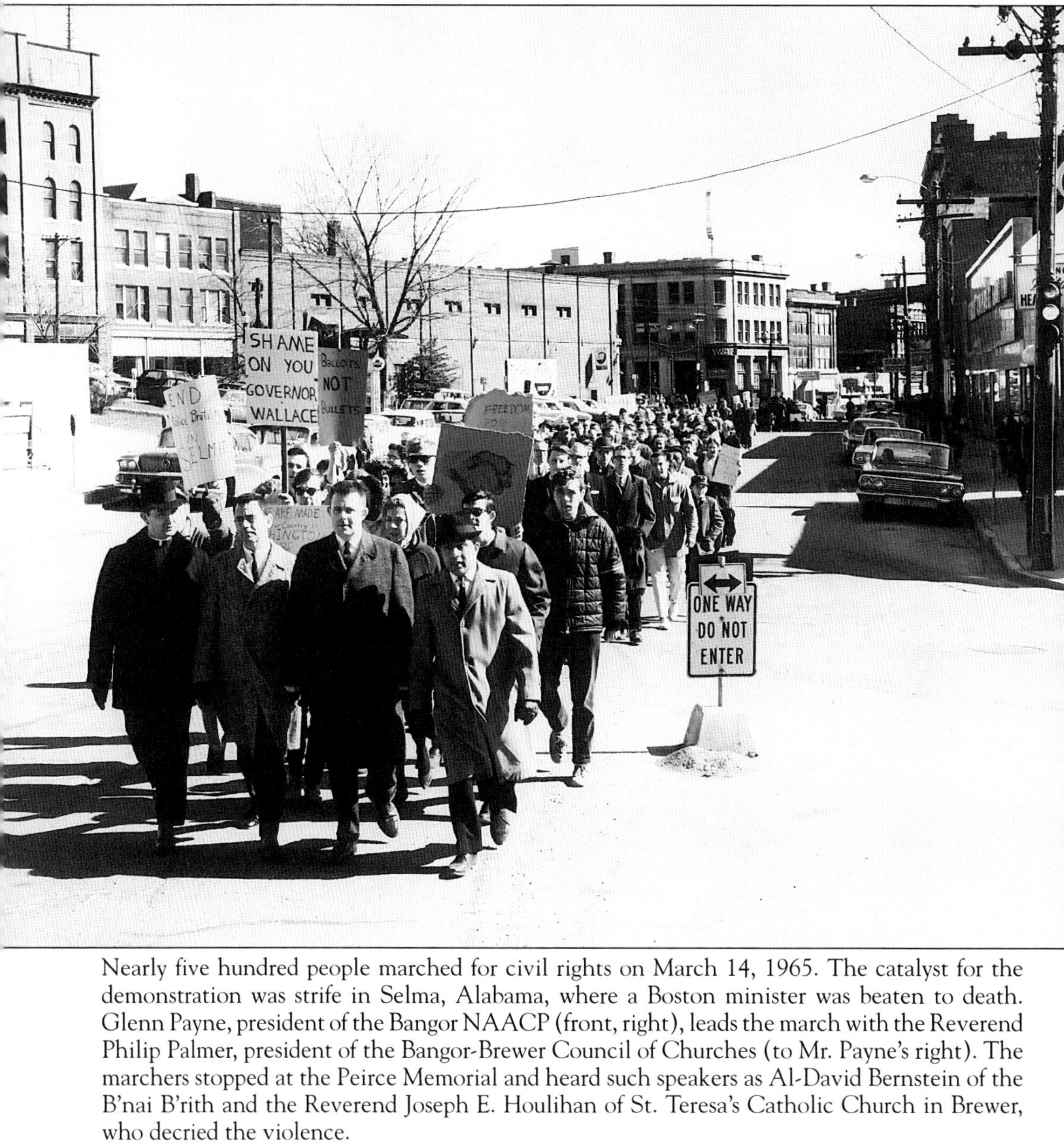

Nearly five hundred people marched for civil rights on March 14, 1965. The catalyst for the demonstration was strife in Selma, Alabama, where a Boston minister was beaten to death. Glenn Payne, president of the Bangor NAACP (front, right), leads the march with the Reverend Philip Palmer, president of the Bangor-Brewer Council of Churches (to Mr. Payne's right). The marchers stopped at the Peirce Memorial and heard such speakers as Al-David Bernstein of the B'nai B'rith and the Reverend Joseph E. Houlihan of St. Teresa's Catholic Church in Brewer, who decried the violence.

Three

Streets and Structures

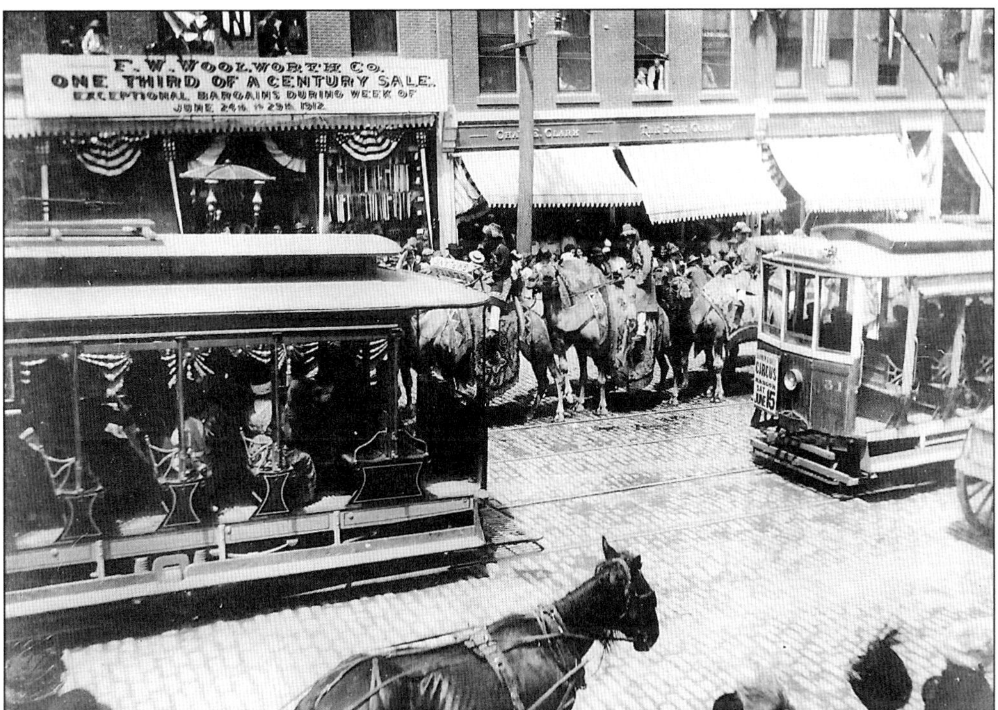

Camels from the Greatest Show on Earth parade down Main Street on June 15, 1912. Streetcar passengers gawk at Barnum and Bailey's mile-long parade that included elephants, horses and Cleopatra and her Maidens from the Nile.

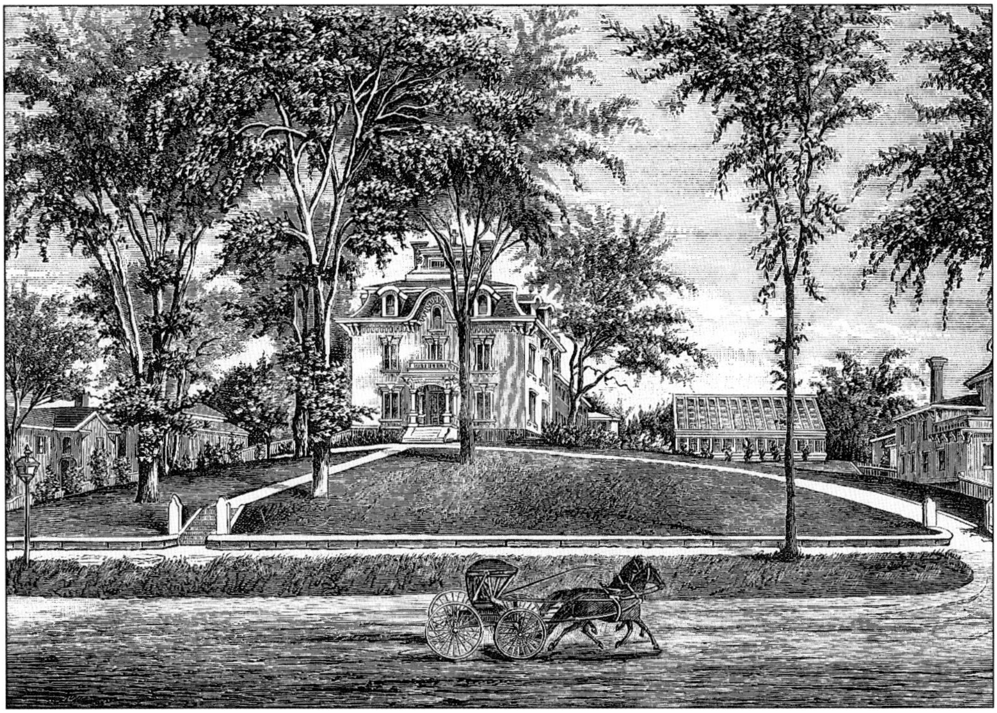

A horse and carriage and graceful elm trees frame this late-nineteenth-century picture of the Convent of Mercy and St. Xavier Academy on State Street. Once the home of Allen Gilman, Bangor's first mayor, and later, Michael Schwartz, who sold hardware, the house was moved to a nearby street and is now a home for senior citizens.

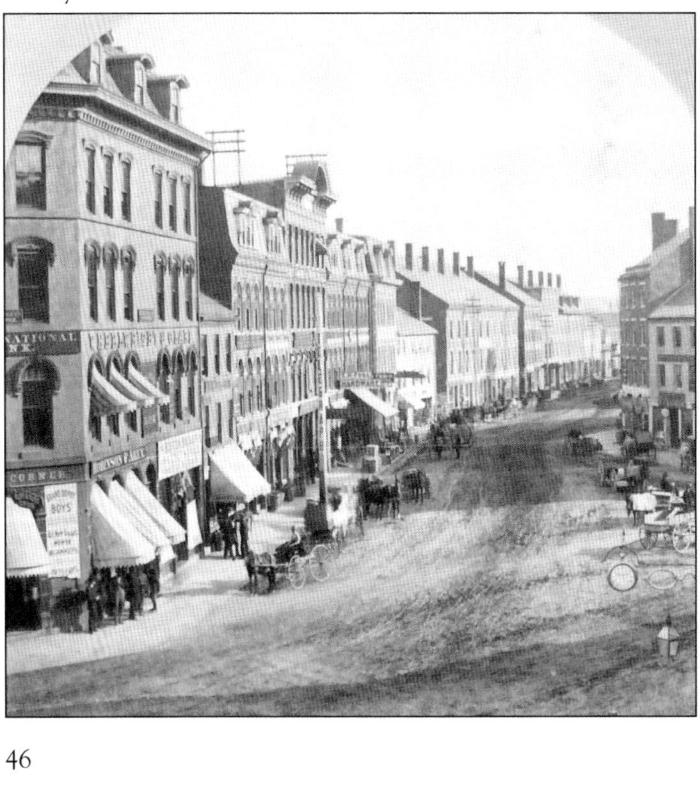

West Market Square in the 1870s, when Bangor was entering its final years as the Lumber Capital of the World. A walk down Broad Street might reveal land speculators, local businessmen, and ordinary shoppers looking for a bargain.

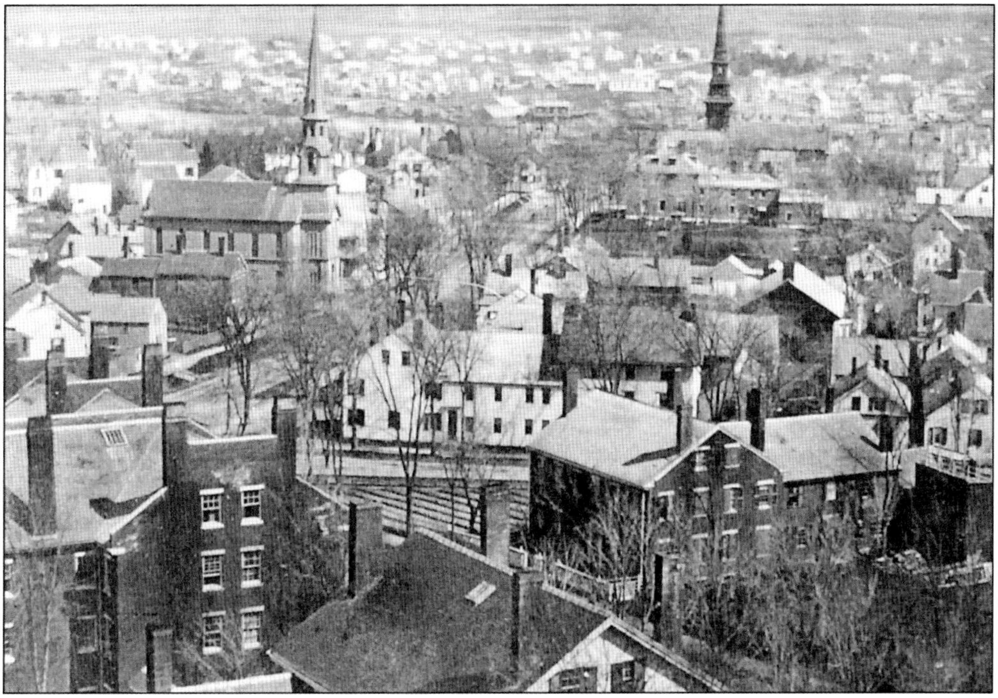

Bangor was a city of church spires, brick homes and dirt streets when this photograph was taken from the belfry of the Bangor Theological Seminary Chapel in the 1870s.

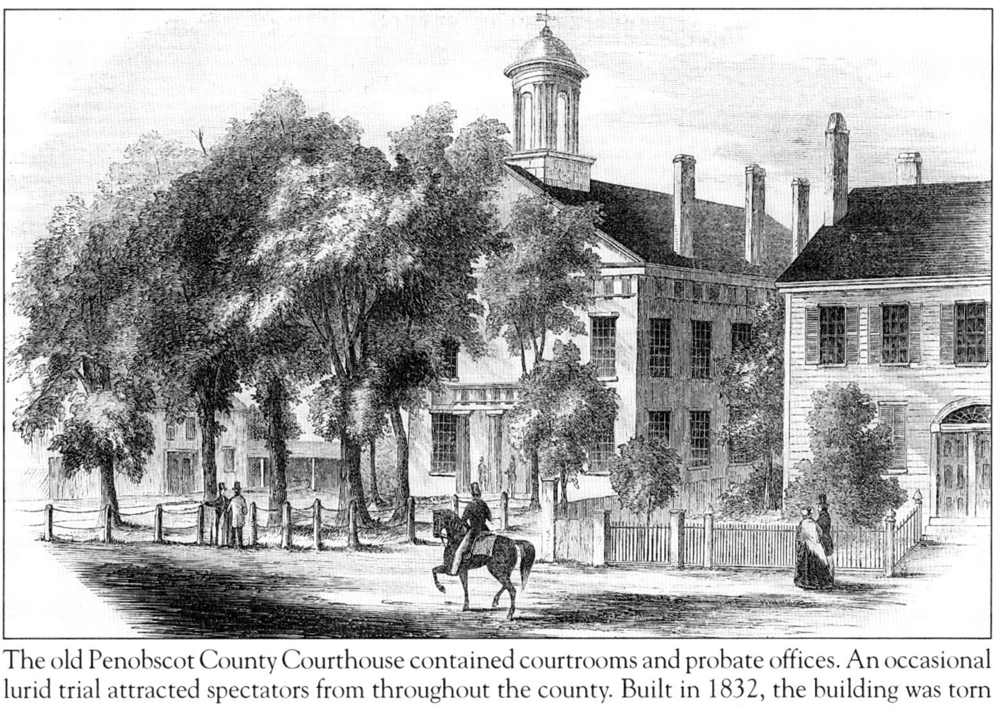

The old Penobscot County Courthouse contained courtrooms and probate offices. An occasional lurid trial attracted spectators from throughout the county. Built in 1832, the building was torn down in the early twentieth century to make way for the present courthouse.

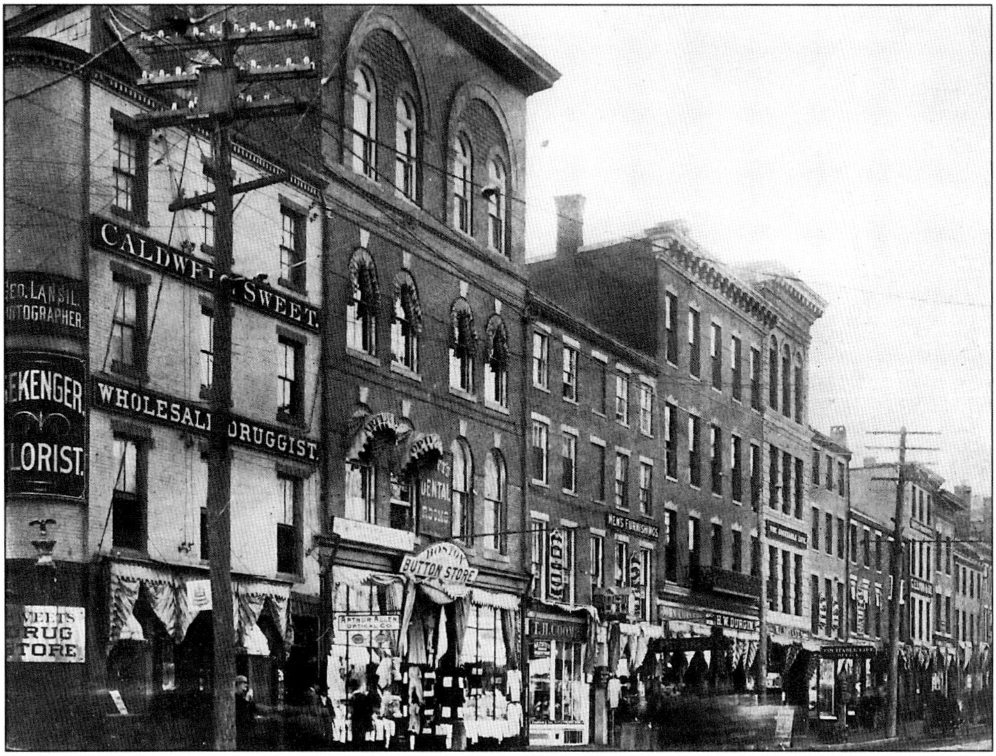

Main Street in the 1890s was a lively place. The Caldwell Sweet Pharmacy and Boston Button Store survived well into the twentieth century.

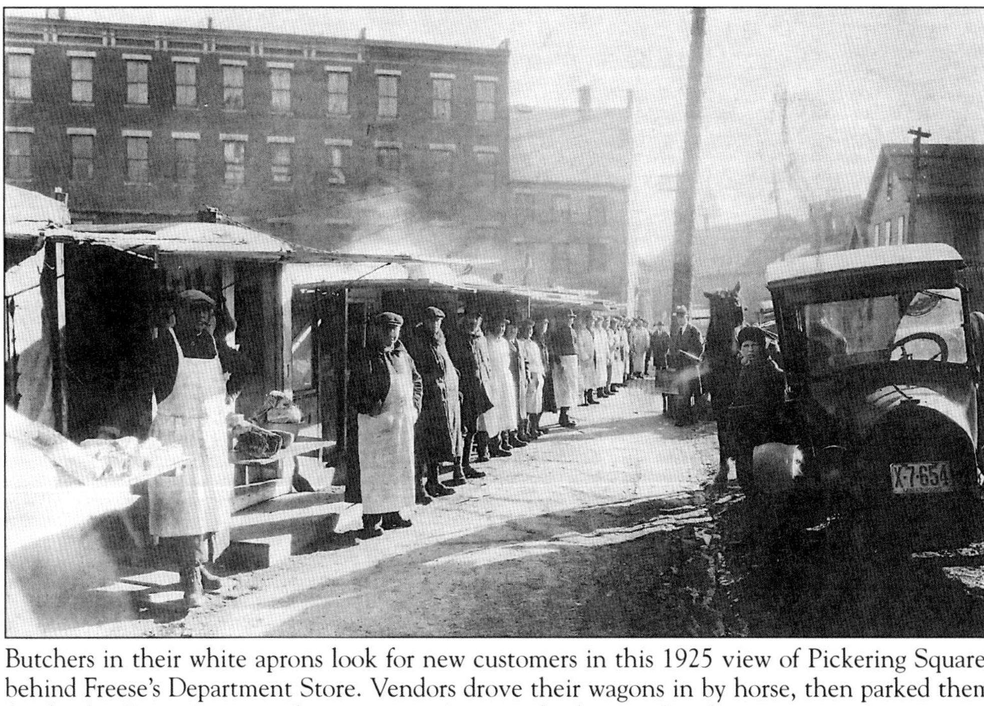

Butchers in their white aprons look for new customers in this 1925 view of Pickering Square, behind Freese's Department Store. Vendors drove their wagons in by horse, then parked them for the day. For many years the square was Bangor's leading marketplace.

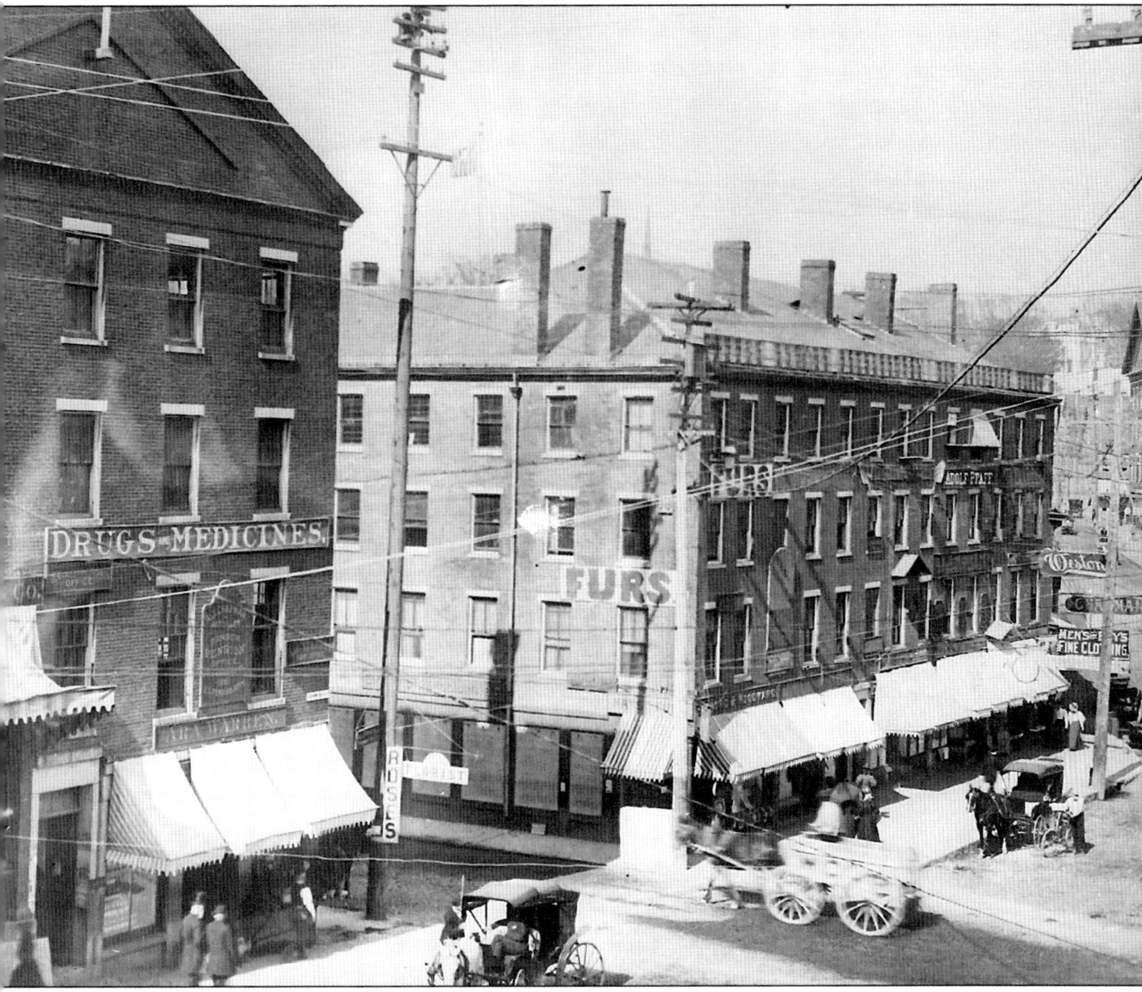

An eclectic assortment of businesses made downtown shopping a treat in the 1880s. Shoppers at the Smith and Bass Blocks at Central and Hammond Streets could buy prescription medicines from Ara Warren, try on a fur coat across the street, or have their portraits taken at Frank C. Weston's studio. On their way home they could pick a rose and browse at Adolf Pfaff's men's clothing store.

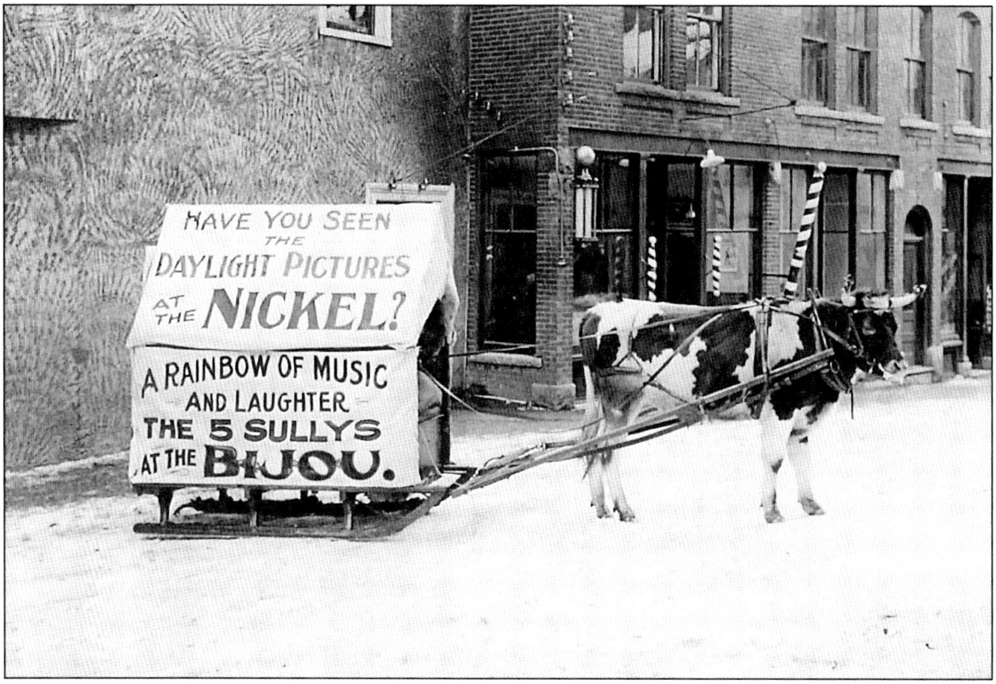

A publicity stunt for two local theaters pulled in customers. Daylight pictures were silent movies shown at the Nickel Theater on Union Street. The 5 Sullys was a vaudeville act appearing at the Bijou, also on Exchange Street. Both were theaters in the Keith Circuit managed locally by Eastport native Stephen Bogrett.

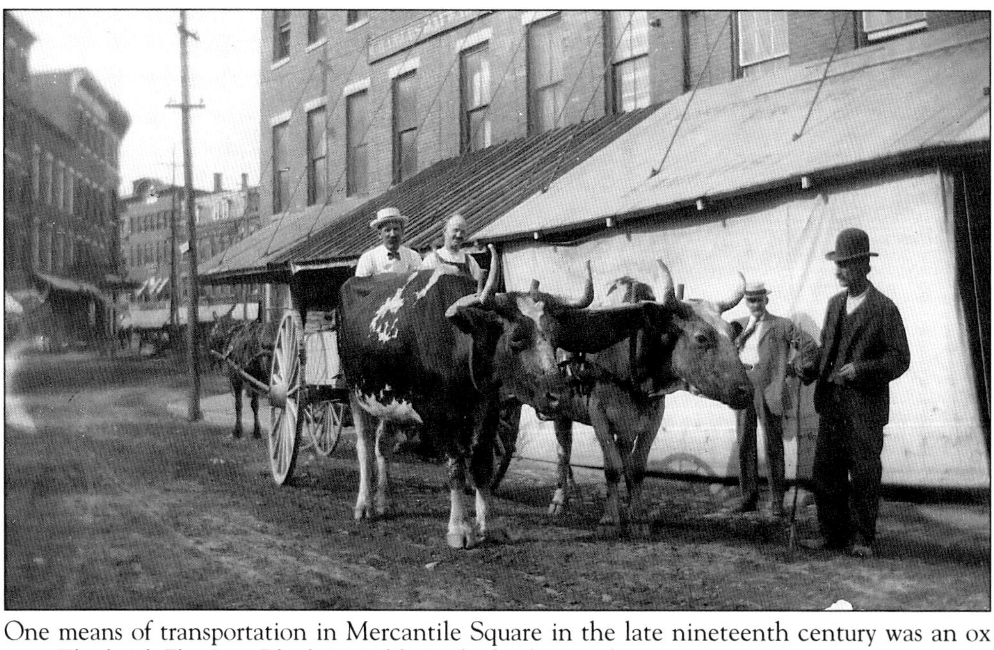

One means of transportation in Mercantile Square in the late nineteenth century was an ox cart. The brick Flat Iron Block is visible in the background.

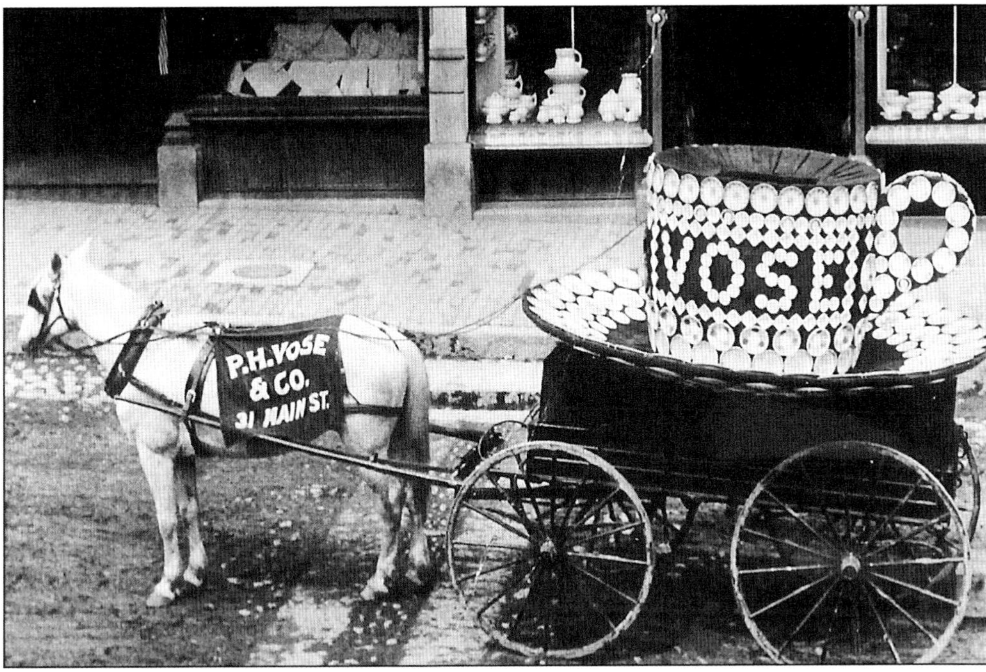

Prescott H. Vose advertised his famous crockery and glassware business with this pony cart. Butter patties from Vose's kiln adorn the giant cup and saucer.

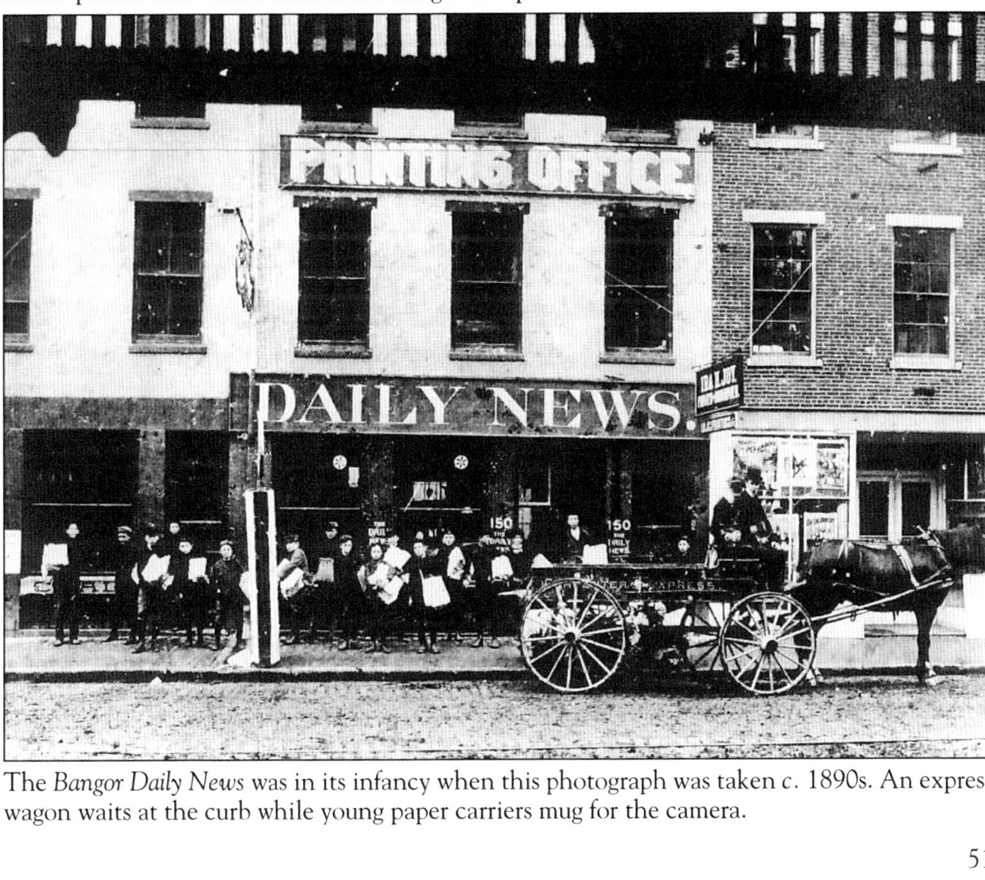

The *Bangor Daily News* was in its infancy when this photograph was taken *c.* 1890s. An express wagon waits at the curb while young paper carriers mug for the camera.

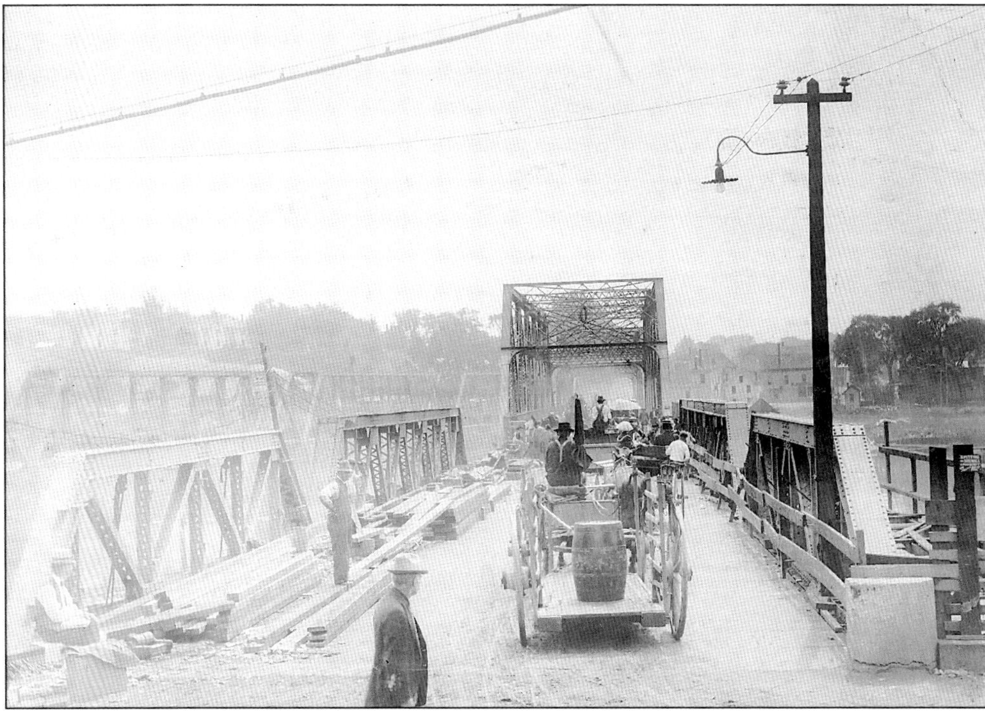

The construction of the Bangor-Brewer Bridge was a sight to behold around 1912. The wagon in the foreground is a jigger, a low vehicle built in Bangor to facilitate the easy removal of potato barrels and other objects.

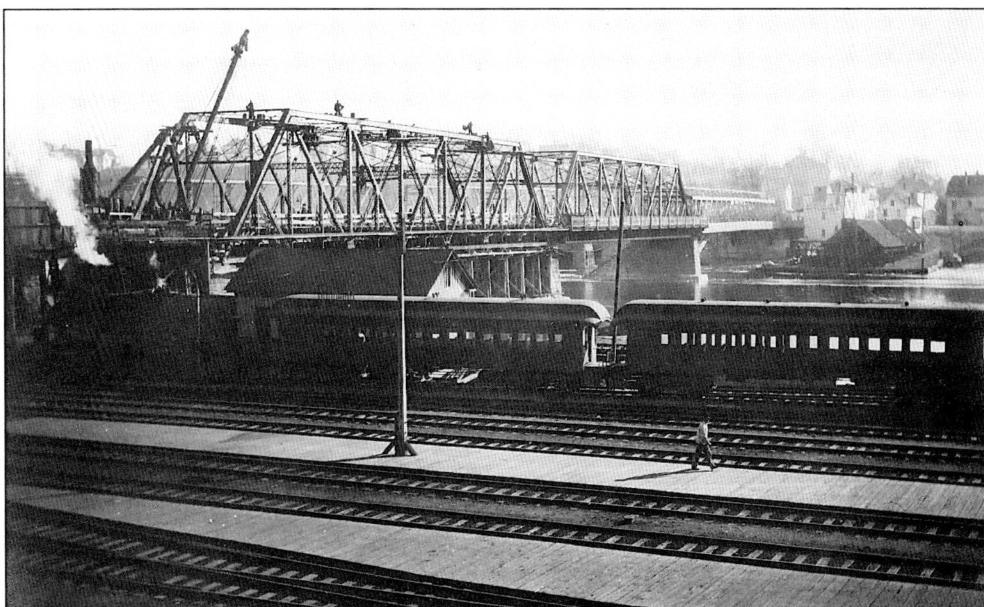

Construction crews put the finishing touches on the "new" bridge which replaced the old covered bridge across the Penobscot which was destroyed in the Flood of 1902. Parlor cars sit on the tracks near Union Station.

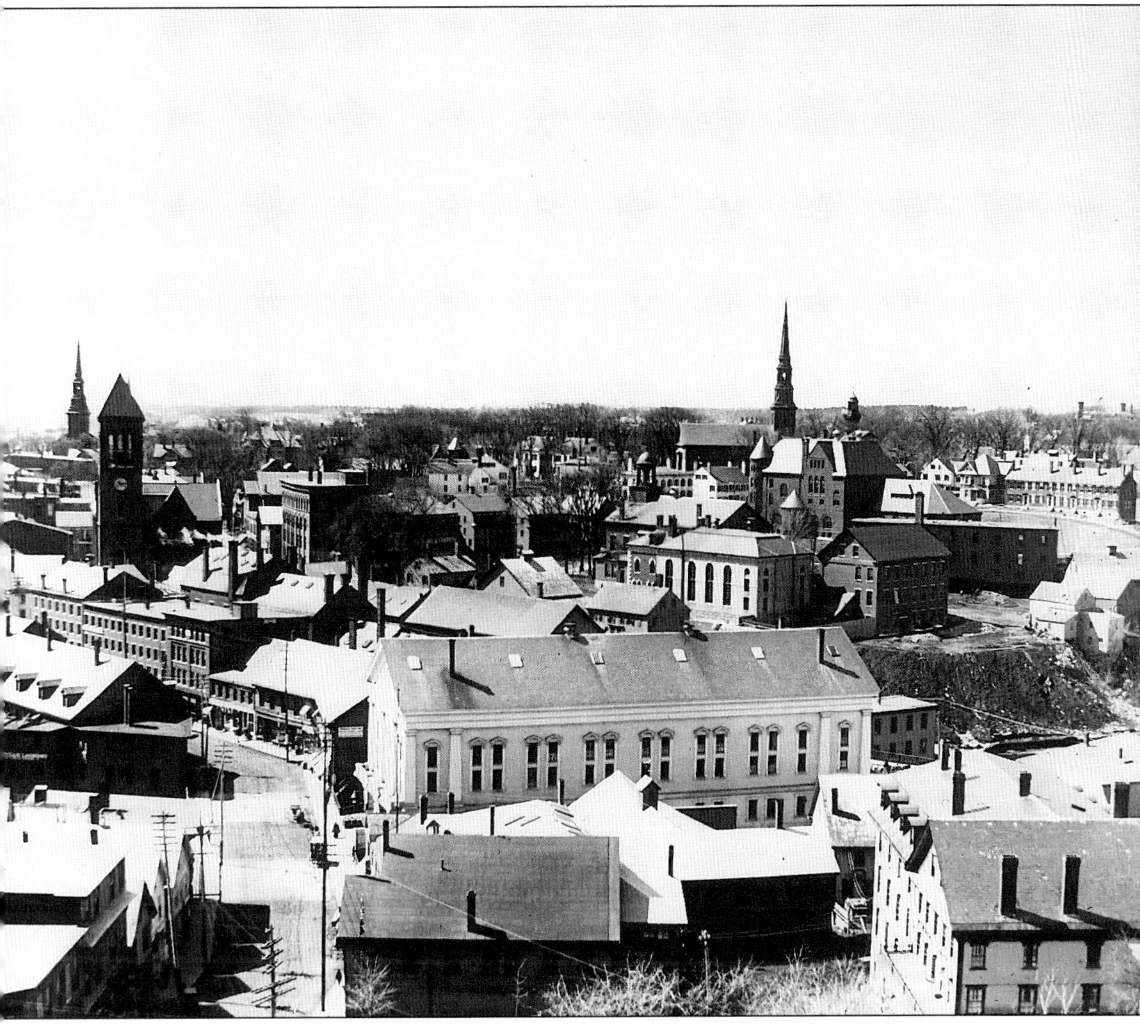

Bangor in full flower before the Great Fire of 1911 laid some of these buildings to ruin. A photographer in the steeple of the Central Congregational Church on French Street (destroyed in the fire) captured the massive Norumbega Hall building at the center, a corner of the Windsor Hotel at the bottom right, as well as the City Hall on the left, and the spires of the Unitarian and Hammond Street Congregational Churches. The fire erased forever the appearance of downtown Bangor as a nineteenth-century city.

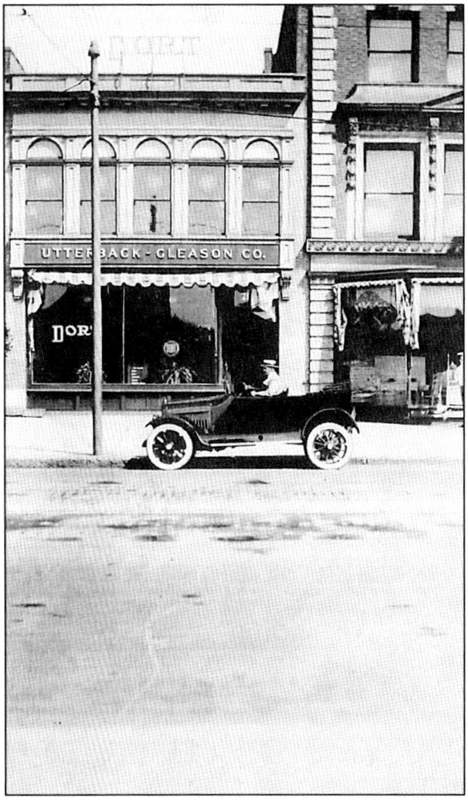

The Dort went the way of the Edsel, but this man enjoyed driving one when he had the chance. The Utterback-Gleason Company sold Dorts c. 1920 from its showroom on Post Office Square.

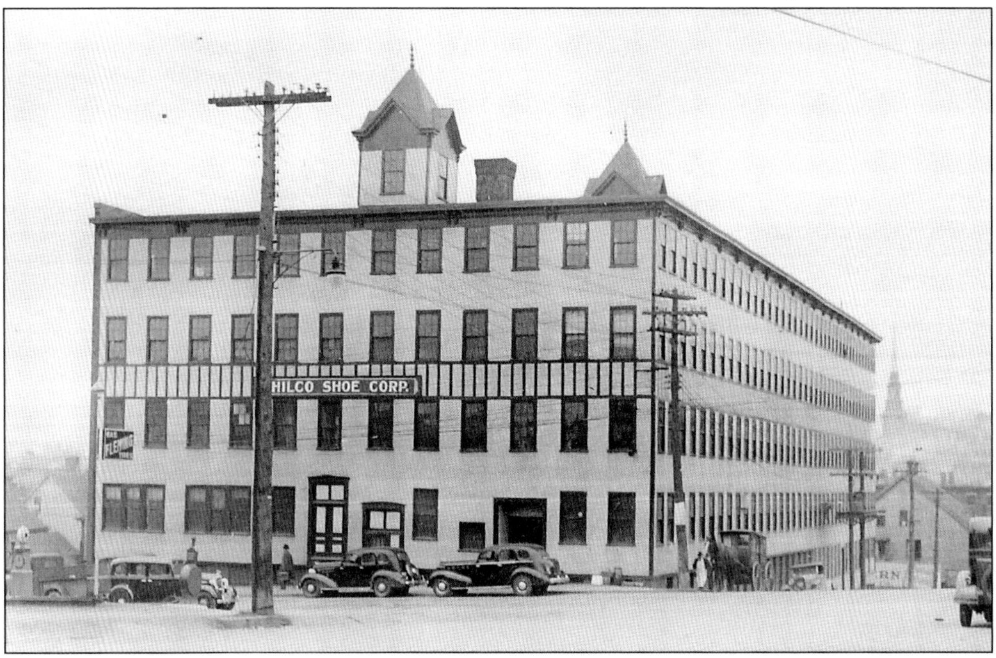

The Philco Shoe Corporation occupied this massive building once located at Hancock and Oak Streets. Built in 1887 for the Parker and Peakes Shoe Company, the building had been greatly enlarged by the time this photograph was taken c. 1930s.

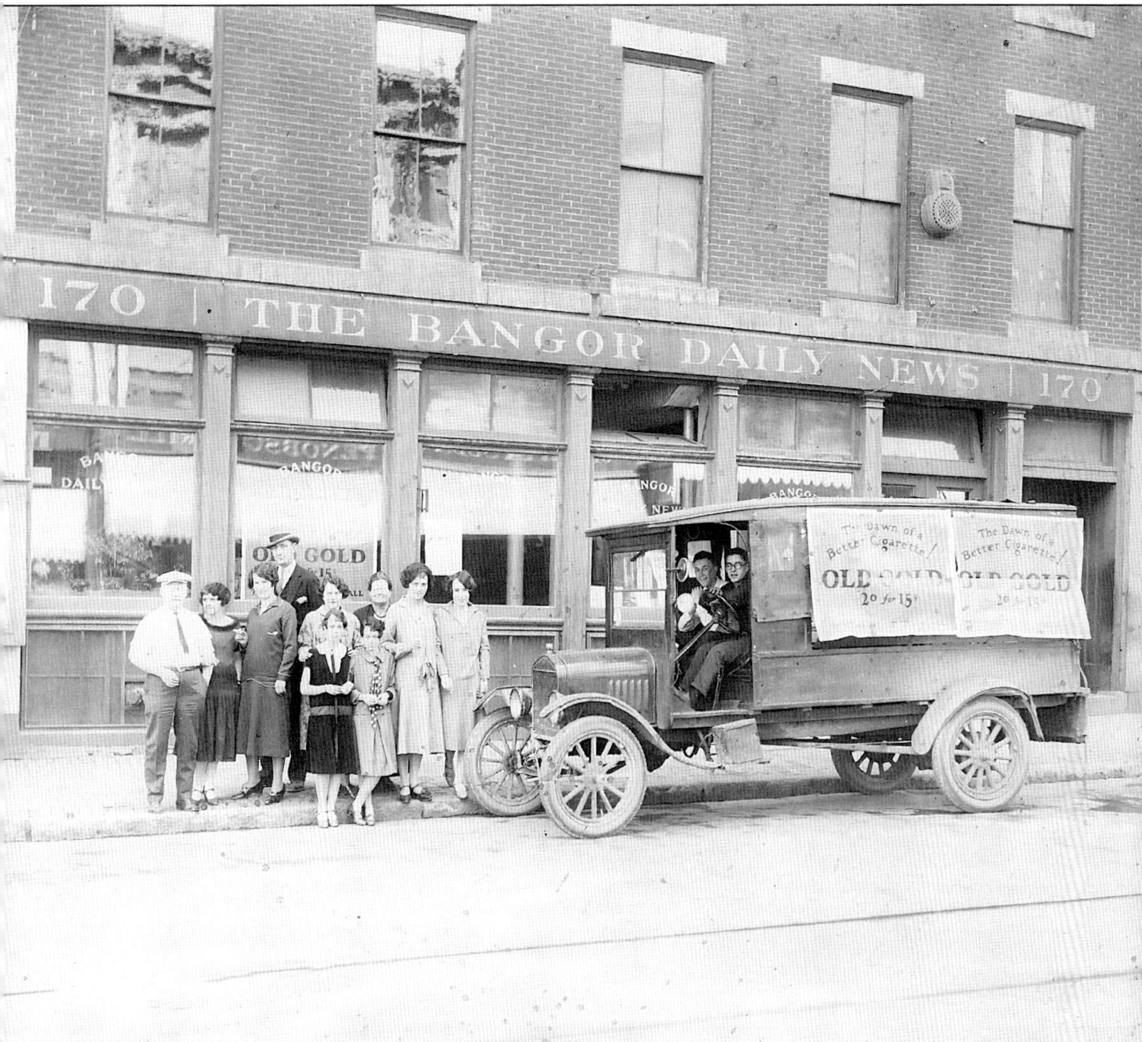

In the 1920s this happy group posed in front of the *Bangor Daily News* building on Exchange Street. The stocky man on the left probably worked for the newspaper while the dashing, tall man in the back may have represented Old Gold Cigarettes, which promised a better cigarette—and twenty for just $.15! Regulations at the time allowed commercial promotion in front of the newspaper office. Today such scenes are taboo. The newspaper has long since banned tobacco advertising, and its Main Street offices and Hampden Printing Press are smoke-free.

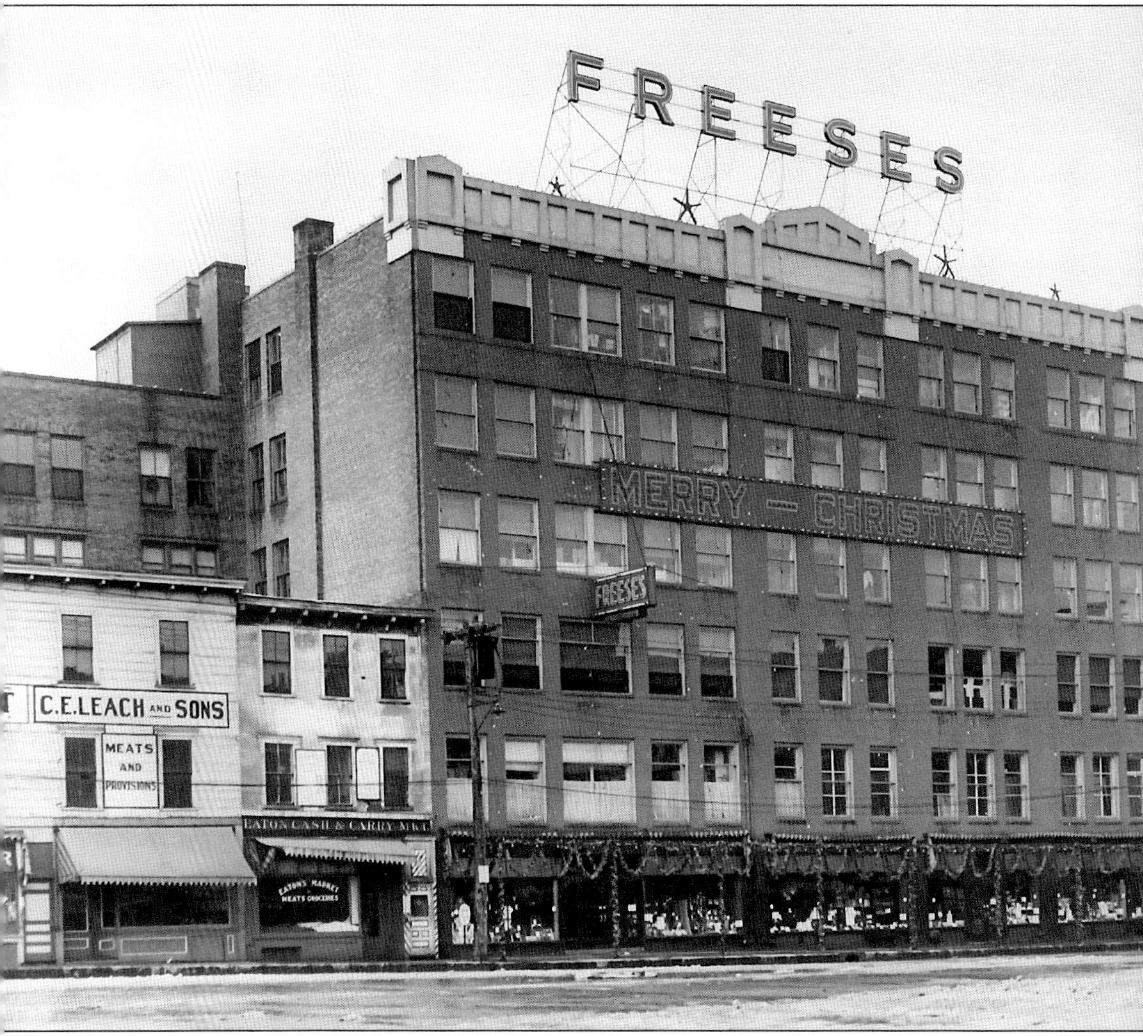

Freese's Department Store decorated for the holidays in the 1930s. Freese's legend grew steadily after A. Langdon Freese opened a clothing store on Main Street in 1892. As business increased, he expanded the store to include the sale of everything from housewares to furniture. After the Santa Claus Parade the day after Thanksgiving, weary shoppers were encouraged by clever store executives to take a short-cut through Freese's from Pickering Square to Main Street. On their way, of course, they often stopped and shopped a while.

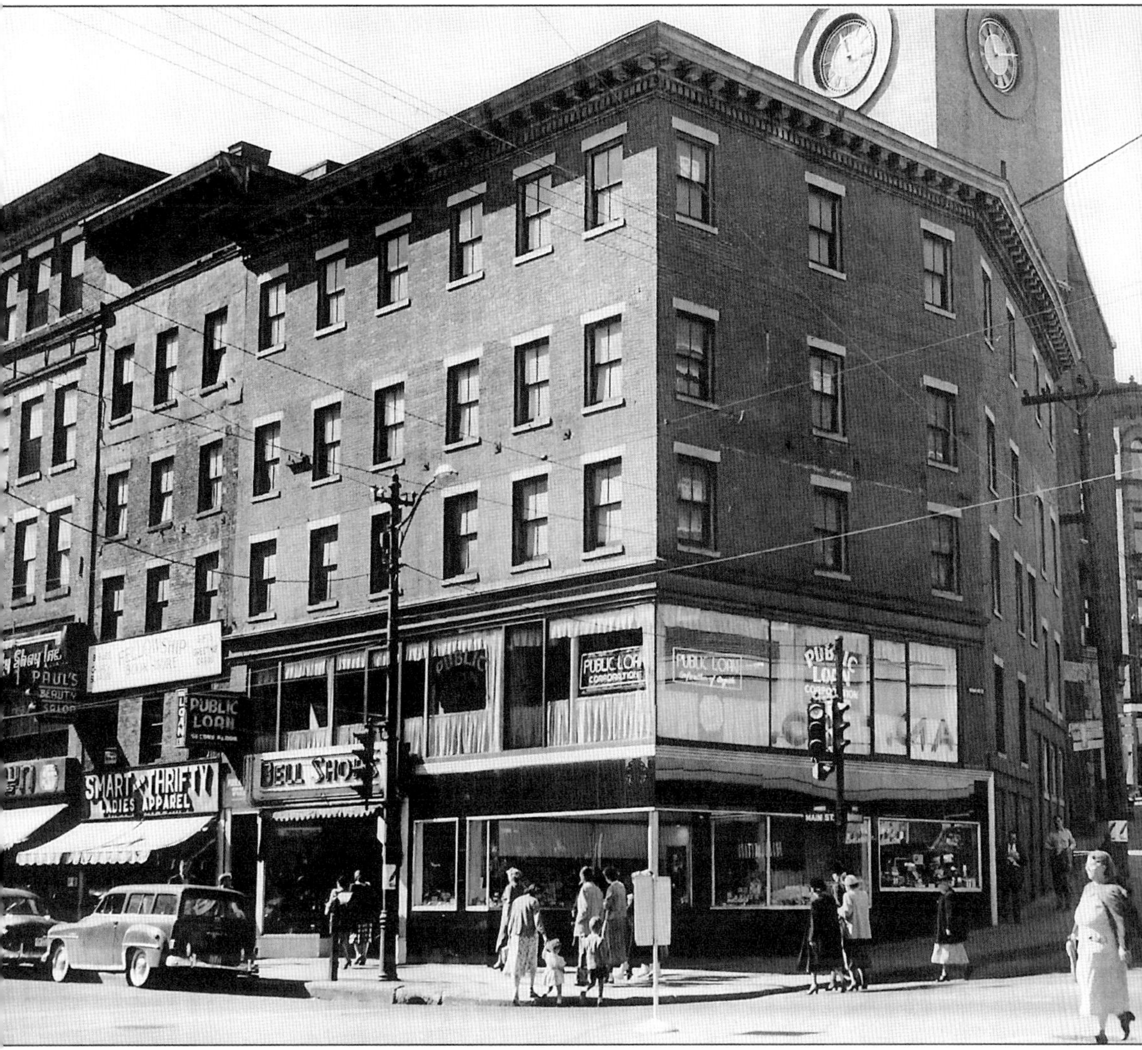

Unlike today's downtown, the Bangor of the 1950s utilized upstairs space with such businesses as Paul and Kitty Shay's Beauty Parlor and the Public Loan Corporation. Ground-floor shopping was still possible, of course. Women liked the affordability of clothing at the Bell Shops and Smart and Thrifty. Crown Jewelers was also easy on the pocketbook. If you lost track of the time the bell tower of the old Bangor City Hall was close by with its huge, illuminated clock.

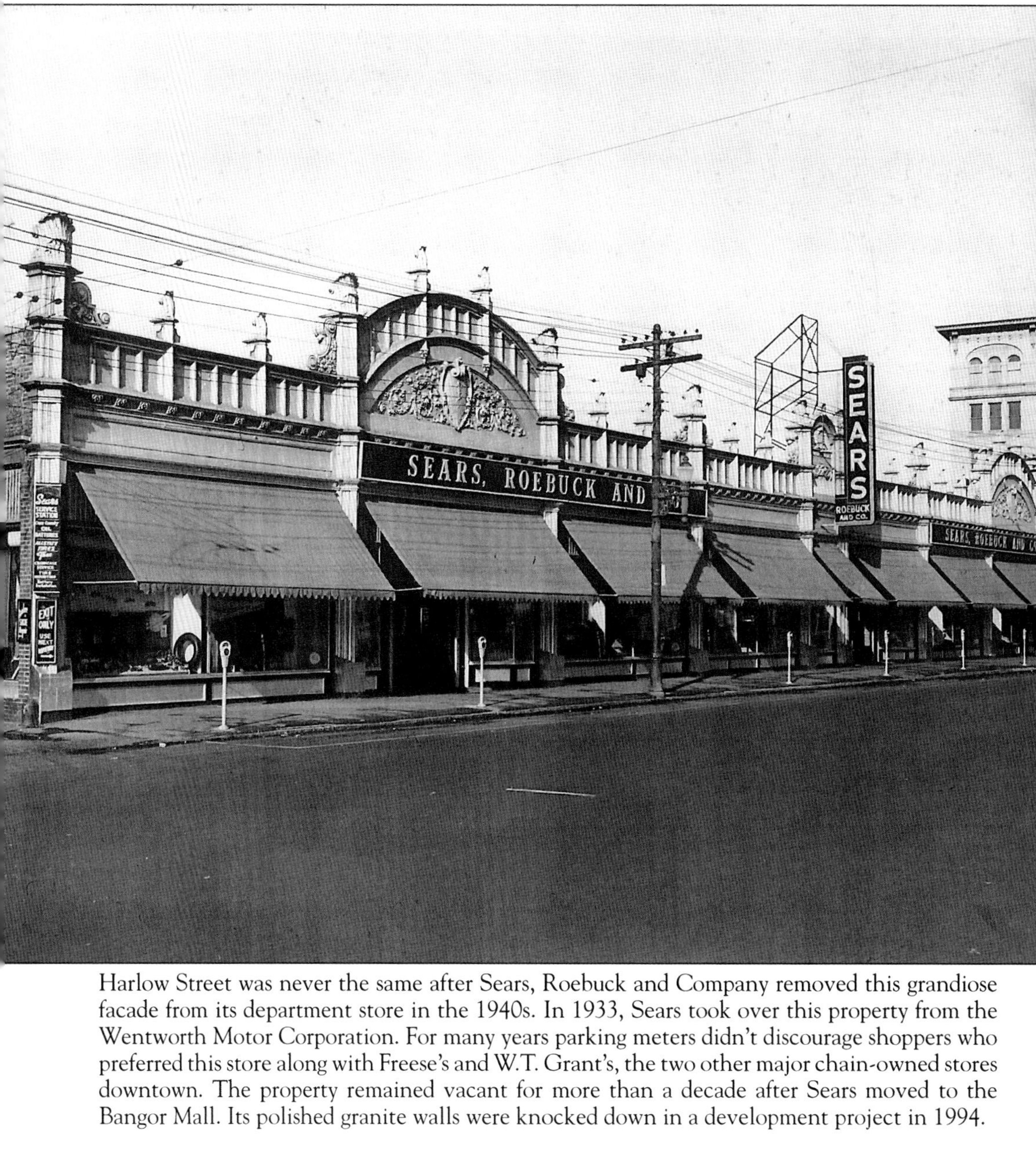

Harlow Street was never the same after Sears, Roebuck and Company removed this grandiose facade from its department store in the 1940s. In 1933, Sears took over this property from the Wentworth Motor Corporation. For many years parking meters didn't discourage shoppers who preferred this store along with Freese's and W.T. Grant's, the two other major chain-owned stores downtown. The property remained vacant for more than a decade after Sears moved to the Bangor Mall. Its polished granite walls were knocked down in a development project in 1994.

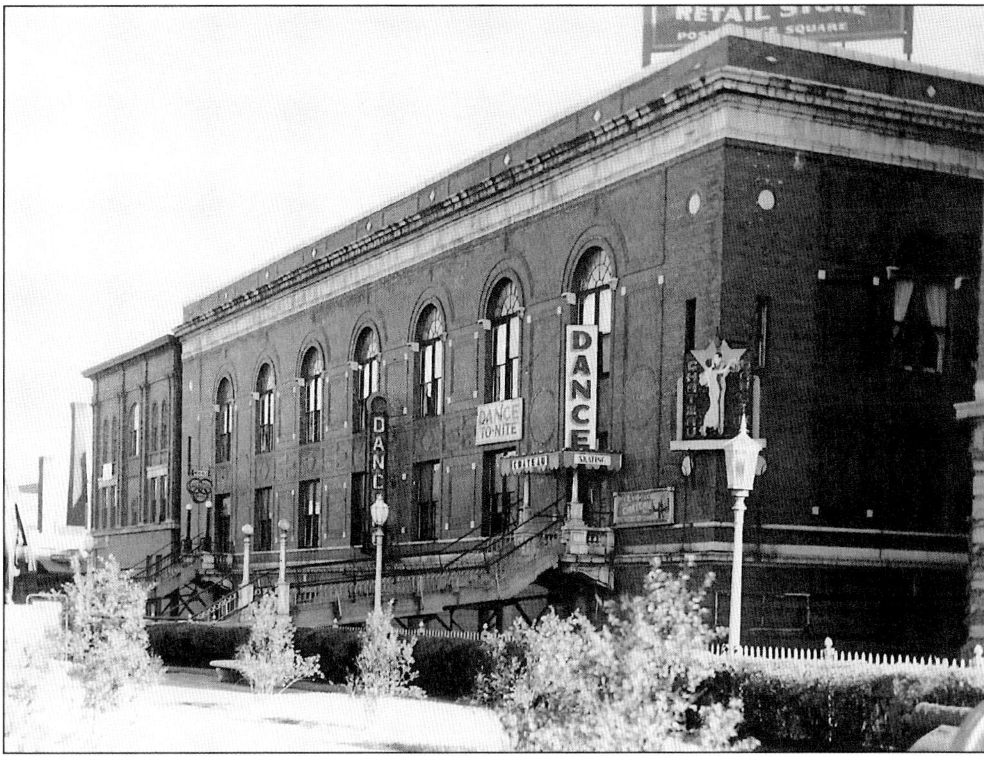

Dancers waltzed their troubles away during the Great Depression at the Chateau Ballroom, managed by Edgar Nickerson. Opposite the Kenduskeag Mall, the ballroom featured a solid wooden dance floor and a crystal ball that spun from the ceiling. Downstairs was the Bowlodrome, a bowling alley and sportsman's club.

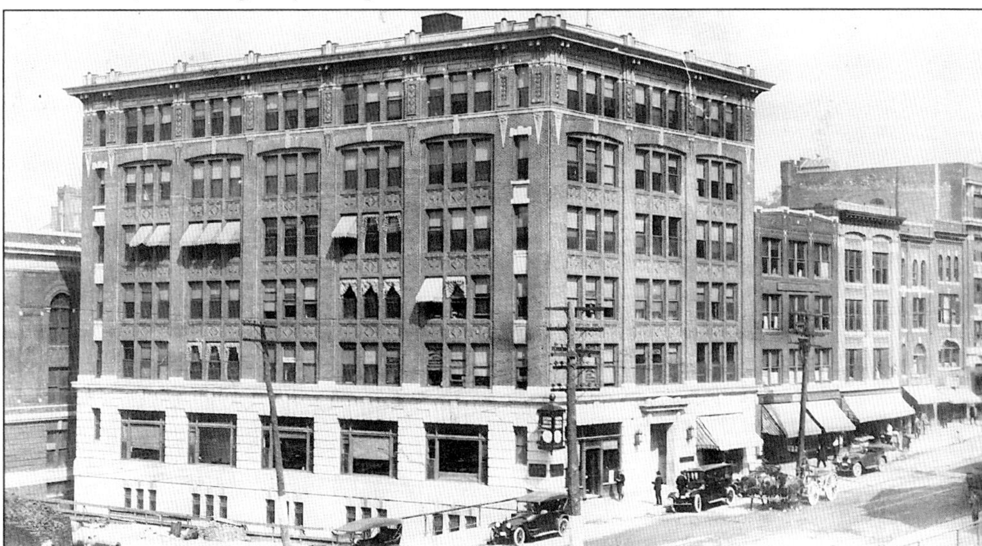

One of the most impressive blocks to rise from the ashes of the 1911 fire was the Eastern Trust and Banking Company Building on State Street. In the upstairs offices millions of dollars were traded in paper company dealings.

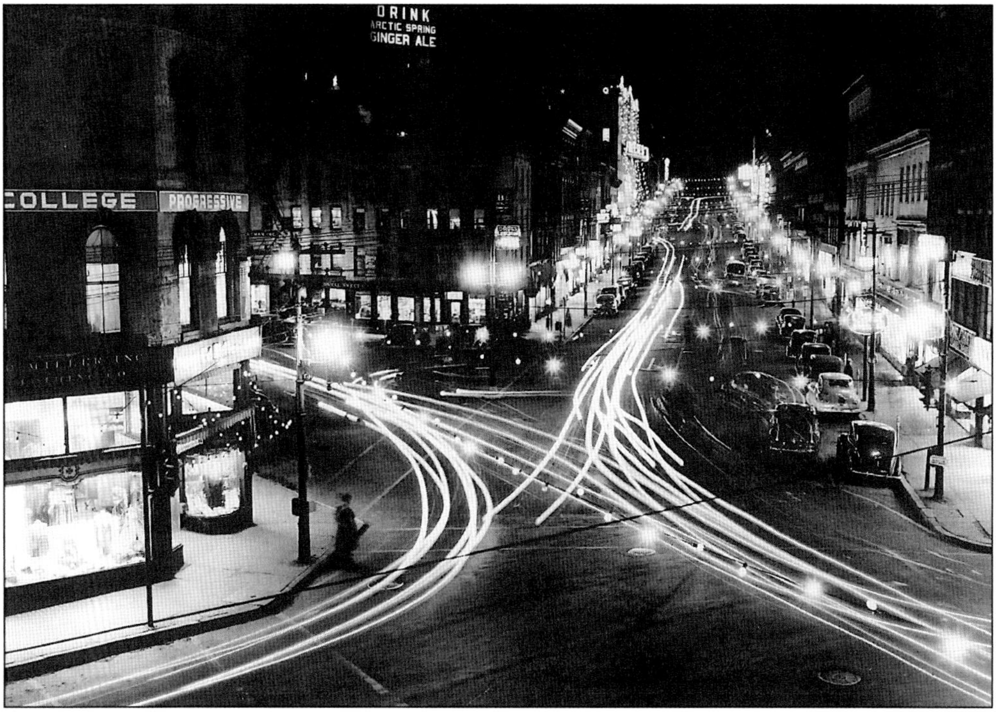

Dan Maher of the *Bangor Daily News*, along with his son (also named Dan), savored nighttime photography. This unique time-lapse scene of Main Street dressed up for Christmas in the 1940s is one of his best.

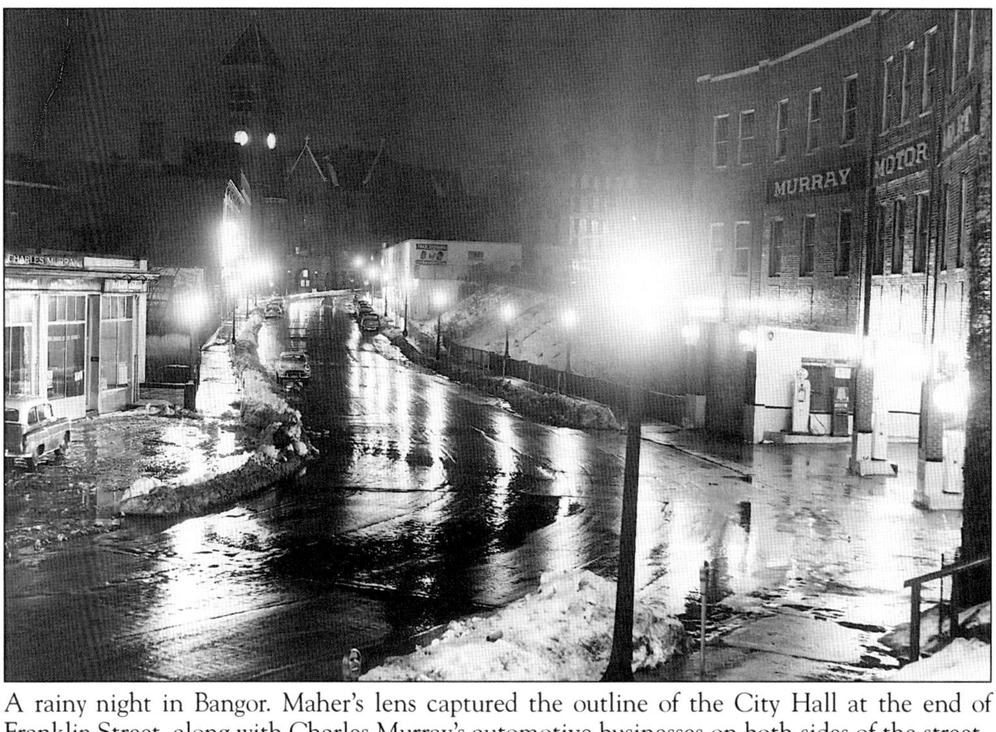

A rainy night in Bangor. Maher's lens captured the outline of the City Hall at the end of Franklin Street, along with Charles Murray's automotive businesses on both sides of the street.

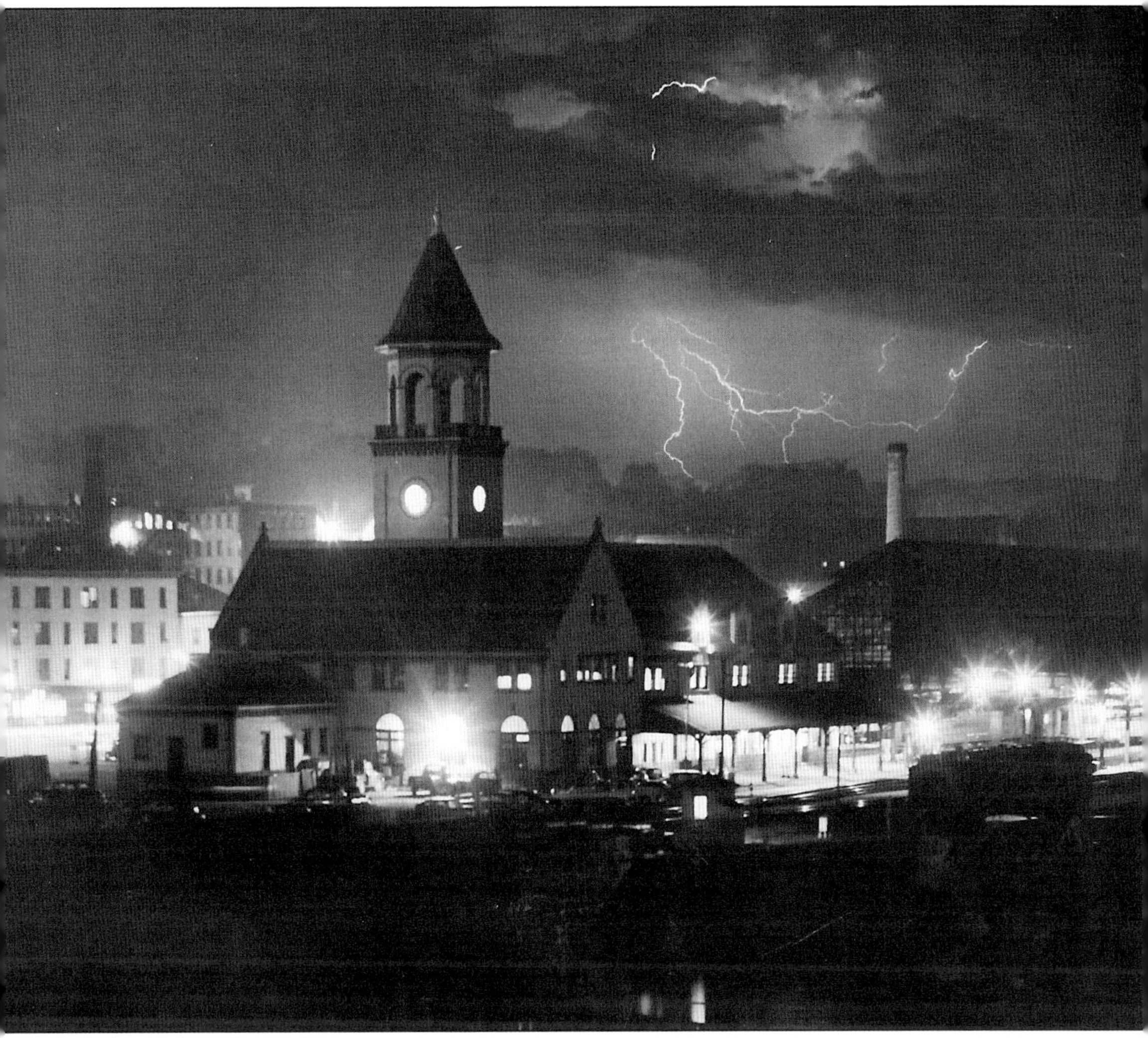

High drama over Union Station in the 1950s. The younger Maher braved the elements, probably standing on the Joshua Chamberlain Bridge, to photograph lightning dancing overhead. Patience and imagination were needed when photographing electrical storms because of their unpredictable nature. Union Station, with its lighted clock tower, was the perfect subject for a Maher photo study. Instantly recognizable, few could mistake its form.

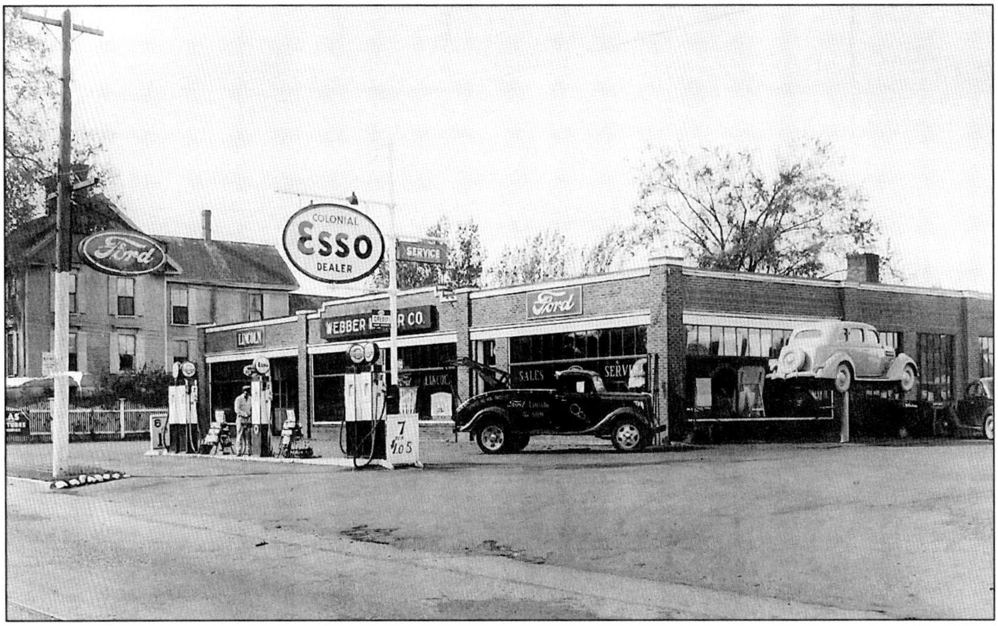

Fill'er up with 7 gallons for $1.05 at the Webber Motor Company's garage on Hammond Street. In the 1930s and 1940s the garage operated a full-service dealership, complete with an outdoor jack.

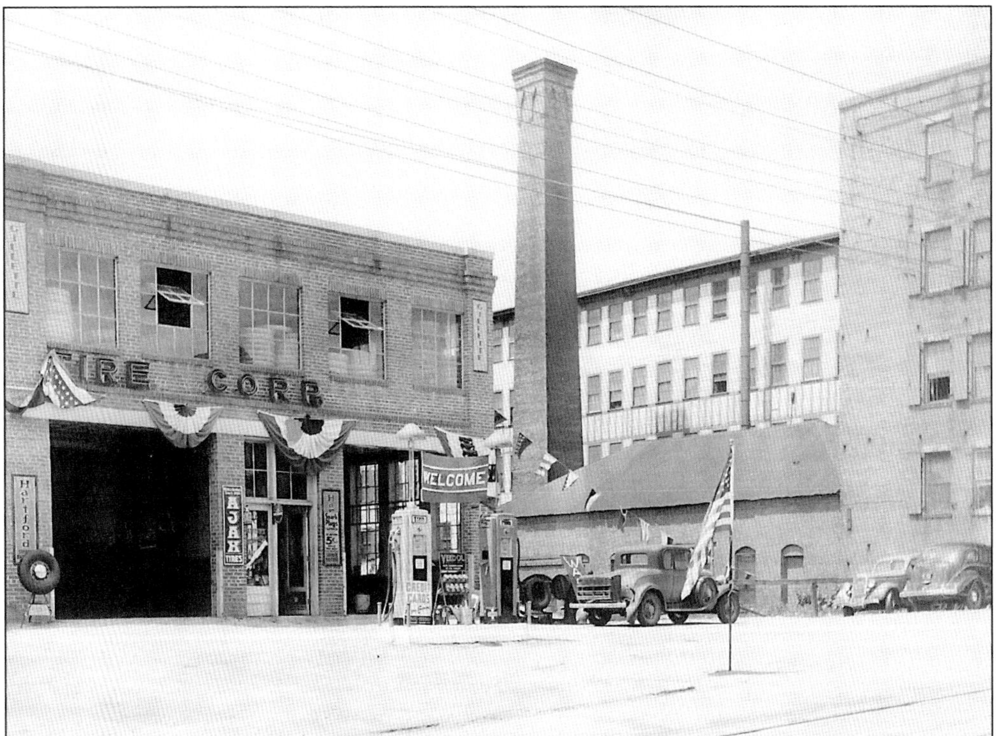

Oak Street was home to the Rapaport Tire Company, which prided itself on being northern New England's largest wholesale distributor.

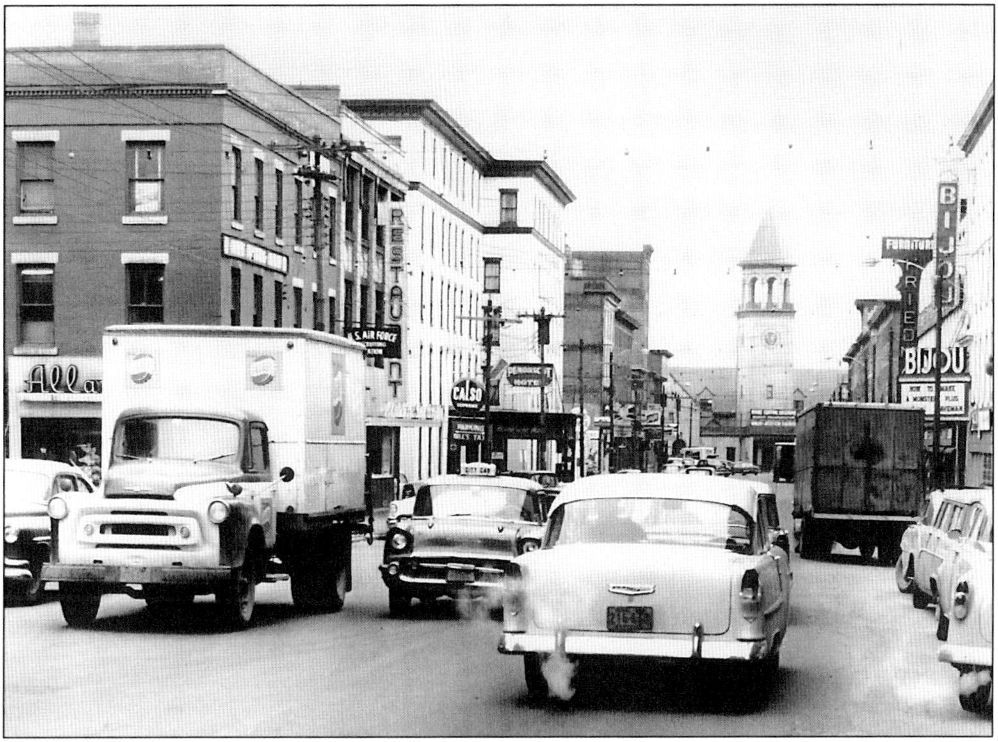

Lining Exchange Street in the 1950s were the Bijou Theater, Friedman Furniture, Allan Lewis Clothiers, the Penobscot Exchange Hotel, the *Bangor Daily News* and many other businesses. All were a minute's walk from Union Station on Washington Street.

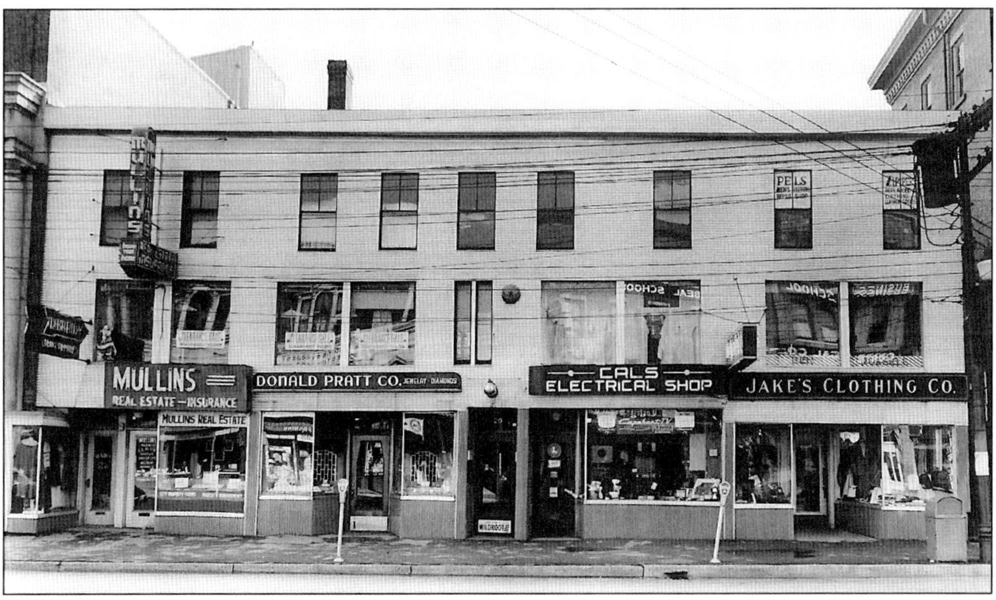

All three stories of this block were occupied by local entrepreneurs in the 1940s. Among others, this wooden building on State Street housed Jake Sclair's Clothing Company, Hubert A. Mullins' Real Estate and Insurance Agency, a walk-in barbershop, and the zipper repair room of Ursula Pels.

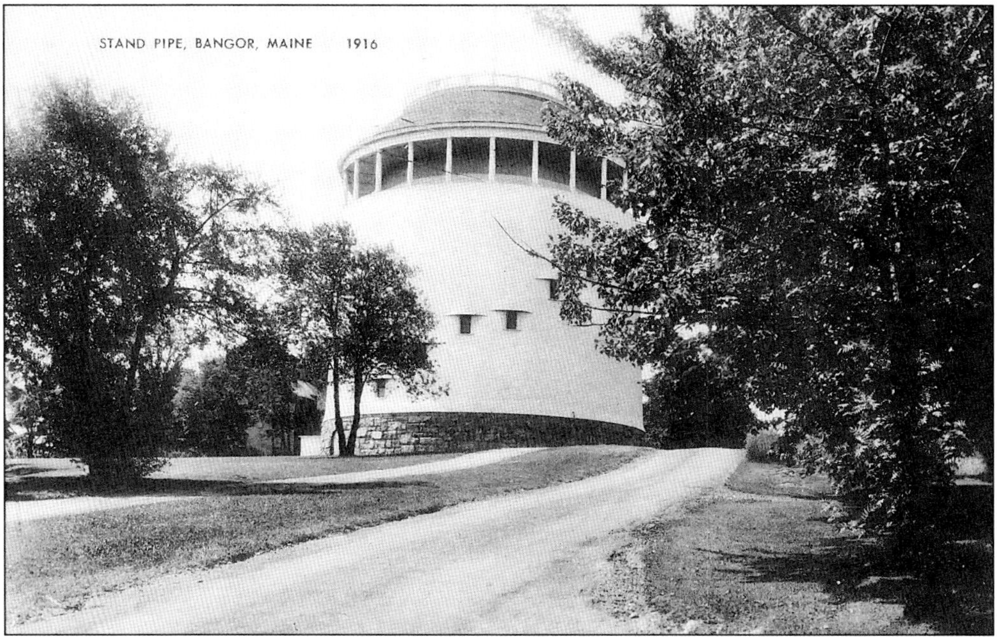

The Bangor Standpipe, still the city's most active water reservoir, sitting atop Thomas Hill filled with more than a million gallons of water. Its observation deck was closed to the public in 1940, after a boy fell to his death inside.

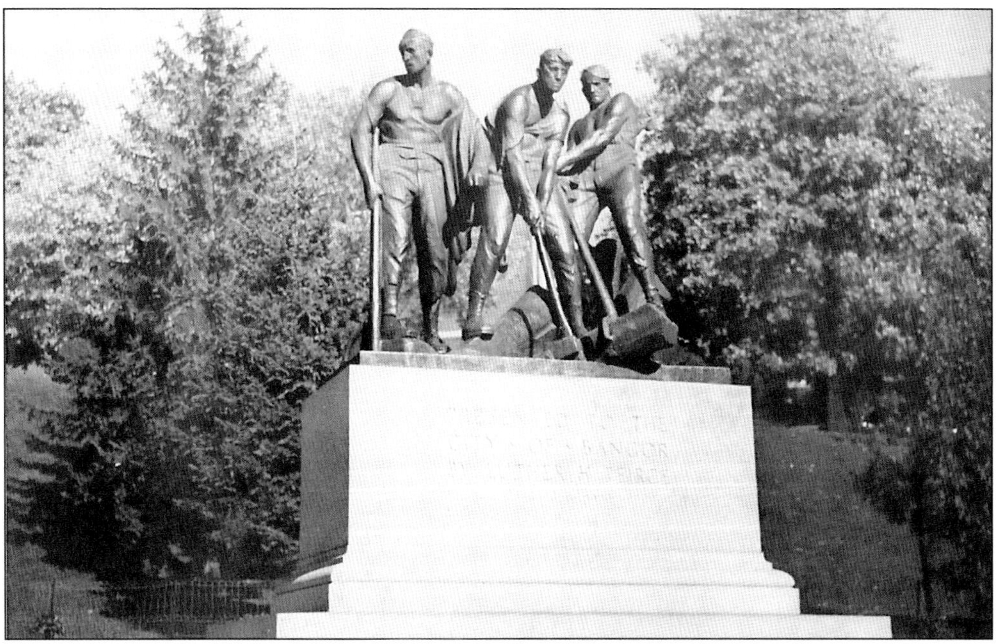

Is this the finest sculpture ever created in Maine? Impressed by its rugged but graceful design, many Bangorites believe it is. Charles Tefft enlisted the help of real-life river drivers as models while creating the Peirce Memorial.

No matter where one was in Bangor it seemed you could always see the copper eagle weathervane that perched atop the old Bangor City Hall on Hammond Street. Built in 1894, the Hersey Memorial Building was the nerve center of Bangor politics until demolition took it down in the 1960s.

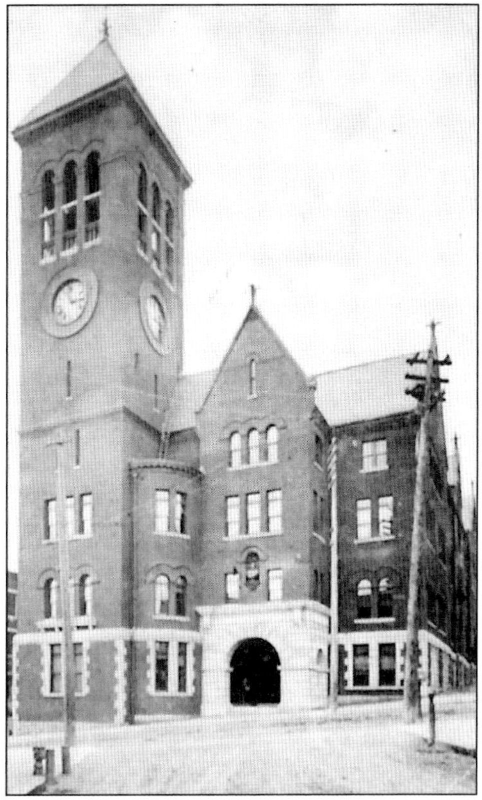

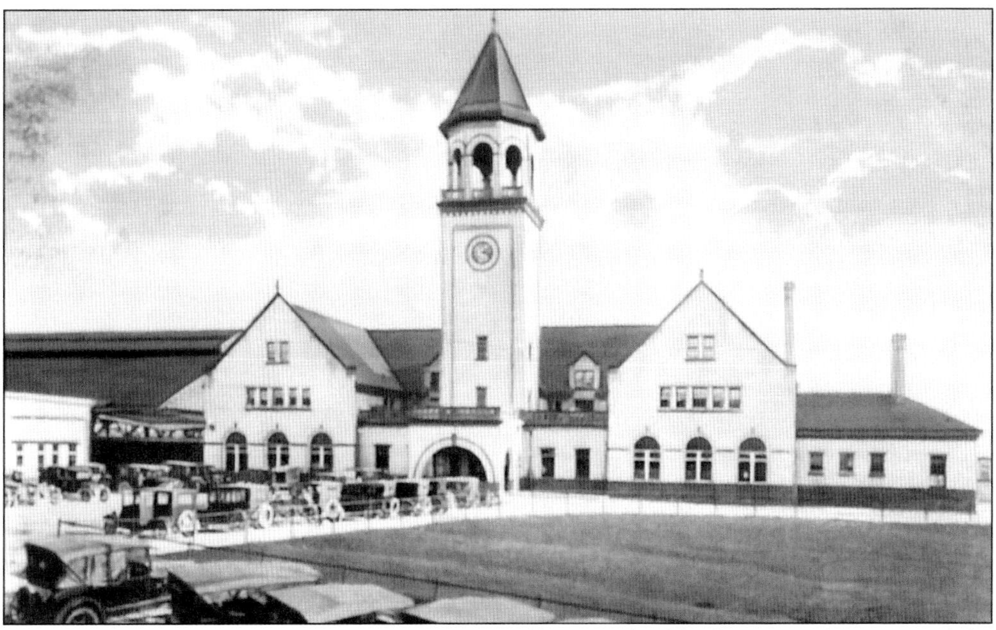

Union Station was the most public of Bangor's buildings in the fifty-four years that it graced the riverfront on Washington Street. The railroad terminal's loss to private demolition was widely regarded locally as the greatest mistake of a decade of downtown destruction.

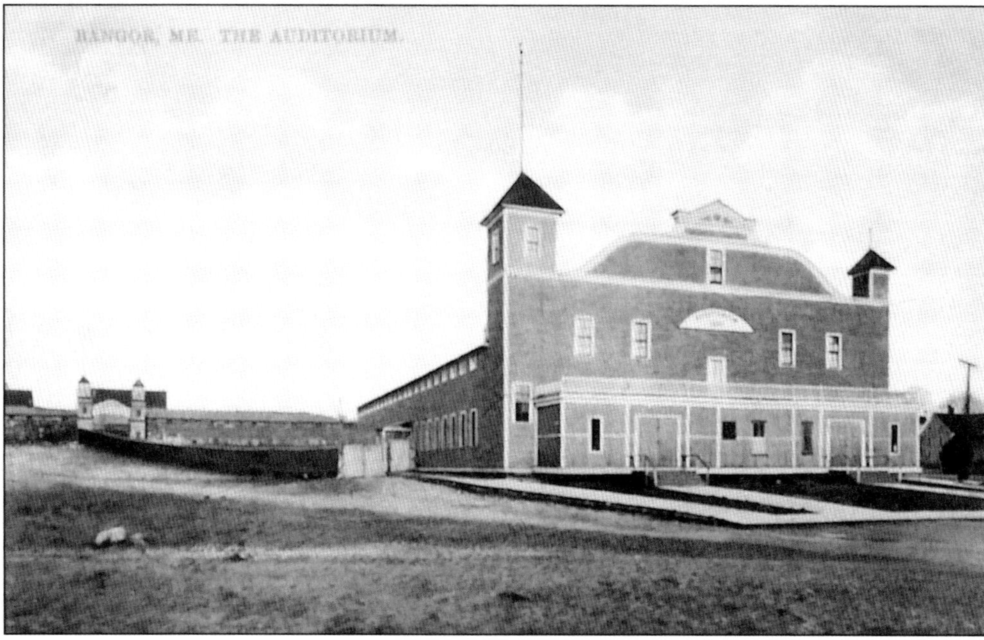

The old Bangor Auditorium was built to last, but the barn-like building lasted only sixty-eight years before it outlived its usefulness and was razed. Famous performers, from Maine prima donna Lillian Nordica to seminal rock stars Bill Haley and His Comets, sang inside the hall, renowned for its crisp acoustics.

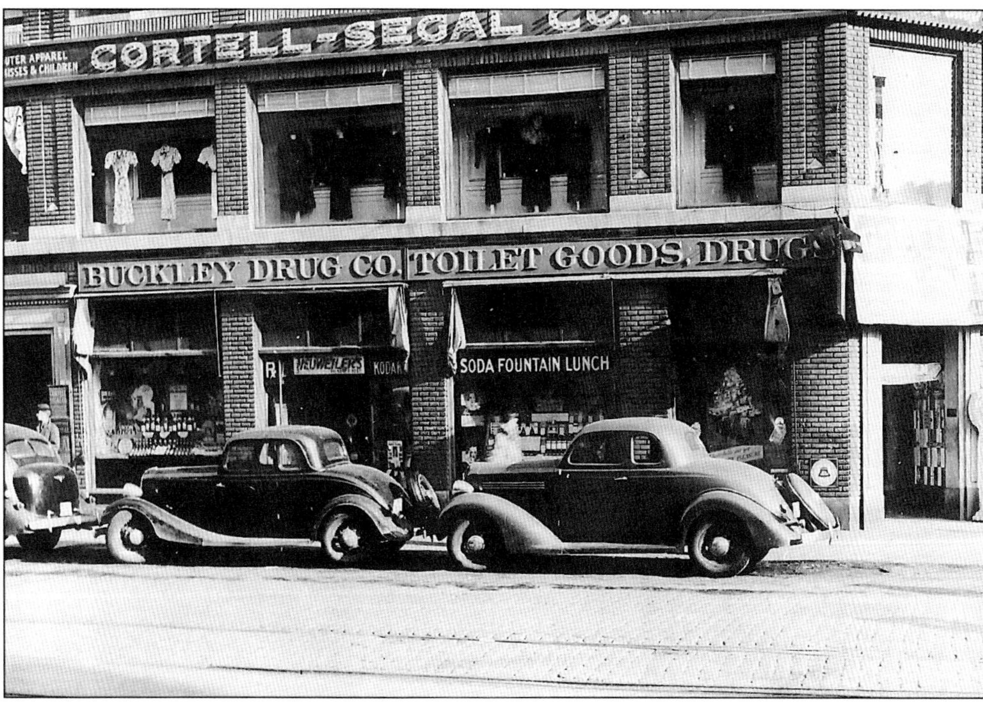

The Buckley Drug Company and the Cortell-Segal Company catered to different clienteles but both prospered at Hammond and Central Streets. At one time there was a pharmacy on all four corners including Buckley's.

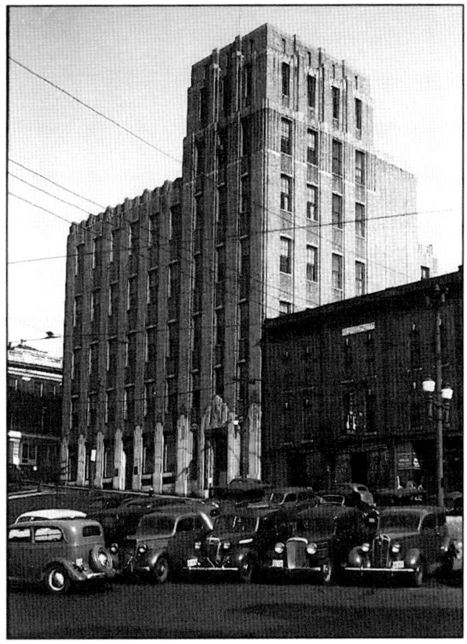

For many years this was Bangor's equivalent of a skyscraper. The Telephone Building, built on Park Street in 1931, resembled telephone buildings in other cities, but on a smaller scale.

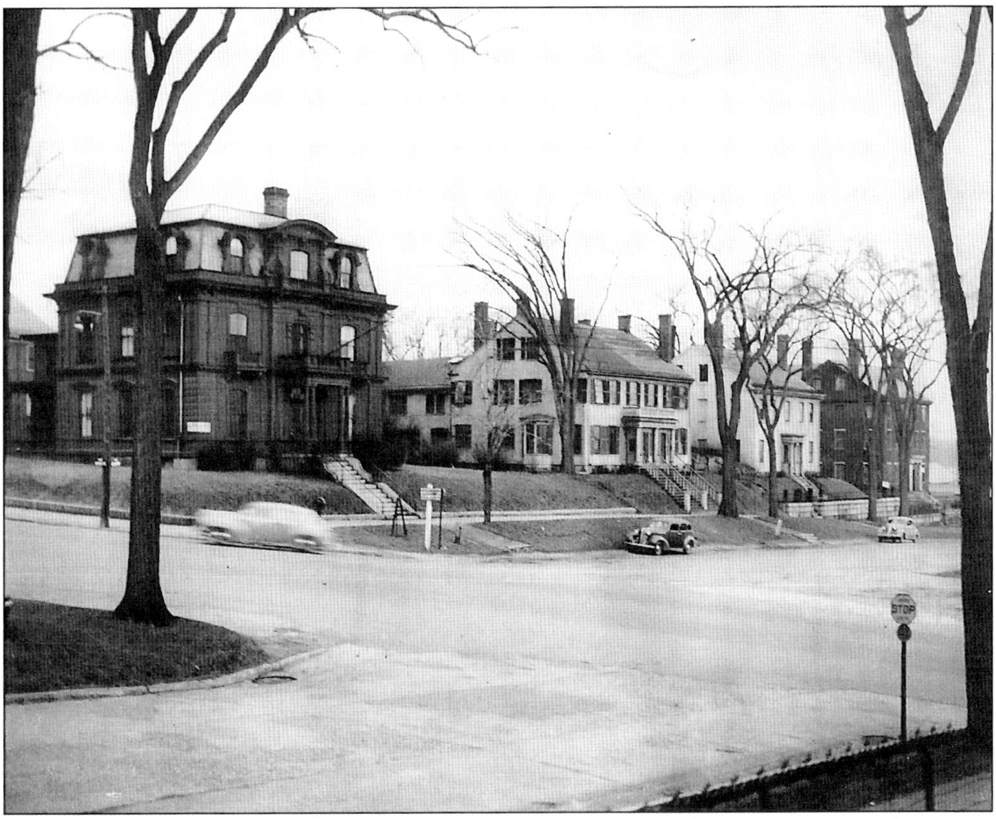

Stetson Square on lower Broadway was once lined with the elegant mansions of Bangor's wealthiest citizens. Local legend holds that timber baron Samuel Veazie built the roofline of his brick home (far right) higher than his rival, neighbor James Crosby's (painted in white, next to Veazie's) so Crosby could never again see the river from his windows.

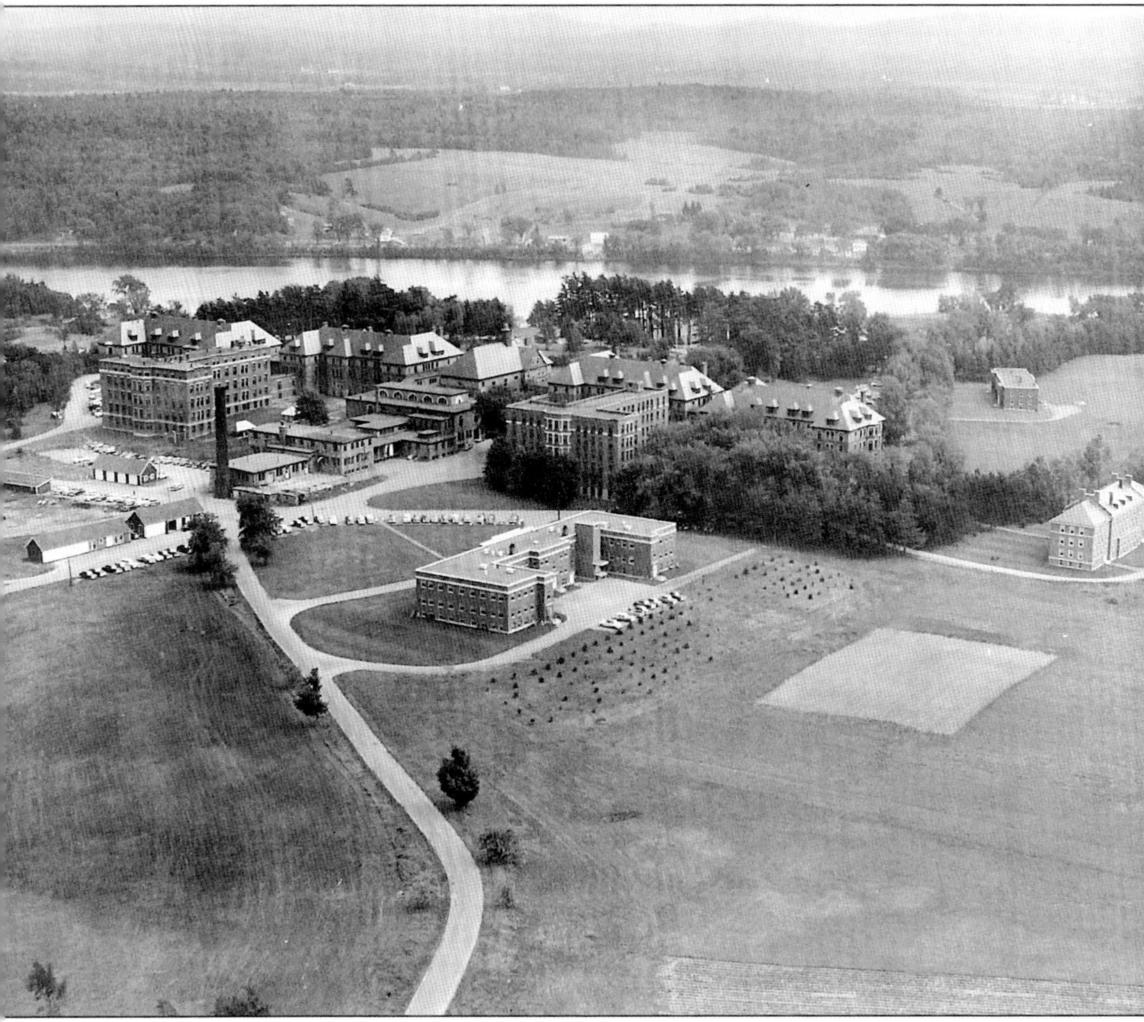

Once called the Eastern Maine Insane Hospital, this impressive set of buildings is now Bangor Mental Health Institute. The hospital admitted its first patients in 1901, and later treated people with tuberculosis when the deadly and incurable disease was claiming the lives of entire families. The property has changed little since this photograph was taken in the early 1950s, but society's attitudes toward treating the mentally ill certainly have. Often at the center of controversy concerning the de-institutionalization of patients, the hospital continues to treat a wide variety of mental and physical problems.

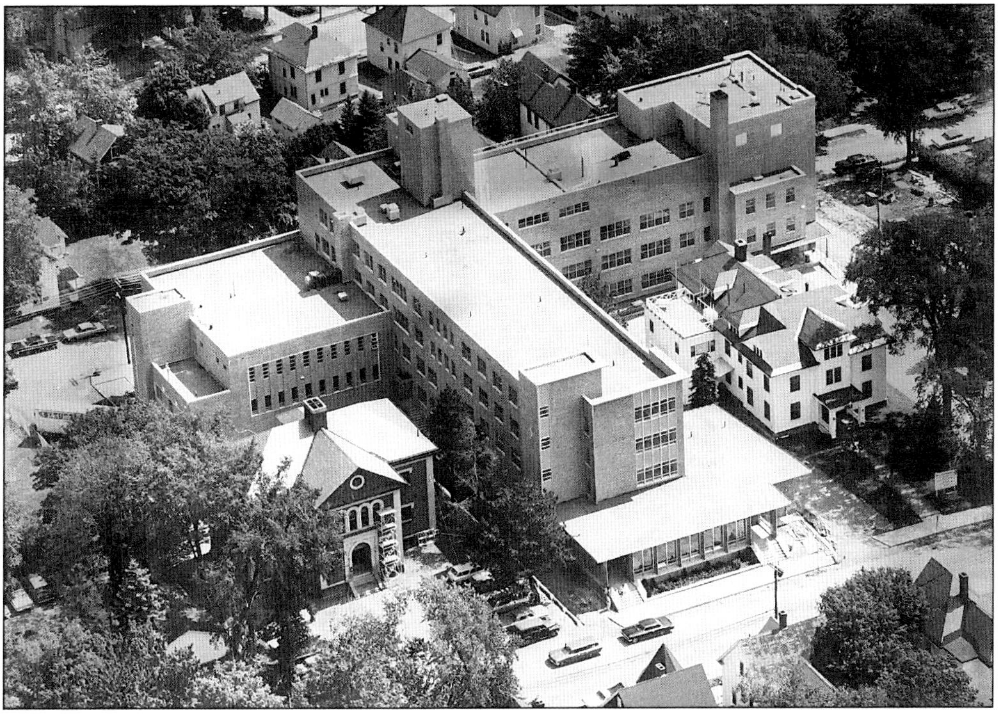

The new St. Joseph Hospital had just opened its doors when this aerial photograph was taken in the 1960s. Its predecessor, the Paine Private Hospital, later bought by the Felician Sisters, is dwarfed at the right. The Longfellow School (kindergarten and first grade) is on the left.

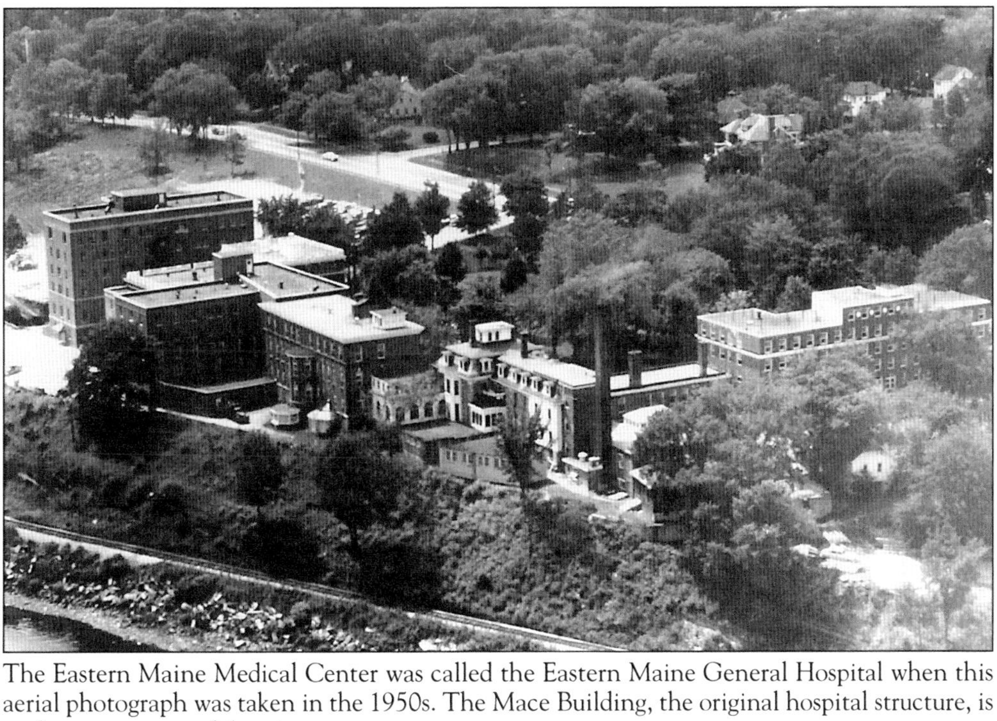

The Eastern Maine Medical Center was called the Eastern Maine General Hospital when this aerial photograph was taken in the 1950s. The Mace Building, the original hospital structure, is at the very center of the picture.

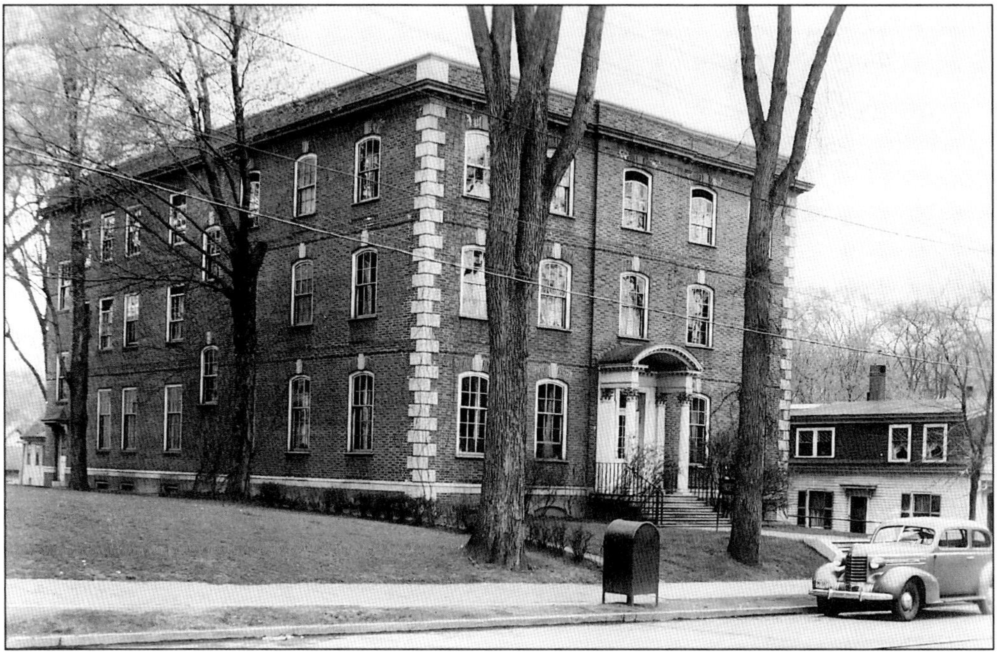

The YWCA Building on Union Street stood by itself in the 1940s. The building, which opened in 1930, now shares the property with newer, more modern additions constructed through diligent fund-raising.

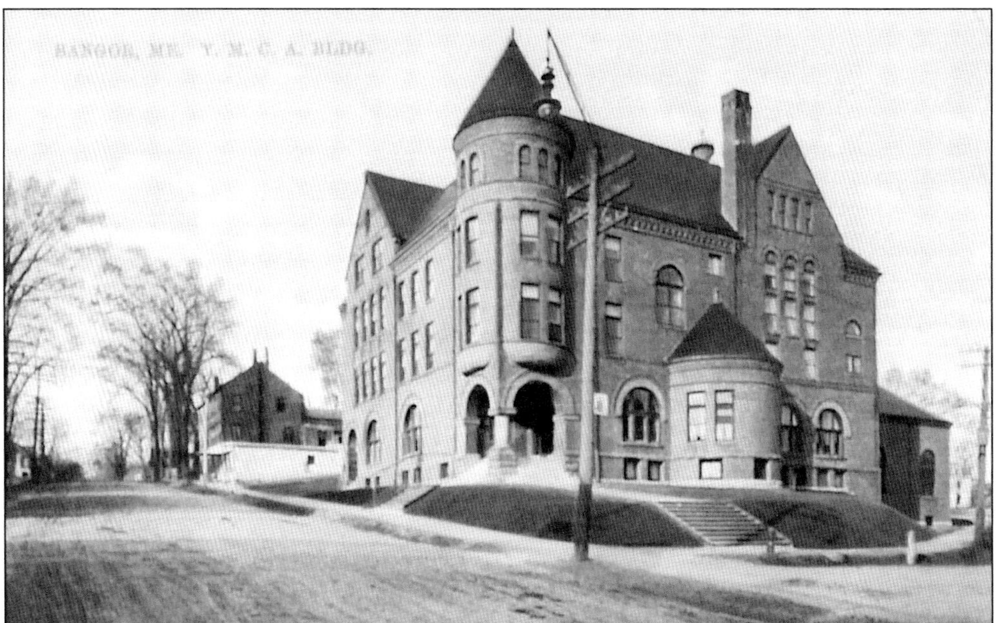

Many men living today received their physical and moral training inside this handsome building that stood at Hammond and Court Streets. Built in 1891, the YMCA was built almost entirely of Bangor and Maine materials, including pine and ash, pressed brick and stained glass.

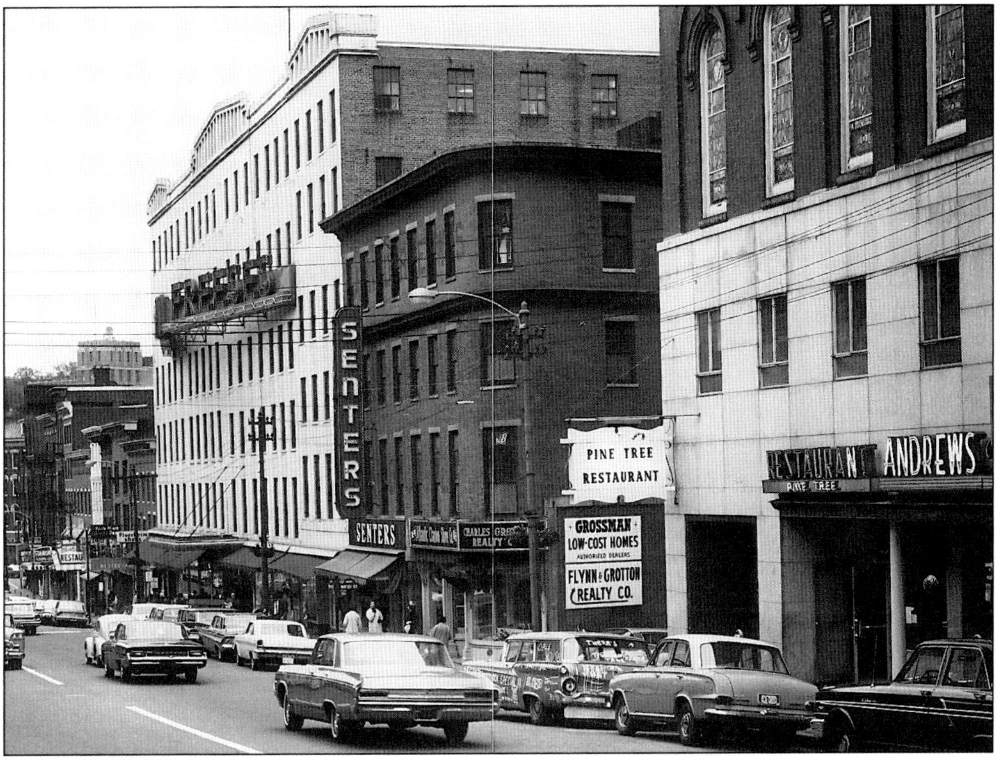

Competition from the Bangor Mall was still a decade and a half away in 1964, and downtown was booming. Freese's Department Store still catered to all ages and tastes, Senters still sold inexpensive clothing, the Pine Tree Restaurant still served the best chicken pie in town and Andrews Music House maintained its reputation as a good place to buy a piano.

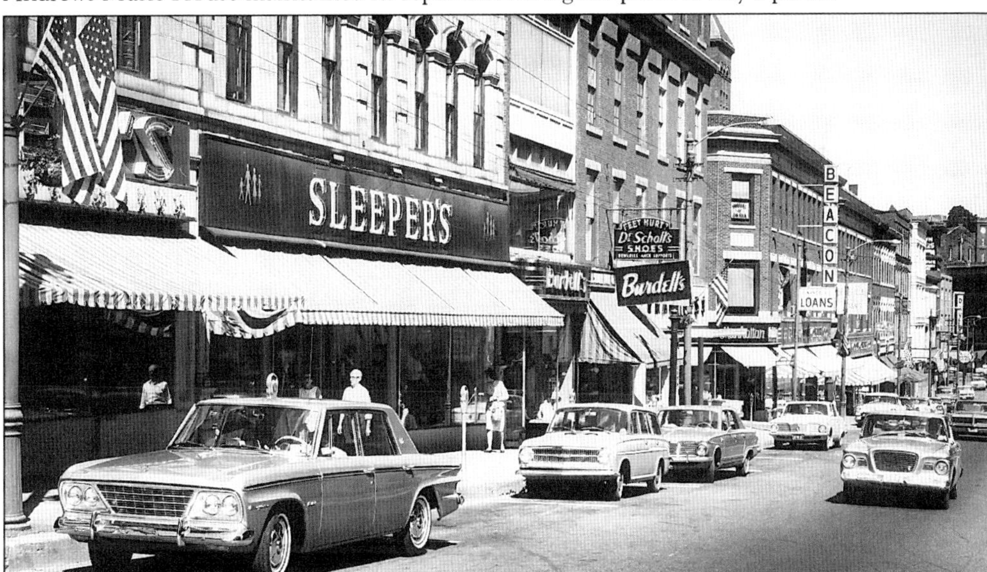

Same day, same street, but the other side. Mitch Sleeper sold men's and women's clothing, Burdell's sold only women's clothing, Dr. Scholl's sold shoes and the Beacon Finance Company sold loans.

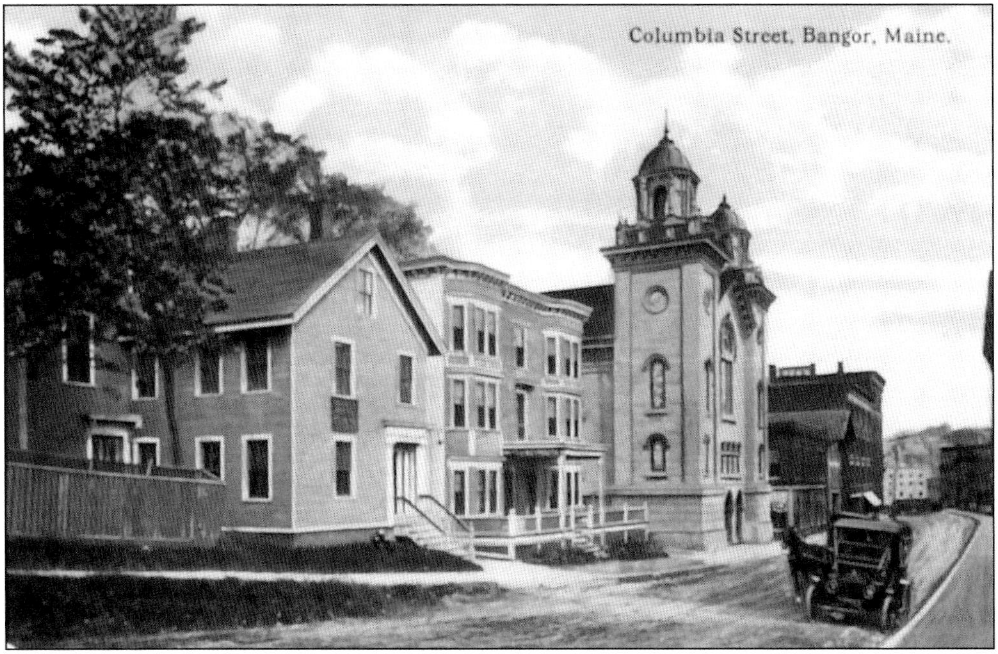

Columbia Street is a short, quiet street although it is located downtown, only a block from Main Street. In 1914 the Columbia Street Baptist Church sat alongside the Weymouth Boarding House and the old GAR Hospital which tended to wounded soldiers during the Civil War.

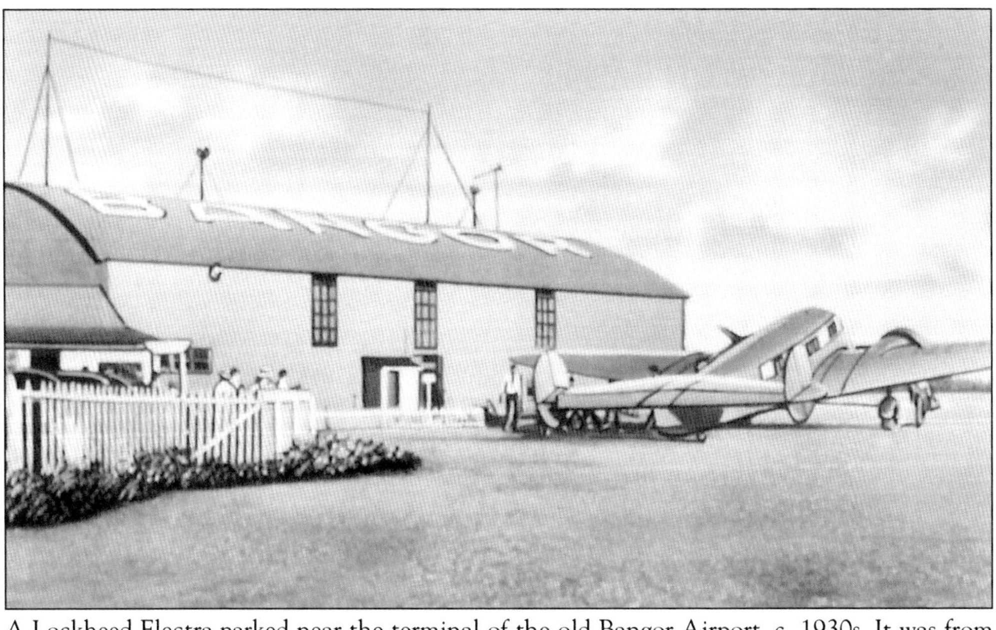

A Lockheed Electra parked near the terminal of the old Bangor Airport, *c.* 1930s. It was from here that Amelia Earhart (see page 79) flew women on "joy hops" over Bangor in 1934.

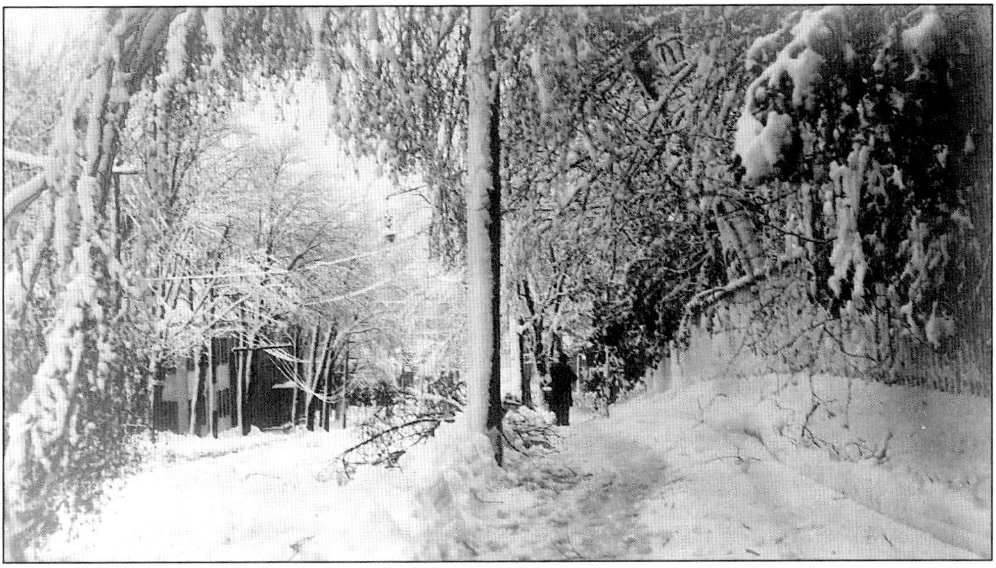

Mother Nature did all the work before this postcard view of a winter ice storm was taken on Hammond Street.

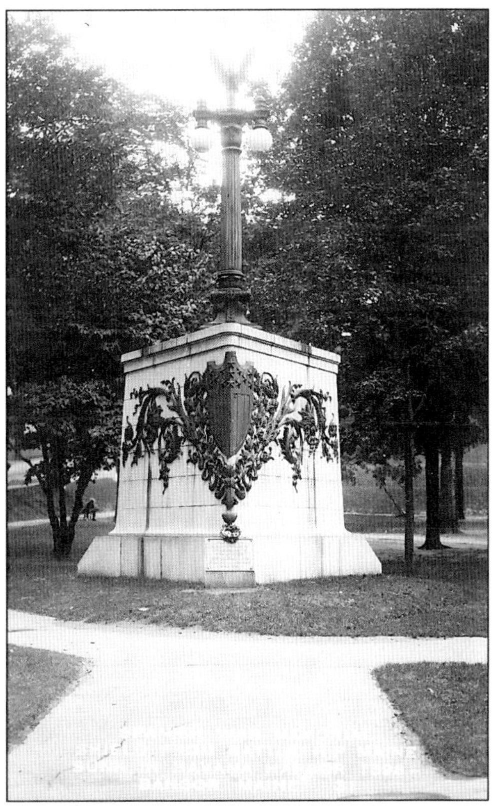

Davenport Park on Main Street attracts visitors because of this Spanish-American War Monument that commemorates the sinking of the battleship *Maine* in Cuba in 1898. The *Maine*'s shield and scrollwork, retrieved from the bottom of Havana Harbor several years after her sinking, are mounted on the monument.

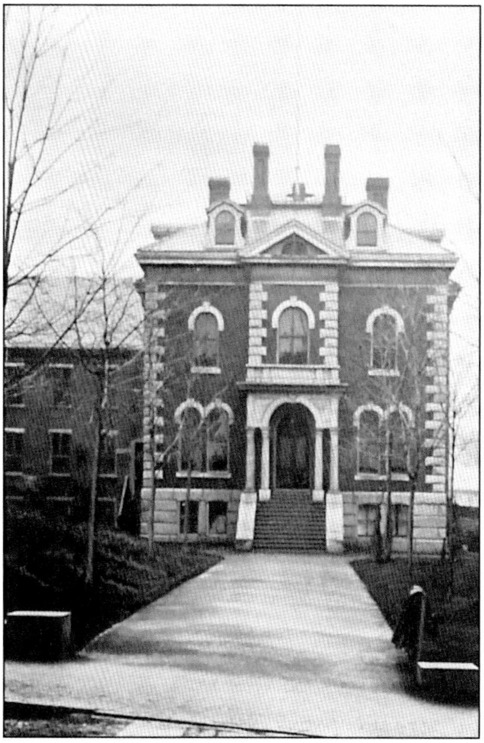

The keeper's house of the Penobscot County Jail, built in 1869, was designed to look inviting. Located near fine downtown homes, pains were taken to have it resemble an Italianate mansion. But life inside the nineteenth-century jail was no holiday. Hardened criminals sometimes broke out, or hanged themselves in their cells.

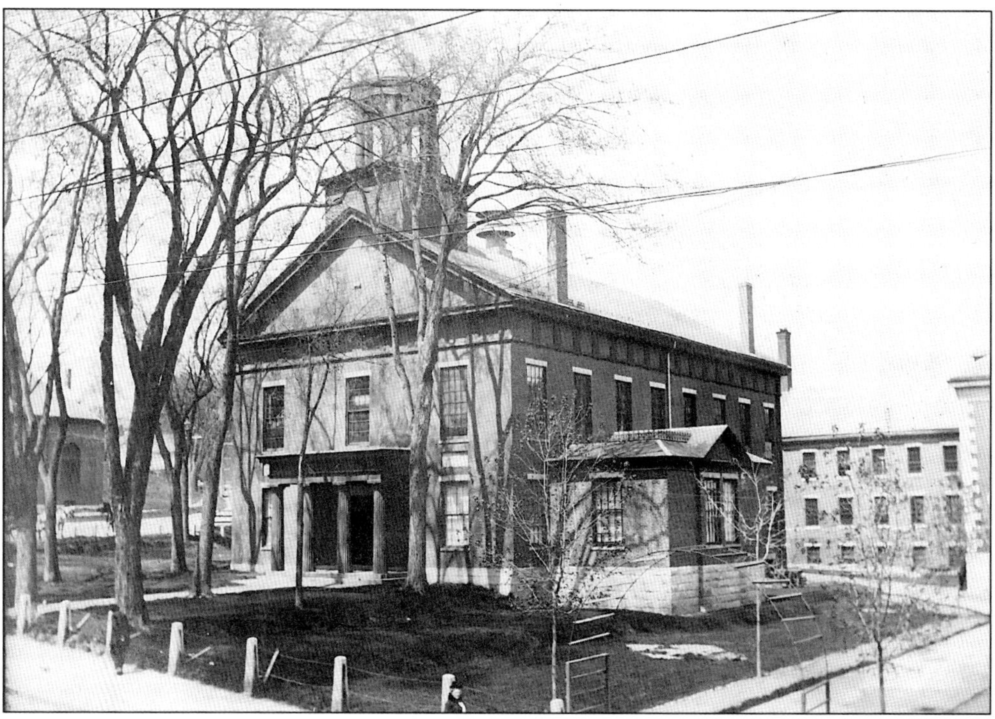

Dutch elm disease has claimed hundreds of trees in Bangor, including these that once helped shade the old Penobscot County Courthouse.

Four

Rich and Famous

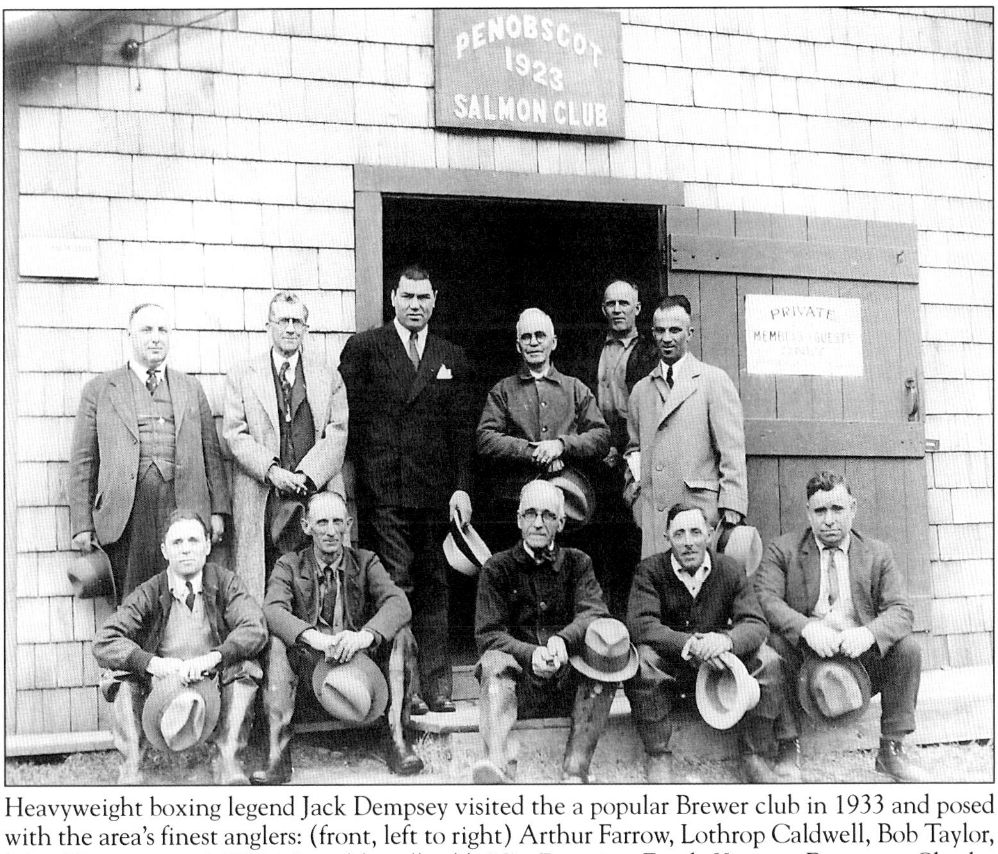

Heavyweight boxing legend Jack Dempsey visited the a popular Brewer club in 1933 and posed with the area's finest anglers: (front, left to right) Arthur Farrow, Lothrop Caldwell, Bob Taylor, John Flanagan and W. McLaughlin; (back) J.D. Derosier, Frank Youngs, Dempsey, Charles Bissell, E. Drinkwater and Charlie Miller.

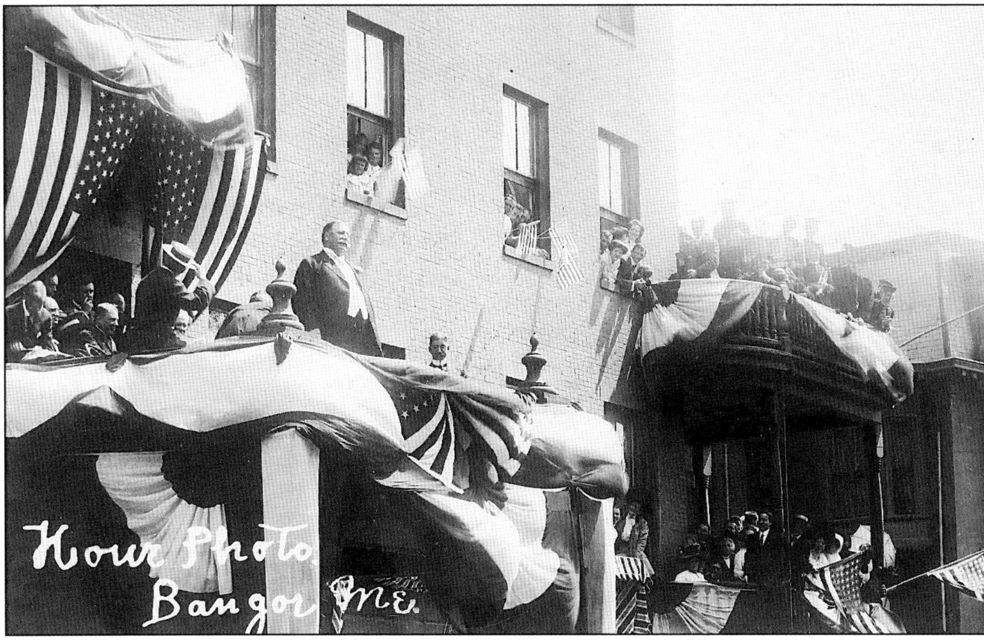

President William Howard Taft delivered a decidedly non-political speech from the front portico of the Bangor House in 1910, speaking at length on the potential of Maine farming.

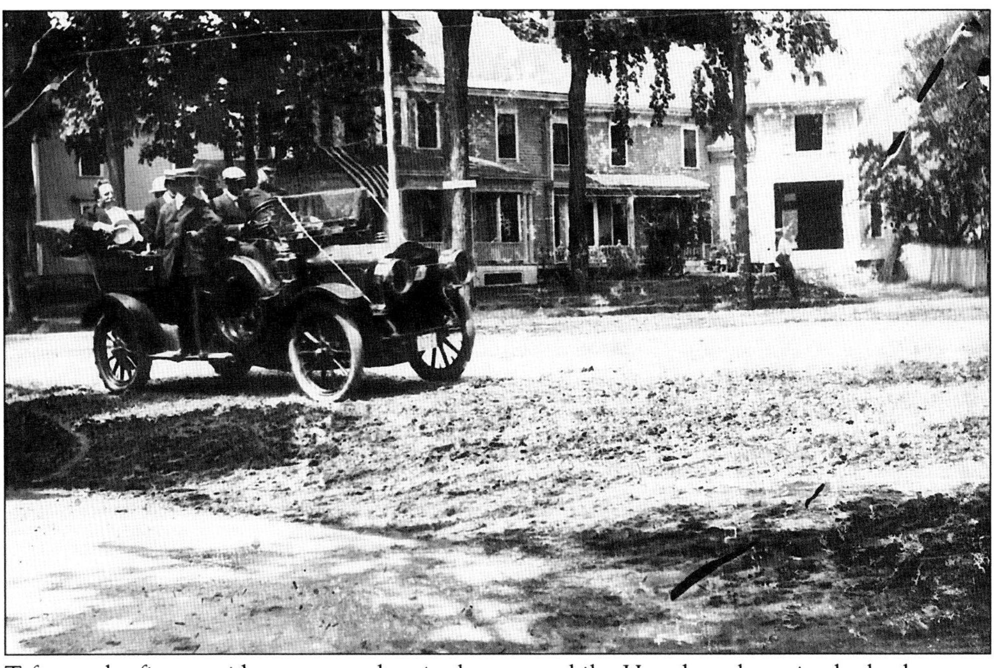

Taft was the first president to tour the city by automobile. Here he relaxes in the back seat at the corner of Cedar and Hammond Streets.

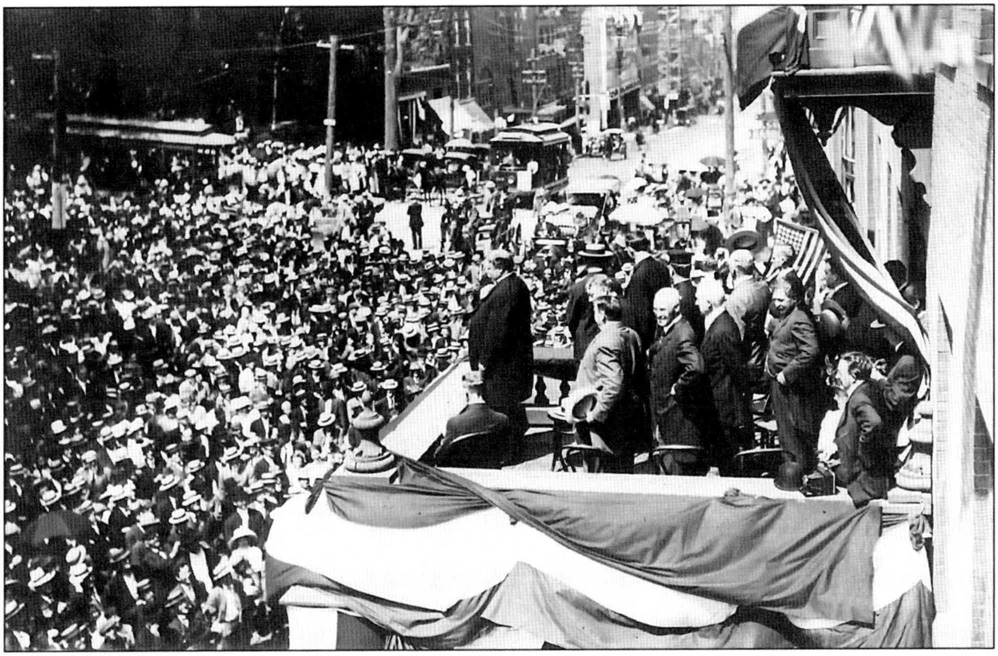

Looking out at the hundreds of spectators who filled Main Street to hear him speak, the *Bangor Daily News* noted, Taft "could only see a white blur of upturned faces." Composing himself, he said, "Bangor is one of the most beautiful cities in the country. . . . I do not wonder you are proud. Great men have come from here—Hannibal Hamlin and others." On the subject of farming Taft said, "There are acres upon acres available for this purpose in Maine. The farmers of today are the millionaires, and there is no reason why Maine should not have farmer millionaires as well as the West." The rotund chief executive then re-entered the Bangor House and dined on melons, breadsticks, Penobscot River salmon, broiled peas, chicken, asparagus and cake.

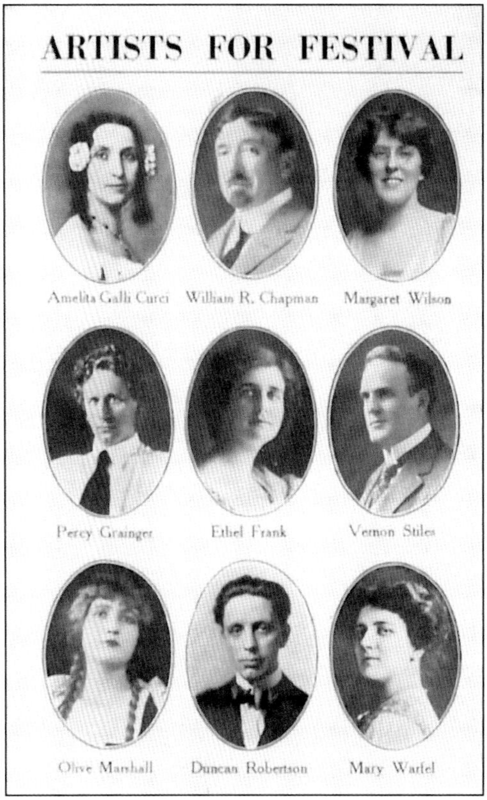

The Maine Music Festival brought famous classical artists to the old Bangor Auditorium, which was built for the purpose of hosting the annual event. Under the direction of William Rogers Chapman, such talents as Percy Grainger and Amelita Galli Curci wowed capacity audiences.

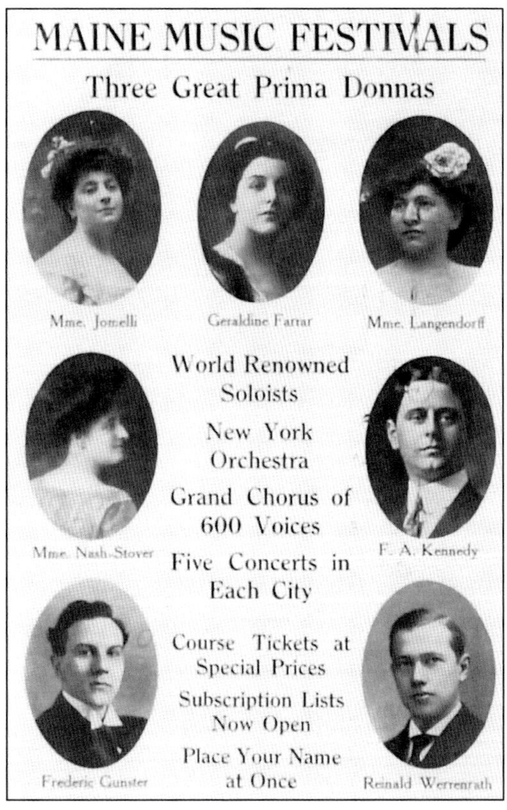

Typical festival ticket prices ran from $5 to $7 dollars for five concerts. The opera stars would then repeat their performances at a festival in Portland.

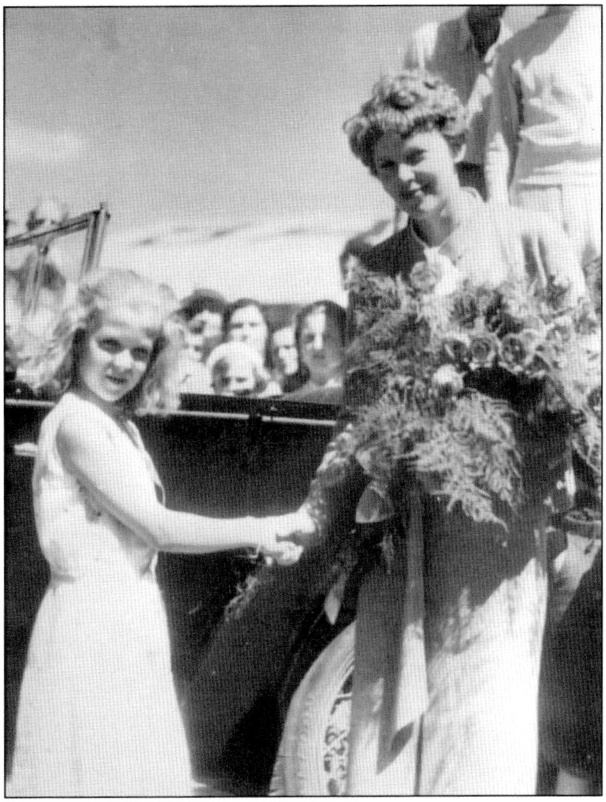

Amelia Earhart greets Joanne Jordan at the Bangor Airport during a publicity visit for Pan American Airlines in 1934. The daughter of *Bangor Daily News* publisher Fred Jordan, Joanne, age ten, was the youngest female to fly with Miss Earhart that day.

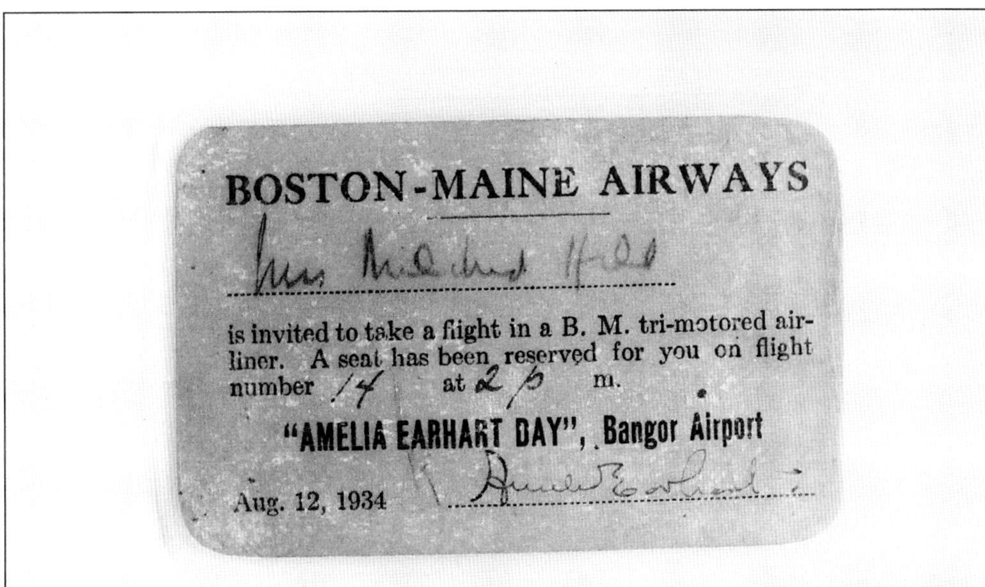

August 12, 1934, is a date that is burned into the memories of many women still living who recall receiving one of these autographed cards from Amelia Earhart. A downtown store promoted the event with a contest that asked entrants to guess the number of beans in a jar.

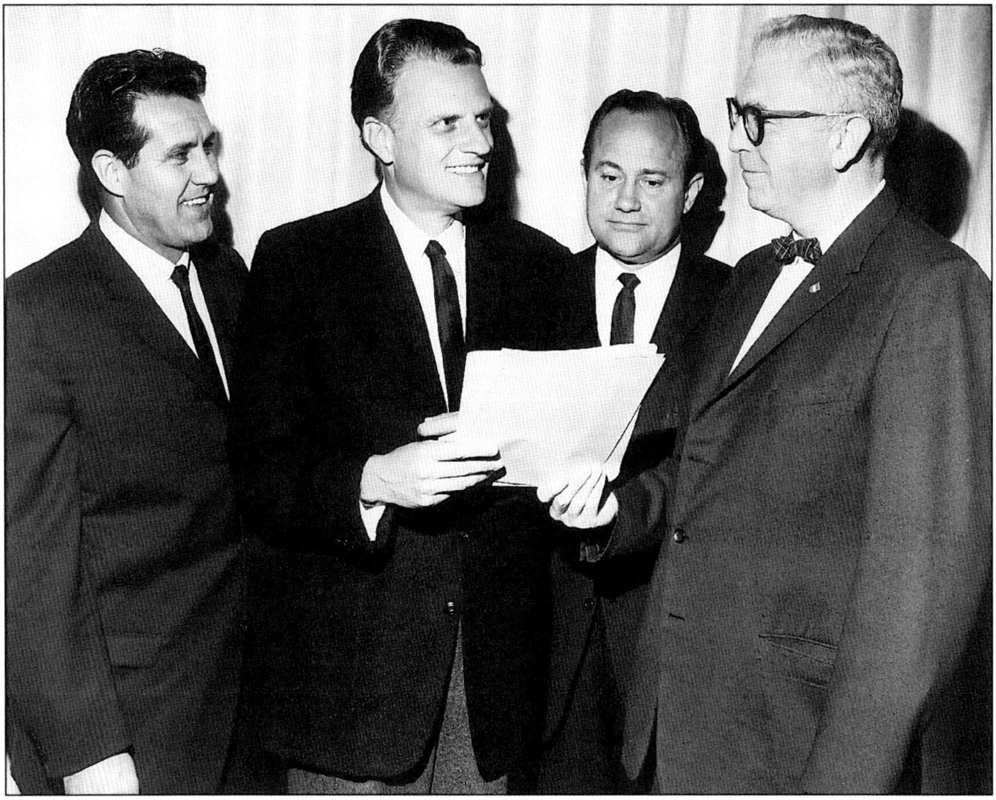

Evangelist Billy Graham discusses final plans with associates before speaking at the Bangor Auditorium on October 21, 1964. With him, from left, are the Reverend Cliff Barrows (master of ceremonies), Dr. Thomas Walter Wilson (evangelist) and Dr. Arthur Fish (a local physician and preacher who helped bring Dr. Graham to Bangor). A crowd of 7,600 with another 300 to 400 huddled outside in the cold, damp weather, and heard Dr. Graham preach on salvation: "There may be only a ten percent chance that there is a hell, but is it worth taking that chance?" asked Dr. Graham. He also spoke on civil rights: "The movement is not all political . . . it involves moral issues. I myself had taken a strong stand on it long before the Supreme Court made its 1954 desegregation decision."

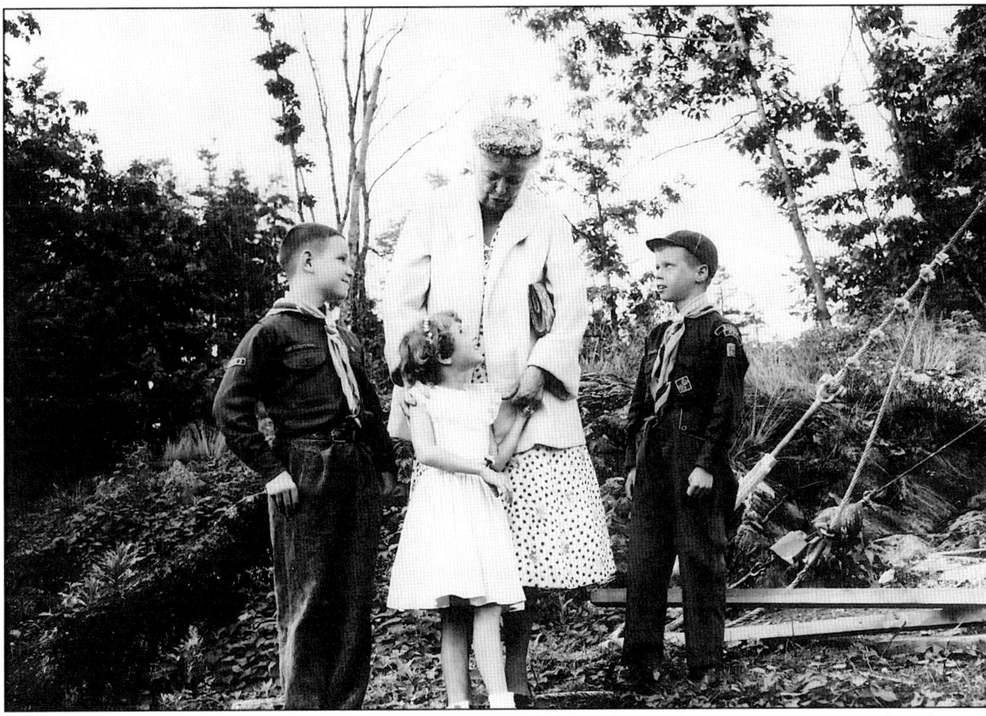

Eleanor Roosevelt met with local Cub Scouts and their friend before speaking at the Bangor Unitarian Church on July 30, 1954.

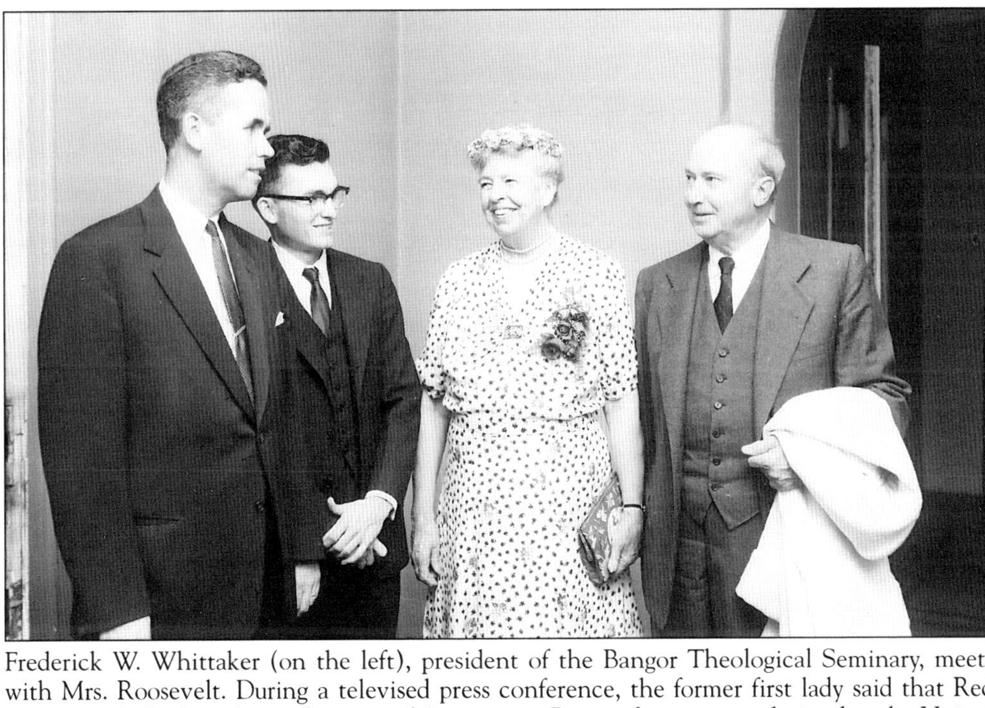

Frederick W. Whittaker (on the left), president of the Bangor Theological Seminary, meets with Mrs. Roosevelt. During a televised press conference, the former first lady said that Red China might be forced into the arms of Communist Russia if it was not admitted to the United Nations. Many recalled Mrs. Roosevelt's official visit to Bangor in 1941.

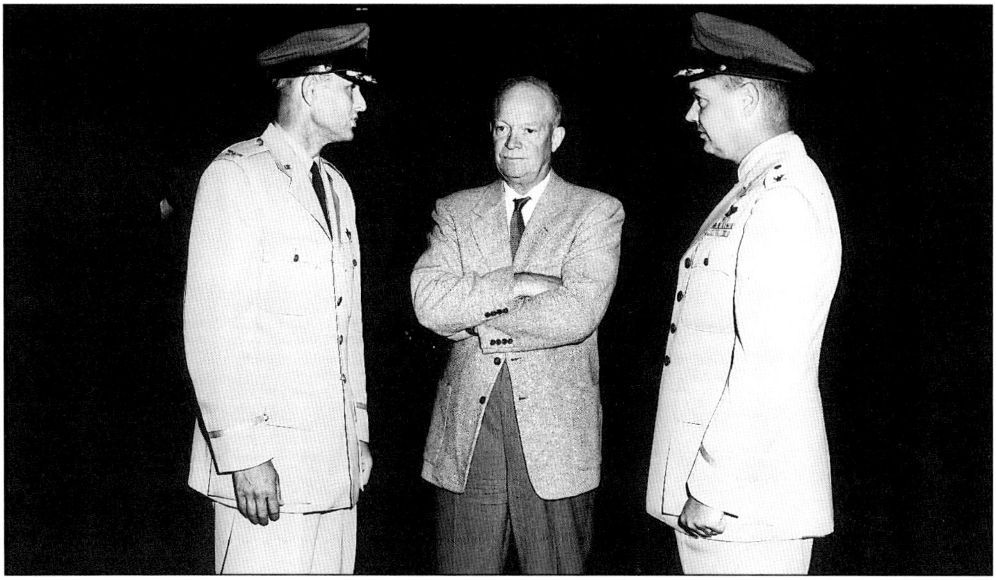

Dwight D. Eisenhower stopped briefly at Dow Air Force Base in Bangor while returning from a history-making summit conference in Geneva. With the president on July 24, 1955, were Colonel Orie O. Schurter (on the left), commander of the 4060th Air Refueling Wing, and Colonel Robert F. Layton, base commander.

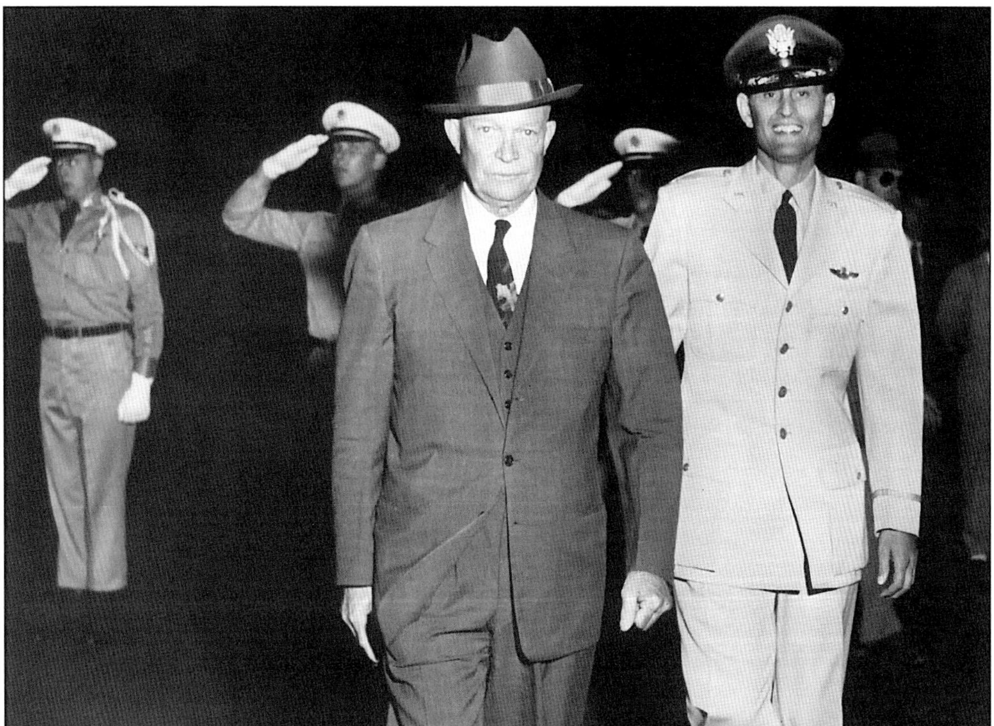

President Eisenhower made an official visit to Bangor in June 1955. Shown here returning from a fishing vacation in western Maine, he passes through an honor guard with Colonel Schurter at Dow Air Force Base.

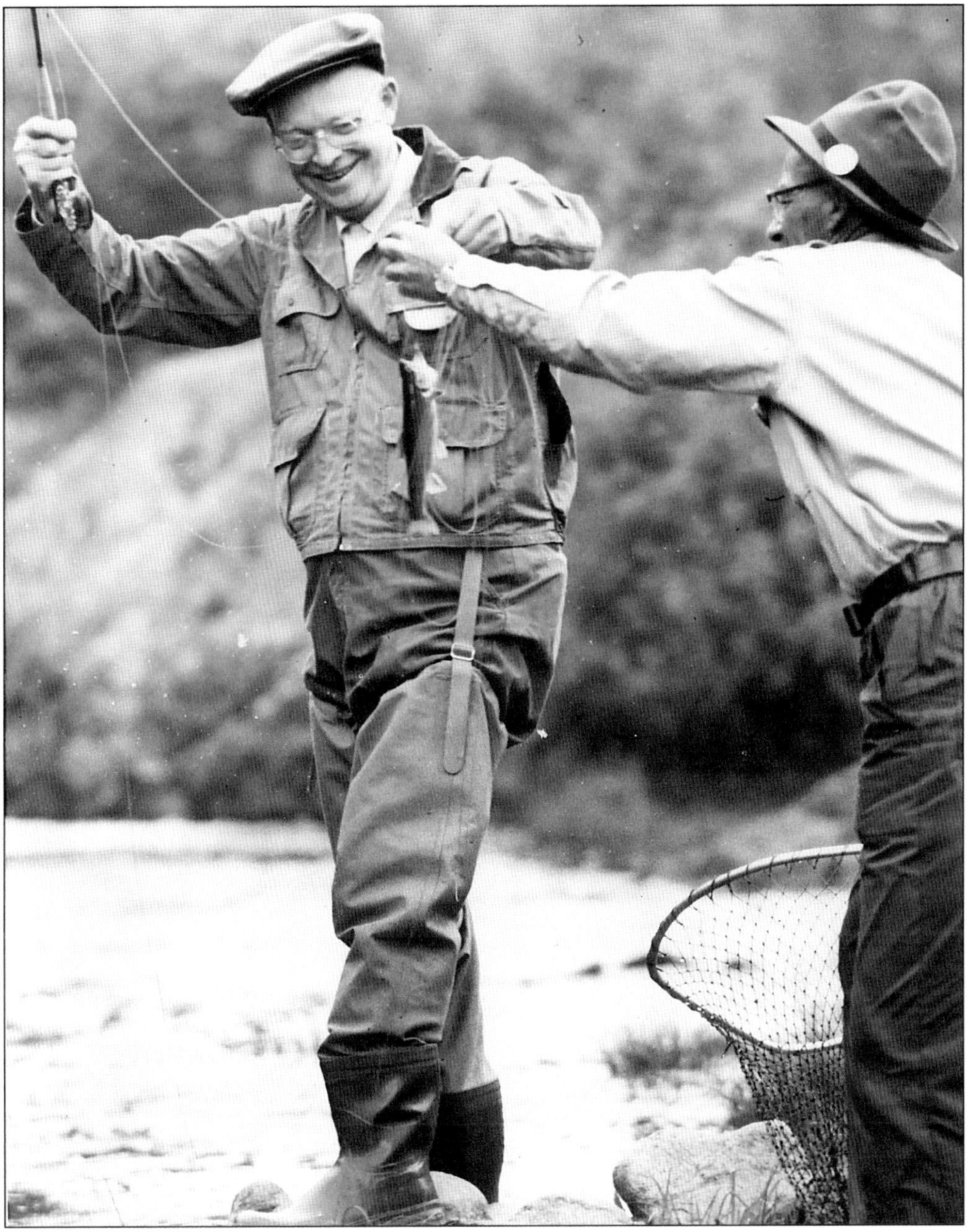

An experienced fisherman, Ike grins like a schoolboy while helping land a fish at Little Boy Falls on the Magalloway River in western Maine during his June 1955 visit to Maine. The President was assisted by his guide, Don Cameron. En route to Bangor, and Washington, D.C. the next day, Eisenhower stopped at the home of Senator Margaret Chase Smith in Skowhegan, Maine, where he enjoyed a clambake and delivered a speech. Ike's fishing vacation was interrupted by an urgent telephone call to his lodge at Parmachenee Lake Club from Secretary of State John Foster Dulles: two Russian MiG jet fighters had just shot down an American Navy plane over international waters between Alaska and Siberia.

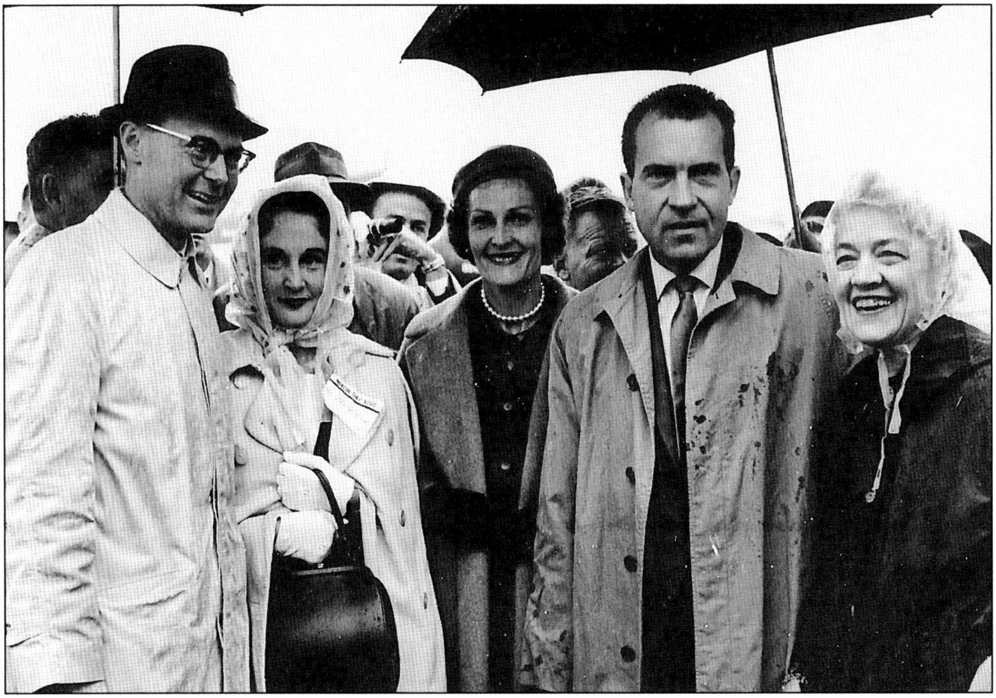

Richard M. Nixon weathers a Bangor rain shower while campaigning for the presidency on September 30, 1960. With him are his wife Pat (center), Governor and Mrs. John H. Reed (on the left), and Senator Margaret Chase Smith (on the right). Nixon lost the election to John F. Kennedy, who also campaigned in the city, the only time both major party candidates appeared in Bangor during an election year.

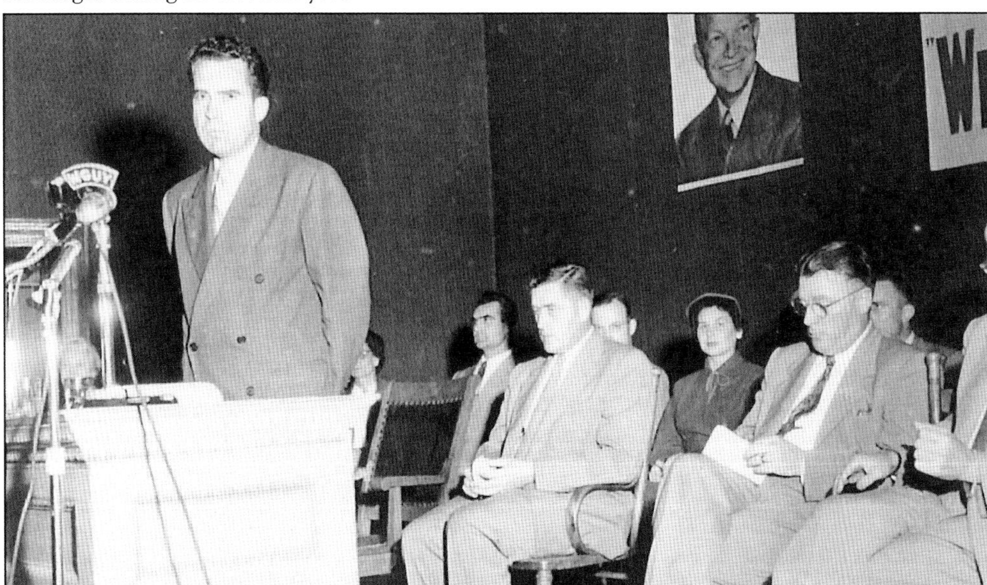

A younger Nixon opens the national Republican presidential campaign in Bangor in September 1952, as Dwight D. Eisenhower's running mate. Republicans Clifford McIntire (on the left) and Robert Haskell sit under Ike's portrait at the Penobscot Exchange Hotel.

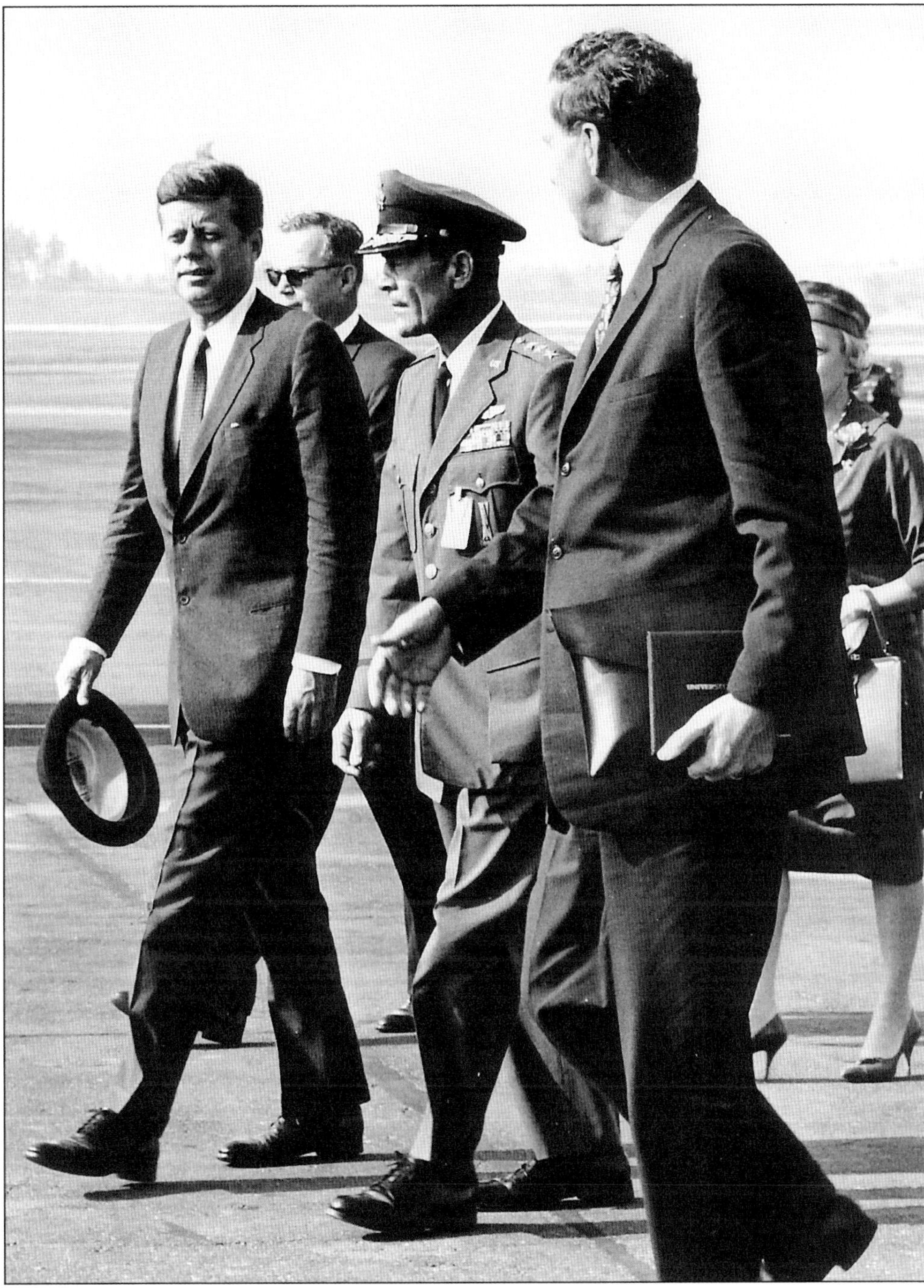

John F. Kennedy's brilliant life was soon to expire, but of course no one knew it as he strode across Dow Air Force Base on October 19, 1963. Accompanied by Senator Edmund S. Muskie (in the foreground) and Senator Margaret Chase Smith (at far right), the president shook hands with children before boarding a helicopter for Orono, where he delivered his last major foreign speech at a University of Maine convocation. Kennedy's aversion to hats was evident in Bangor and in Orono, where he declined to wear a mortarboard while speaking.

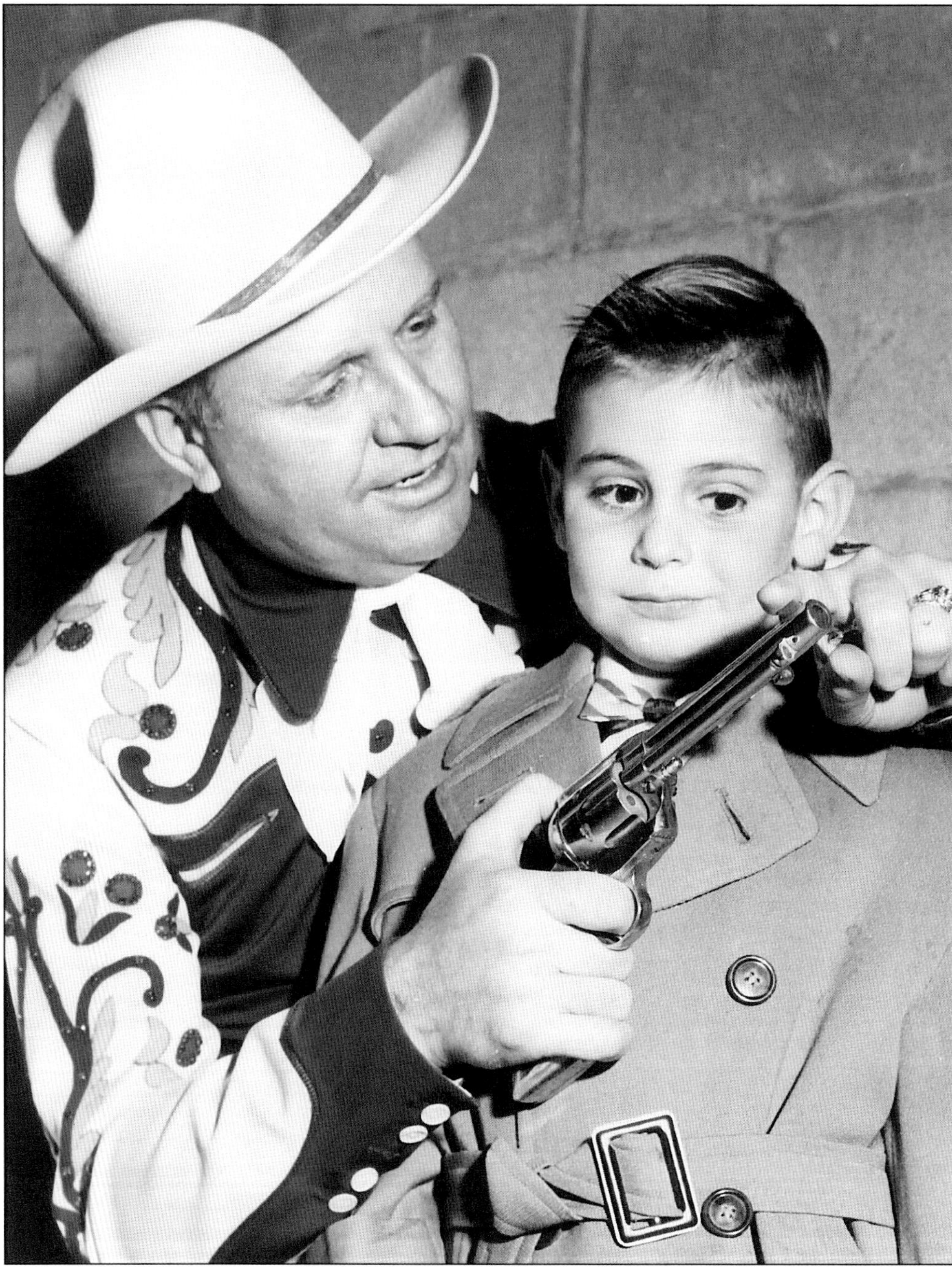

Gene Autry, star of many a difficult movie sequence, shows Gene Swimmer, son of Major and Mrs. Adolph Swimmer of Bangor, how to handle a six-shooter backstage during the Autry show at the Bangor Auditorium. Autry drew the first capacity crowd (eight thousand) at the newly opened auditorium on February 4, 1956.

Five

War and Peace

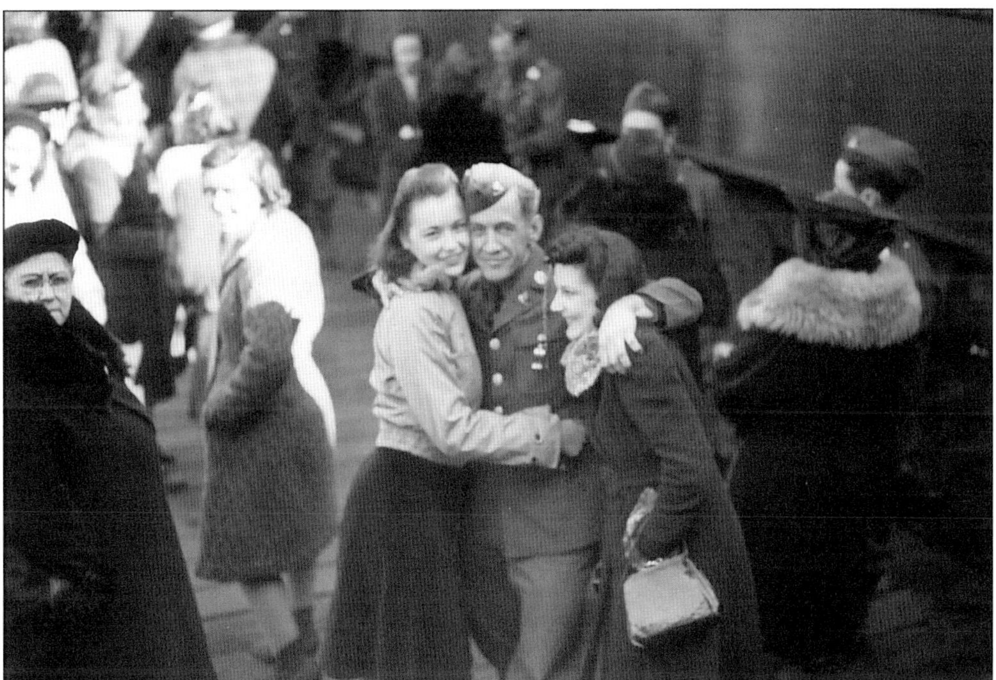

On a cold morning in March 1941, an officer of the 152nd Army Field Artillery says his farewells before boarding a train for Camp Blanding, Florida. Three hundred men and 109 vehicles left Bangor that day, nine months before the entry of the United States into World War II.

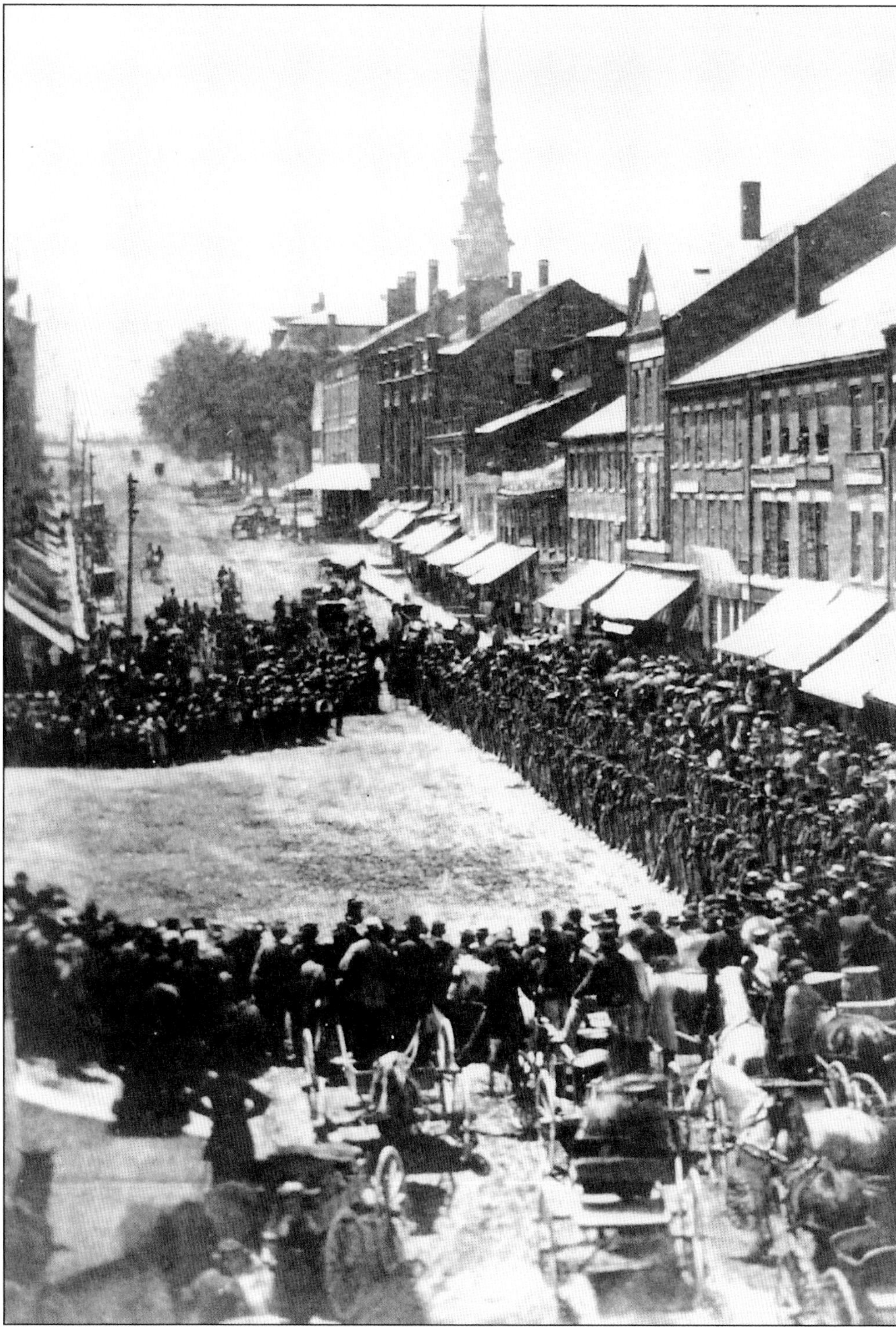

Soldiers of the Second Maine Regiment stand in formation on Main Street while hundreds of spectators look on. The Bangor unit, the first in Maine to march off to war in 1861, shed blood at the Battles of Antietam, Fredericksburg, Bull Run and others.

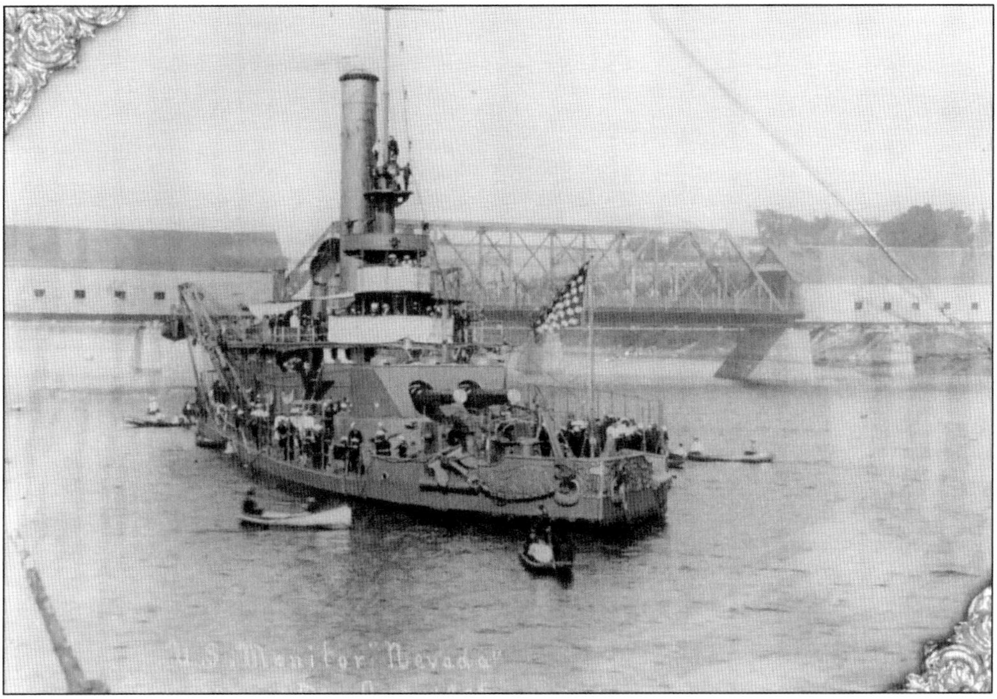

Bangor appeared to be under siege on August 7, 1905, when the monitor *Nevada*, shown here, and the torpedo boat destroyer *Lawrence* were berthed at the Toll Bridge for public inspection. Thousands of people poured onto the war vessels, the first in twenty-three years to visit the city.

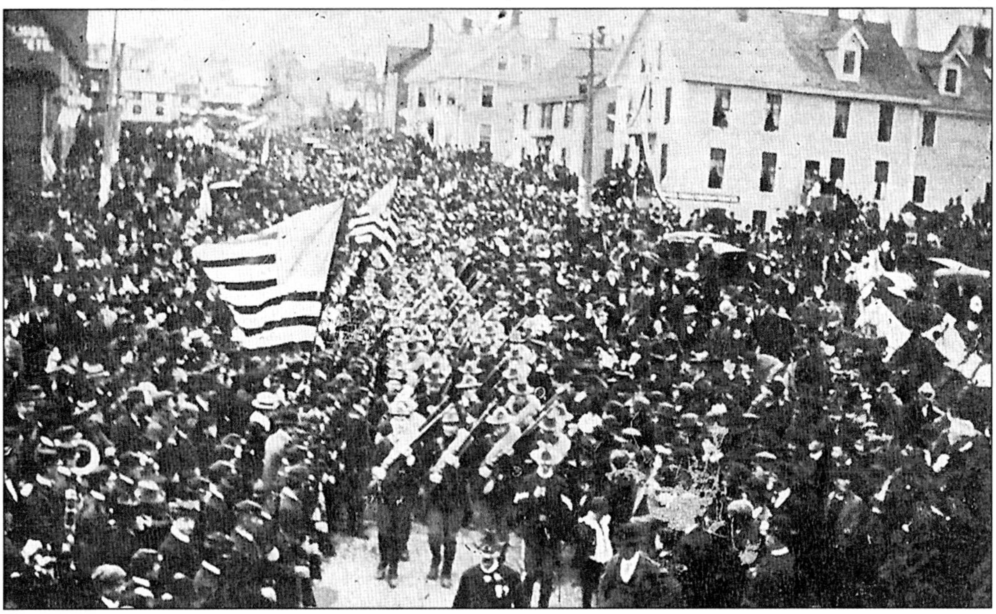

Bangor was awash with bunting on May 2, 1898, as more than a thousand men, many with the Company G National Guard Unit, marched through the city to the railroad station during the Spanish-American War. The procession stopped at the Bangor House Park—where the Bangor Band played "America"—and then continued on to the station which displayed a banner that urged citizens to "Remember the Maine."

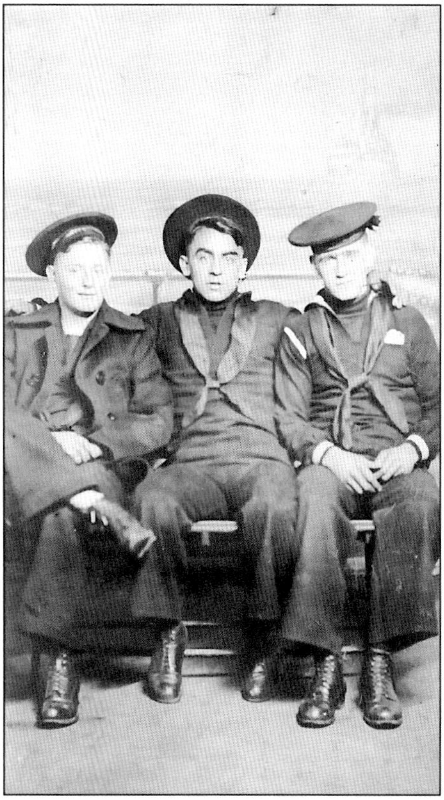

Bangor area sailors stop off at a photographic studio in Norfolk, Virginia, in 1916. It was a time when many Americans braced for a war with Mexico after insurgents led by Mexican bandit "Pancho" Villa killed some Americans in a New Mexico town.

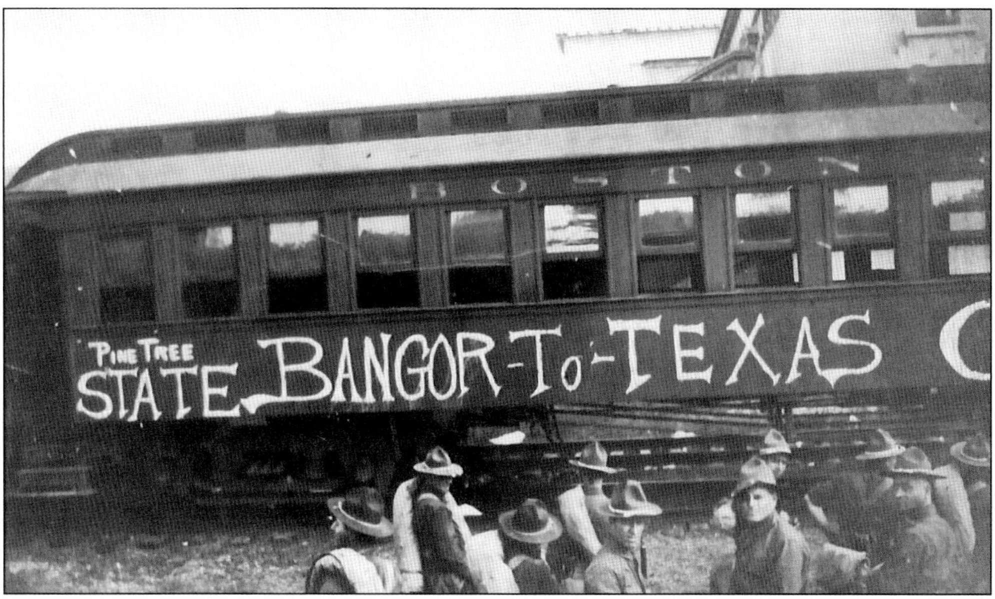

The men of Company G and the Machine Gun Company leave Bangor in Pullman cars on June 22, 1916, prepared to fight Villa's forces at the border.

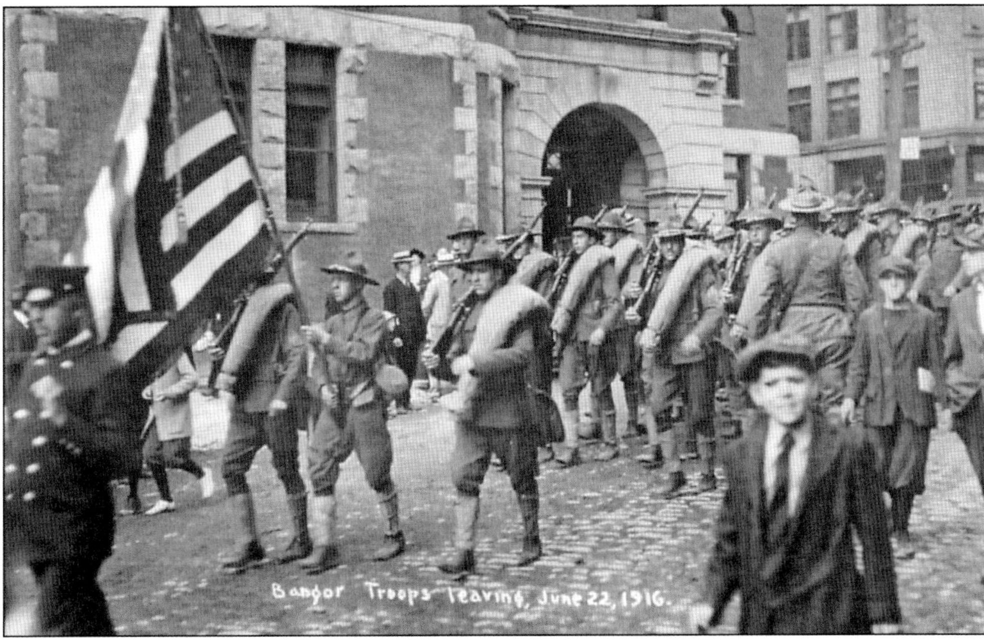

Bangor troops march past the old City Hall in 1916 ready for the worst with the crisis in Mexico.

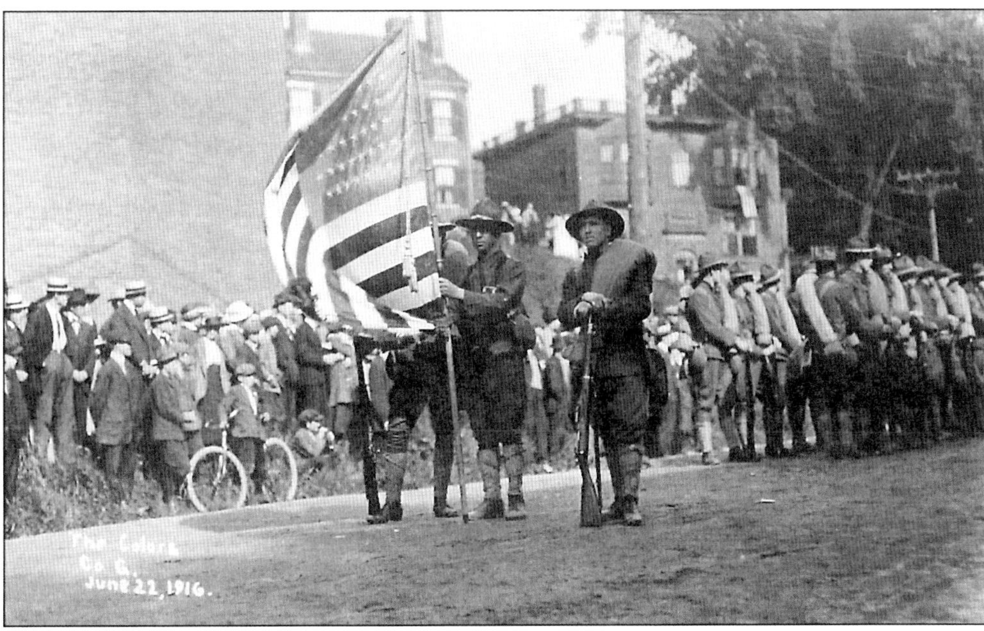

The troops pause with the colors before heading south in 1916. By October they were back in Bangor after the crisis was defused without a war. Many of these same men donned their uniforms again in 1917 and marched off to Europe to fight the Germans.

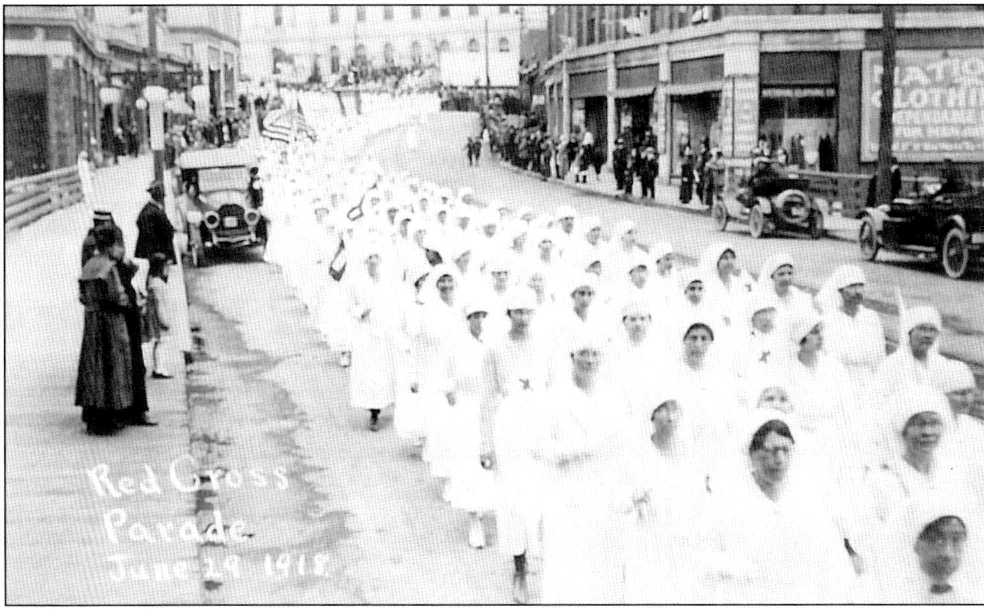

A benefit parade for the Penobscot Chapter of the American Red Cross proceeds down Central Street during World War I. More than 1,200 Red Cross women marched, joined by members of the United Commercial Travelers. Bangor nurses saw distinguished service on the battlefields of Europe.

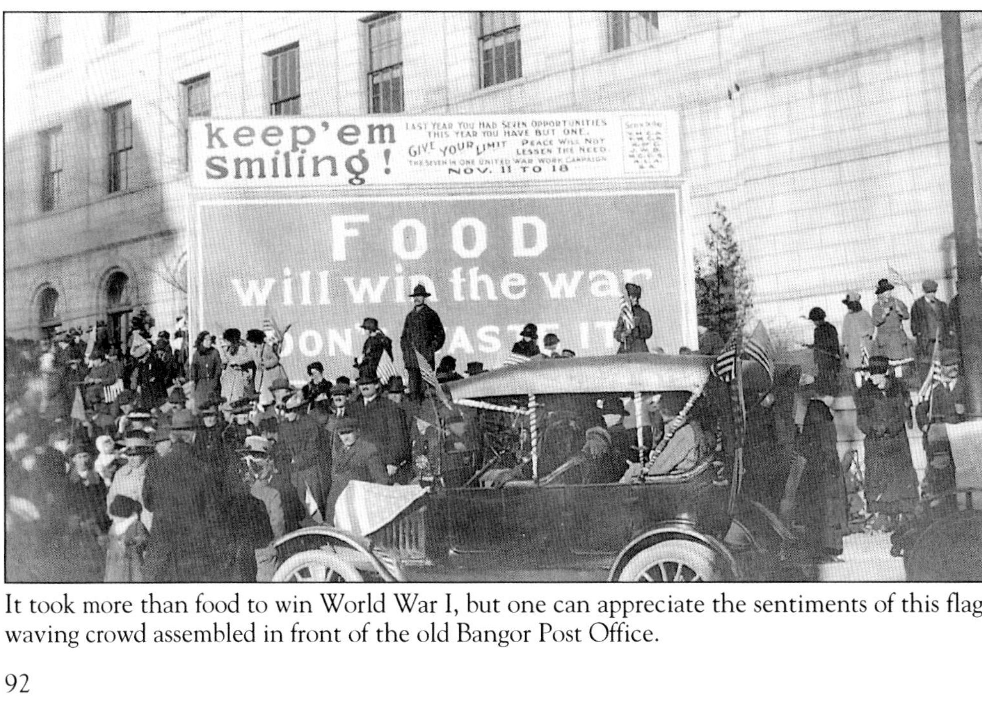

It took more than food to win World War I, but one can appreciate the sentiments of this flag-waving crowd assembled in front of the old Bangor Post Office.

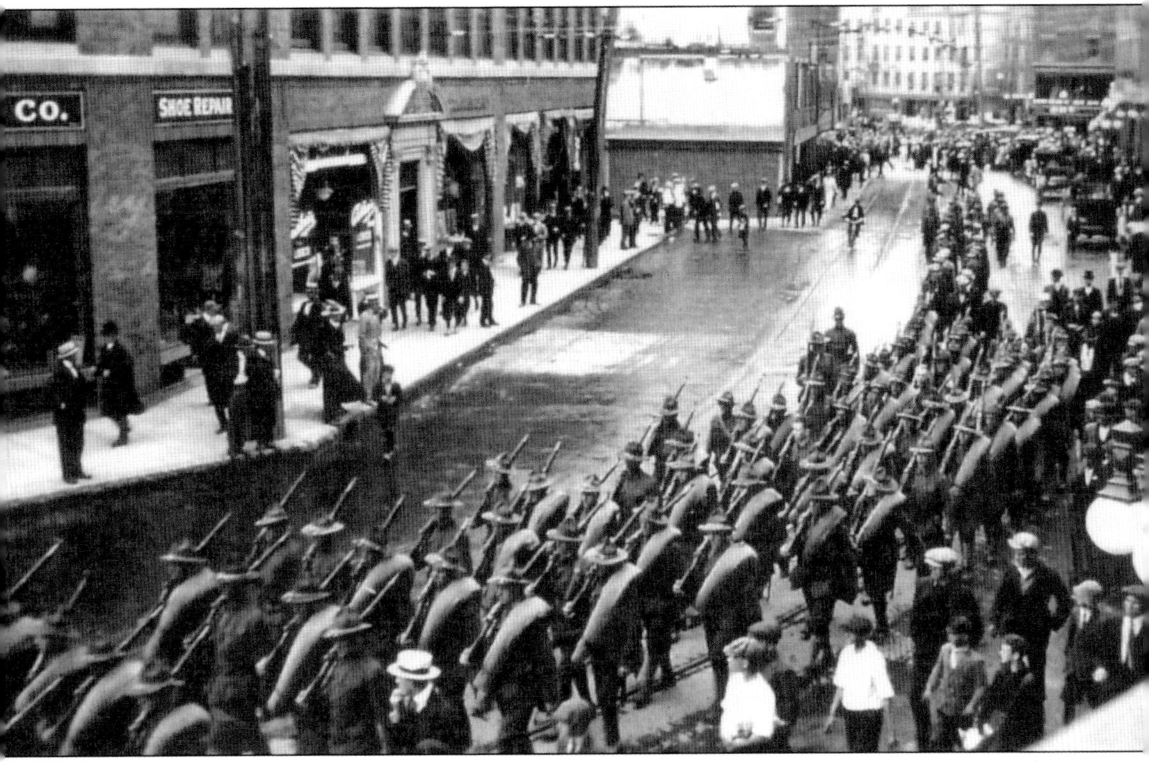

A seemingly endless stream of infantrymen marches through Central Street during World War I. Such parades always brought out thousands of spectators and inspired residents to decorate their homes with red, white and blue bunting. During one parade a unit of soldiers at rest began singing "It's a Long Way to Tipperary." Invariably, old Civil War soldiers stood by the curbing and remembered when the Second Maine Regiment marched off to war in 1861. Ten Bangor men were killed in action and nine died of war wounds during World War I; another thirteen died of pneumonia.

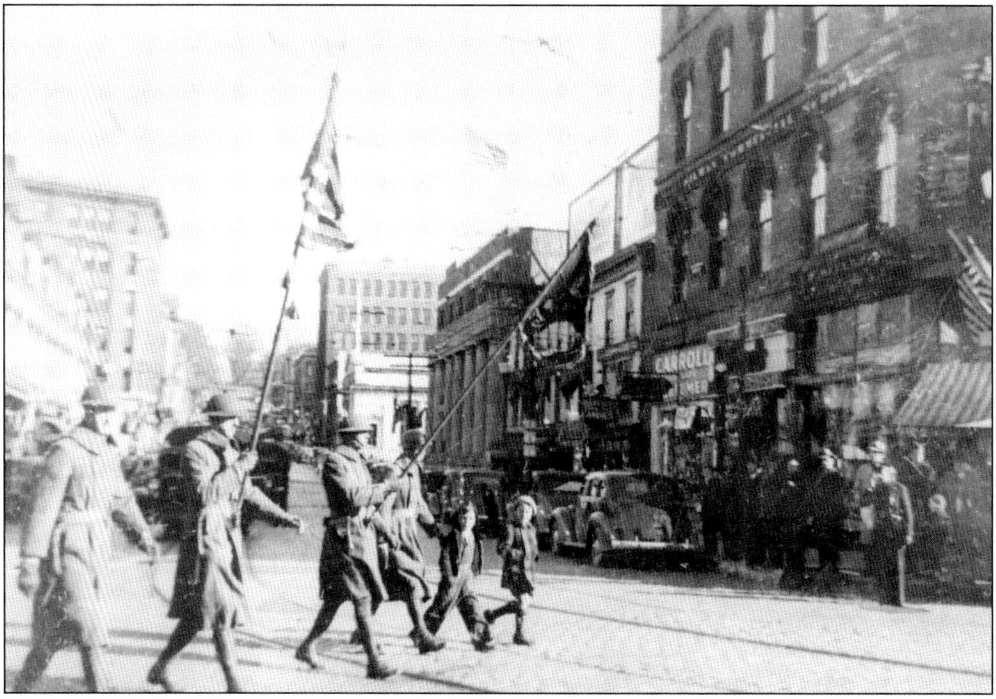

Nineteen years after the armistice ended World War I, former doughboys march across Hammond Street in the 1937 Veterans Day Parade. The buttons on the soldiers' uniforms resembled dumplings of earlier times, known as doughboys (or so the story goes).

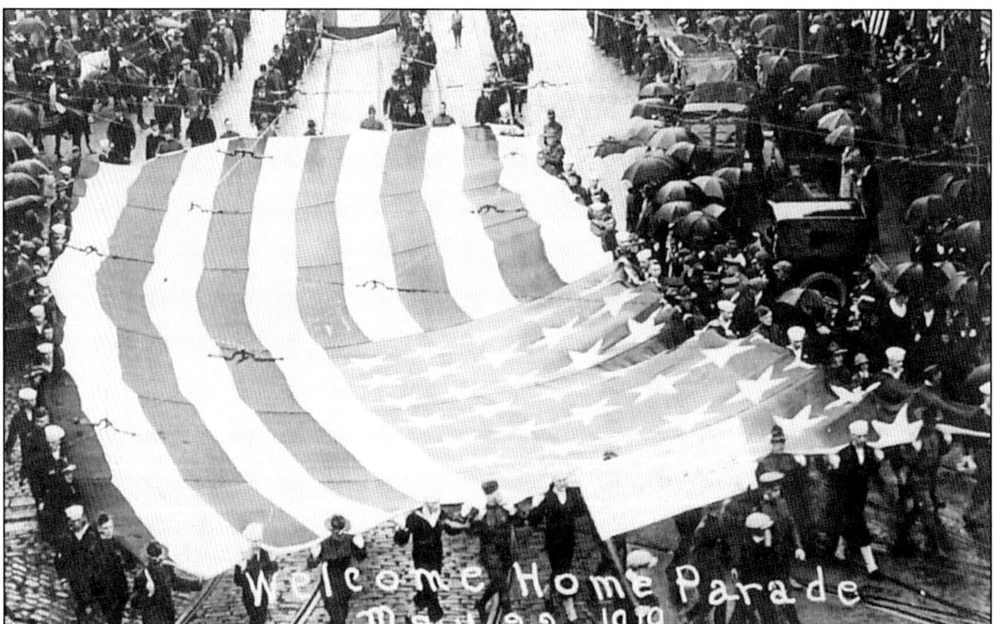

History must surely have been made on May 22, 1919, when local sailors carried the largest American flag ever seen in Bangor.

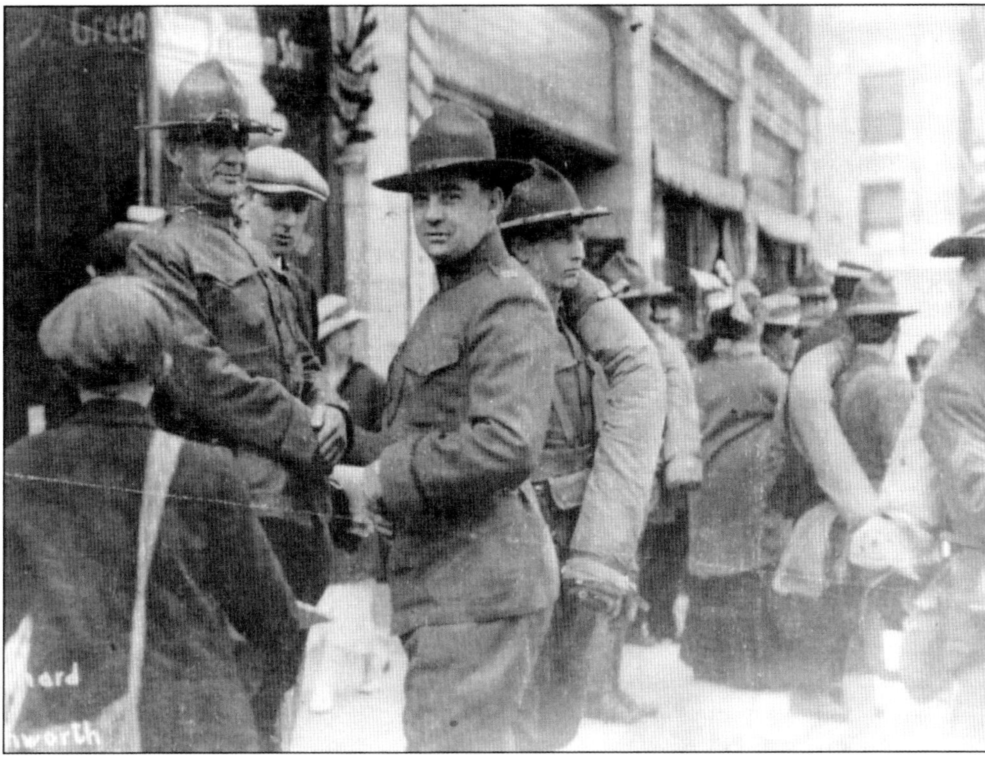

A familiar downtown sight during World War I was local doughboys either going to war or returning home. Many carried their own bedrolls to the railroad station.

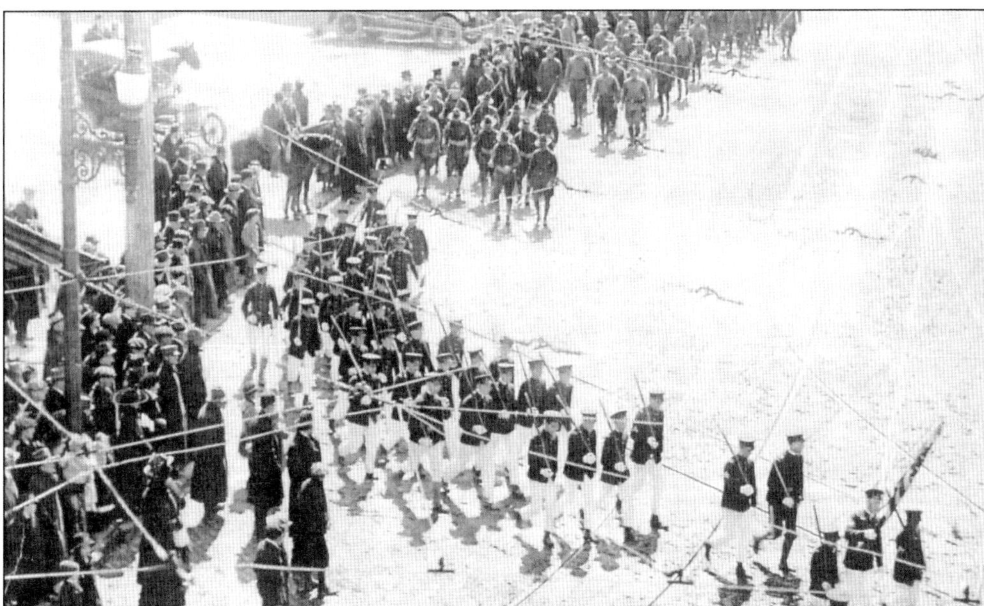

Patriot's Day in 1917. This bird's-eye view shows soldiers and sailors marching across West Market Square and up Hammond Street.

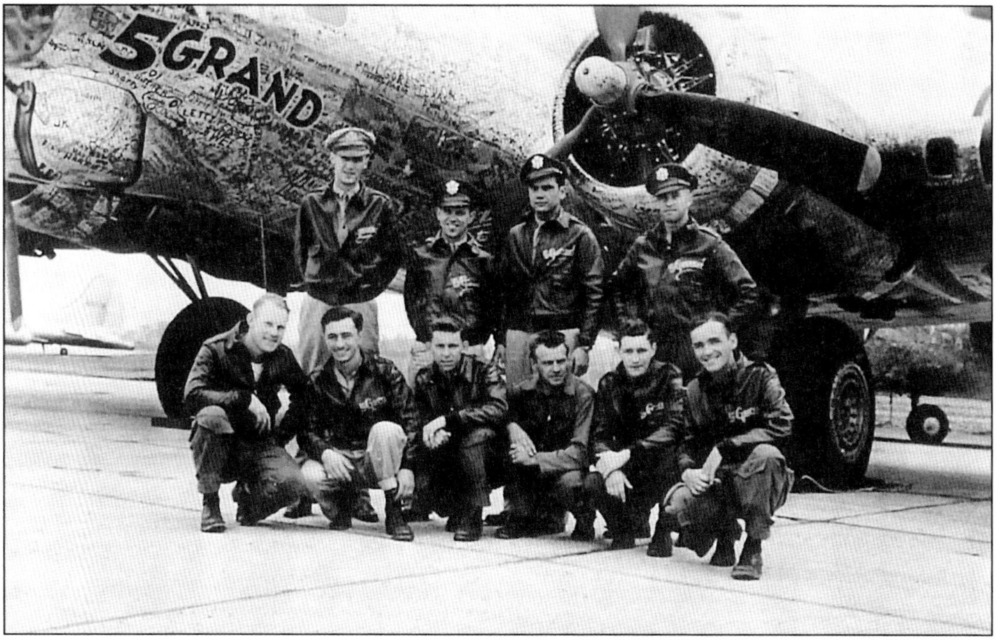

Good luck graffiti blankets the fuselage of a war plane at Dow Field during World War II. Other planes were adorned with the pictures of nude or semi-nude pinup girls.

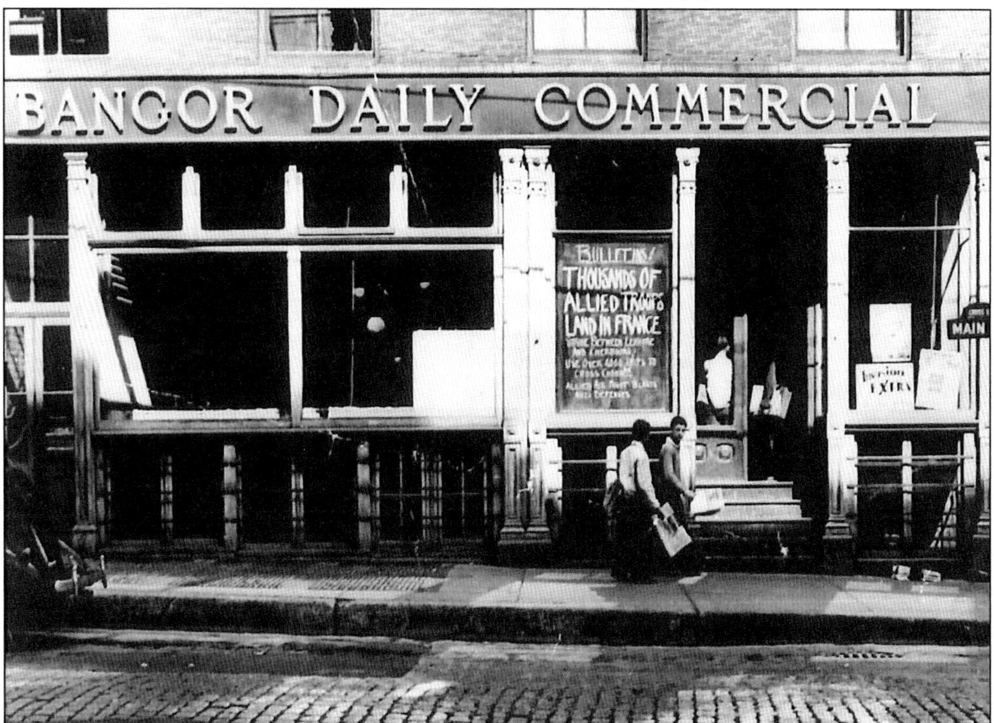

D-Day, June 6, 1944, on Main Street. Thousands of "extra" editions announcing the Allied invasion of Europe were sold by eager young paper carriers. The *Bangor Daily Commercial* competed with the *Bangor Daily News* for many years.

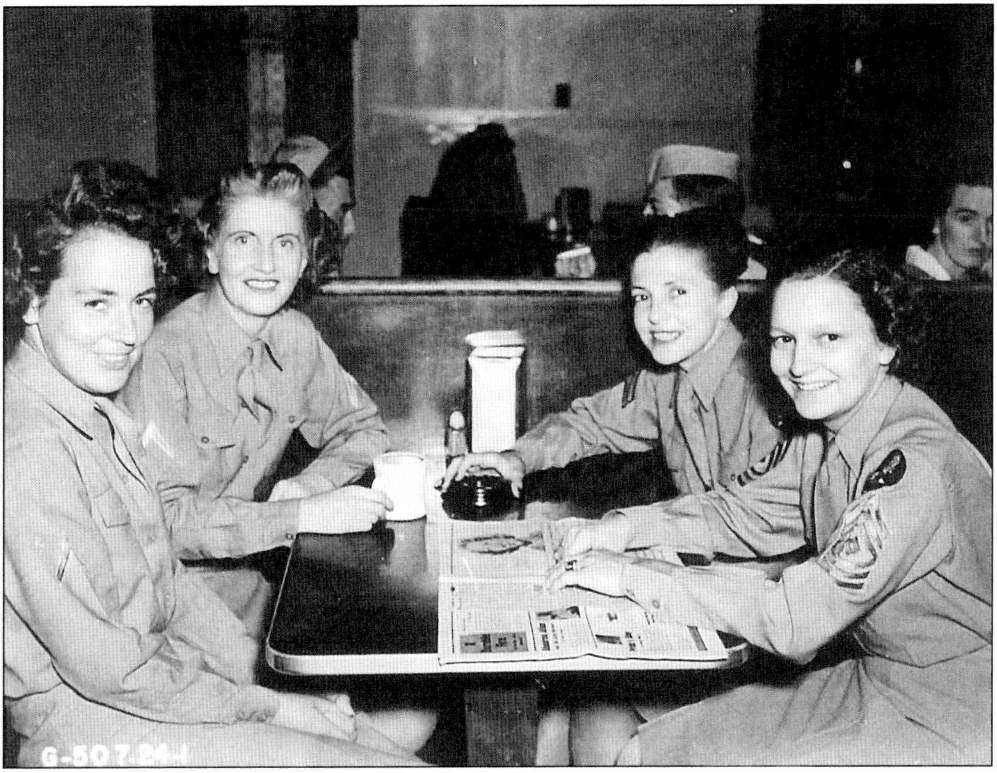

Smiling Army Air WACS at the Dow Air Force Base canteen made the war years more tolerable for the thousands of troops that passed through the base since its inception early in 1942.

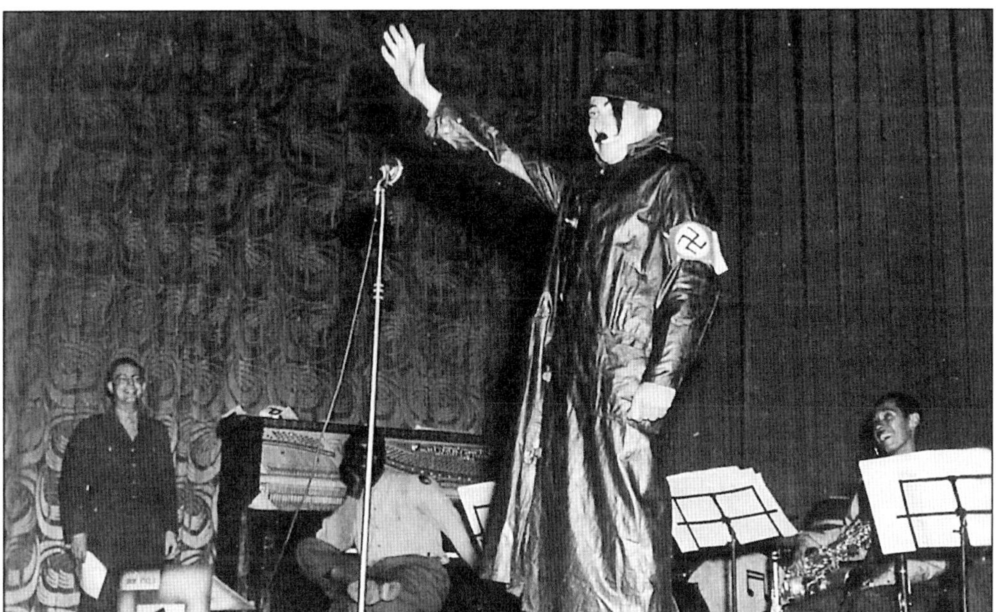

Sieg Heil! was the order of the evening at the Bangor City Hall Auditorium during an army skit spoofing the leader of the Third Reich.

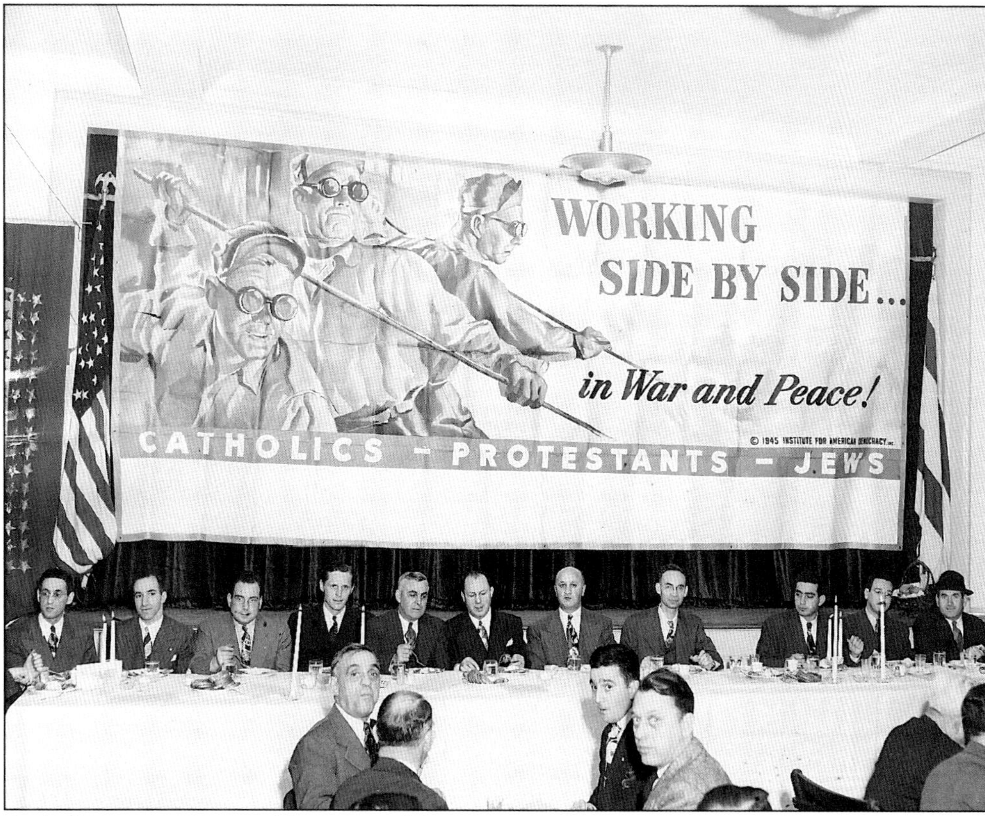

Catholics, Protestants and Jews joined forces in Bangor *c.* 1945 at a dinner attended by such notable men as attorneys Edward Stern and Edward Gross (on the far left), and local businessmen and civil leaders.

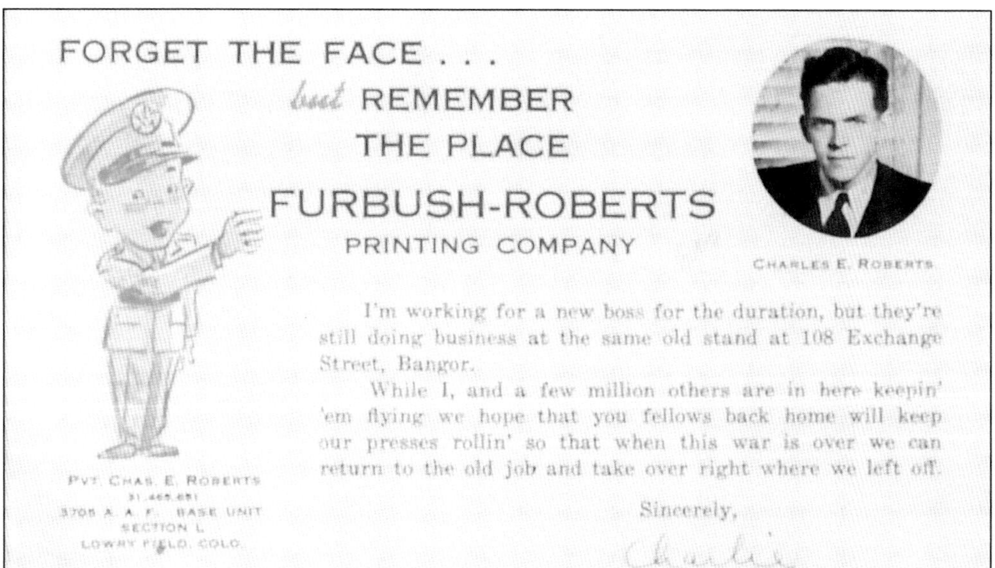

Charles Roberts chose this novel way of informing customers that he was in the employ of Uncle Sam during the war years. The family business is still going strong.

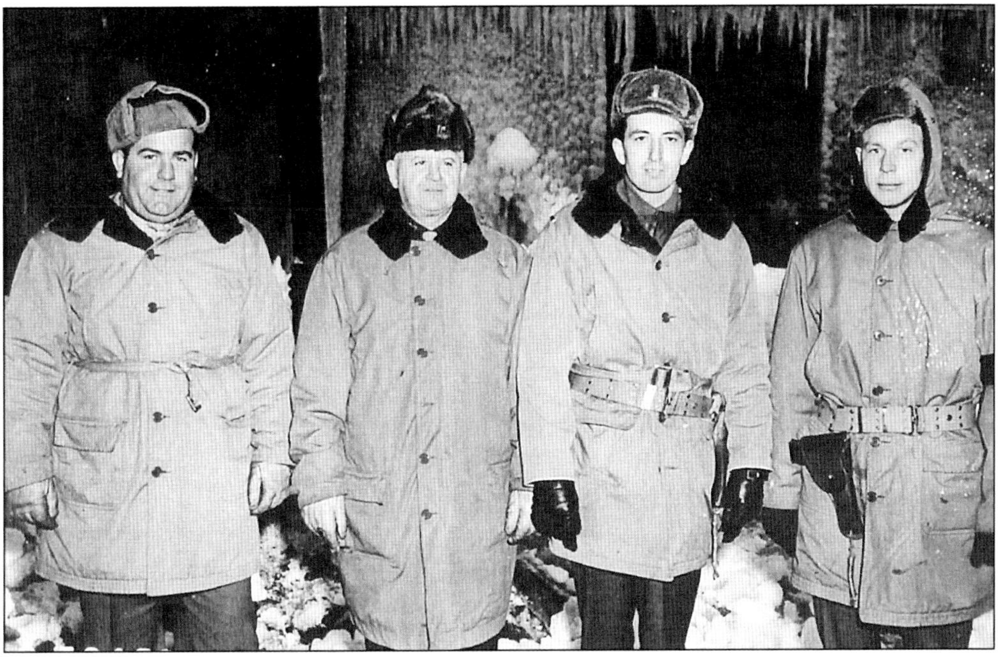

German prisoners of war were trucked to Bangor from a camp in Houlton, Maine, in January 1945 to clean up debris after a fire destroyed two blocks on Exchange Street. It was the first time German POWs were seen openly in the business center of an American city.

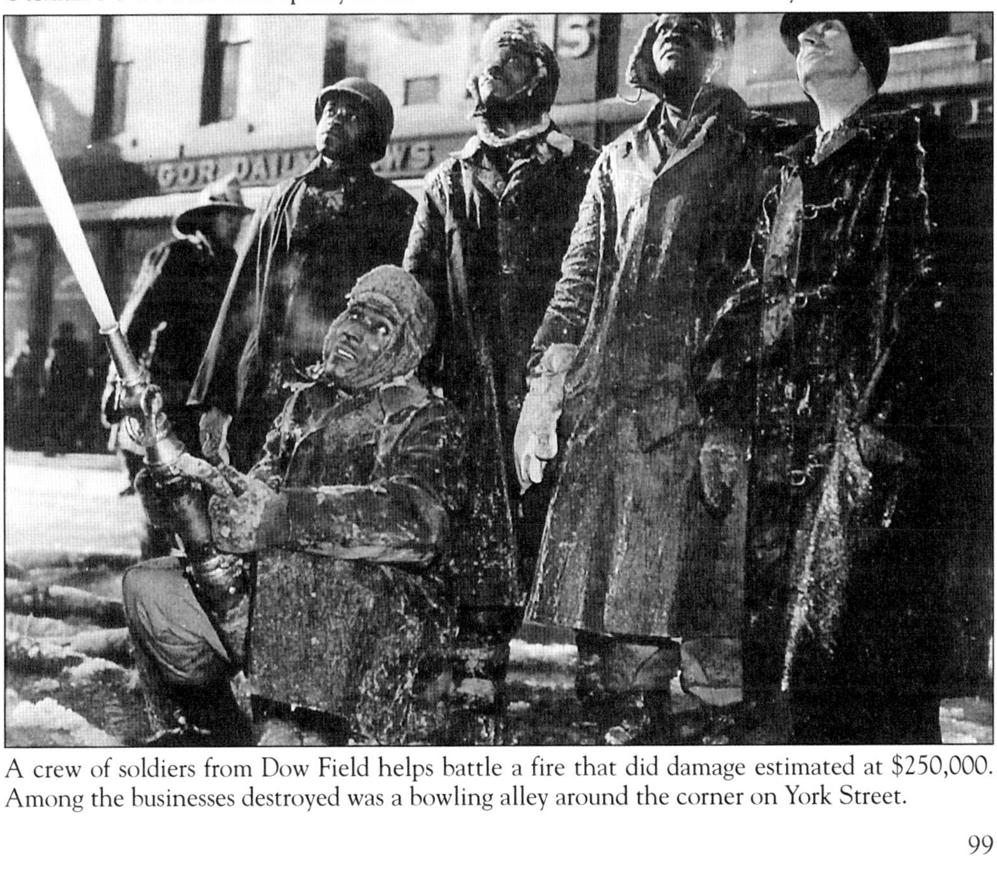

A crew of soldiers from Dow Field helps battle a fire that did damage estimated at $250,000. Among the businesses destroyed was a bowling alley around the corner on York Street.

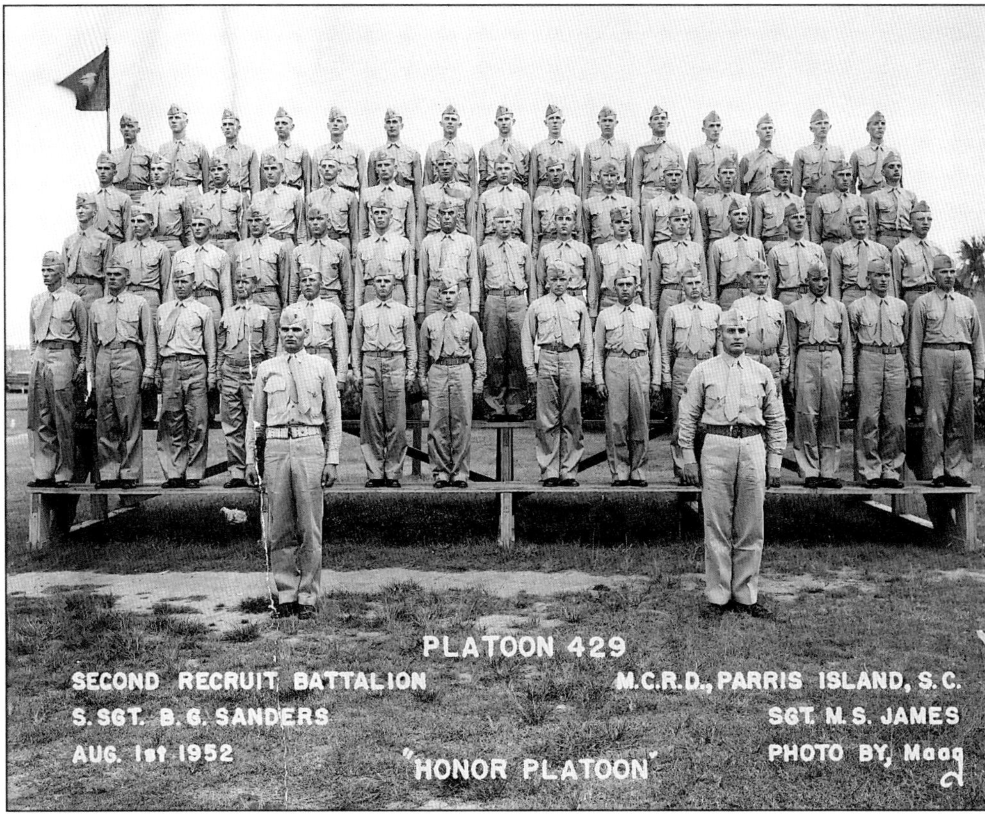

Parris Island, South Carolina was the setting for this photograph showing a battalion of Maine Marines trained to battle Korean forces in the "Forgotten War." Among the Second Recruit Battalion Honor Platoon that posed on August 1, 1952, were Ken Buckley of Bangor (second row, third from right), Len Thompson of Portland and Maurice Guay of Old Town (to Buckley's right and left).

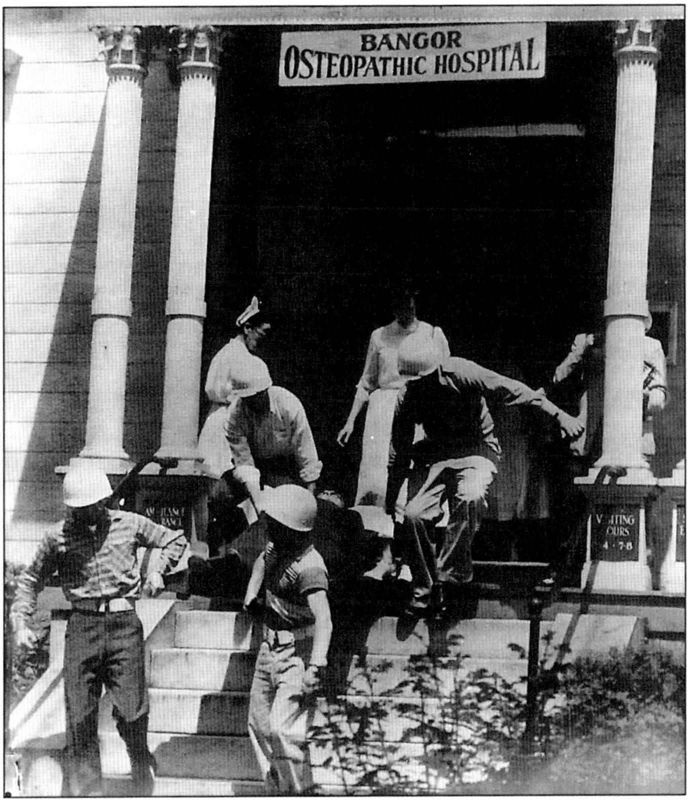

The Cold War was raging in 1955 when the Civilian Defense program tested Bangor's ability to mobilize. Patients at the Osteopathic Hospital on State Street were evacuated along with twenty-two thousand other residents in the first test of its kind in the Eastern United States.

WHEN THE WARNING SOUNDS

A STEADY BLAST OF 3 TO 5 MINUTES

This means: **ATTACK ALERT—TAKE ACTION AS DIRECTED BY LOCAL GOVERNMENT.**

Tune your AM radio to a **Conelrad** frequency **(640 or 1240)** for official directions. Proceed according to your community's emergency action plan. **Don't use the telephone.**

WAILING TONE OR SHORT BLASTS FOR 3 MINUTES

This means: **ATTACK—TAKE COVER IMMEDIATELY IN BEST AVAILABLE SHELTER.**

In a building: If there is no prepared shelter, go into a basement or to an interior first floor room. Stay in shelter until you get word you can leave.

Outdoors or in a car: Go to nearest shelter. If you cannot reach prepared shelter lie flat on the ground face down, or crouch on floor of car.

Small cards were given out explaining the difference between a wailing tone and a short blast. Knowing the difference, it was thought, could save many lives.

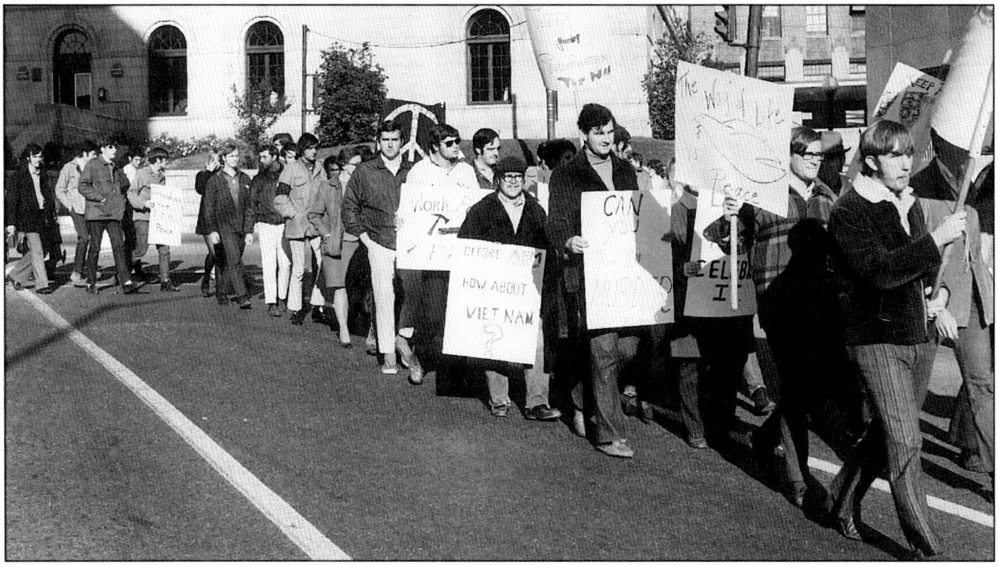

The Vietnam War separated people by ideology as no conflict had done before. In 1969 local protesters, as well as students and faculty from the University of Maine, marched down Central Street in a simple plea for peace.

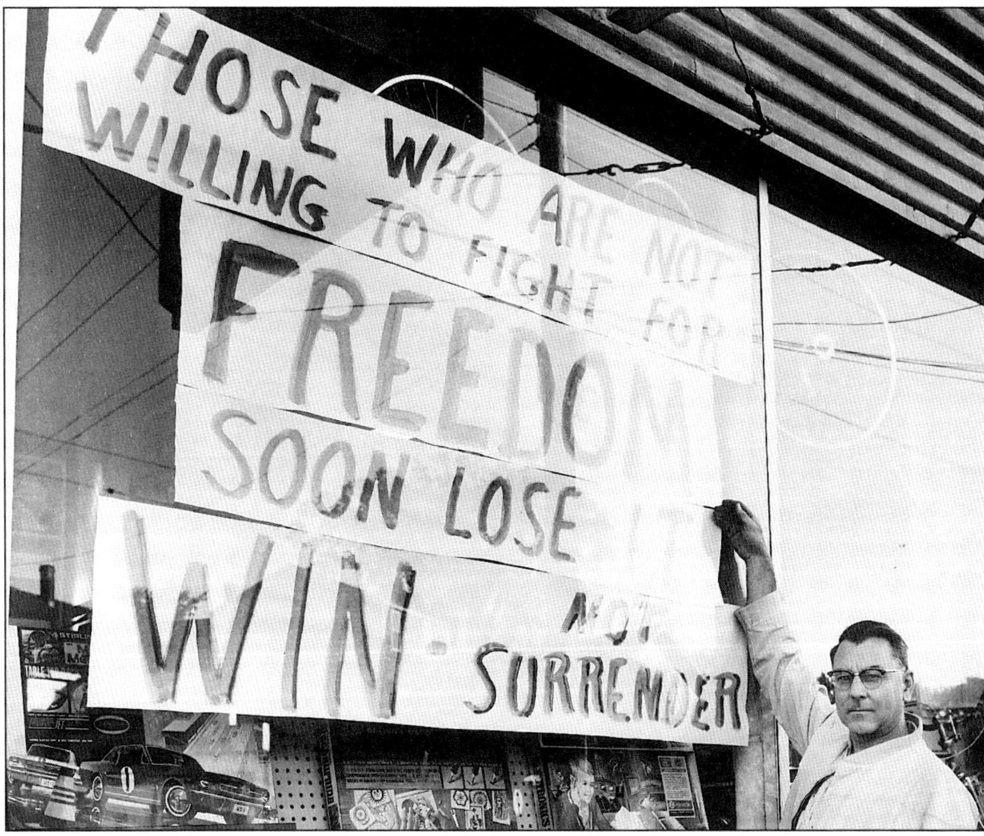

This local merchant had other ideas about the Vietnam War in 1969. While protesters marched in the streets, he argued for perseverance in Southeast Asia.

Six

Bed and Board

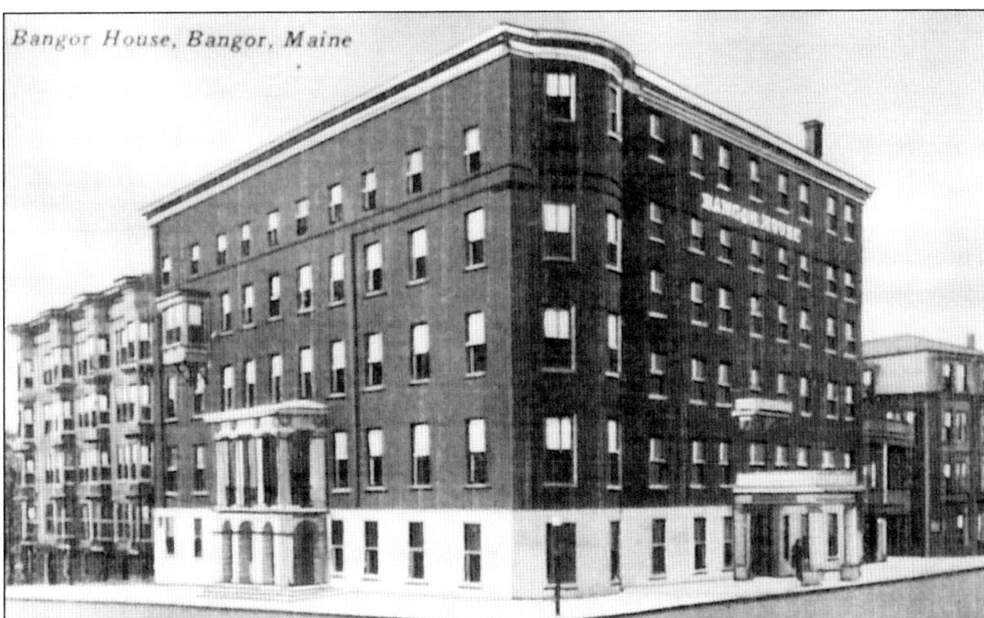

The Bangor House was the *crème de la crème* of Bangor hotels after it opened its doors in 1834. Each room was heated by a fireplace, and guests could enjoy ladies' drawing and dining rooms, a smoking room and a gentlemen's parlor.

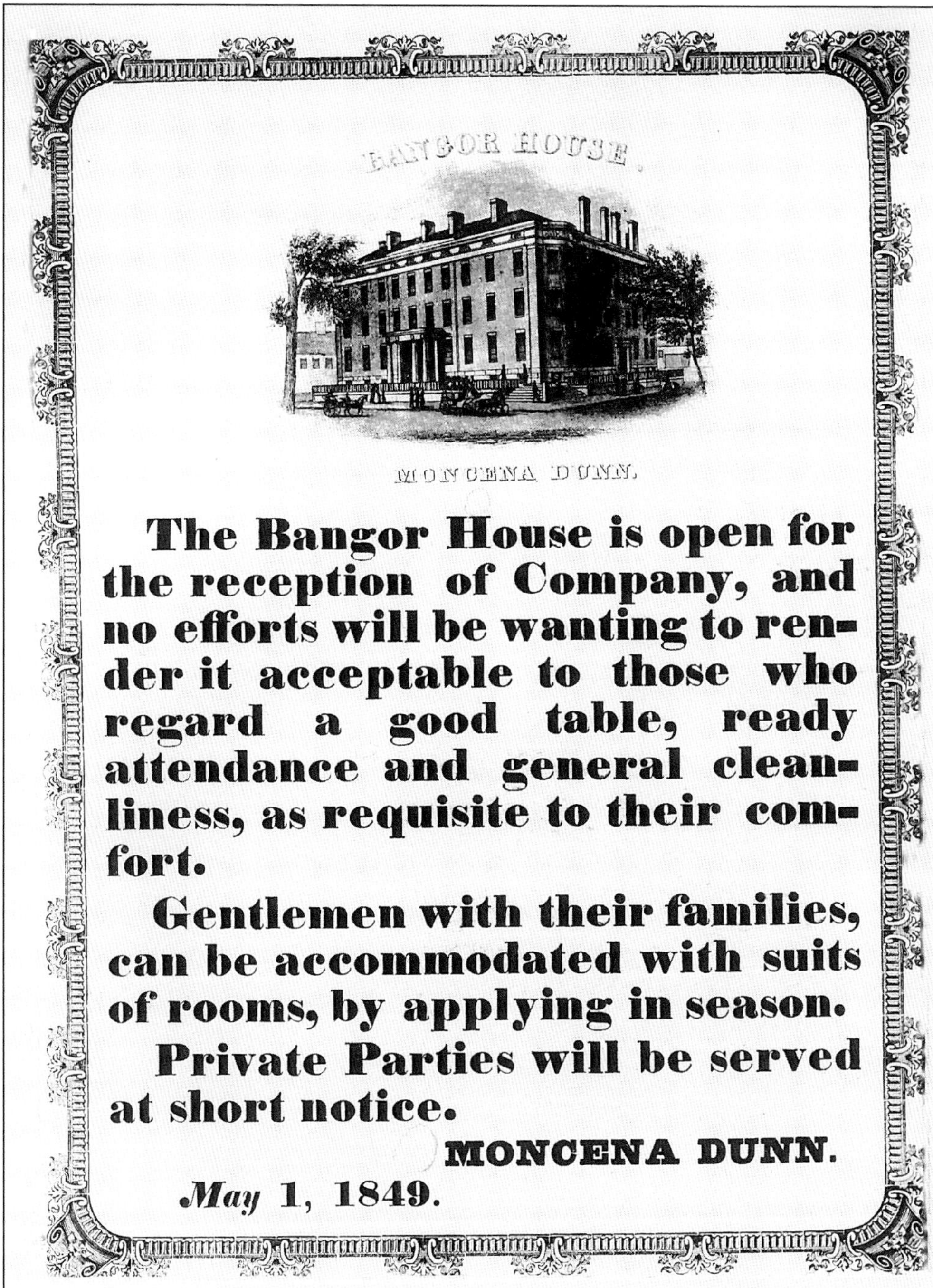
BANGOR HOUSE.

MONCENA DUNN.

The Bangor House is open for the reception of Company, and no efforts will be wanting to render it acceptable to those who regard a good table, ready attendance and general cleanliness, as requisite to their comfort.

Gentlemen with their families, can be accommodated with suits of rooms, by applying in season.

Private Parties will be served at short notice.

MONCENA DUNN.

***May* 1, 1849.**

Moncena Dunn, an early manager of the Bangor House, wasn't exaggerating in this 1849 advertisement. No other hotel for miles around could touch the hotel's elegance and comfort. "General cleanliness" was a deciding factor in choosing a hotel at a time when many weren't inspected on a regular basis.

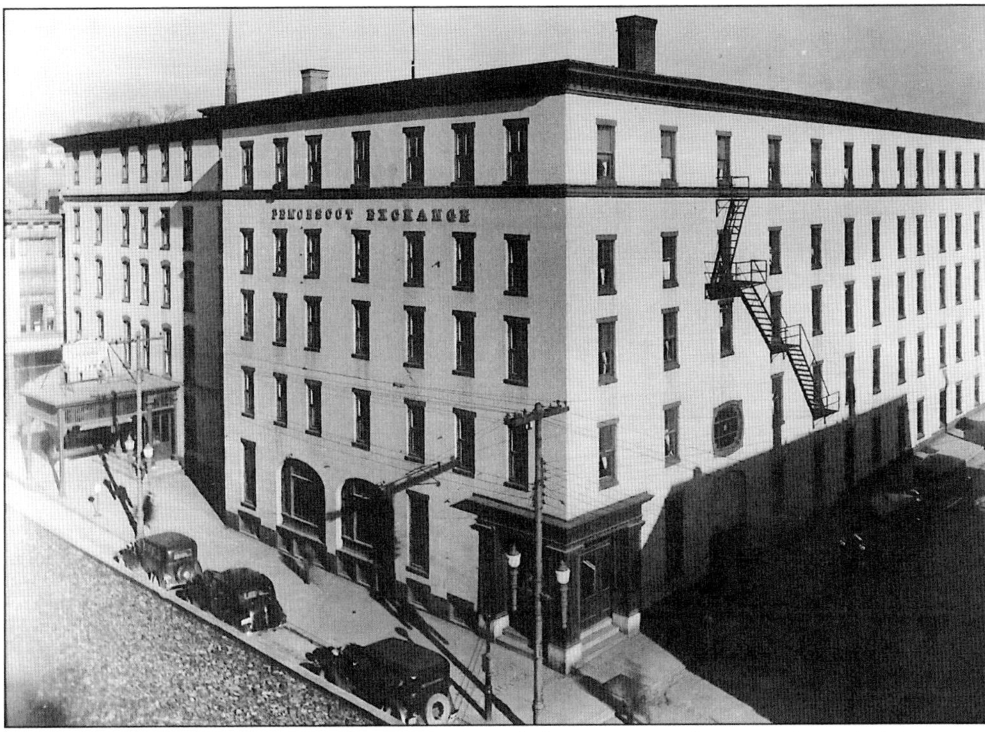

The Penobscot Exchange Hotel, or the "Penoby" as guests affectionately called it, was a landmark on working-class Exchange Street that catered to traveling men as well as Boston and New York society. Built in 1827, the hotel was remodeled several times over the years, including the flattening of the roof *c.* 1900 to prevent street injuries from falling snow and ice.

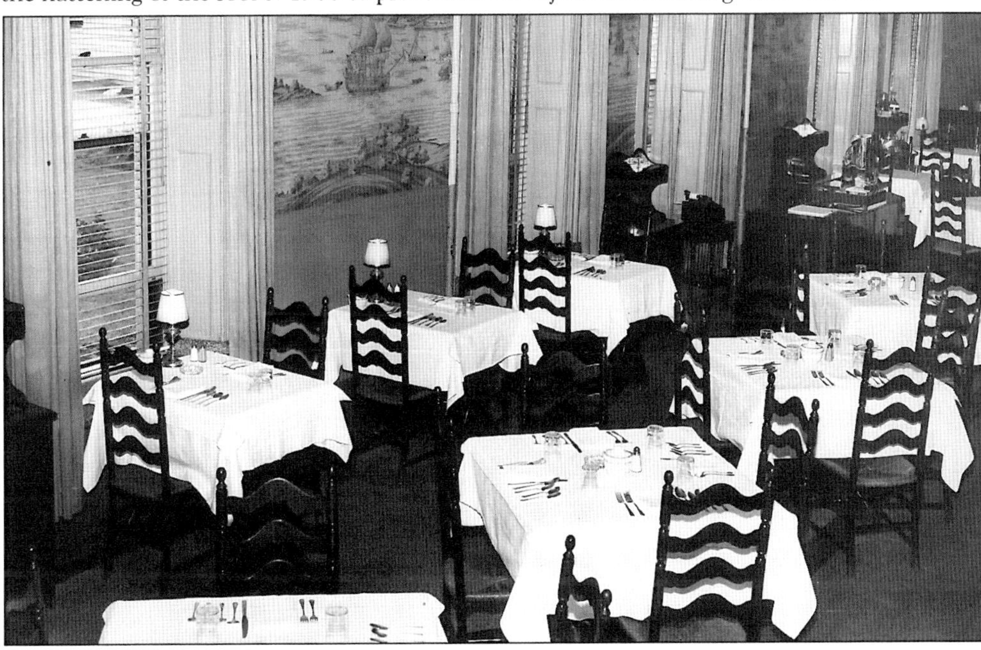

Eating in the Penobscot Exchange's dining room was always a treat. Moon and Cratty, the two men who operated the hotel for decades, spared no expense in the meals they served.

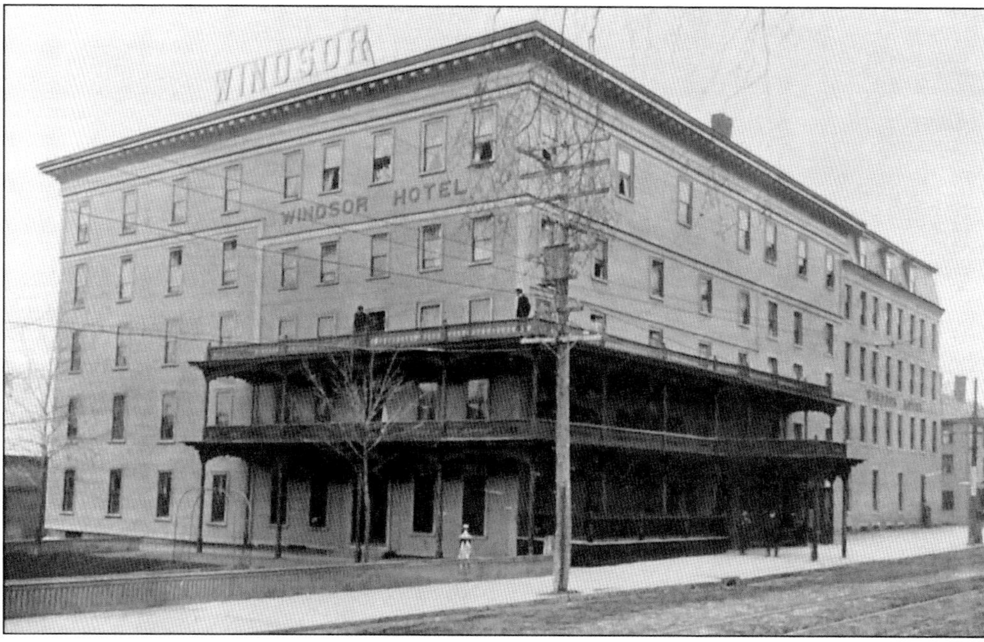

Rooms at the Windsor Hotel on Harlow Street went for $1.50 in the 1800s, including three good meals. If a guest desired heat in his room he had to tip a porter $.50; the porter would then bring up kindling and a hodful of coal and light a fire.

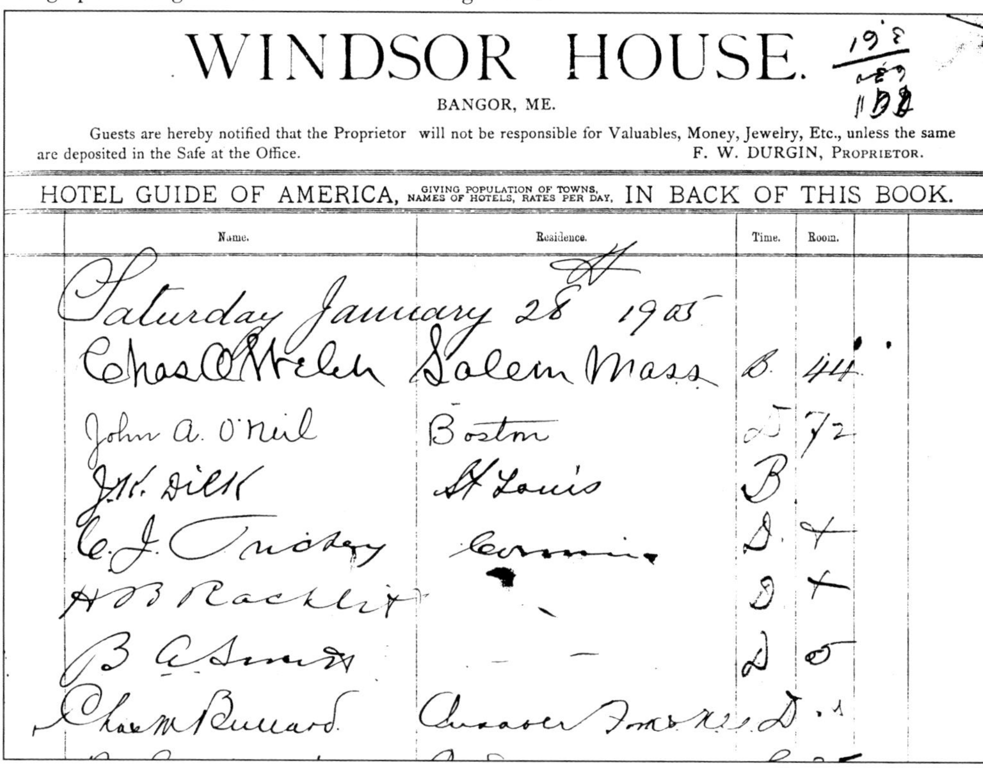

WINDSOR HOUSE.

BANGOR, ME.

Guests are hereby notified that the Proprietor will not be responsible for Valuables, Money, Jewelry, Etc., unless the same are deposited in the Safe at the Office.

F. W. DURGIN, PROPRIETOR.

HOTEL GUIDE OF AMERICA, GIVING POPULATION OF TOWNS, NAMES OF HOTELS, RATES PER DAY, IN BACK OF THIS BOOK.

Saturday January 28 1905

Name.	Residence.	Time.	Room.
Chas O Welch	Salem Mass	B.	44
John A. O'Neil	Boston	D	72
J. K. Dilk	St Louis	B	
C. J. [illegible]	[illegible]	D.	
H B Racklift		D	
B A Smith	—	D	
Chas M Bullard	[illegible]	D.	

Horace Chase's hotel put up guests from as far away as Boston, Portland and Eastport in 1905. Chase named the hotel after the elegant Windsor in Montréal.

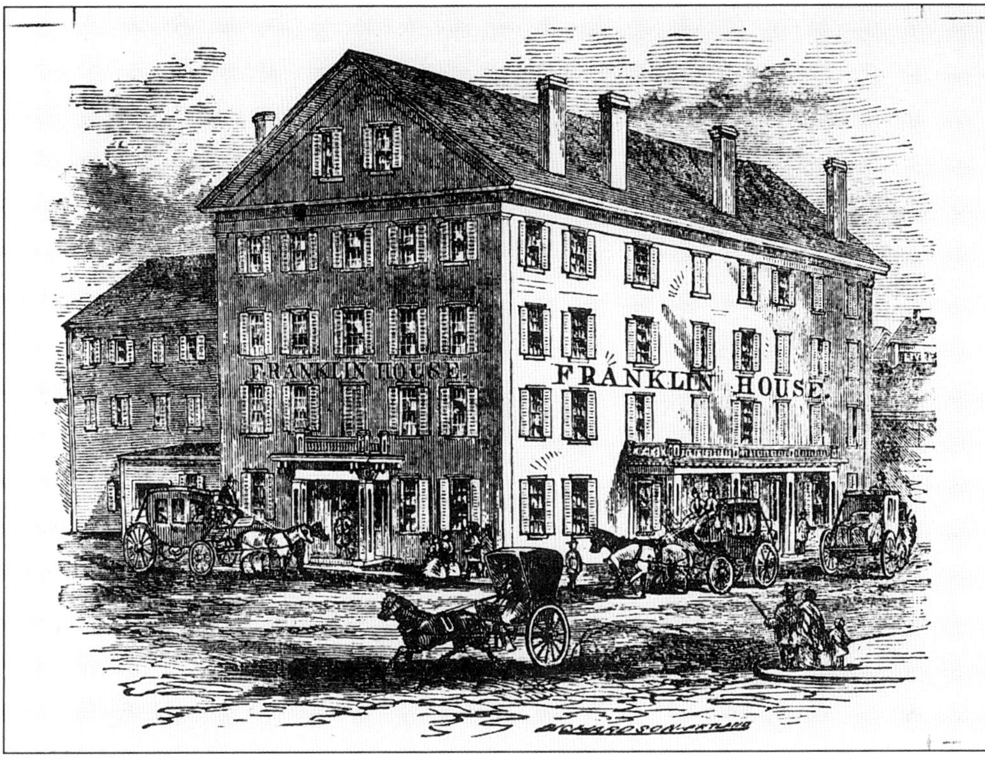

The Franklin House was an earlier identity of the Windsor at Harlow and Franklin Streets. Built in 1825, it was briefly renamed the American House before Horace Chase changed the name. The hotel and all the surrounding buildings were leveled in the Great Fire of 1911.

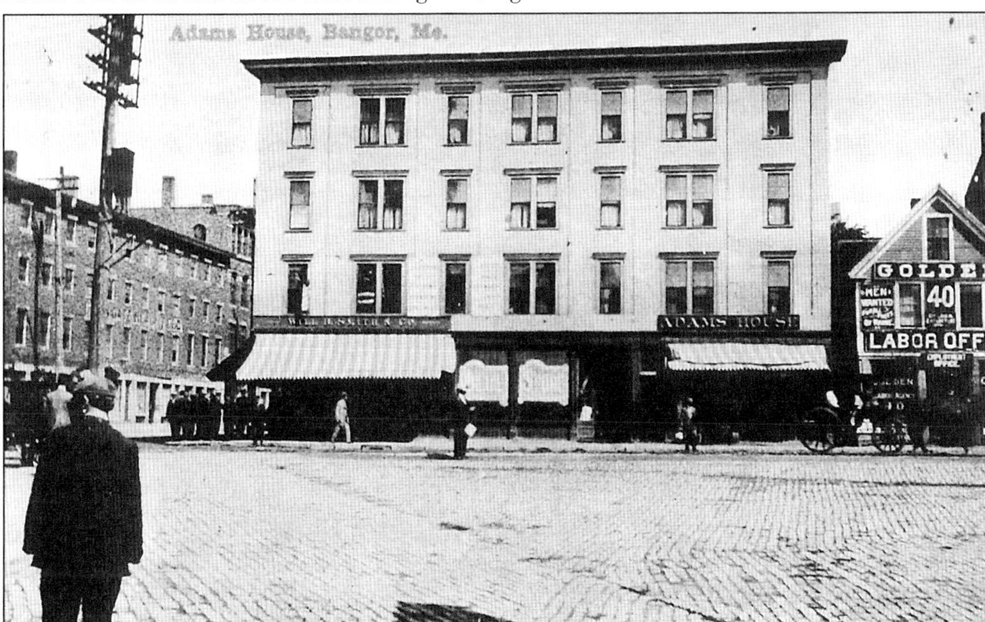

Visitors and residents could get a warm meal and a clean room cheap at Charles Adams' hotel located on Washington Street directly across from the railroad station.

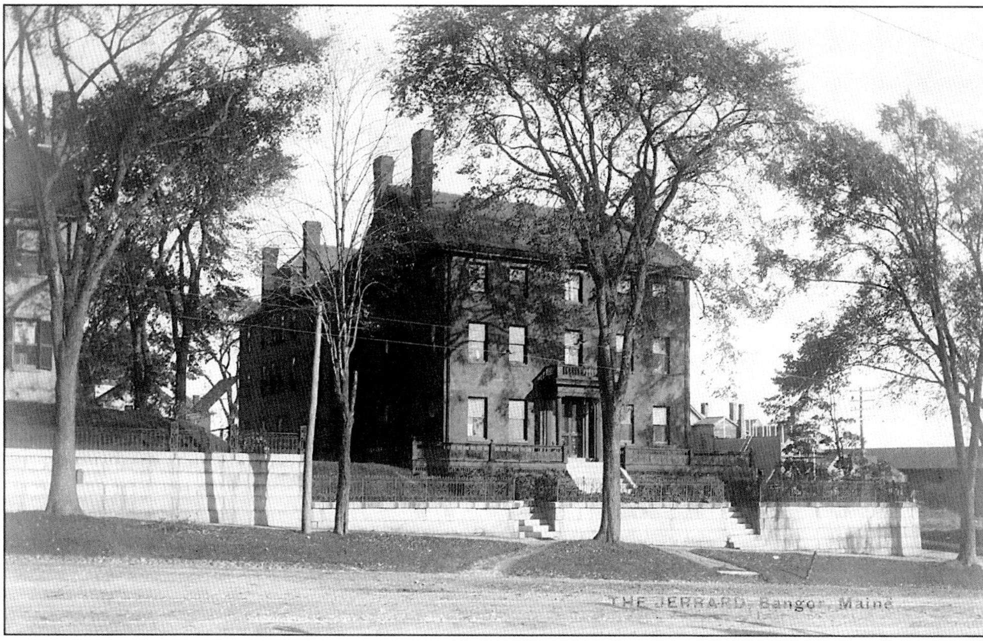

Sam Veazie's mansion at Broadway and York Streets lived on as the Jerrard Hotel in the twentieth century. Anson Jerrard's family hotel was sold to Lillian Bowden and Jennie Leighton, who operated it for several years.

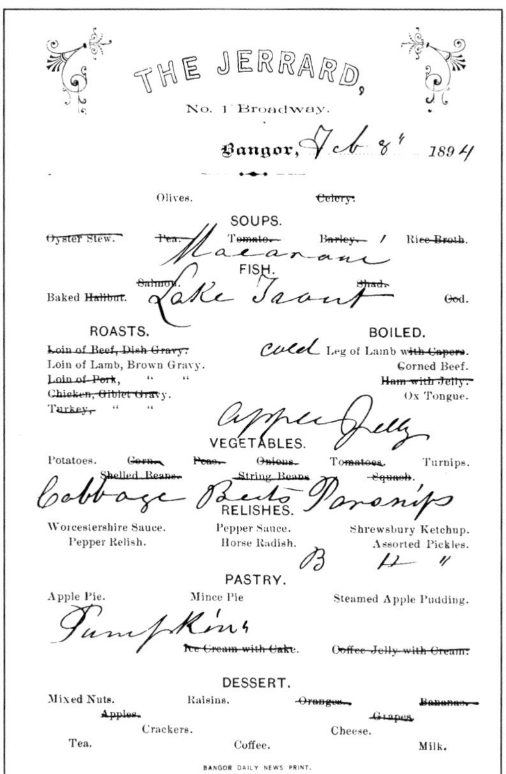

THE JERRARD,

No. 1 Broadway.

Bangor, Feb 8th 1894

Olives. Celery.

SOUPS.

Oyster Stew. Pea. Tomato. Barley. Rice Broth.

Macaroni

FISH.

Baked Halibut. Salmon. Lake Trout Shad. Cod.

ROASTS.

Loin of Beef, Dish Gravy.
Loin of Lamb, Brown Gravy.
Loin of Pork, " "
Chicken, Giblet Gravy.
Turkey, " "

BOILED.

cold Leg of Lamb with Capers.
Corned Beef.
Ham with Jelly.
Ox Tongue.

Apple Jelly

VEGETABLES.

Potatoes. Corn. Peas. Onions. Tomatoes. Turnips.
Shelled Beans. String Beans. Squash.
Cabbage Beets Parsnips

RELISHES.

Worcestershire Sauce. Pepper Sauce. Shrewsbury Ketchup.
Pepper Relish. Horse Radish. Assorted Pickles.

PASTRY.

Apple Pie. Mince Pie Steamed Apple Pudding.
Pumpkins Ice Cream with Cake. Coffee Jelly with Cream.

DESSERT.

Mixed Nuts. Raisins. Oranges. Bananas.
Apples. Grapes.
Crackers. Cheese.
Tea. Coffee. Milk.

BANGOR DAILY NEWS PRINT.

Lake trout, cold leg of lamb and macaroni soup were served at the Jerrard on February 8, 1894.

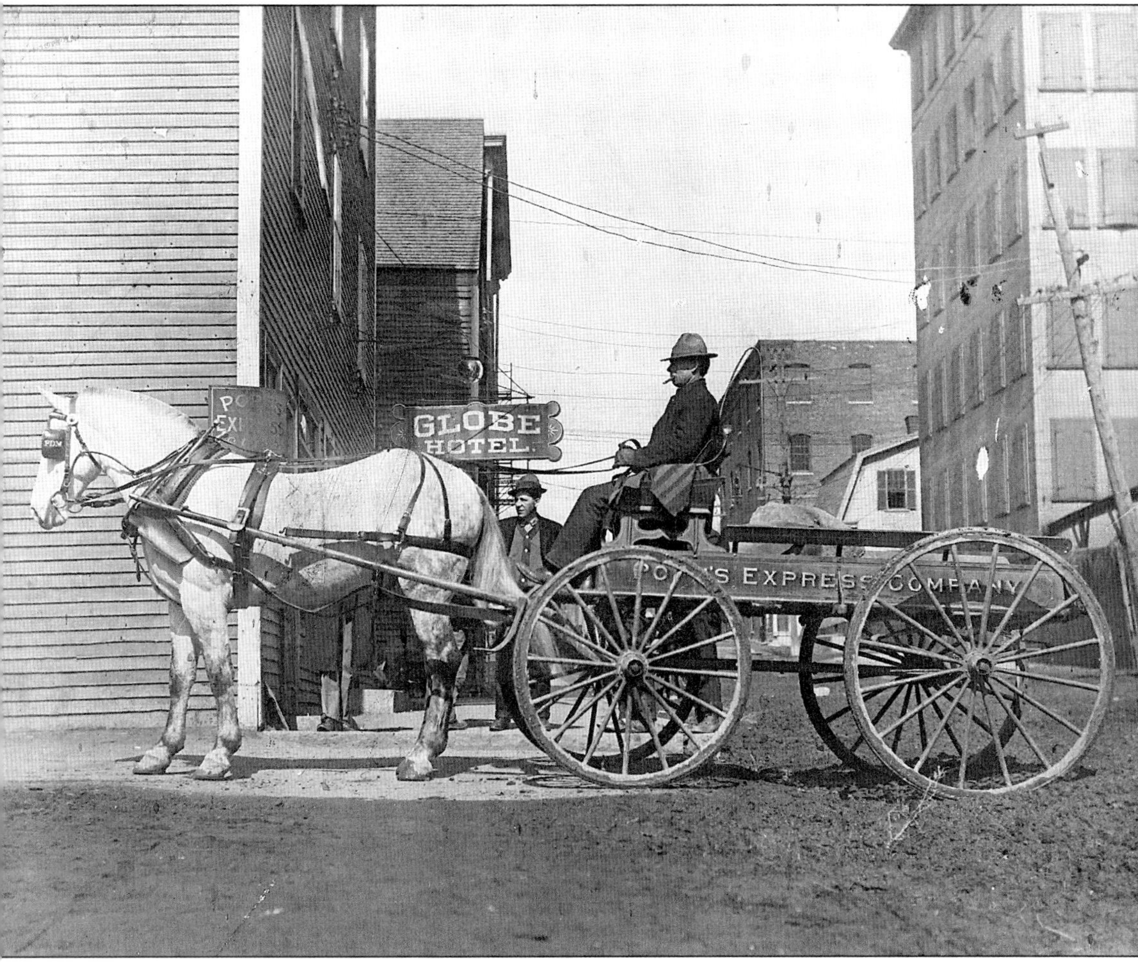

Pope D. McKinnon owned the Globe Hotel on French Street, ran his own express company, and manufactured cigars such as the stogie he's seen smoking in this *c.* 1914 photograph. He also managed the Palace and Star Theaters. In stark contrast to the elegance of the Penobscot Exchange and Bangor House Hotels, the Globe was nestled among the bars and brothels of the city's earthy district. Apparently McKinnon was wily enough to make a profit operating under these conditions.

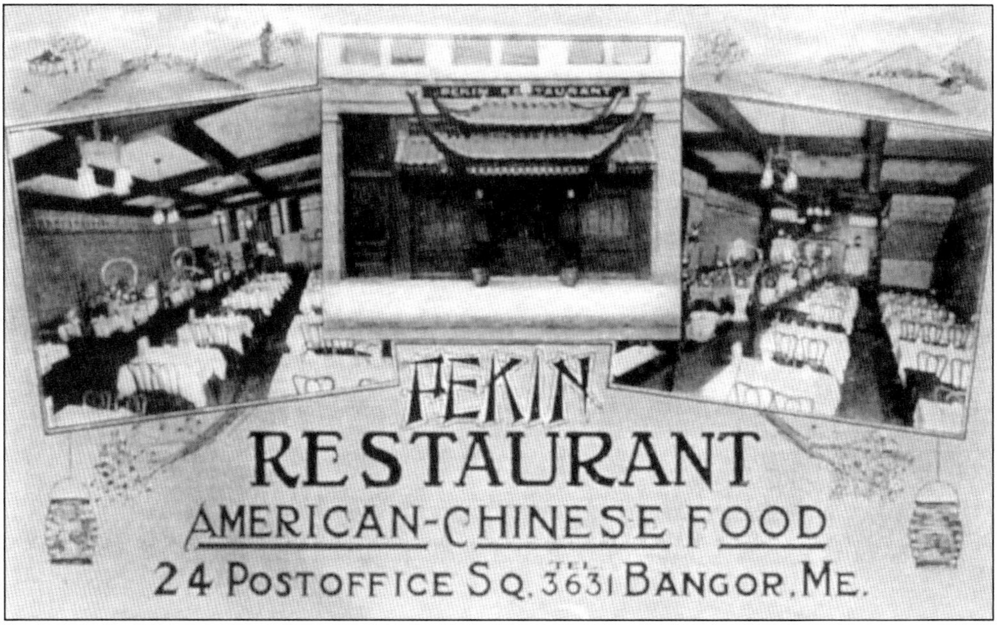

Many Bangor patrons got their first taste of Mandarin-style cuisine at the Pekin Restaurant on Harlow Street, started in 1924 by Wong Hee and Wong J. Jones.

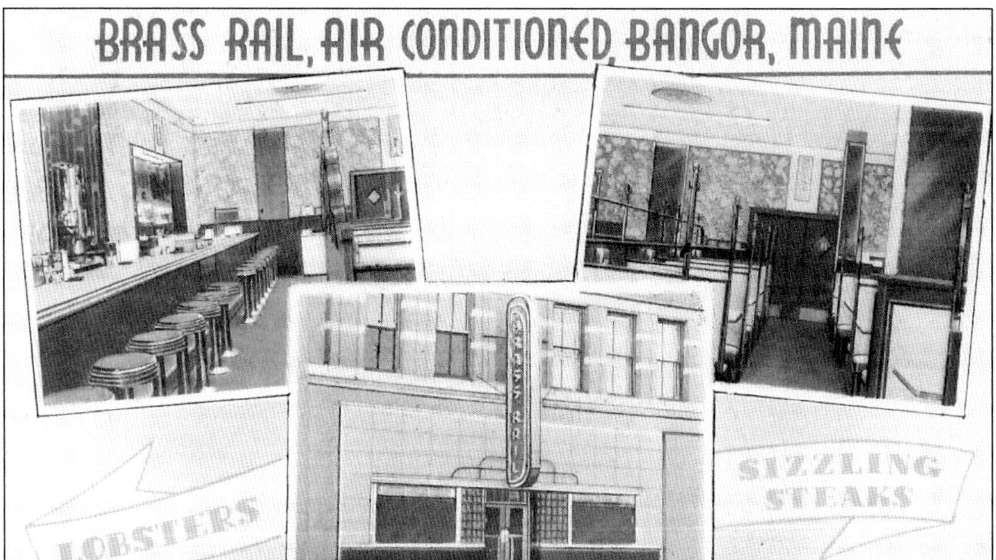

Max Kominsky and Louis Stavron were two of the names associated with the operation of the Brass Rail on Exchange Street, which opened in 1931. Who could resist "a completely air-conditioned and sound-proof restaurant serving delicious foods at popular prices. Featuring charcoal broiled steaks and all seafoods, free parking facilities, excellent service."

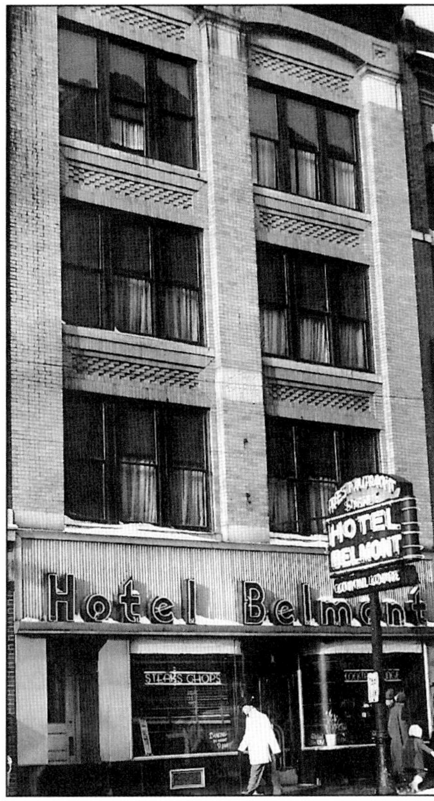

The Cocktail Lounge was a magnet that attracted many to the Hotel Belmont at 18 State Street. Bill Cyr operated the establishment in 1957 when this photograph was taken. Charles Cummings managed it in the late 1940s.

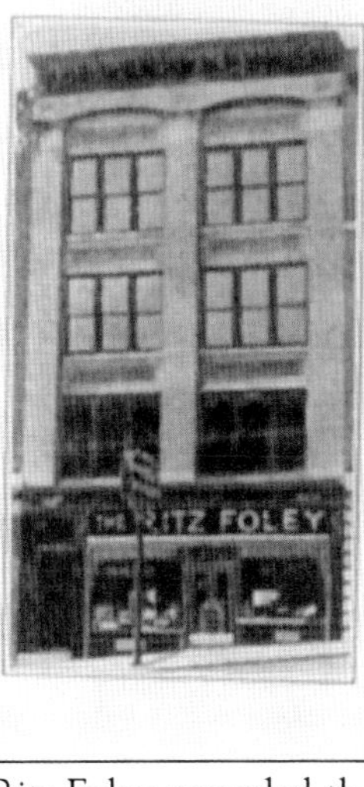

.·. "The Home of Good Food" .·.

The Ritz-Foley

J. Edward Foley, Manager

Bangor's Newest . . . Modern . . . Up-to-Date

HOTEL ◆ RESTAURANT

COCKTAIL LOUNGE

Reasonable Rates

18-20 State Street — Bangor, Maine

The Ritz-Foley preceded the Hotel Belmont on lower State Street. J. Edward Foley, who ran the business in the 1930s and early 1940s, advertised reasonable room rates despite the hotel's high-society name.

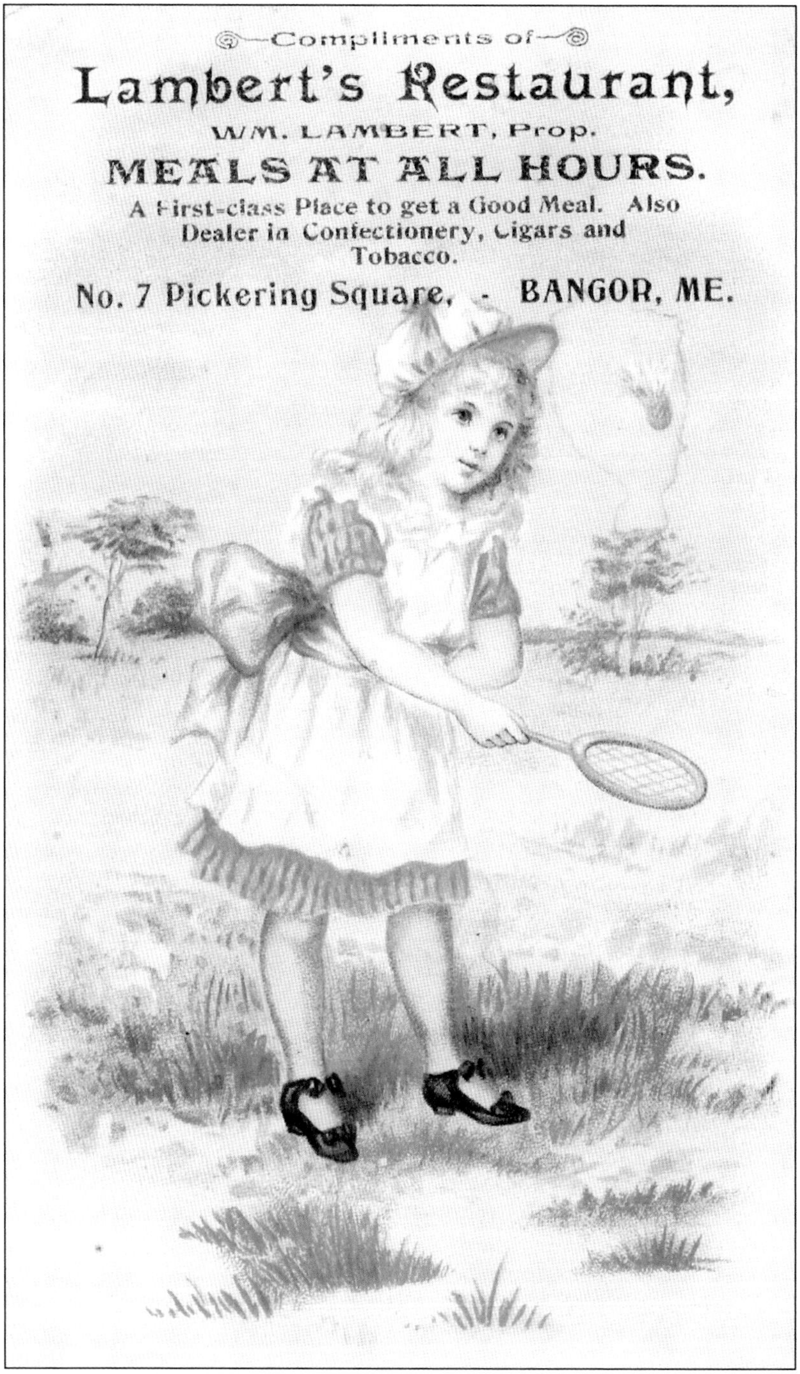

Little girls playing badminton had nothing to do with William Lambert's popular Pickering Square restaurant, but charming advertising cards helped pull in the customers. The square behind Freese's at the turn of the century was an interesting mix of smelly fish markets, butcher shops, wholesale merchants and restaurants like Lambert's. Note that one could also purchase candy and tobacco at the restaurant, a service that lasted well into the twentieth century until vending machines disappeared from many places.

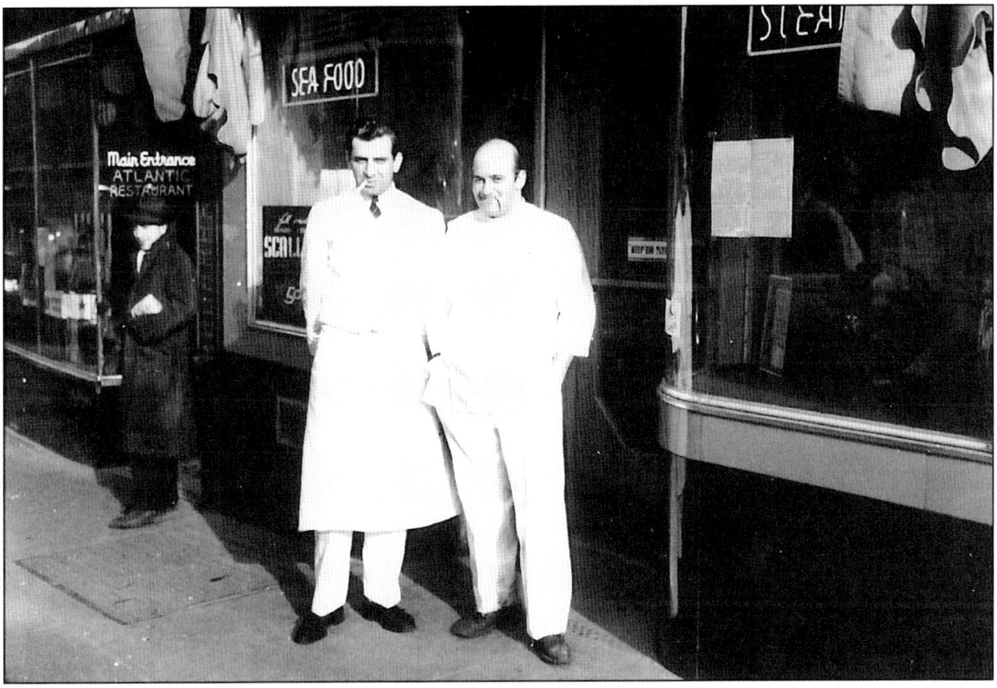

Jim Vomvoris (left) and Pete Vafiades, short-order cooks, enjoy a smoke outside the Brountas Restaurant, *c.* 1940s. George N. Brountas and his family specialized in steak and seafood. Next door on Main Street was the New Atlantic Restaurant operated by Tom Mourkas.

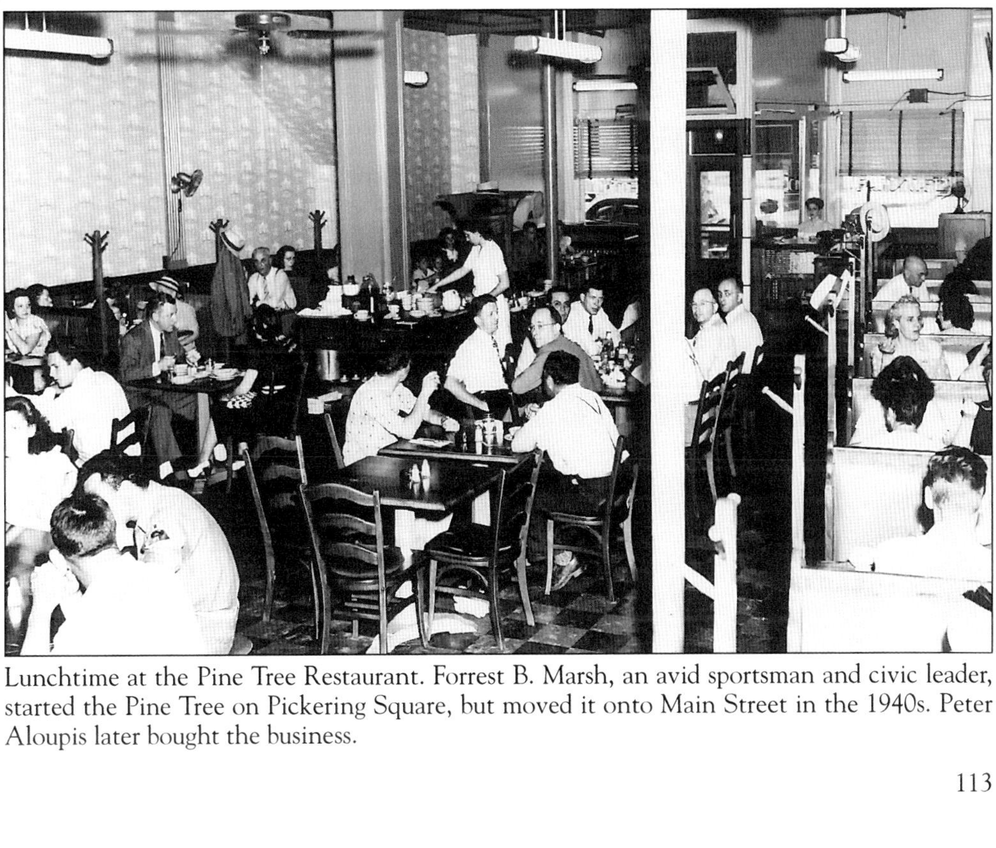
Lunchtime at the Pine Tree Restaurant. Forrest B. Marsh, an avid sportsman and civic leader, started the Pine Tree on Pickering Square, but moved it onto Main Street in the 1940s. Peter Aloupis later bought the business.

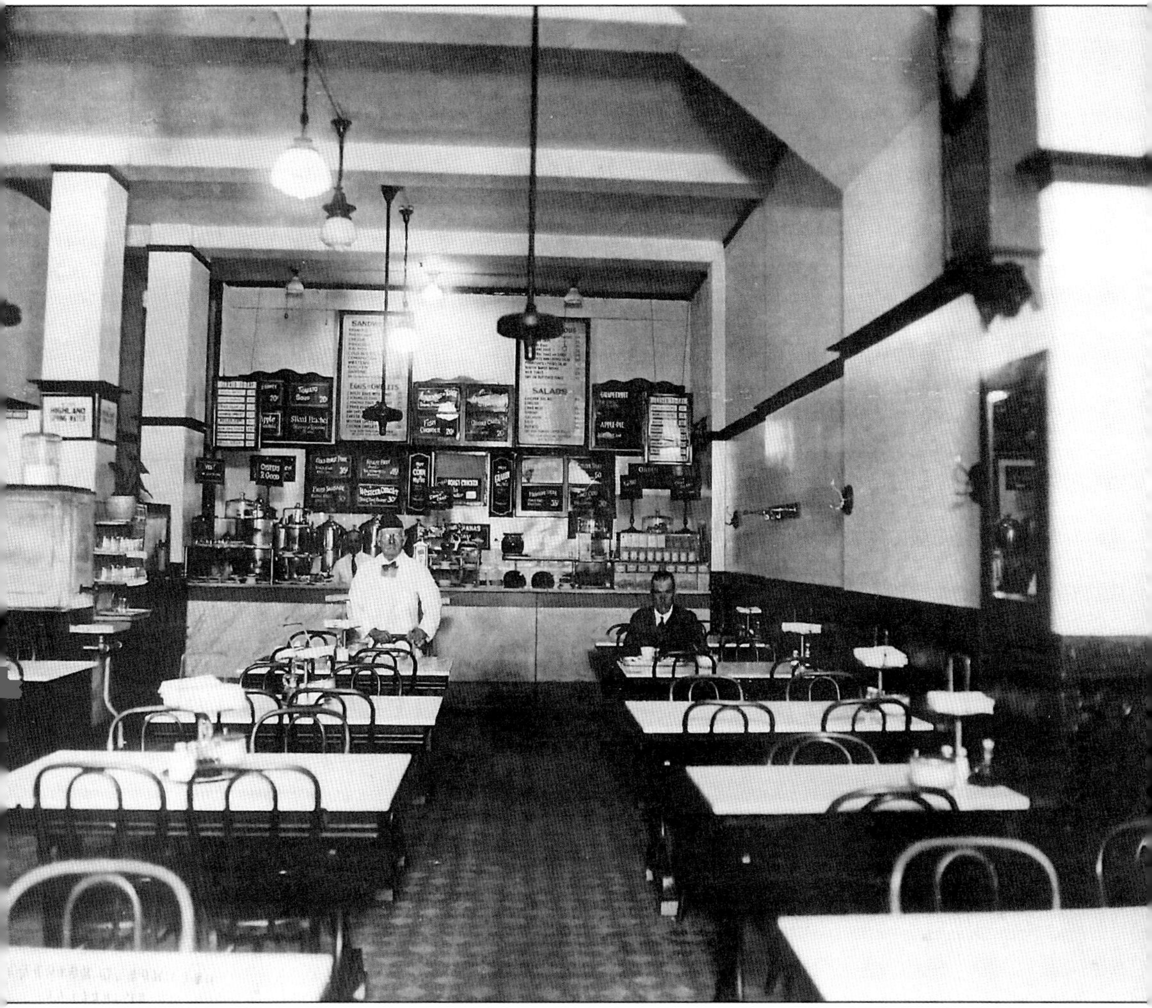

Louis and Annie Amatruda started this little cafeteria in 1915 with high hopes and a glorious name: The Astoria Dairy Lunch Co. When this photograph was taken *c.* 1930s the business was serving tomato soup and fish chowder for $.20 a bowl, and western omelette for $.30. Also on the menu were cold roast pork, oysters, grapefruit, apple pie, and asparagus on toast. Edward Karam bought the Central Street business from the Amatruda family in the early 1950s, and later moved it several blocks away to Clinton Street after the building was damaged by a flood.

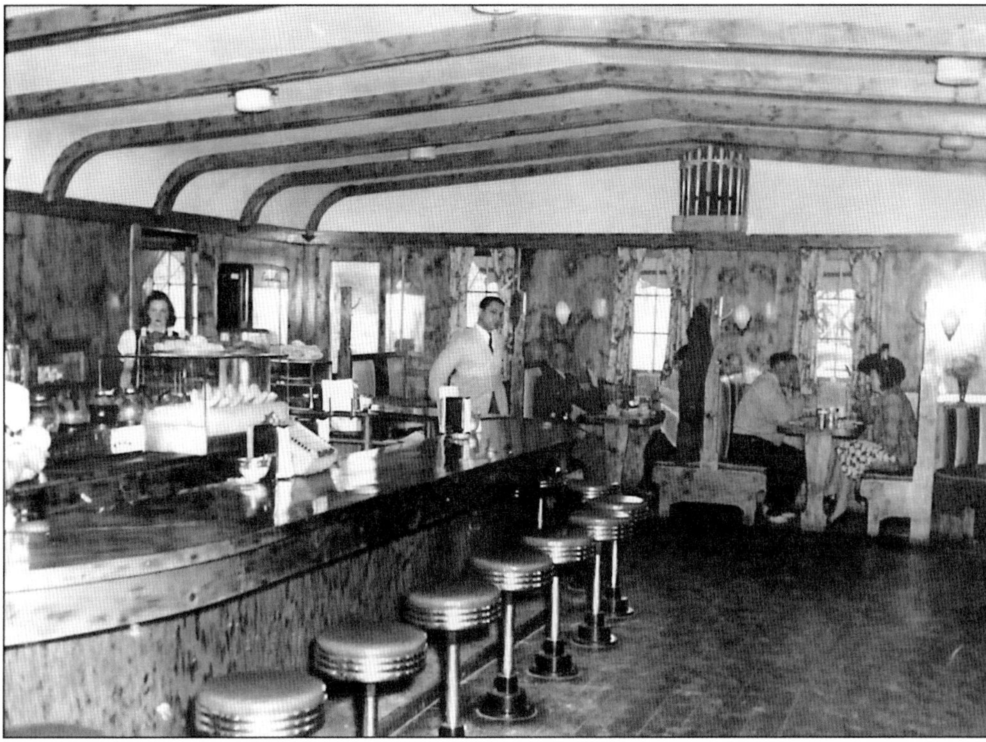

Paul Zoidis founded the Pilots Grill in 1940 near the runway of the old Bangor Airfield, later catering to servicemen from Dow Air Force Base. Soon Paul was joined by brothers Ernie and Peter (shown here in the 1940s). In 1957 the restaurant, now managed by Bill Zoidis, was moved to its present location on outer Hammond Street.

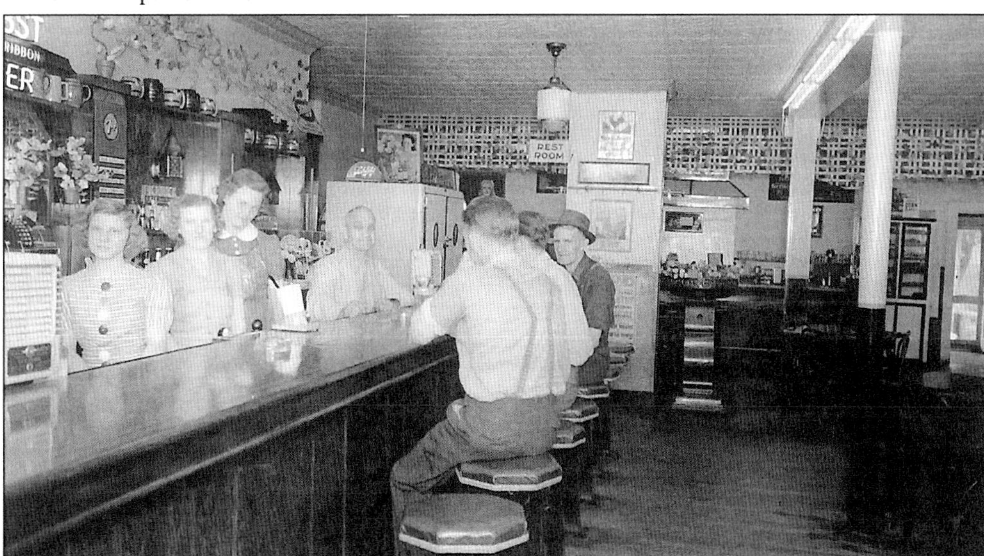

The wooden counter top of the Northern Hotel at 91 Exchange Street shines in this view showing the restaurant's jukebox, Blue Ribbon Beer clock sign and tin ceiling. The hotel's legacy ended one cold night in 1962 when a $100,000 fire that claimed the life of a guest staying upstairs gutted the six-story building.

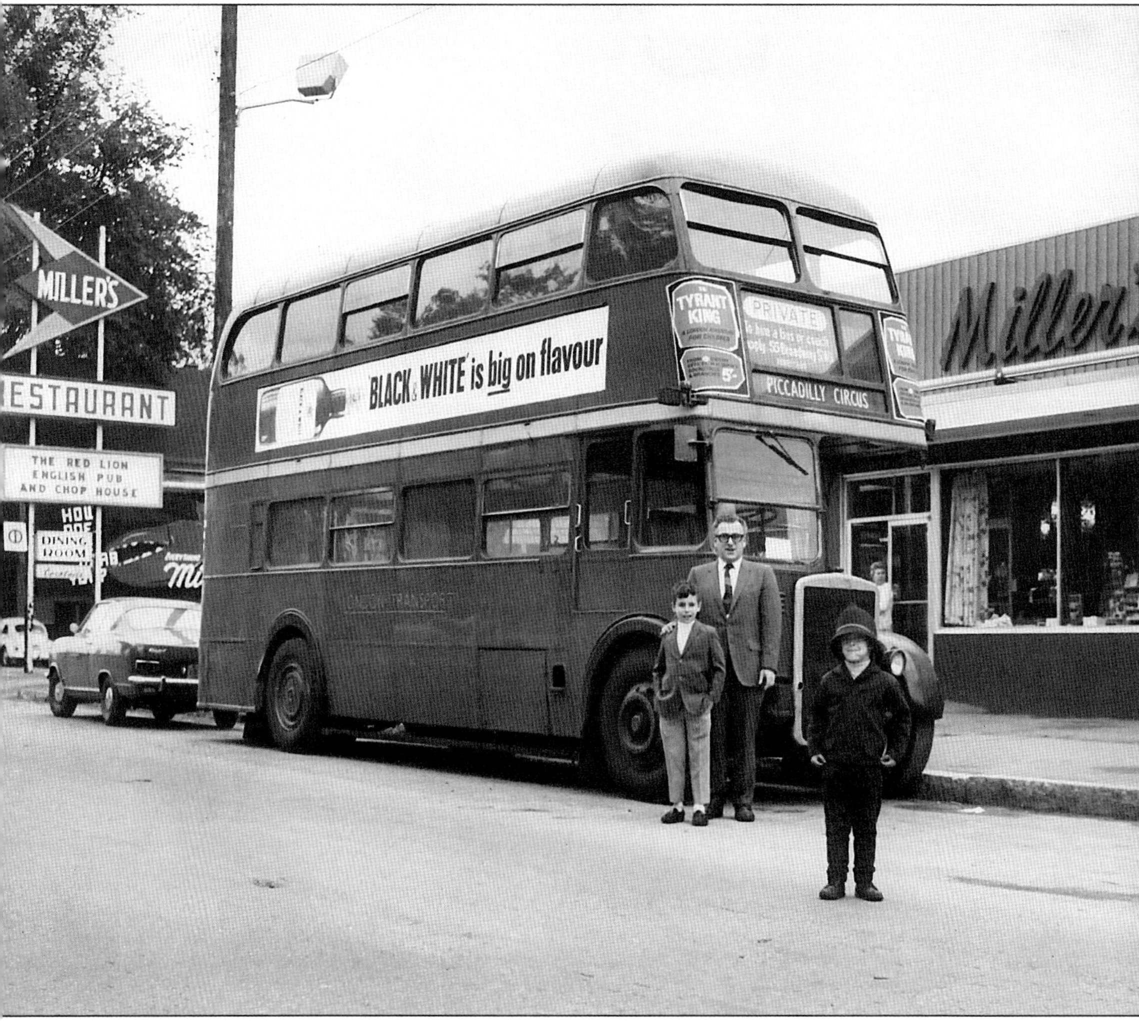

Sonny Miller and his sons, Jon (with his father) and Scot, in front of the family restaurant in 1969. The double-decker bus was a promotion for the Red Lion, an extension of Miller's Restaurant that featured an English pub and chop house. Jon is now president of Miller's Inc. and brother Scot is the treasurer. Sonny is still involved in the business, appearing at the restaurant daily to oversee its operation. Meyer and Rena Miller, Sonny's parents, opened Miller's Luncheonette on Washington Street in 1951, moving four years later to a second location on Main Street. When that restaurant burned in 1962, Sonny bought this property at 427 Main Street, the former Aunt Molly's Restaurant.

Seven

Fire and Ice

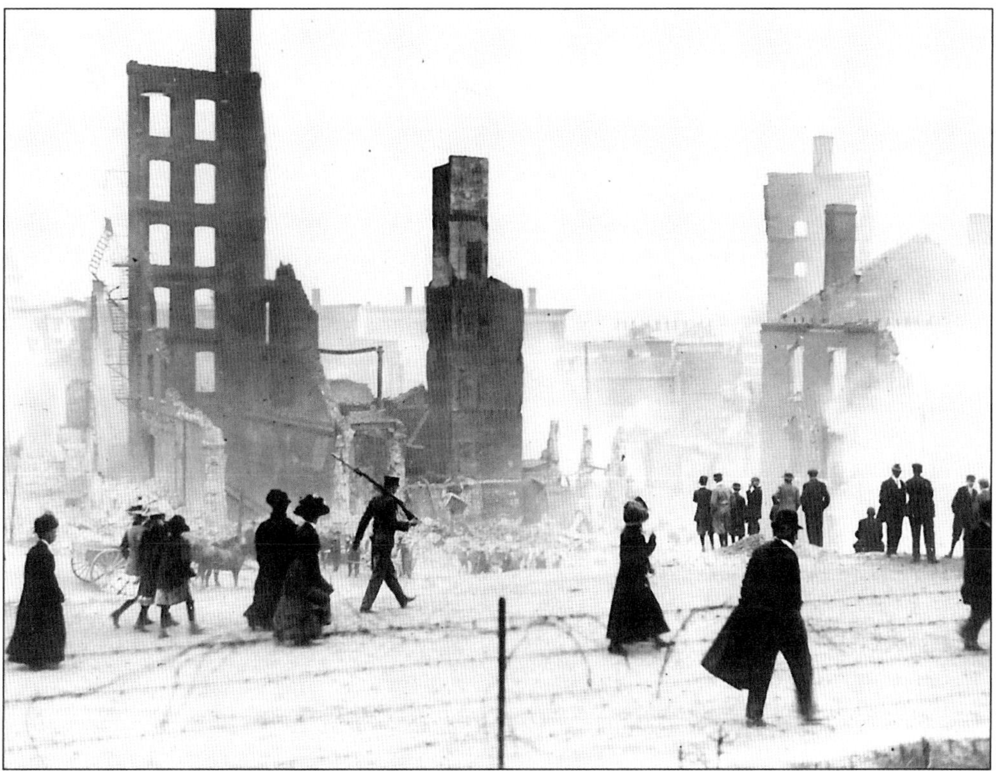

Bangor residents walked the streets in disbelief after the Great Fire of April 30, 1911, reduced most of downtown to a smouldering ruin. Two lives and nearly $3 million in property were lost.

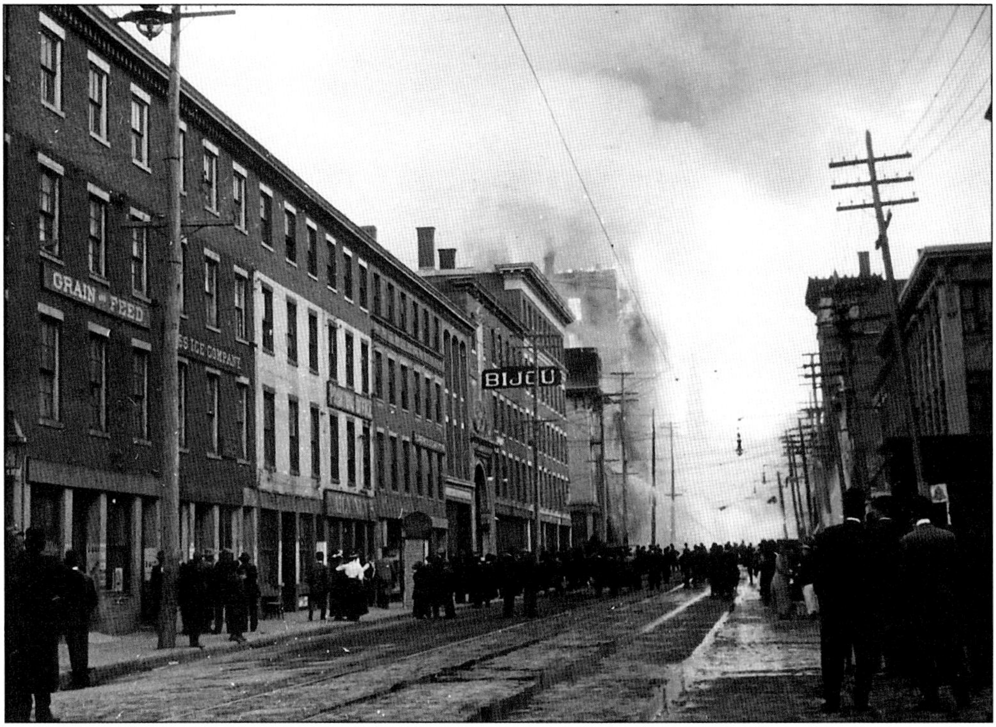

Soon after the fire started in a hay shed on Broad Street a stiff southeast wind carried the embers over the stream and onto Exchange Street. Buildings such as the Bijou Theater were saved; property owners on the upper end of the street weren't so fortunate.

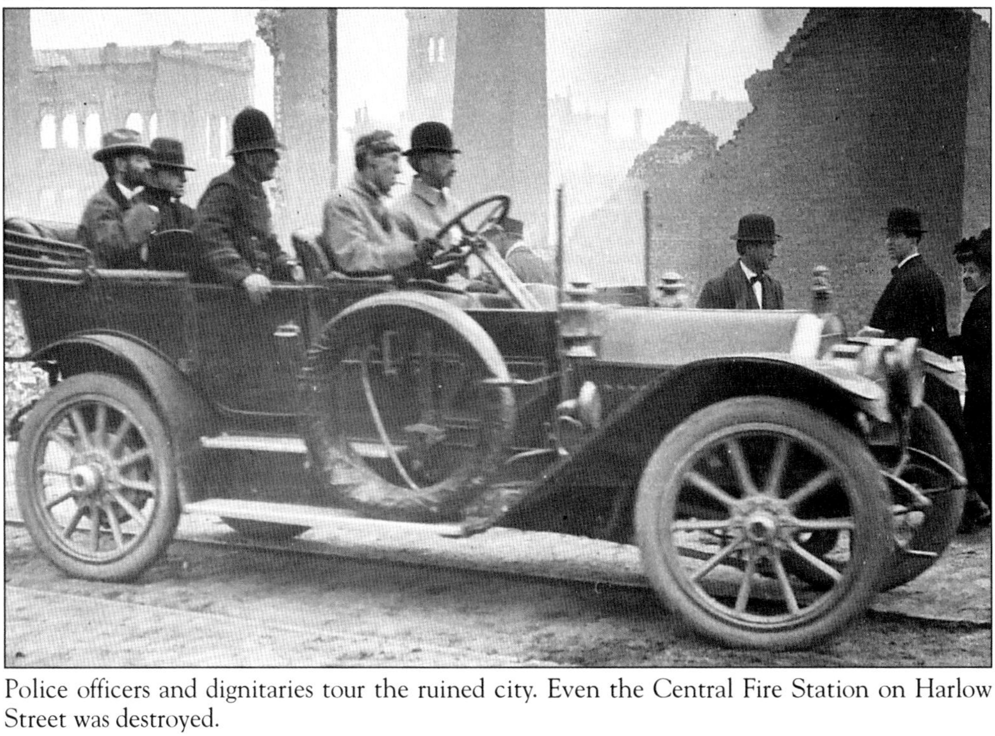

Police officers and dignitaries tour the ruined city. Even the Central Fire Station on Harlow Street was destroyed.

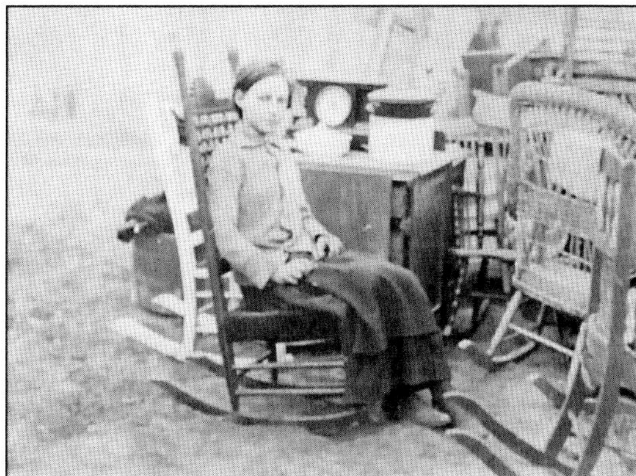

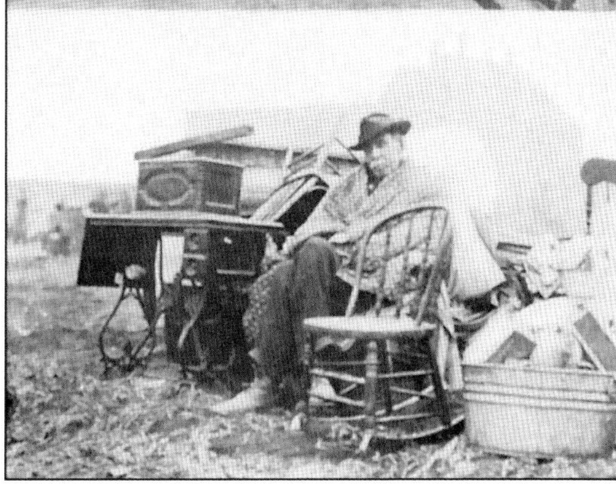

Looting was a more serious problem than many might have believed in the days following the Bangor Fire. Some property owners stood guard over the few household belongings they were able to rescue.

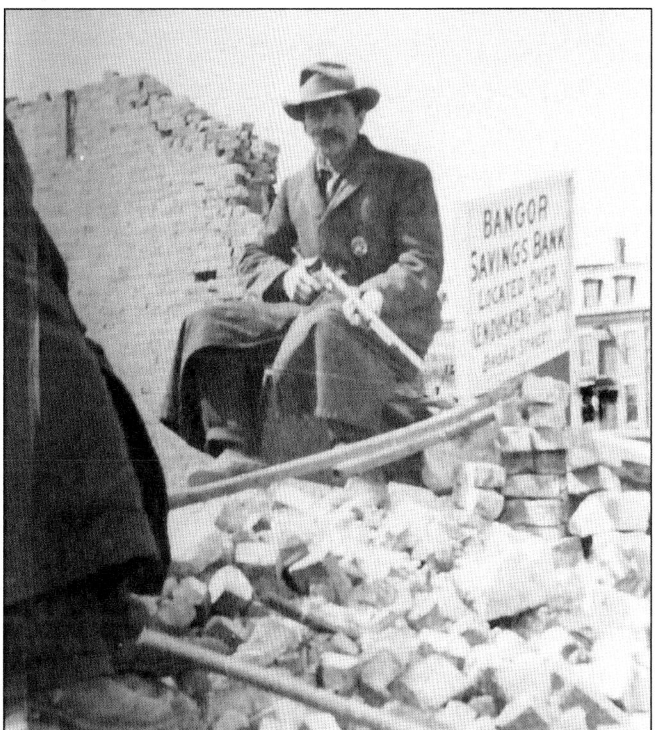

A looter approaching the vault of the destroyed Bangor Savings Bank on State Street would have found himself looking down the business end of this lawman's rifle. The Merrill Trust Company was also ruined in the fire.

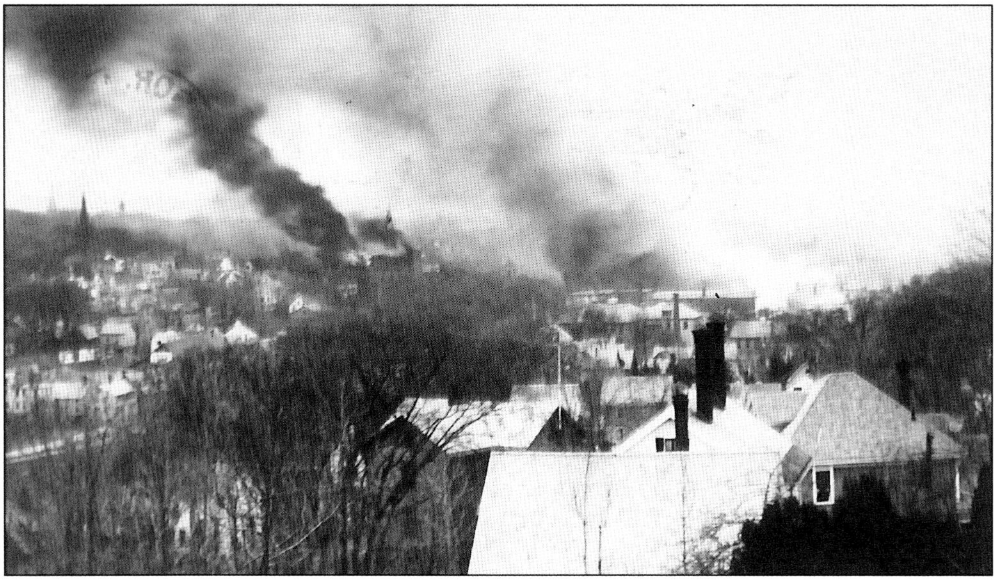

This unusual photograph of the fire in progress was taken from a respectable distance on that Sunday afternoon. Firefighters from as far away as Portland bravely fought the intense fire.

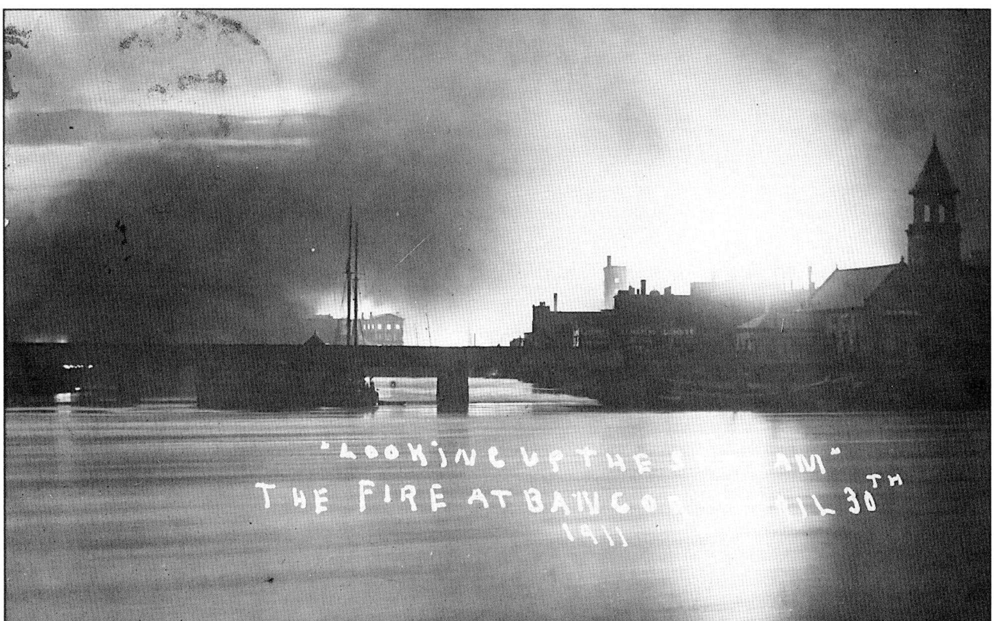

By nightfall the city resembled a scene from Dante's *Inferno*. The glow was visible for many miles.

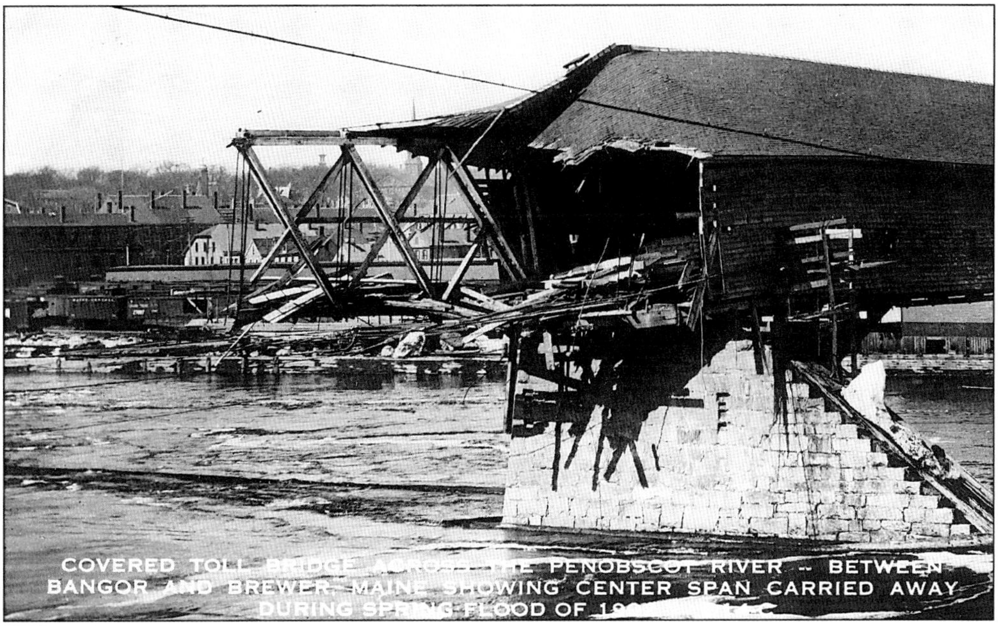

History repeated itself in 1902 when huge chunks of ice raced down the Penobscot River and took out the middle span of the Bangor-Brewer Bridge. The Great Flood of 1846 destroyed an earlier covered bridge at this location.

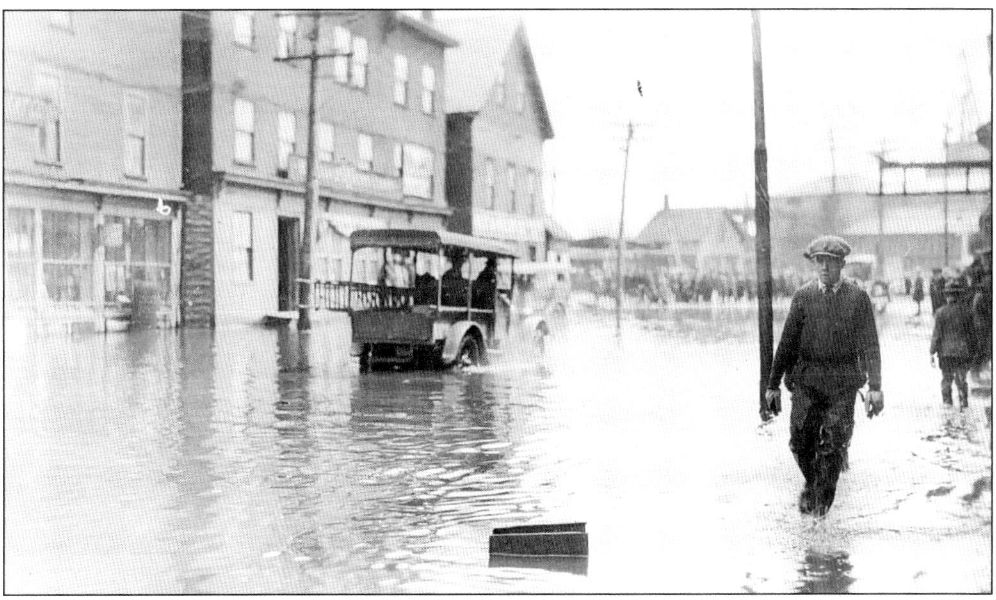

Lower Broad Street in 1923. Another flood made for rough driving and walking in the stream and waterfront areas.

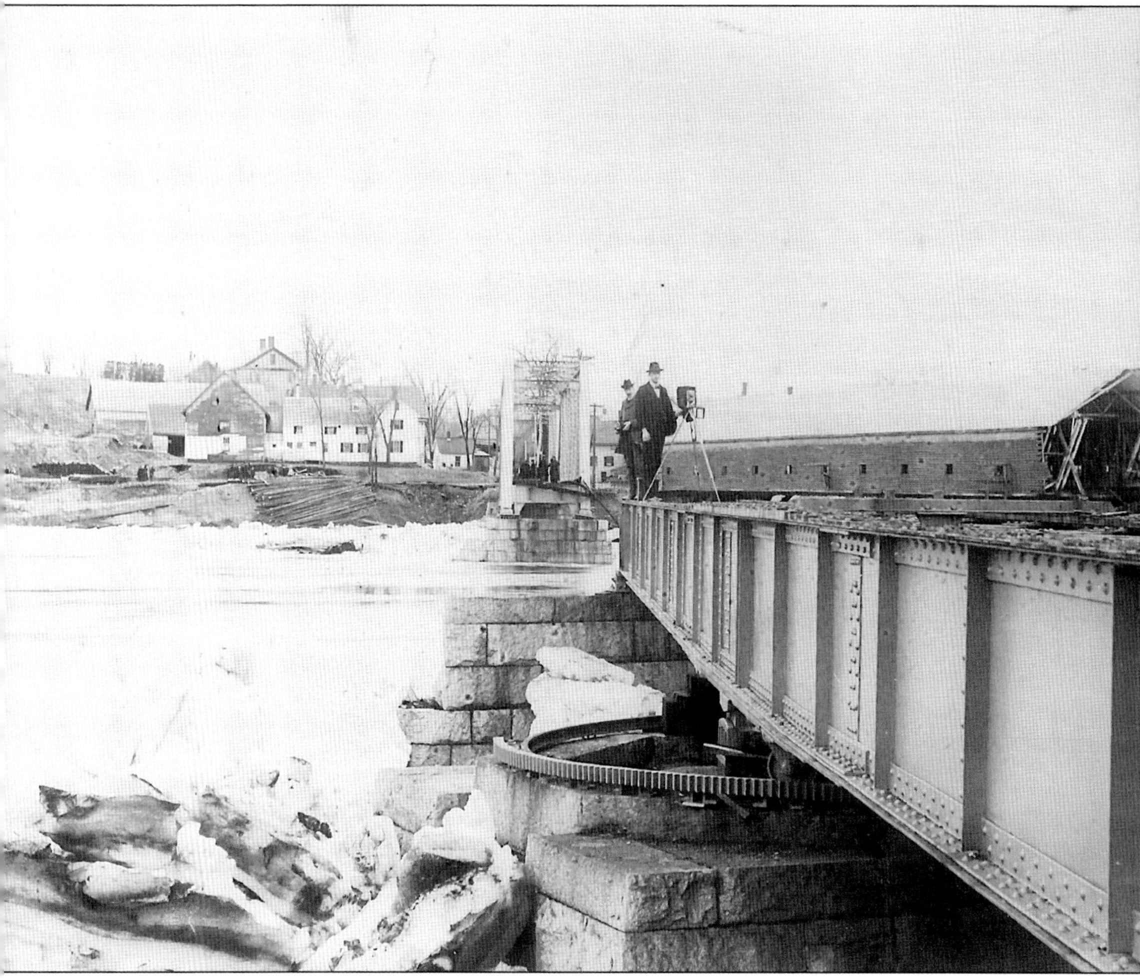

Remnants of the mammoth ice jam that destroyed the Bangor-Brewer Bridge are visible in this photograph taken after the 1902 spring freshet. Intrepid photographers set up their equipment on a section of the railroad bridge, also destroyed in the disaster. Spectators panicked and ran screaming from this bridge when the chunks of ice moved down the river. There were many close calls, but no one died in the disaster.

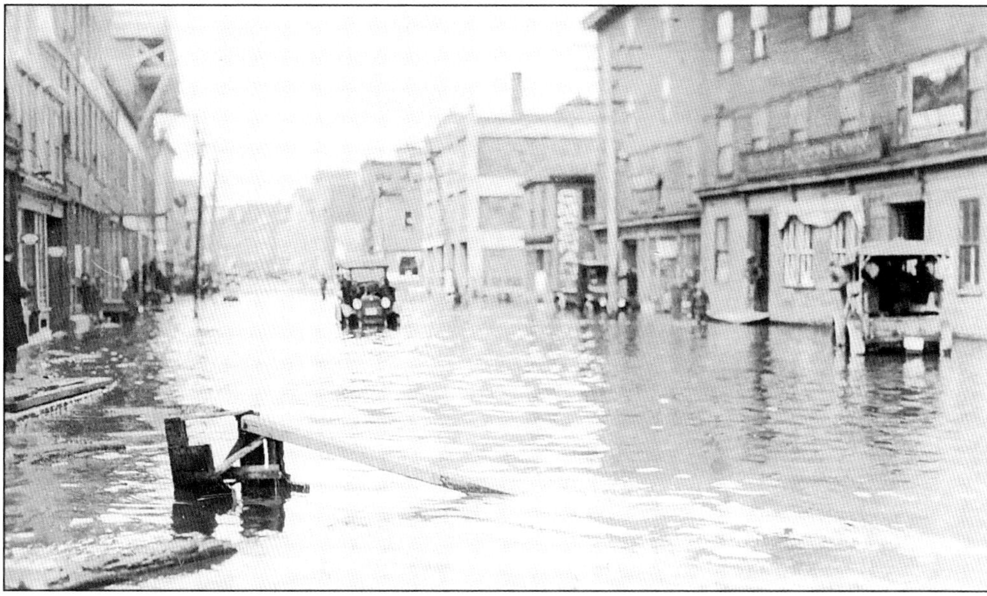

The ferocity of a spring freshet is evident in this 1923 view of Broad Street. Many basements of area businesses were flooded.

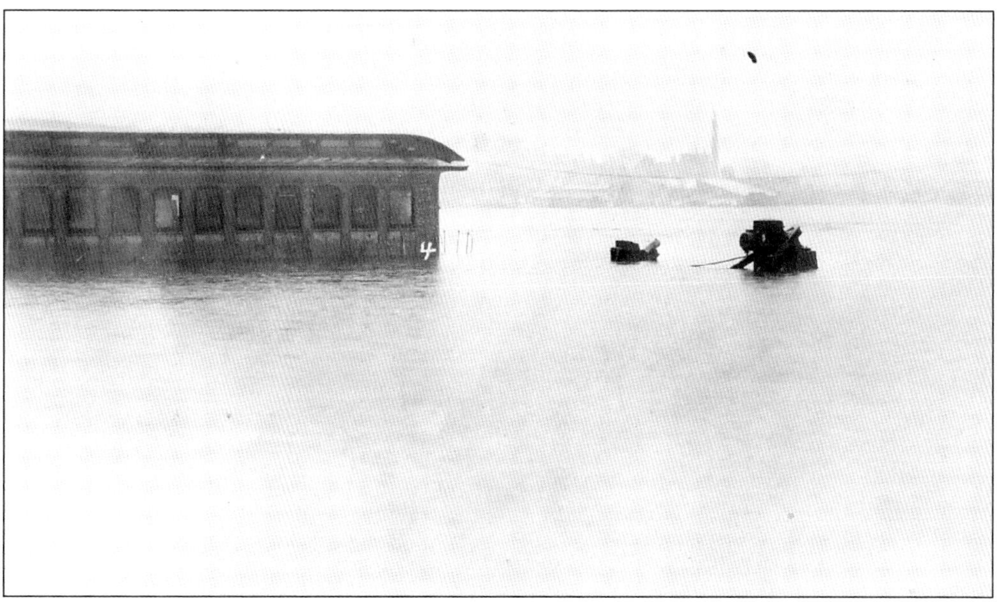

Parlor cars and railroad tracks were submerged in the flood of 1923.

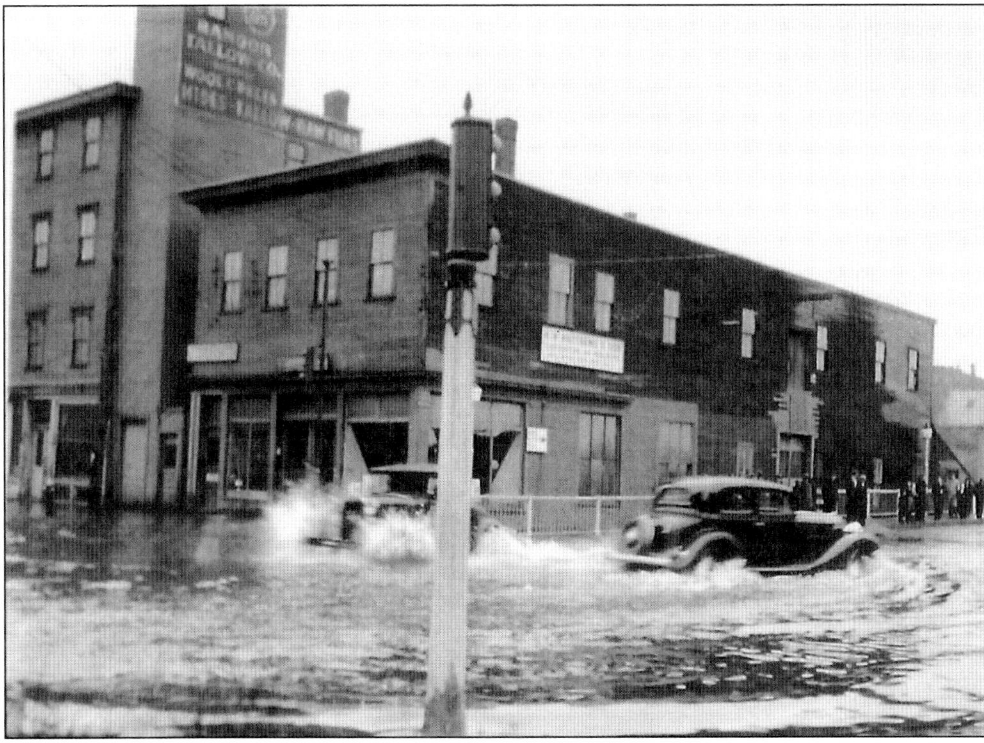

Flood waters rose again in 1936. Vehicles slogged through the water of the overflowed Kenduskeag Stream as seen here at Broad Street near the Washington Street Bridge.

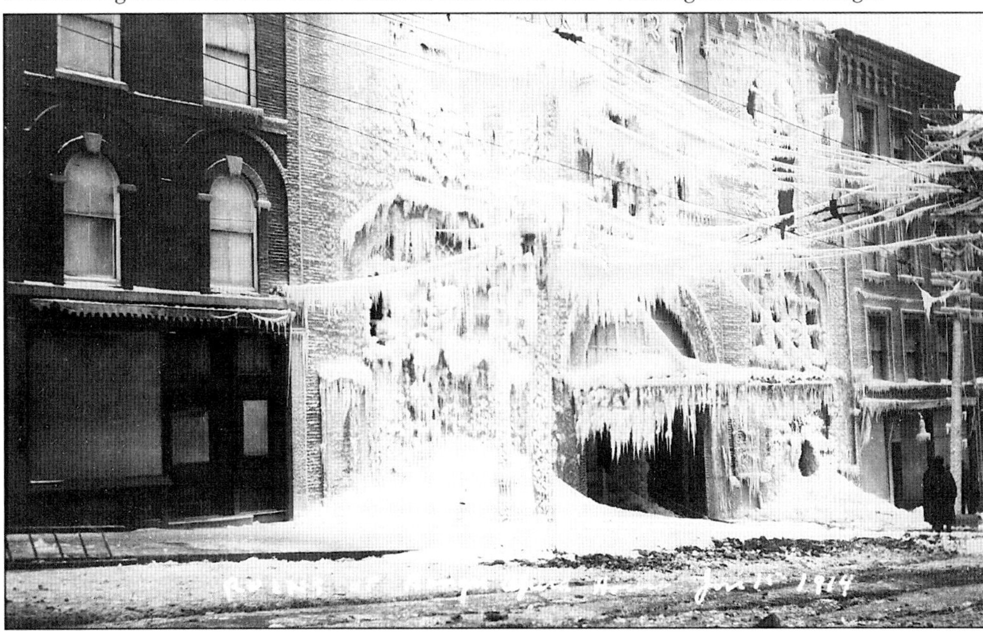

Two firemen were killed by a falling wall when the old Bangor Opera House caught fire one frigid night in 1914. The fire started in the basement boilers, then roared up the stairs which acted like funnels. Scenery coated with inflammable paint behind the stage added to the fire's intensity. Not until 1920 was the present Opera House built on the site.

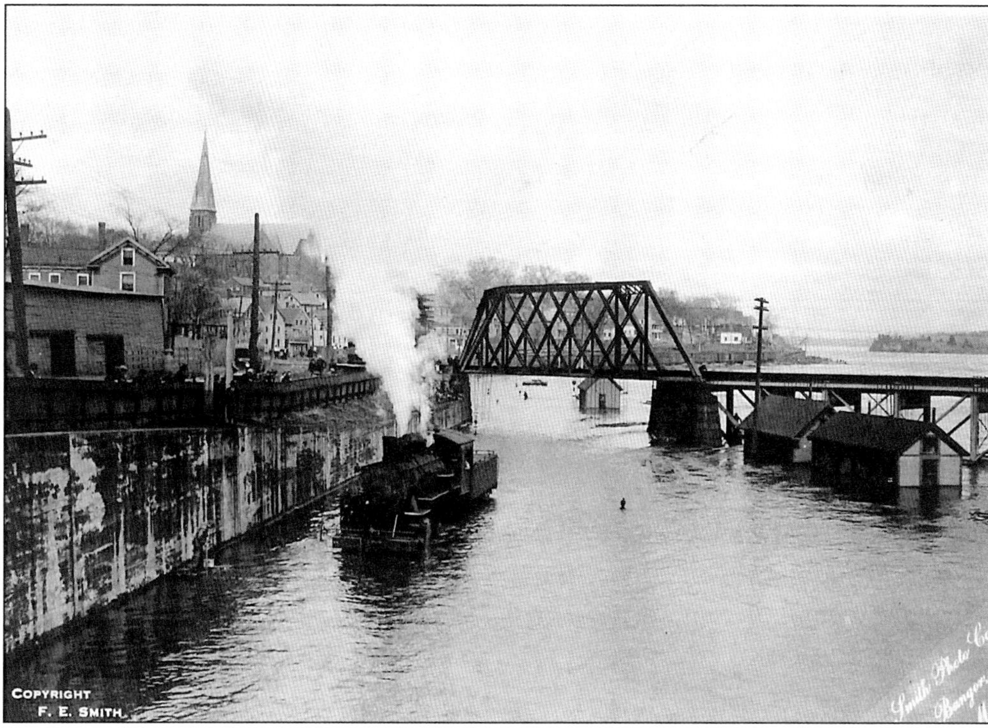

A steam engine makes its way under the Bangor-Brewer Bridge during the 1923 flood. Buildings on higher land such as St. John's Catholic Church, visible in the distance, were not damaged.

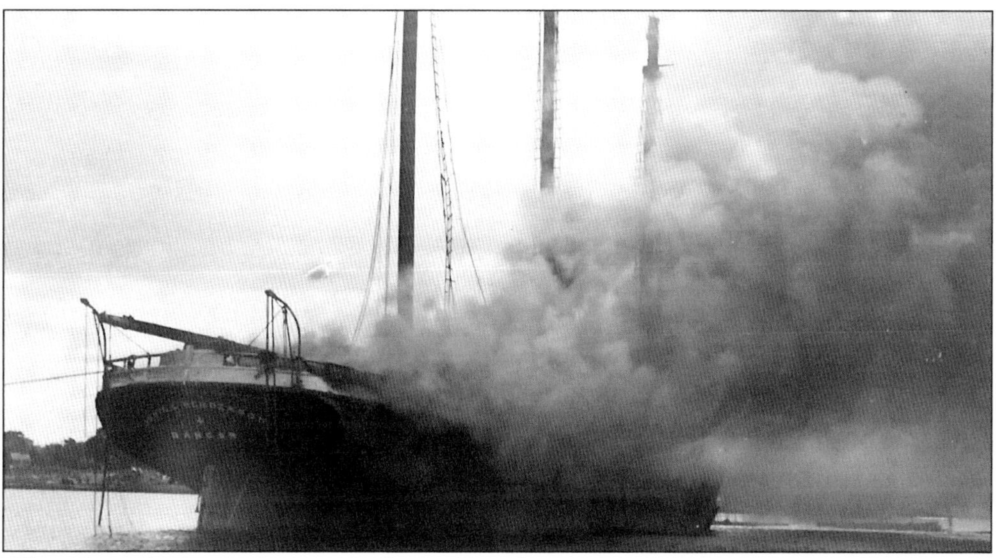

When the schooner *Annie L. Henderson* burned in Bangor Harbor on September 1, 1906, spectators knew they were witnessing an event that would be talked about for years to come.

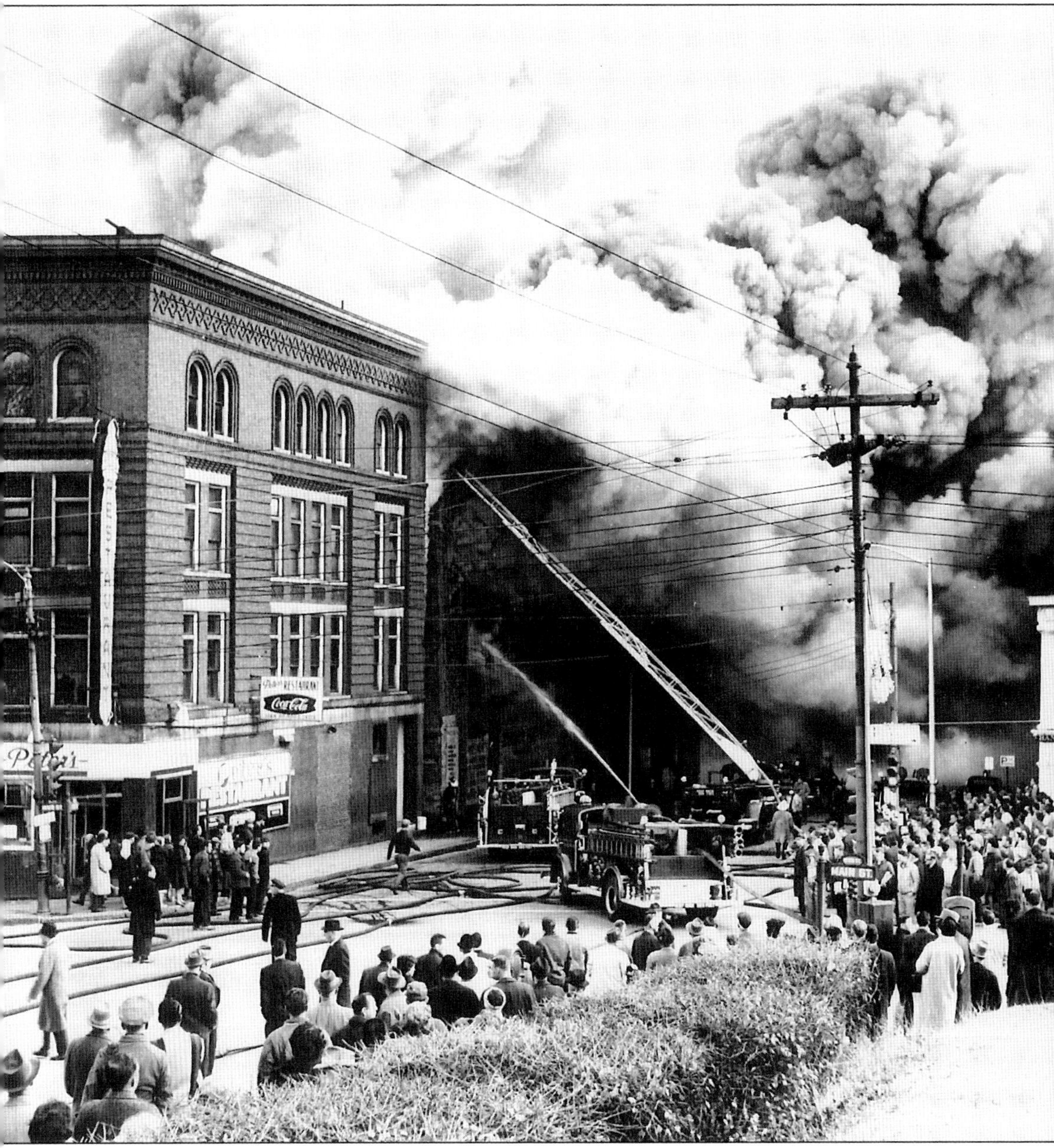

A spectacular fire consumed the Olympia Theater Building in 1963. One fireman was seriously injured when a ladder collapsed, and scores of others battled the stubborn blaze that threatened surrounding buildings such as the Bangor House (partially visible at right) and even the Central Fire Station next door. The old wooden theater, affectionately called the "Rat Hole" by anyone who ever watched a movie inside, had seen better days. It had been years since area youngsters sat in the dingy darkness and marveled at the movies of Hopalong Cassidy, Gene Autry, and Roy Rogers and his horse Trigger, while munching on the best popcorn in town.

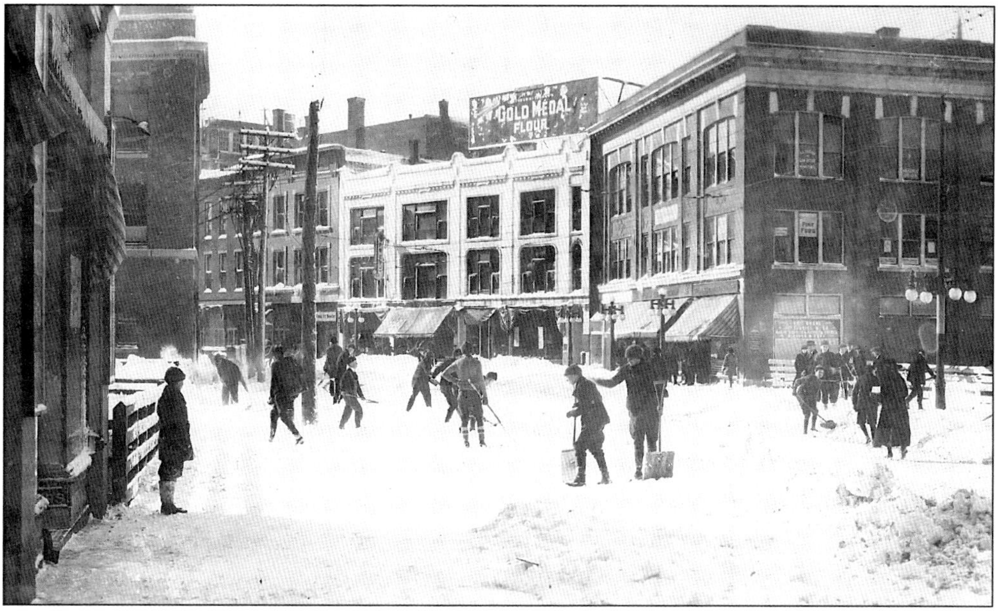

Local businessmen got out their shovels and cleared Central Street of snow in the 1920s.

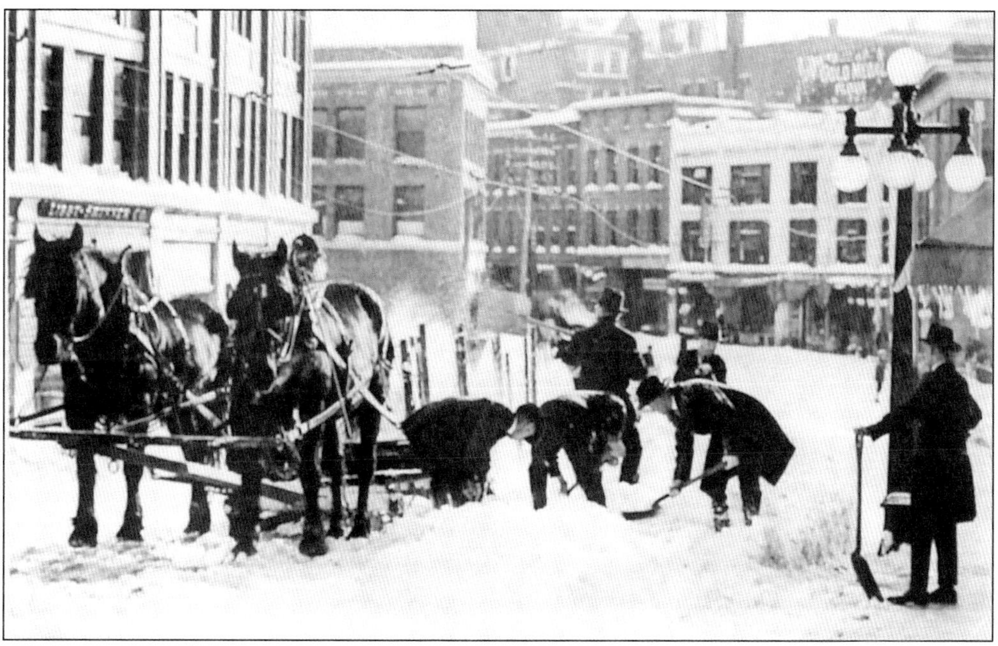
While a man at the right takes a break from shoveling the sidewalk near his business, other merchants load snow into a wagon. The Libby-Skinner Company on the left sold pianos and Pathe Phonographs.

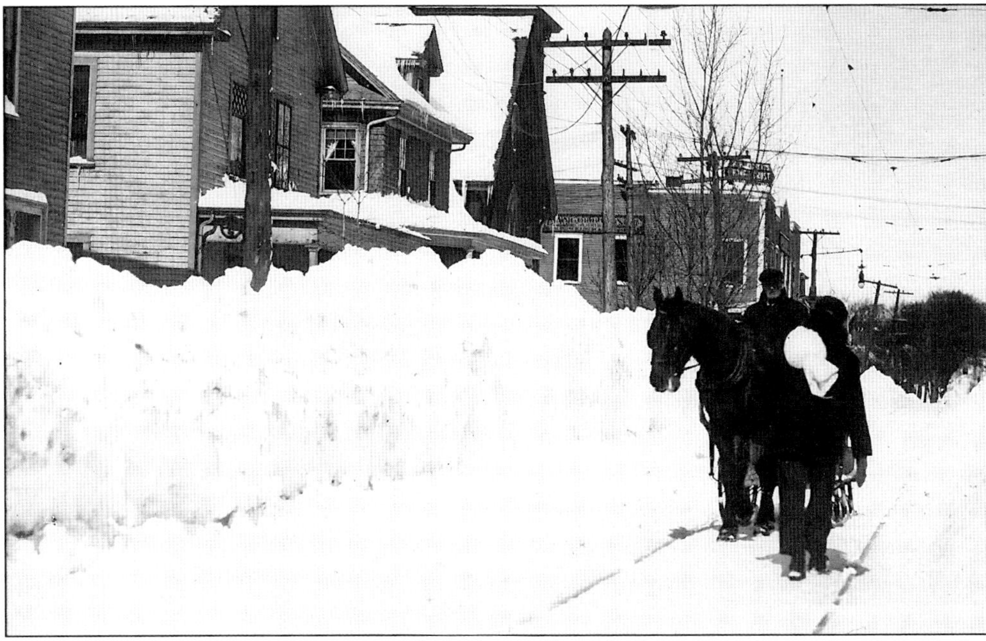

The streetcar tracks on Center Street have been cleared of snow in this postcard view that seems to prove the old adage, "We don't have Nor'easters like we used to."

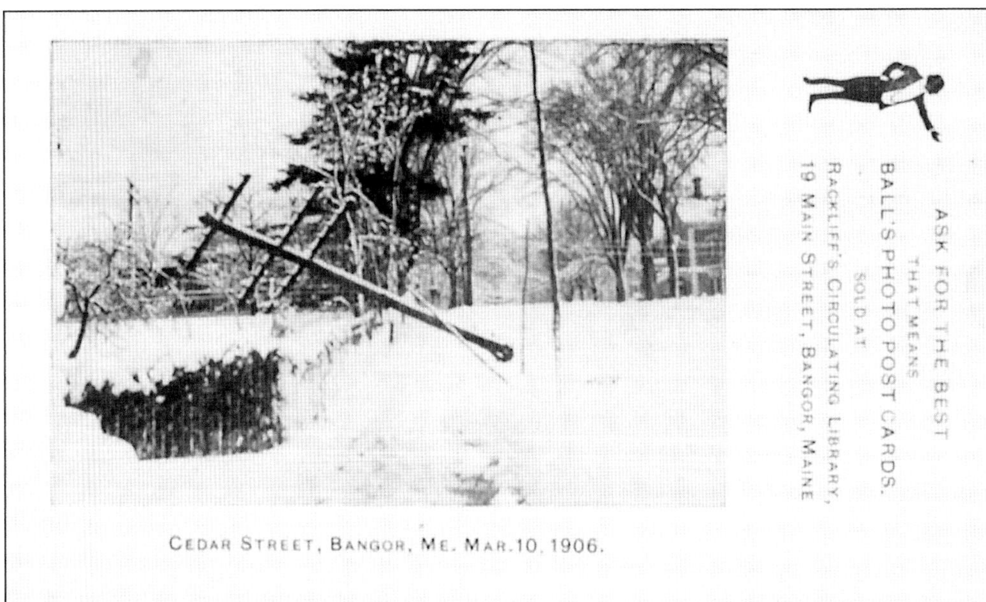

A March snowstorm felled telephone poles and tree limbs in 1906. Electrical and telephone services were often interrupted for days after such storms.

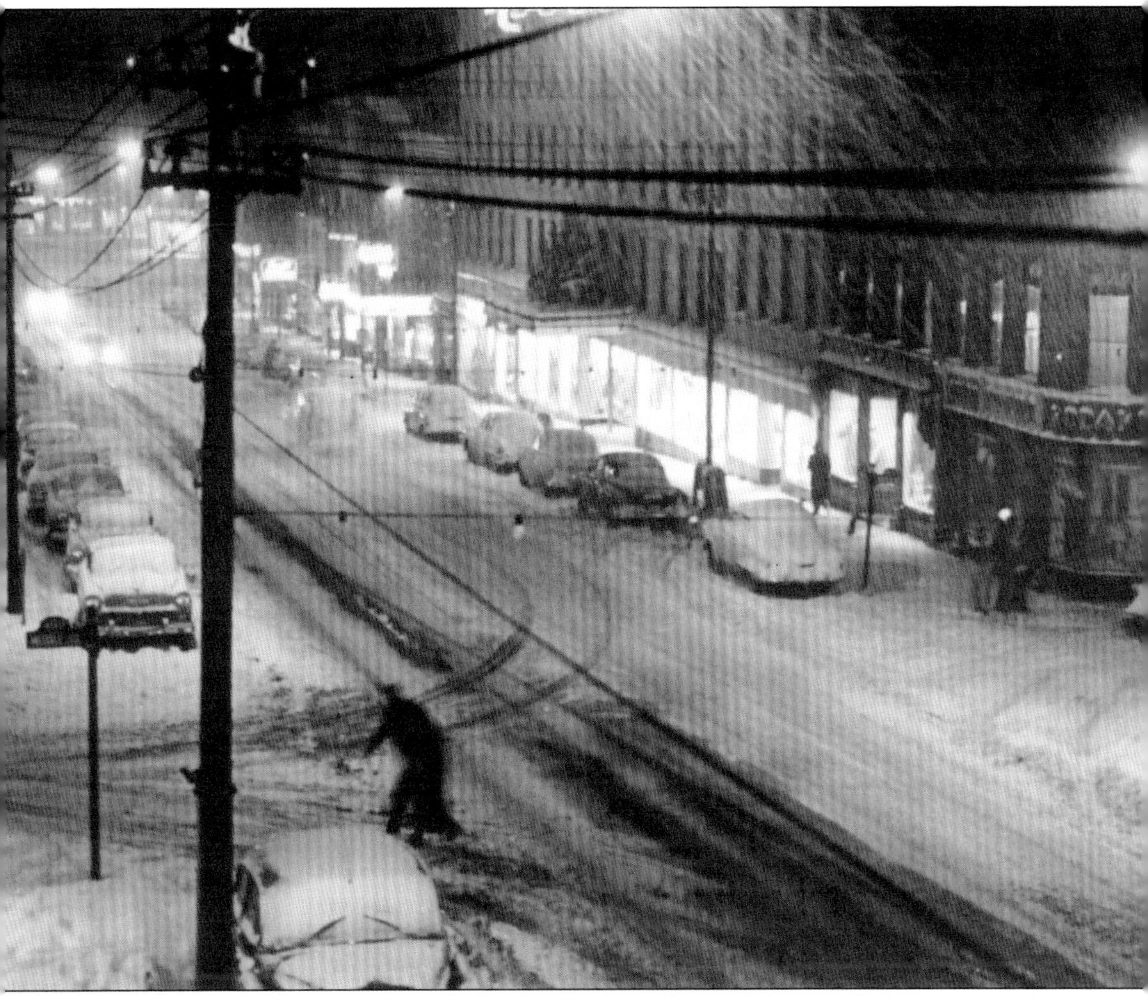

Main Street *c.* 1950s was a forbidding-looking place the night Dan Maher took this photograph of a Nor'easter in progress. The lights in Freese's Department Store illuminate the sidewalk, indicating that downtown businesses weren't intimidated by the furious storm. The most famous blizzard in memory occurred around New Year's Day, 1963, when a storm buried much of Maine under several feet of snow, closing businesses and schools for days. It was the only time the *Bangor Daily News* did not publish a newspaper since its inception in 1889.

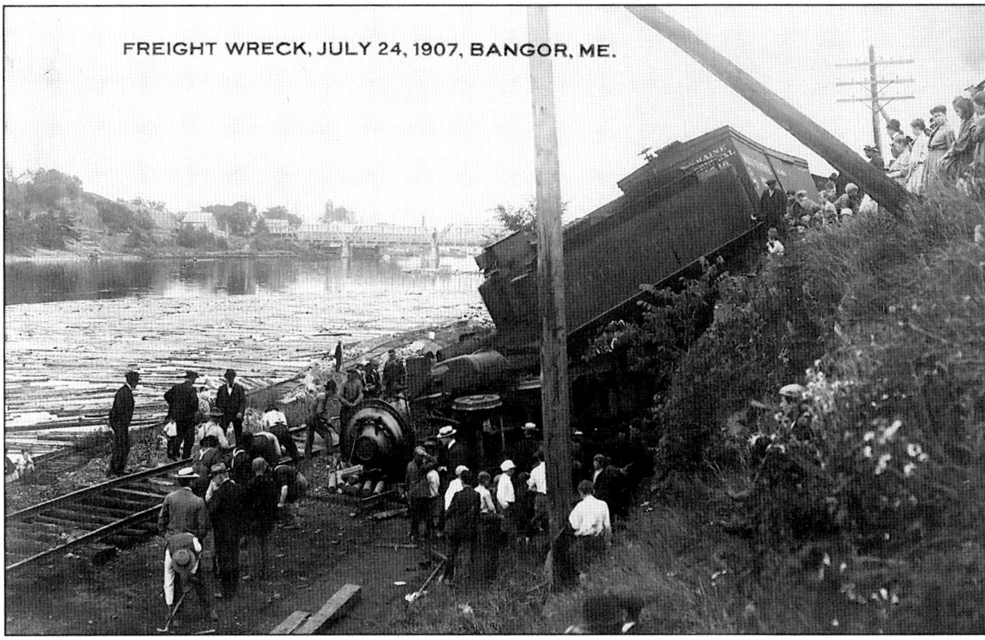

Maine Central Railroad Engine Number 318 was hauling seventeen freight cars from Washington County when it derailed near Newbury Street in 1907. Engineer Adam J. Markley was killed and Fireman Roger M. Welch shaken up and bruised. Brake failure was blamed for the mishap.

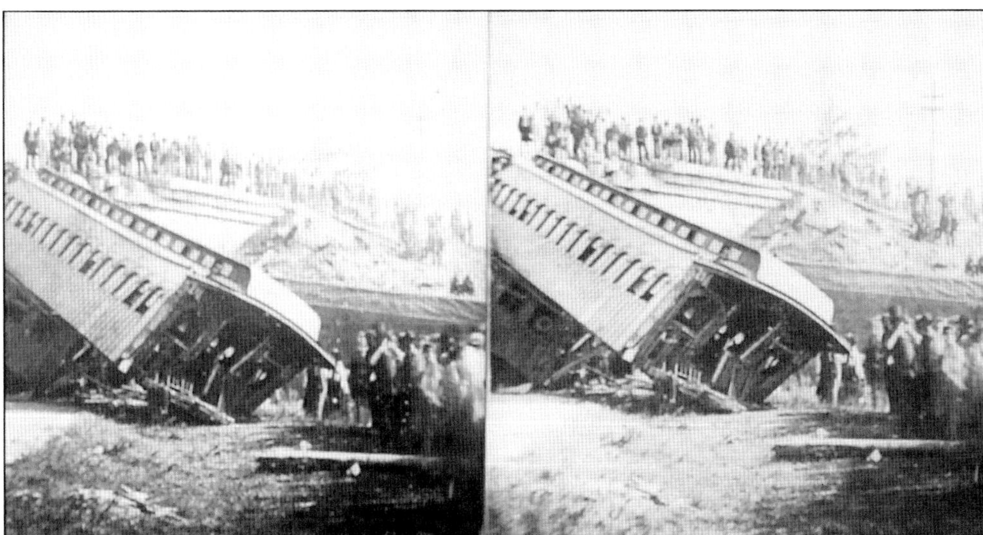

Rotten bridge timbers caused this tragic accident at the "Tin Bridge" on August 9, 1871. A brakeman and a passenger died when the Bangor Express tumbled off the defective bridge, located near the Hampden town line on lower Main Street.

Eight

Portraits from the Past

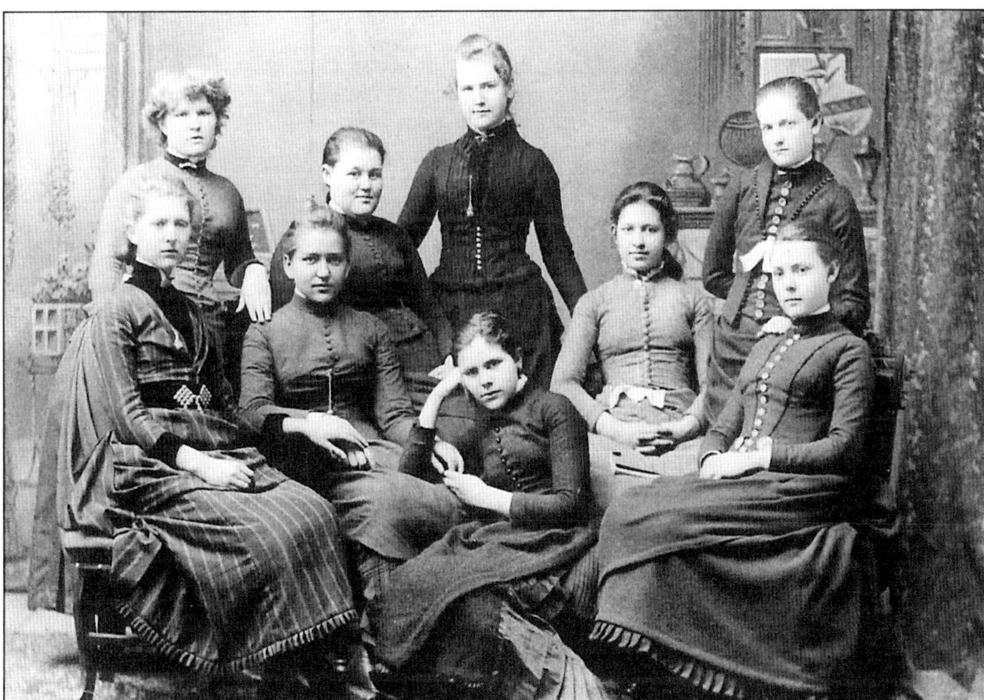

Nine wealthy young women, all unmarried, pose for a Bangor photographer in the 1800s. They are: (top row) Nina Howard, Louise Sargent, Charlotte Roberts and Mary Farnum; (front row) Nan Goodenow, Angela Godfrey, Marie Leavitt, Edithe Lesley and Lovere Veazie.

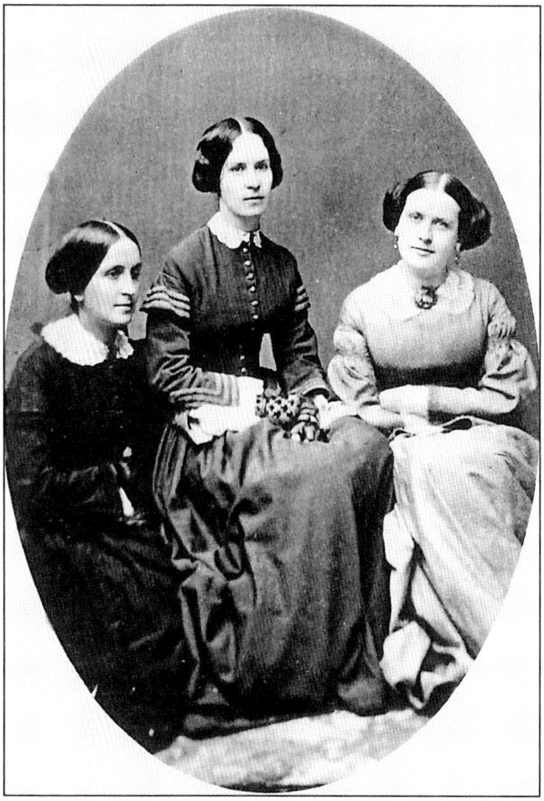

Bangor belles in the 1850s. Mary, Sally and Robina McRuer were the daughters of Daniel McRuer, a prominent Bangor doctor who went on to become a Civil War surgeon.

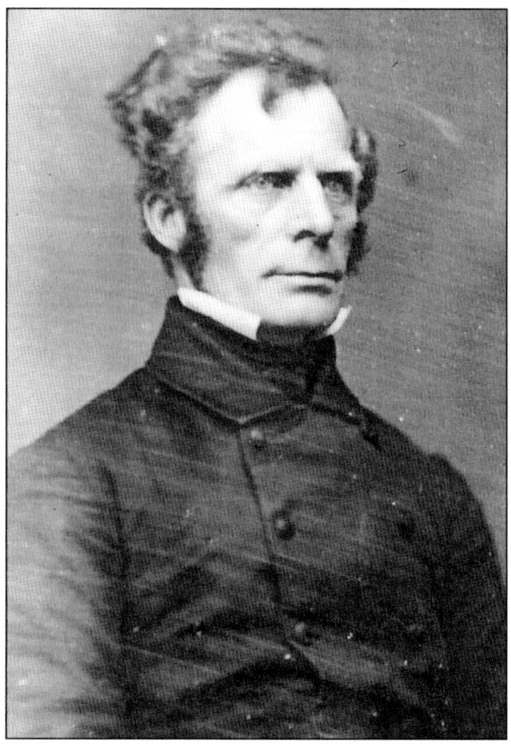

George A. Thatcher was a well-known Bangor businessman from 1822 until his retirement in 1847. But it was his later anti-slavery views as a local deacon and trustee of the Bangor Theological Seminary that set him apart from most men. His wife, Rebecca Billings, was a cousin of Henry David Thoreau, whom Thatcher guided through the North Woods during his visits to Maine.

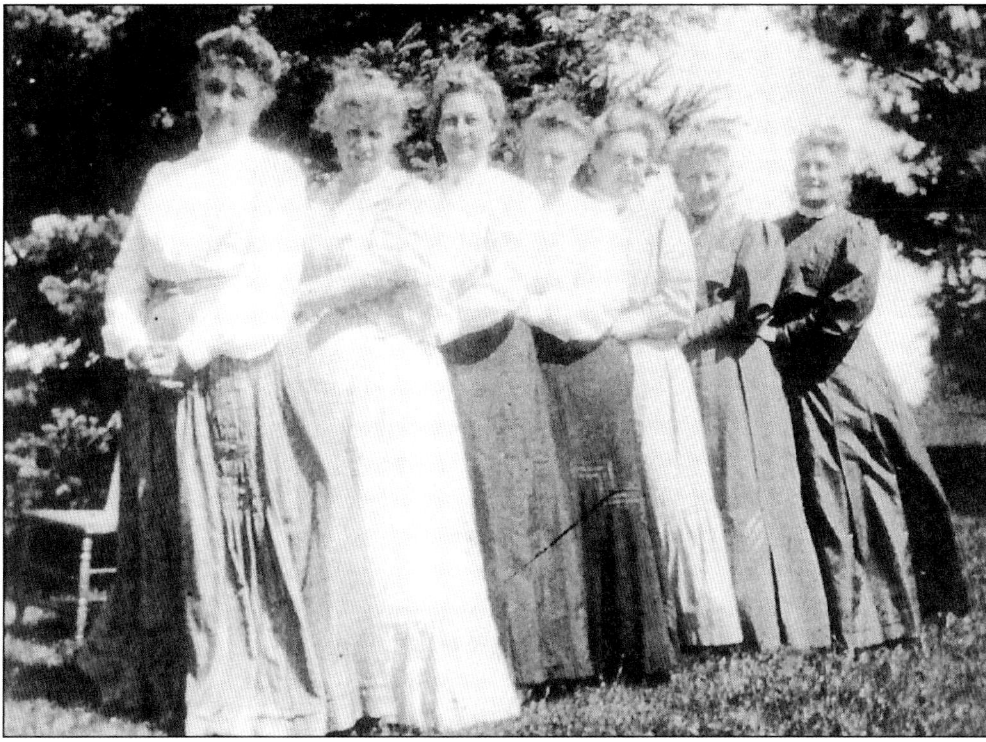

Two names that stand out in this old family portrait are Cynthia P. Taylor Adams (second from right) and Laura Taylor French (third from left).

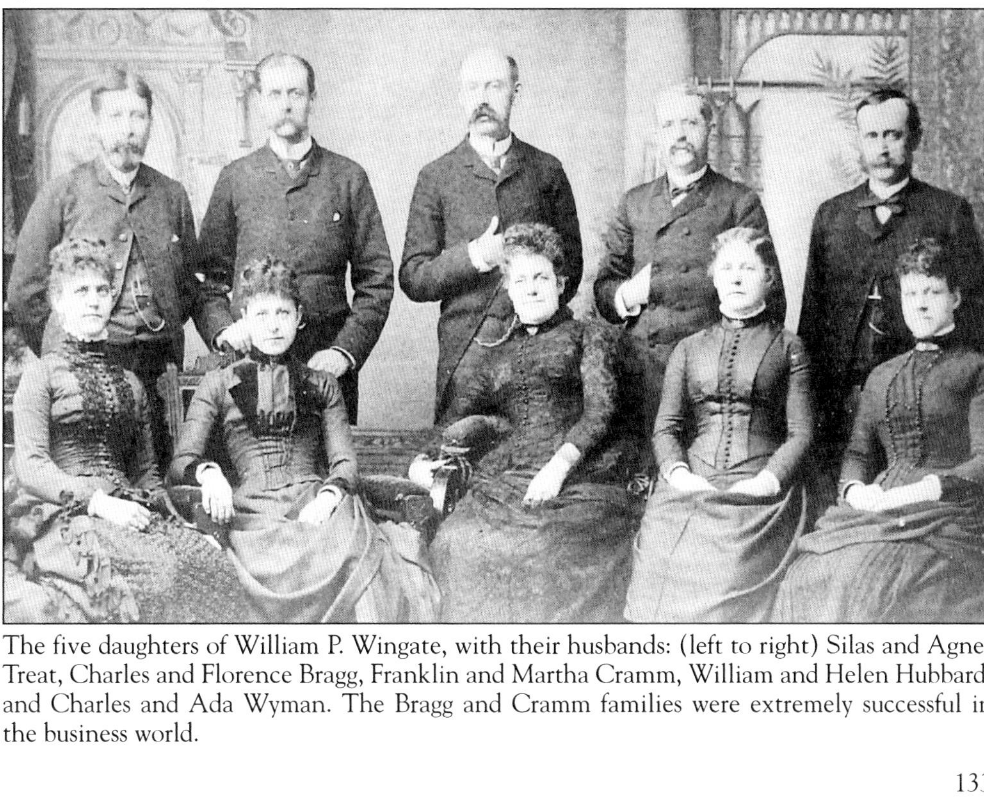

The five daughters of William P. Wingate, with their husbands: (left to right) Silas and Agnes Treat, Charles and Florence Bragg, Franklin and Martha Cramm, William and Helen Hubbard, and Charles and Ada Wyman. The Bragg and Cramm families were extremely successful in the business world.

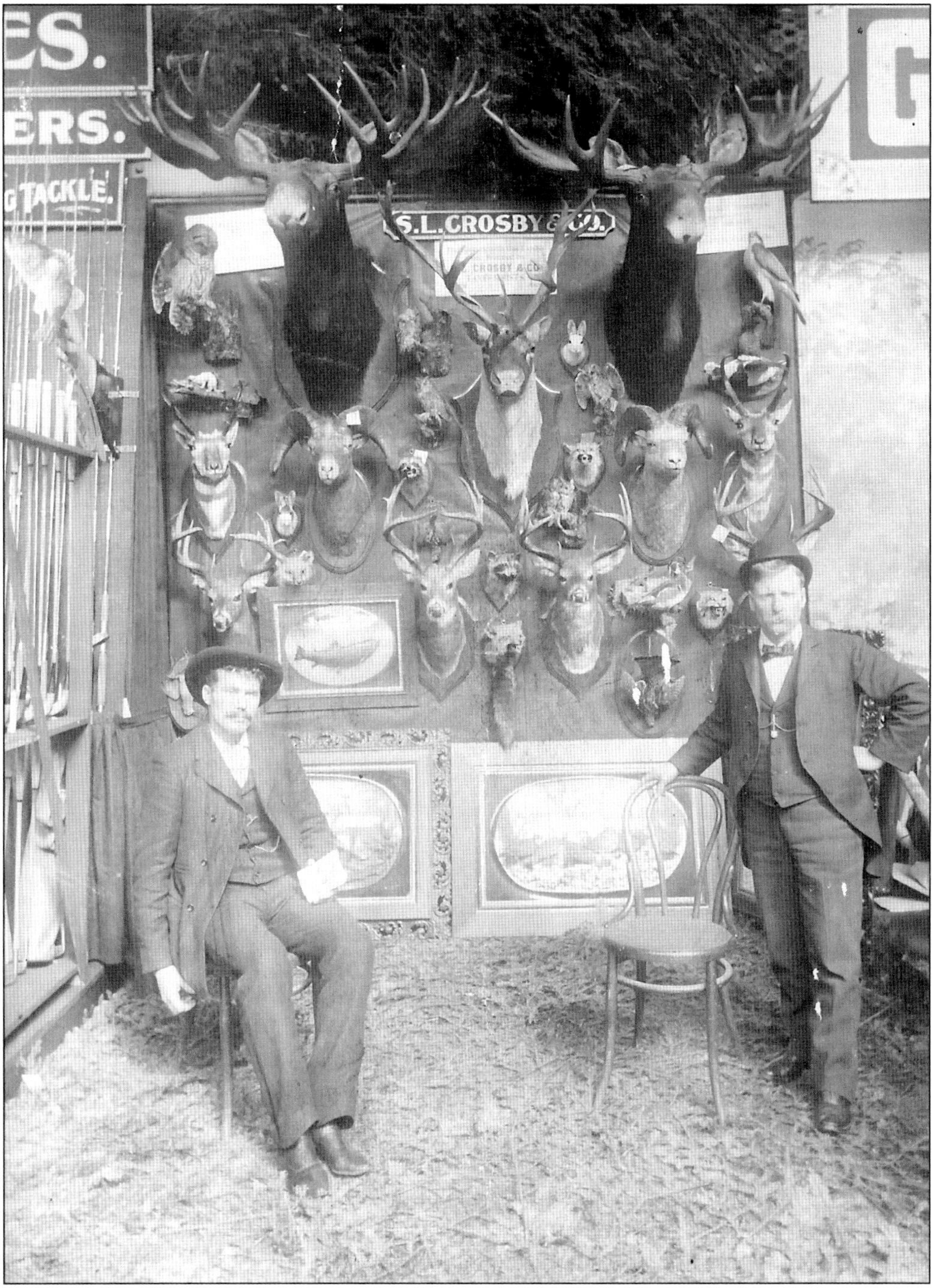

The stuffed heads of raccoons, elk and martens are displayed along with mounted birds and fish in this nineteenth-century photograph, probably taken at an exposition or sportsmen's show. One of the many businesses operated by the S.L. Crosby Co., a taxidermy shop was set up at 124 Main Street when E.S. Bowler (a taxidermist) sold out to Crosby. An 1887 advertisement notes that all specimens would be cured with arsenic, the only preventive against moths.

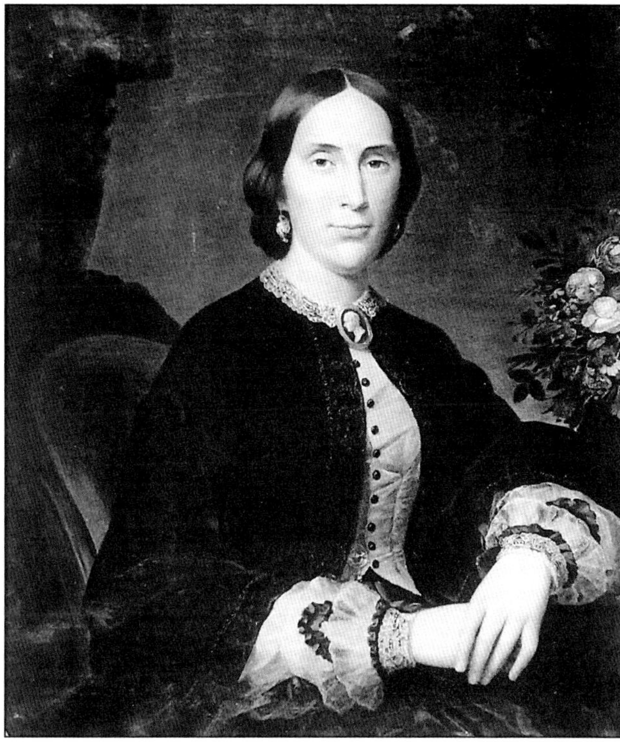

The second wife of Hannibal Hamlin was, according to one New York newspaper, "of medium height, possessing a fine form and figure, with auburn hair, a clear, fair complexion, expressive eyes, and a voice at once mild, musical and sweet." The future vice president married Ellen Emery in 1856. Ellen was the younger half-sister of Hamlin's first wife, Sarah.

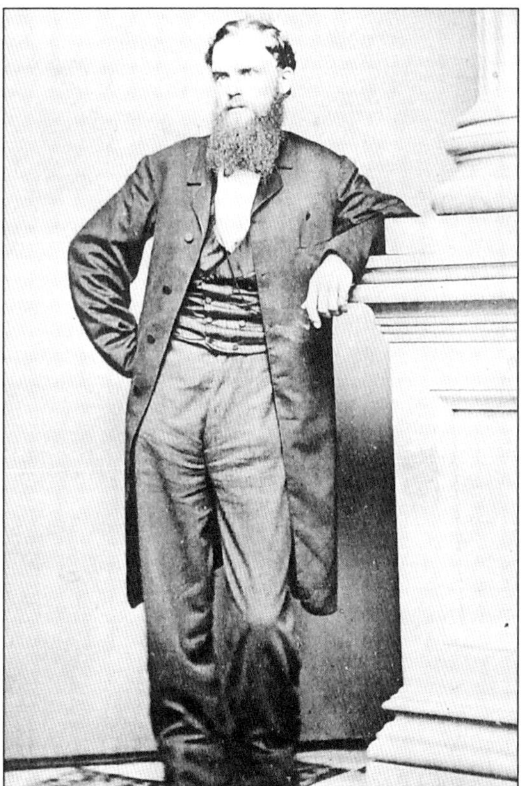

George Zadoc French cut quite a figure in Bangor society. Born in 1834, he died in 1909. Eventually French's family would have an East Side street named after them.

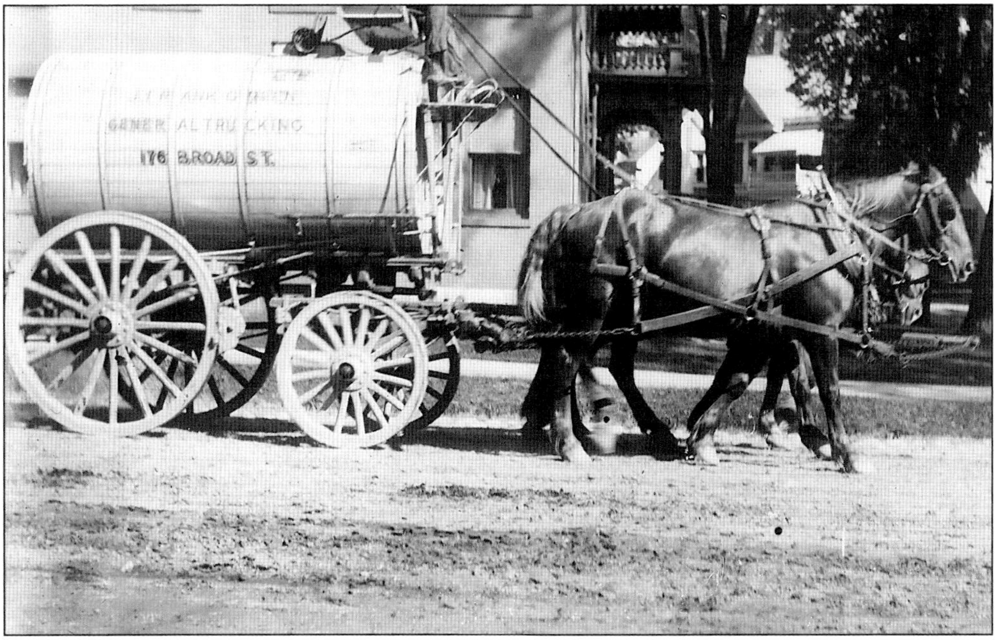

Watering Hammond Street before asphalt paving was an important job for J. Frank Green, who operated a general trucking business in Bangor. The Great Fire of 1911 started in Green's Broad Street hay shed.

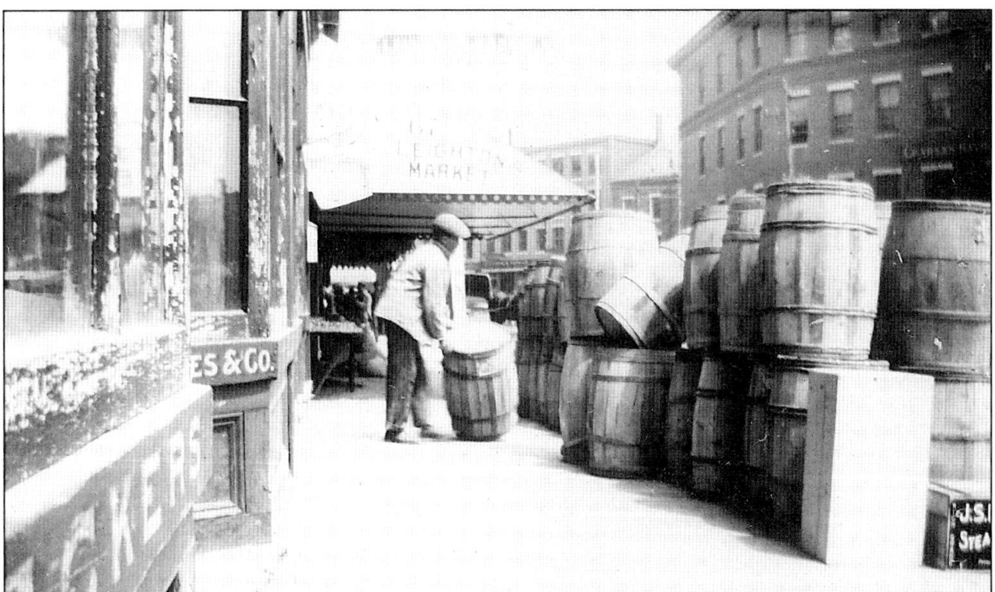

Crackers, or perhaps salt cod, were stored inside these barrels photographed in Pickering Square in the late nineteenth century. F.L. Jones and Company, whose store is on the left, manufactured butter and oyster crackers, as well as soda, milk and graham and oatmeal biscuits.

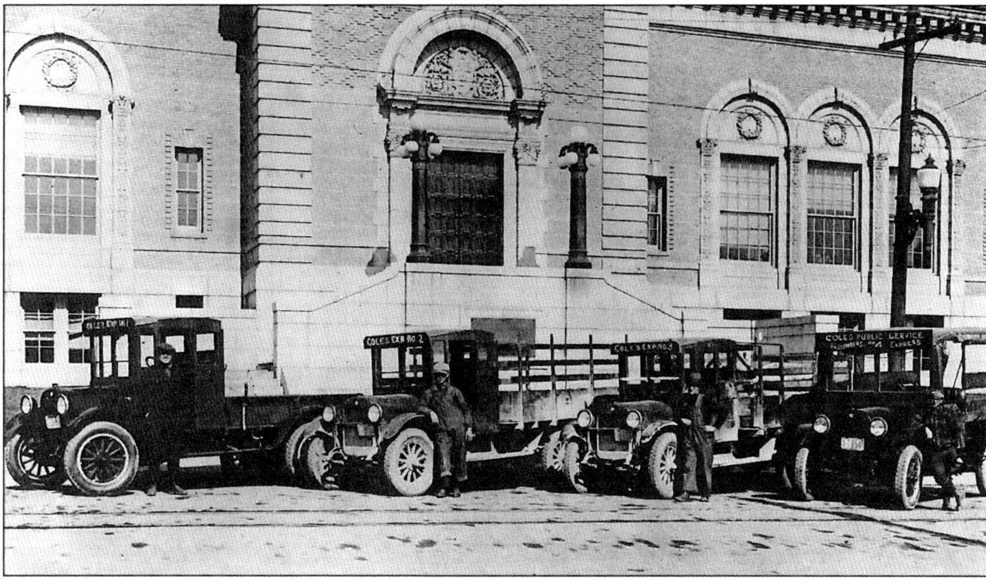

Allie Cole and Mark Ginn (far left, second from right) would become friendly trucking rivals in the years following 1925, when this photograph was taken in front of the Bangor Public Library. Also identified with one of Cole's trucks is Mel Boyd (on the far right).

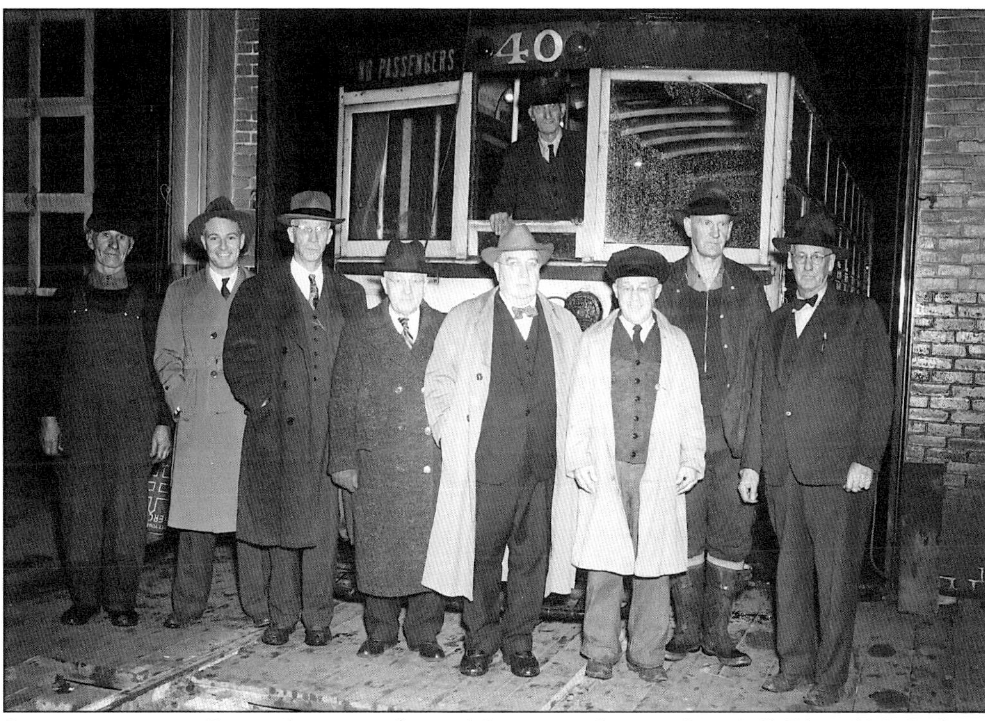

Streetcar service in Bangor became a thing of the past on January 31, 1945. Edward M. Graham, president of the Bangor Hydro-Electric Company, which built the line in 1889, is shown in front of Car 40 after it made one last run around the city. Veteran motorman Thomas Davis is standing inside the trolley.

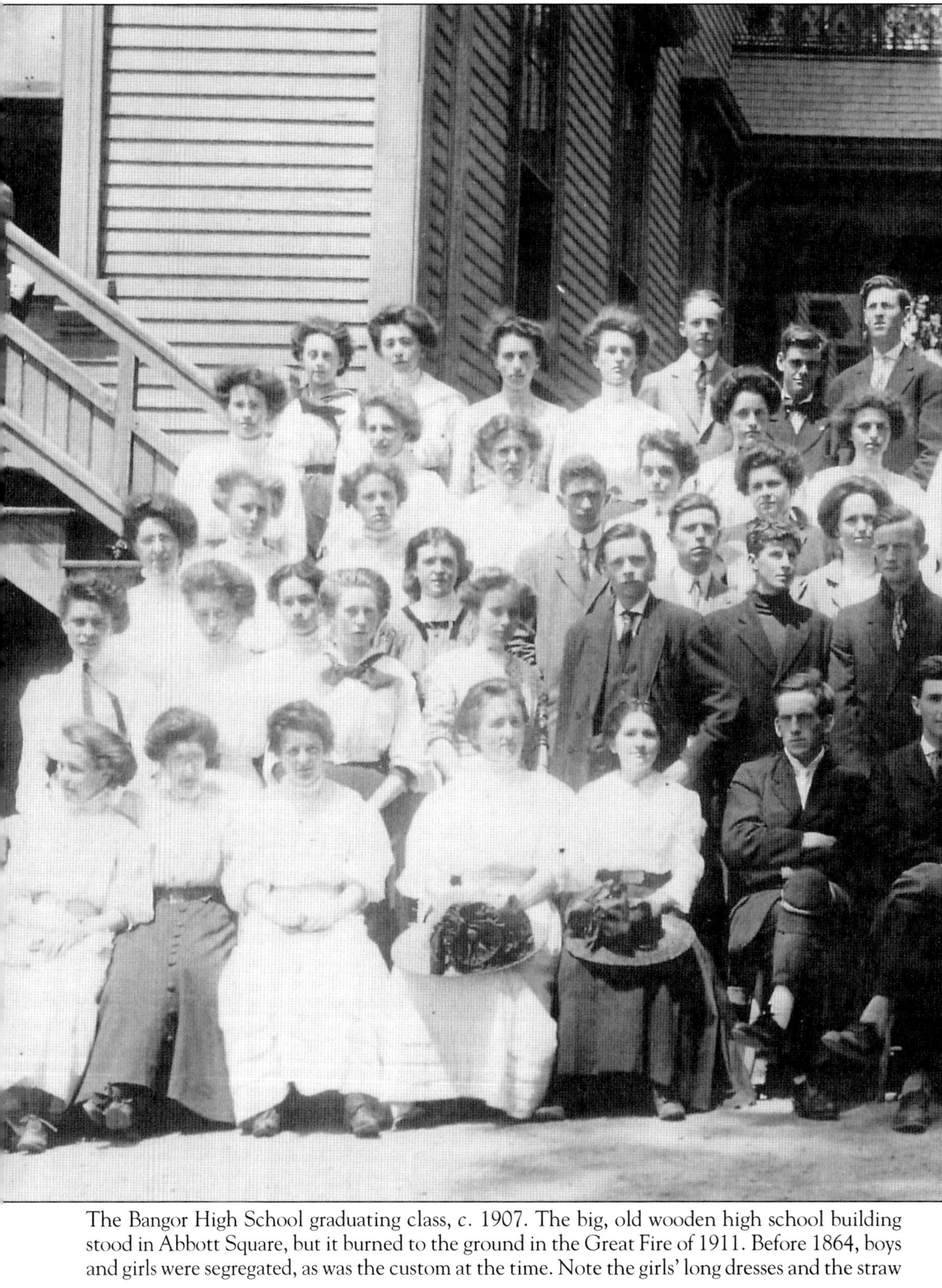

The Bangor High School graduating class, *c.* 1907. The big, old wooden high school building stood in Abbott Square, but it burned to the ground in the Great Fire of 1911. Before 1864, boys and girls were segregated, as was the custom at the time. Note the girls' long dresses and the straw

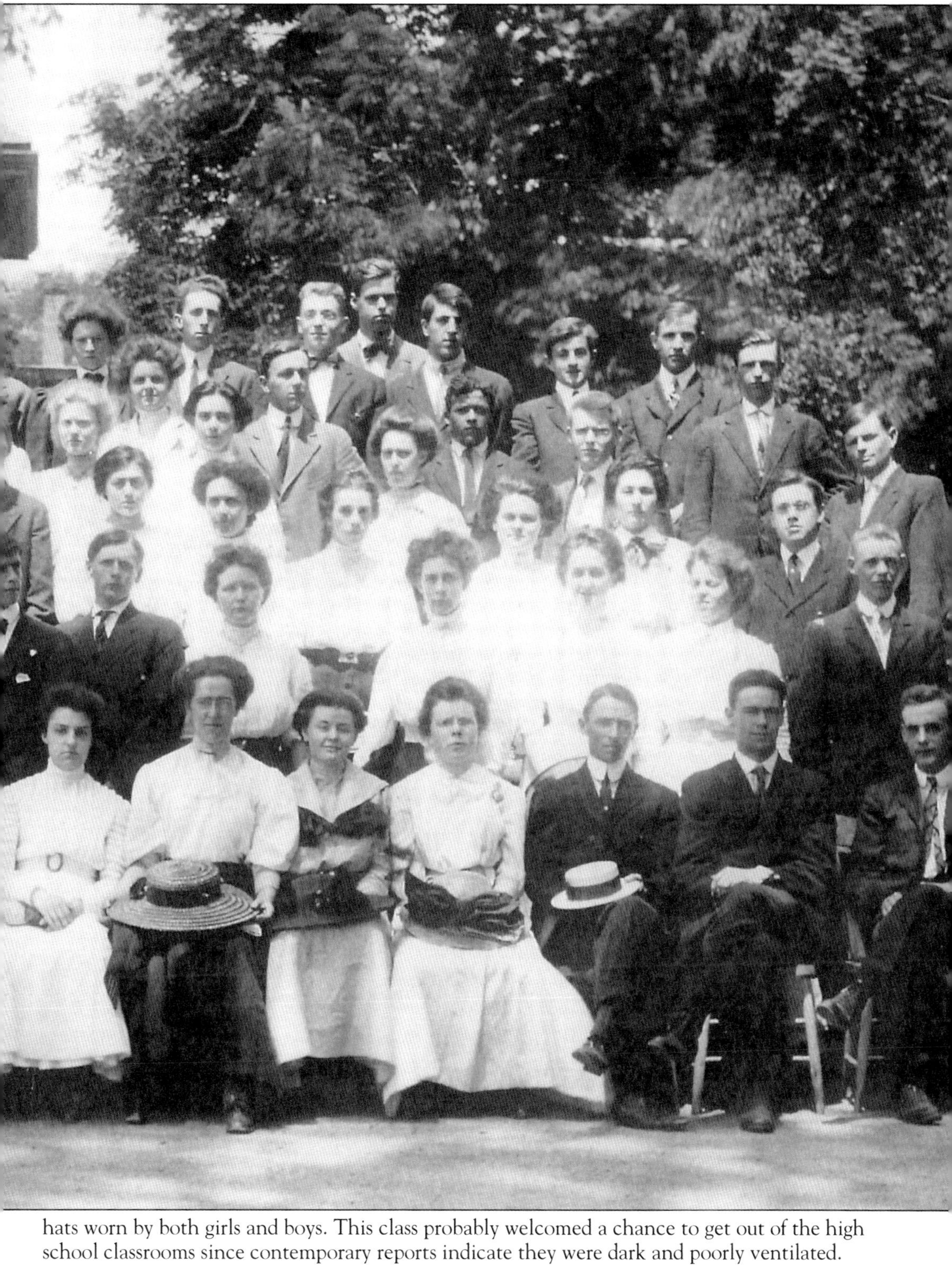

hats worn by both girls and boys. This class probably welcomed a chance to get out of the high school classrooms since contemporary reports indicate they were dark and poorly ventilated.

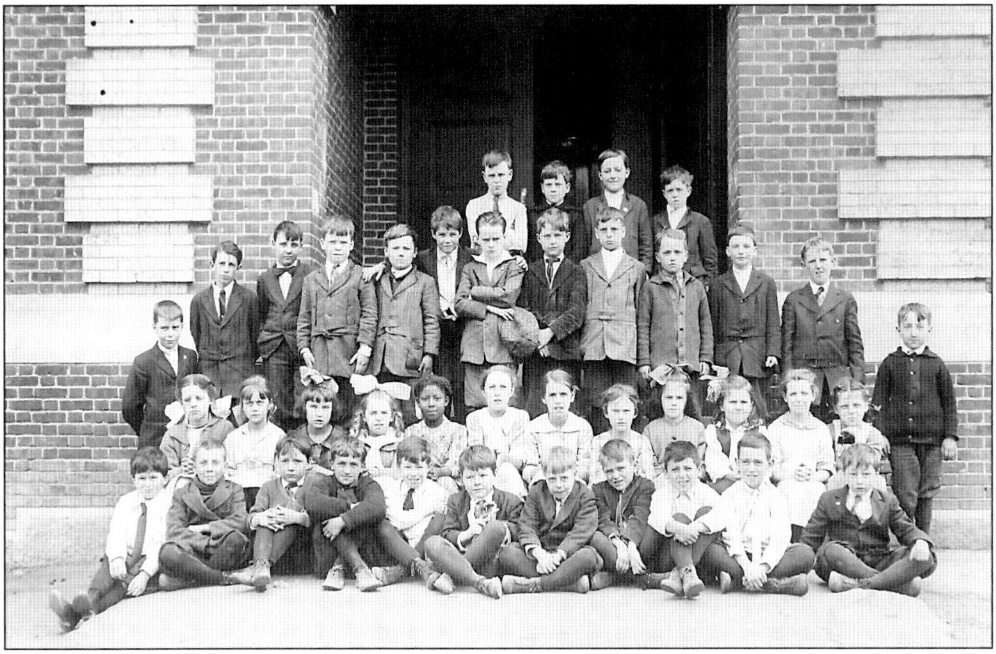

Grannie Nickerson's third grade class poses proudly in front of the Valentine School at Union and First Streets in 1916. No cut-offs and T-shirts for these children; a dress code mandated suits and ties for the boys, and clean, light-colored dresses for the girls.

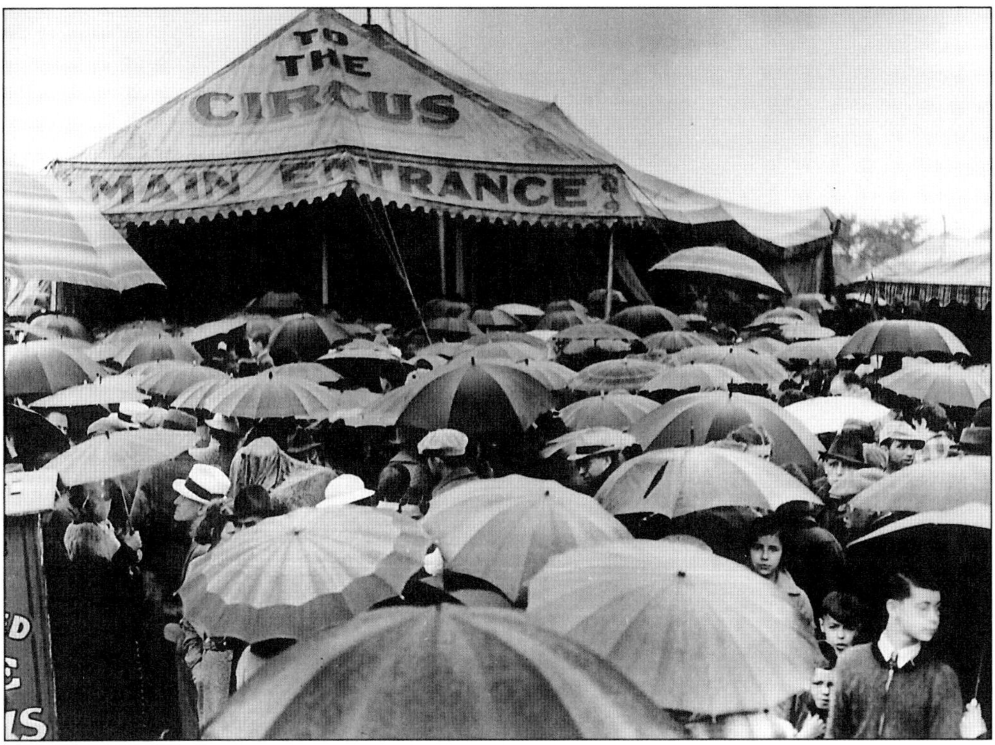

A day at the circus was every child's dream, even if it meant waiting in the rain at the Bangor Fairgrounds.

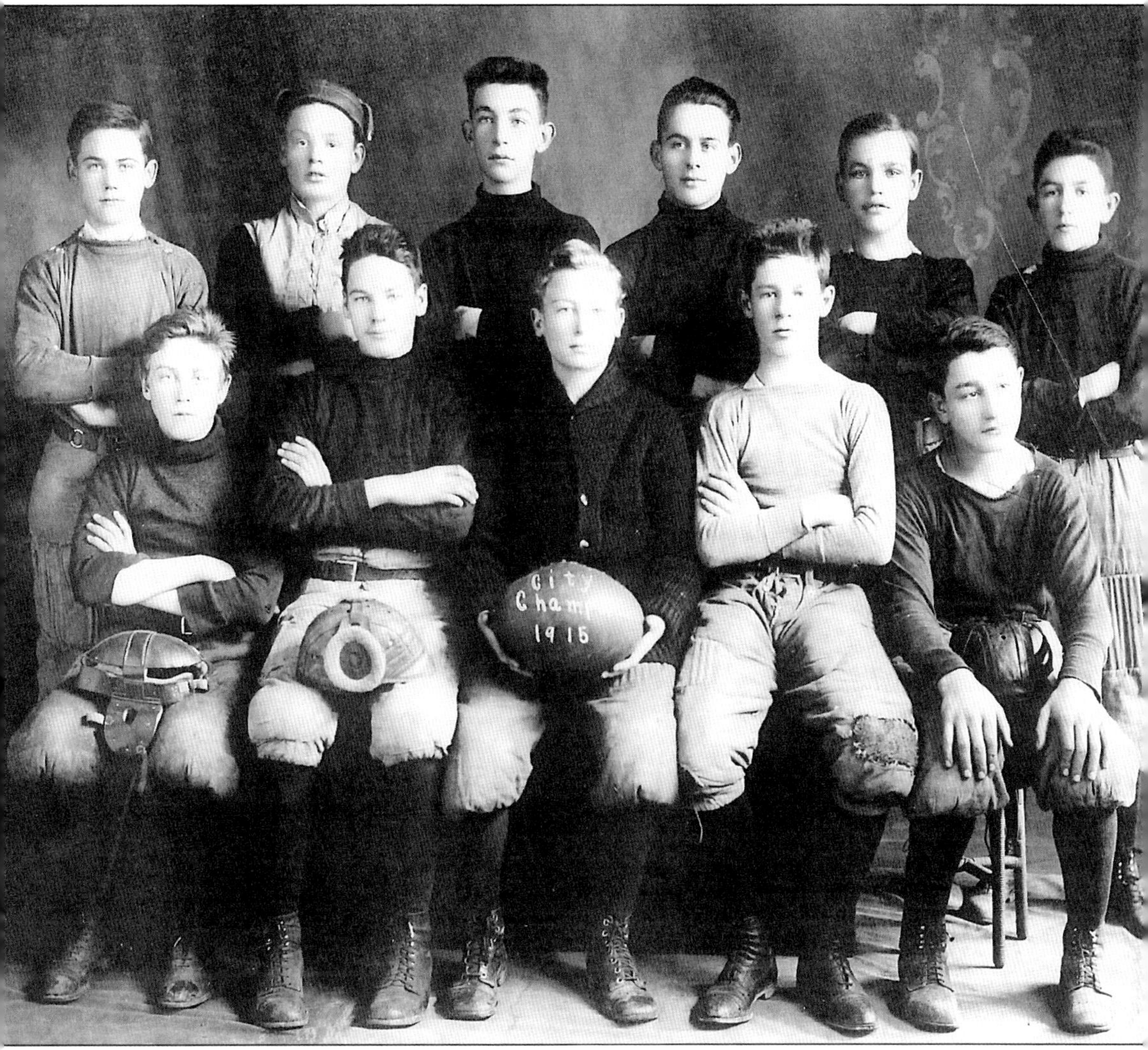

Football became a spectator sport in Bangor in the 1890s. Before that it was purely a street game for young people. By 1915, when these local teenagers became the city champions, football enjoyed a strong following locally. These uniforms, though, would bring howls of laughter at Cameron Stadium, where Bangor's high school games are played today. The shoes alone would be reason enough to throw a player off the field.

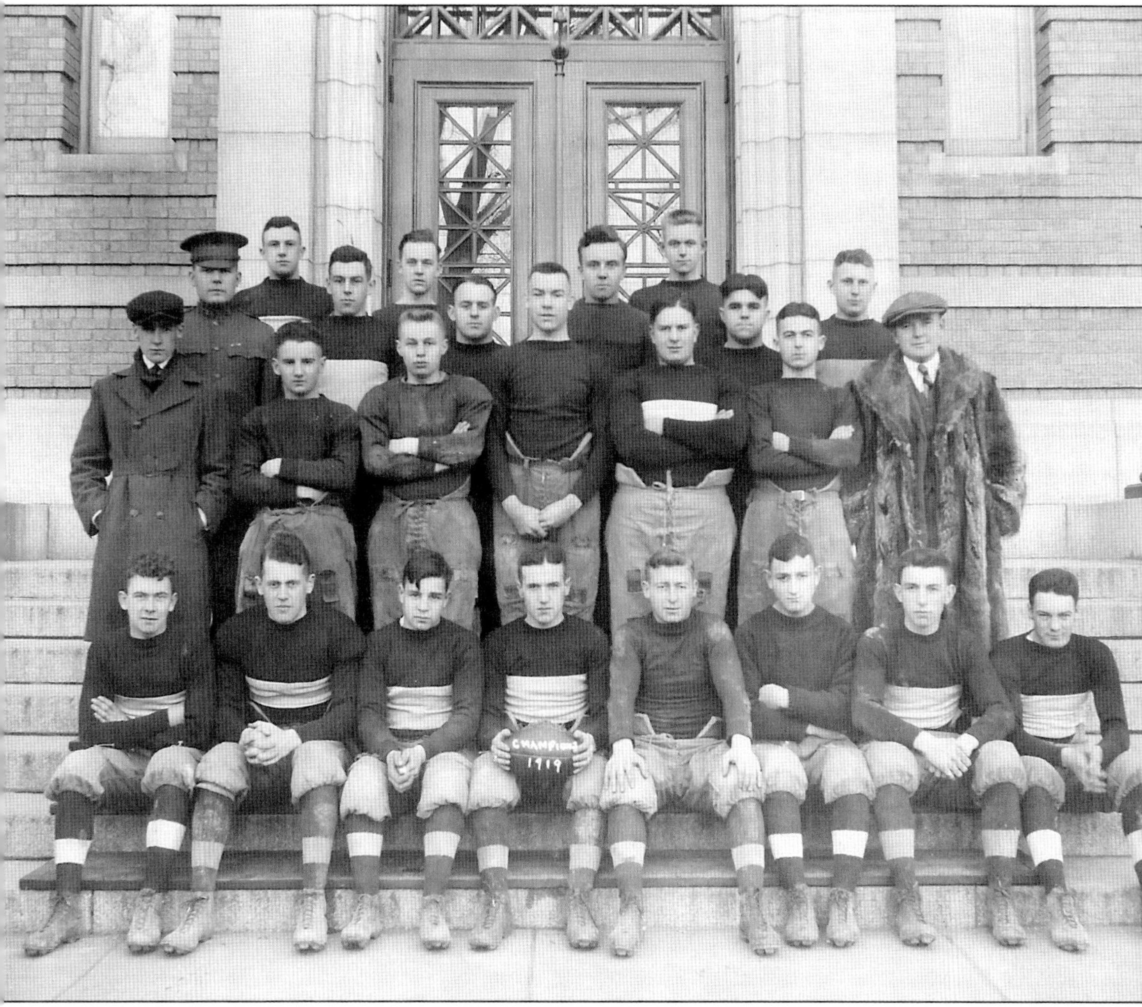

In 1890 football was introduced at Bangor High School. Bangor won state championships consistently partly because players above high school age were allowed to join the team. The school defeated the Maine State College and Bates varsity teams with the older players' help, and later beat college freshman and sophomore teams. This team, shown in 1919 in front of the high school on Harlow Street, were proud champions. Note the World War I-era uniform and the raccoon coat.

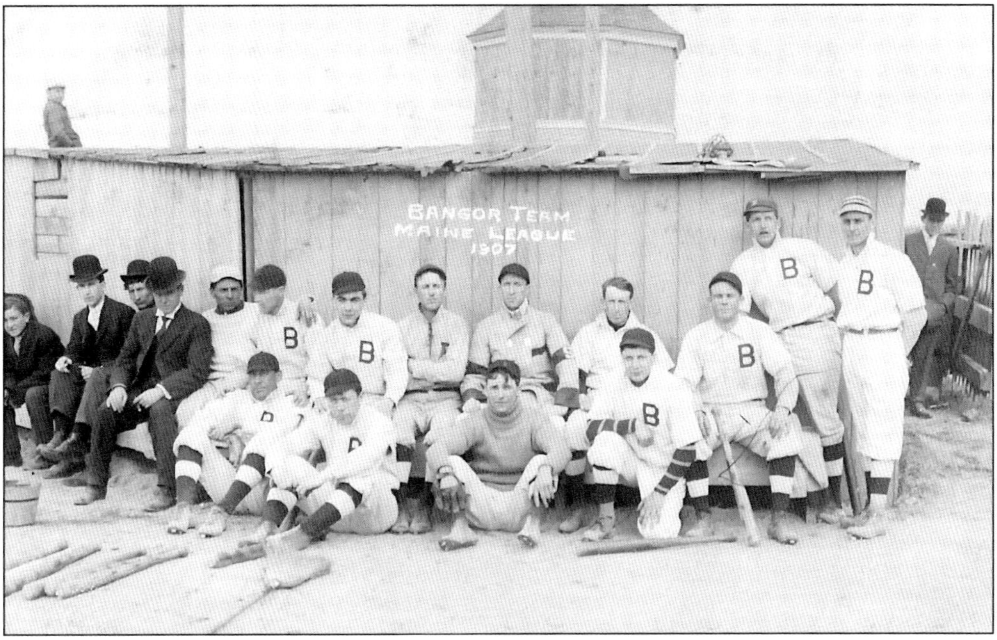

A Bangor baseball team played in the Maine League in 1907. At Maplewood Park they played the Augusta team in new uniforms. For only $.25 ($.35 would buy you a seat in the grandstand), fans could see a Penobscot Indian named Sockalexis play right field.

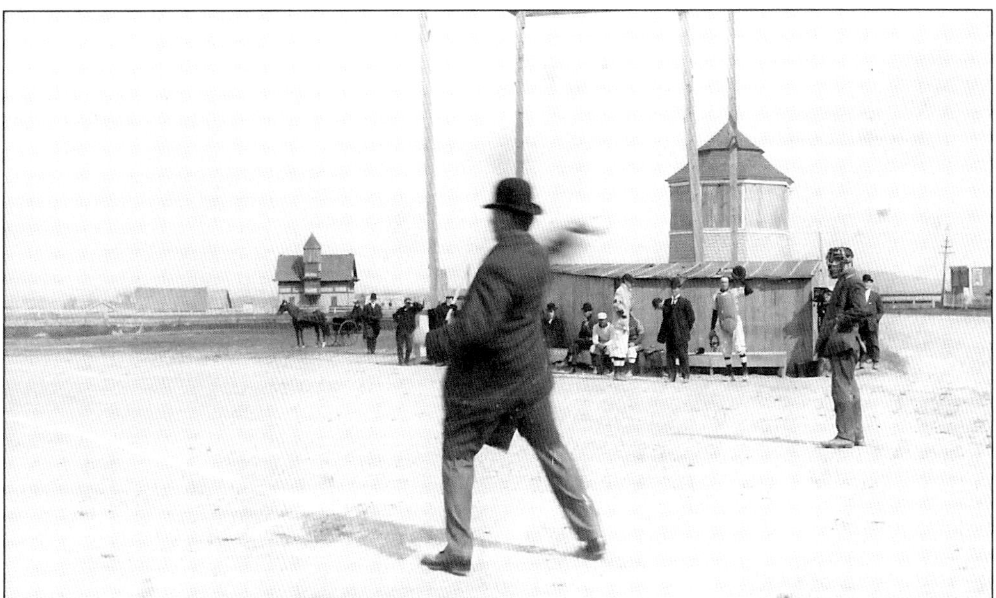

Mayor John F. Woodman throws out the first ball in 1907 at the Maine League game in Bangor. A new scoreboard was a highlight of the season.

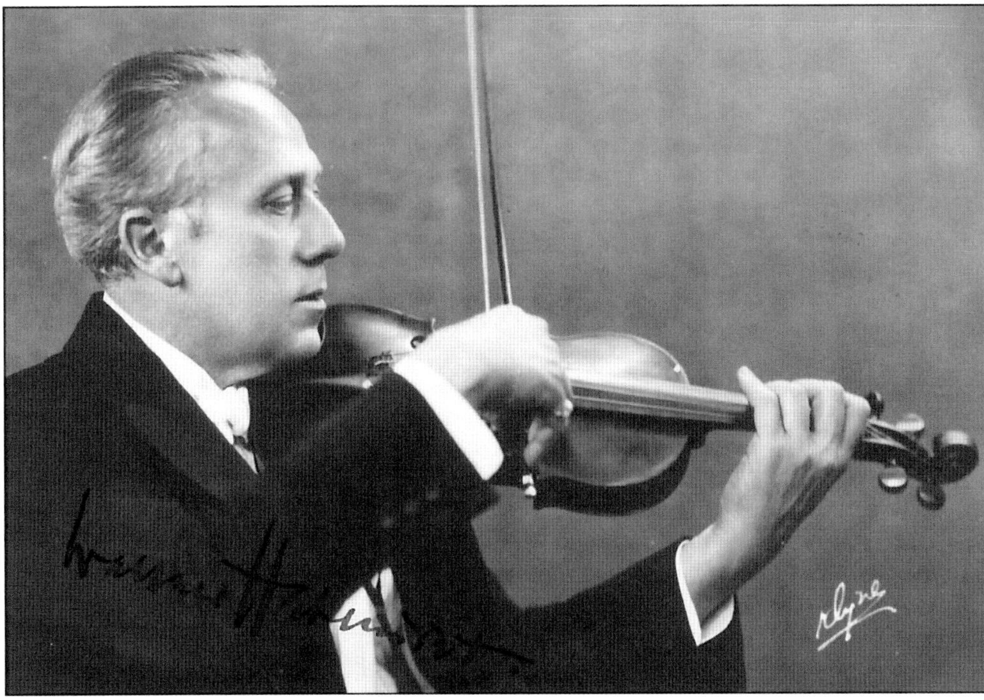

Walter Habenicht was a German native who emigrated to the United States to play in the Boston Symphony. When World War I broke out he was unable to return to Germany, so he moved to Bangor where he lived for many years with his wife, Estelle. He shared his love of the violin at public recitals and gave private lessons.

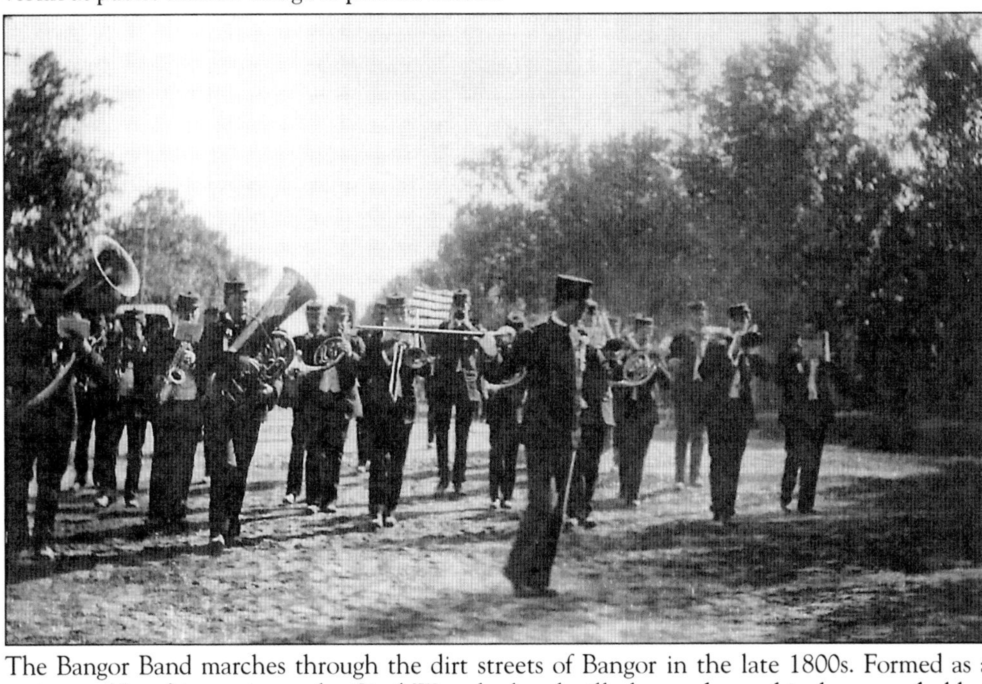

The Bangor Band marches through the dirt streets of Bangor in the late 1800s. Formed as a regimental band just prior to the Civil War, the band still plays today and is the second oldest town band in the nation.

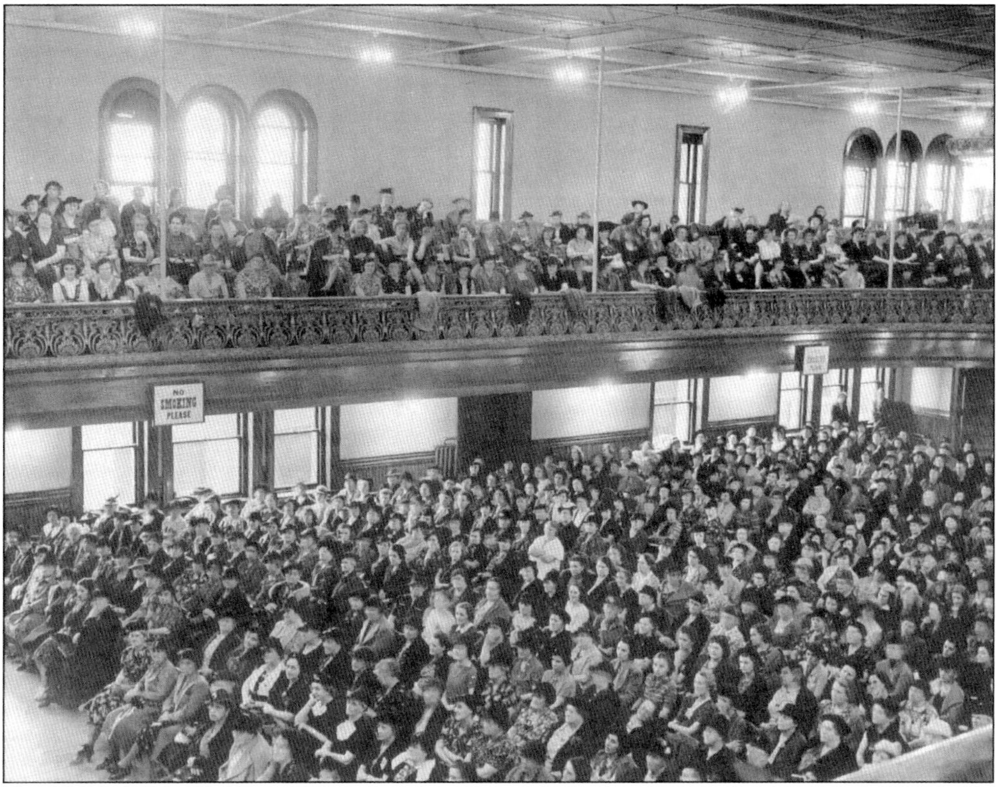

The Bangor City Hall Auditorium was a wonderful place to hear a symphony concert, a political speech or a traveling evangelist. Perhaps this audience is listening to the Trapp Family Singers, who performed at the auditorium in 1941.

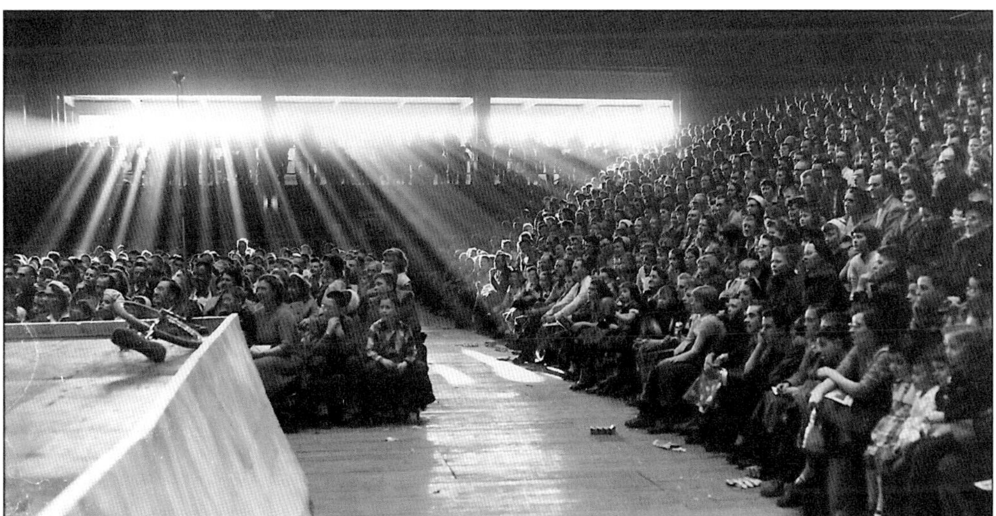

A unicycle near the apron of the stage at the old Bangor Auditorium suggests that a vaudeville show or circus is in town.

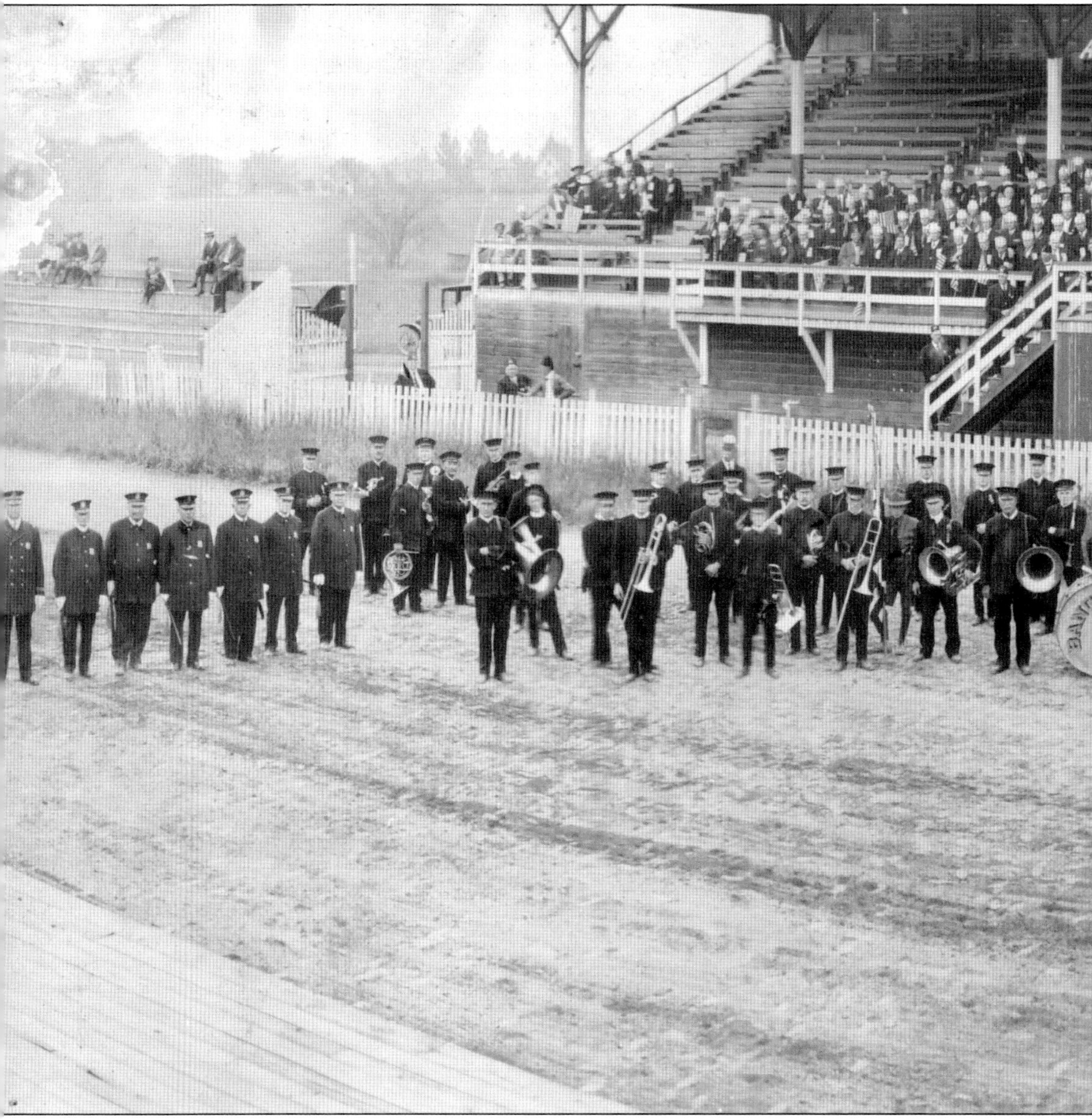

The birth of the Anah Temple shrine at Bass Park on July 21, 1921, was an occasion of brilliant pageantry and mystic rites. The institution of a new temple in Bangor was attended by thousands who came by car, boat and train from as far away as Savannah, Georgia.

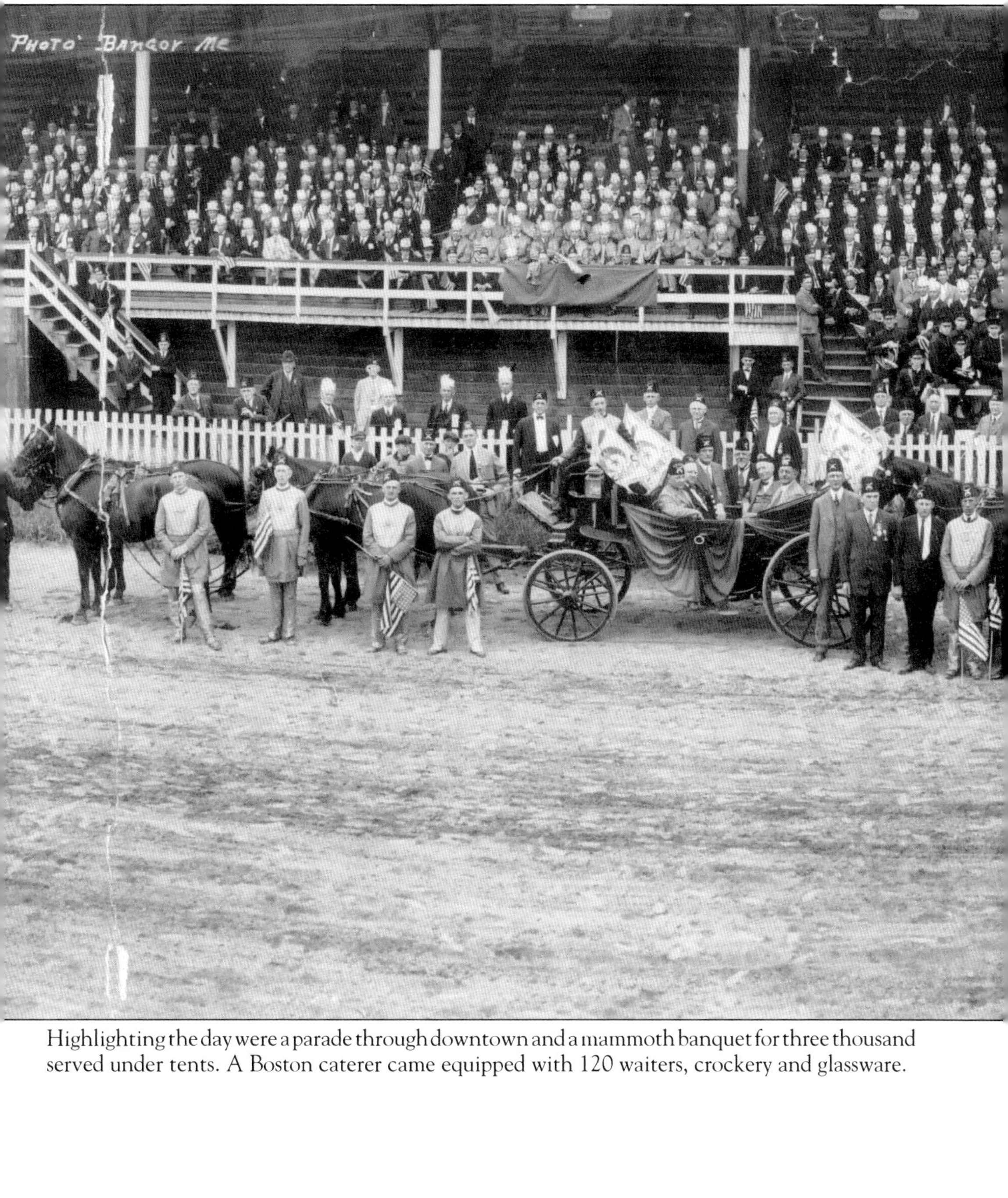

Highlighting the day were a parade through downtown and a mammoth banquet for three thousand served under tents. A Boston caterer came equipped with 120 waiters, crockery and glassware.

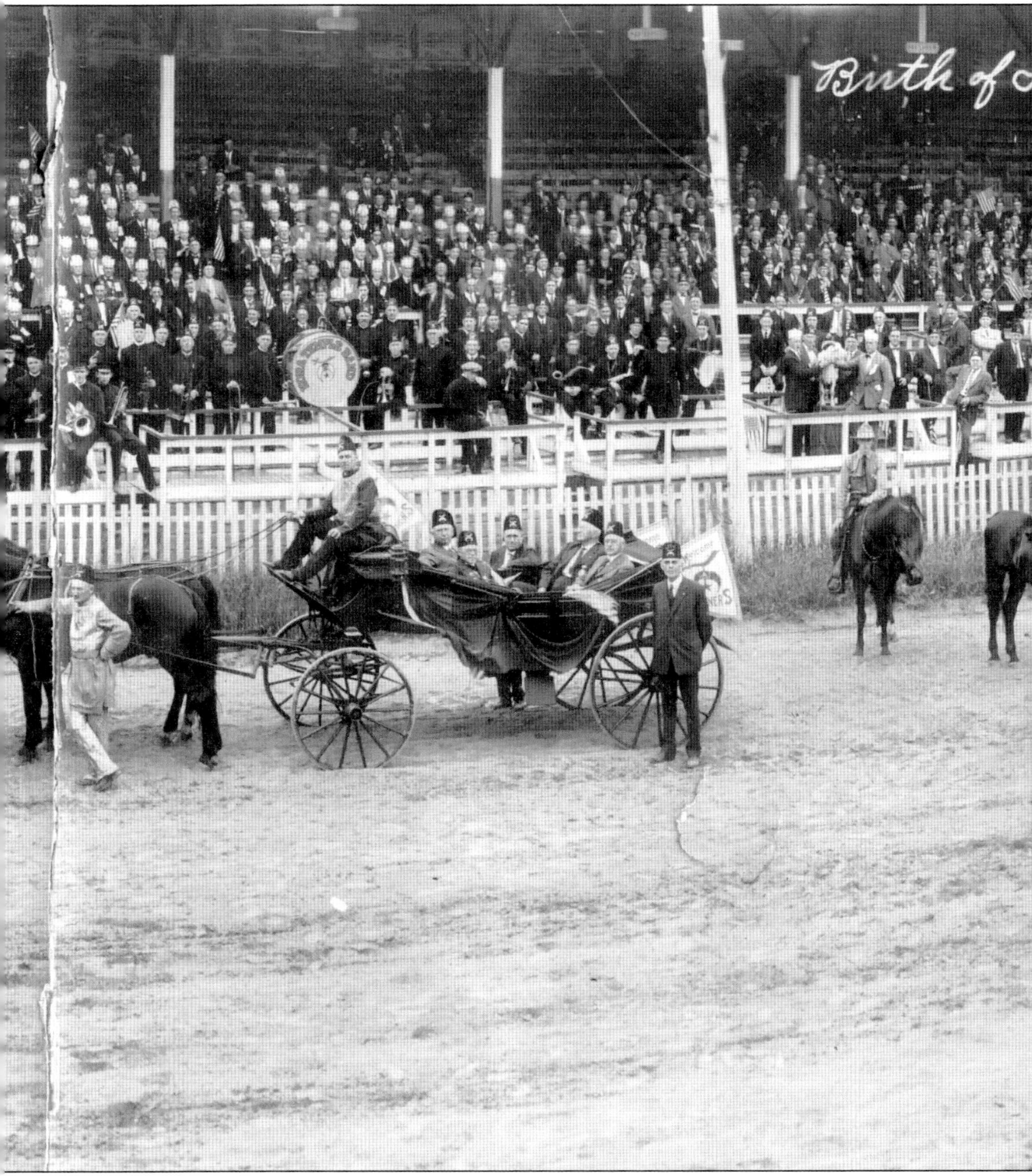

This panoramic photograph, shot by A.F. Orr of Old Town, was taken soon after the Shriners entered the Third Street gate to Bass Park and assembled in the grandstand. Orr rotated his big, heavy camera around several times to take several shots of the crowd.

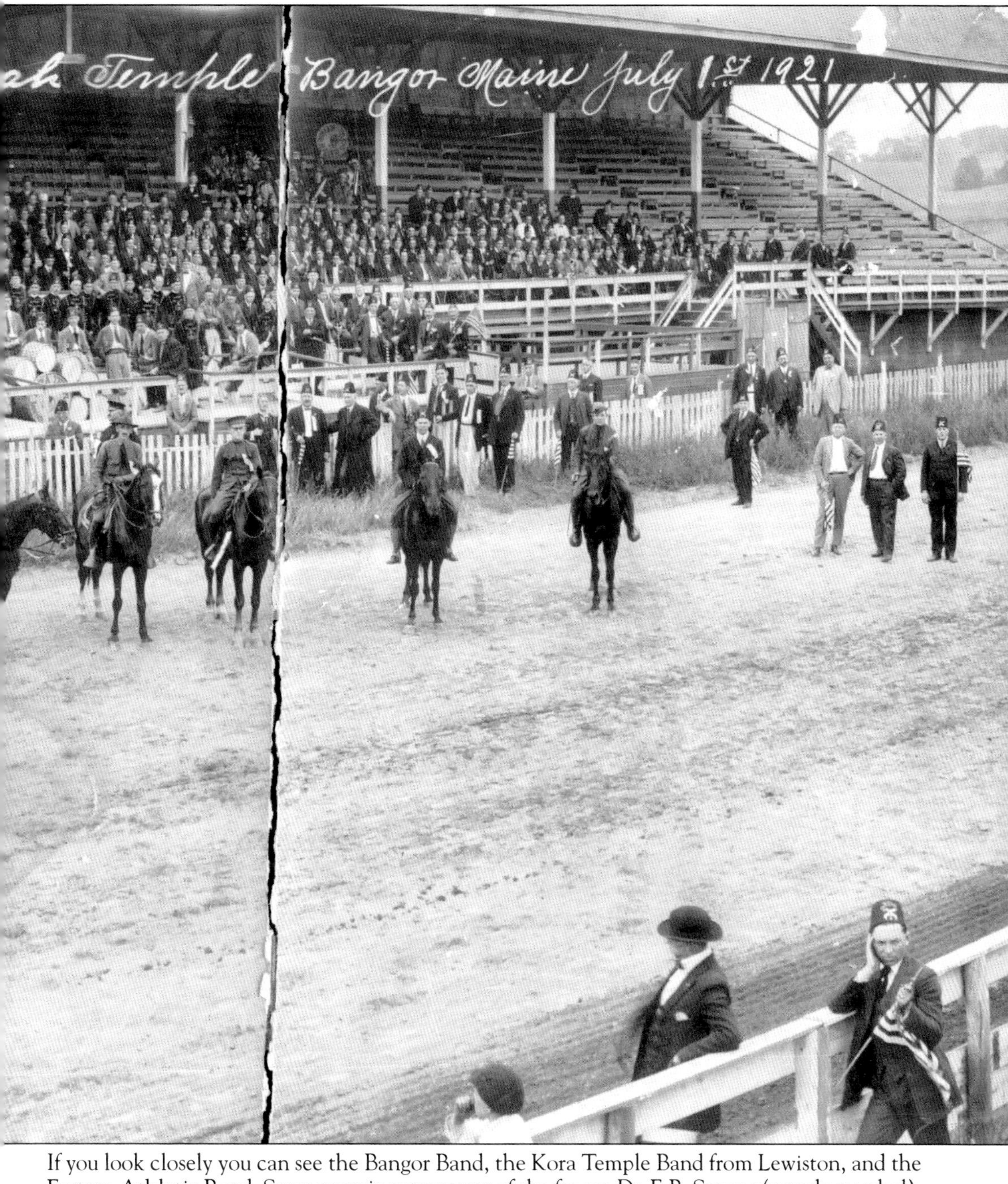

If you look closely you can see the Bangor Band, the Kora Temple Band from Lewiston, and the Eastern Athletic Band. Some prominent wearers of the fez are Dr. E.B. Sanger (parade marshal), Orman B. Fernandez, and Harry Chapman (chairman of the Reception Committee).

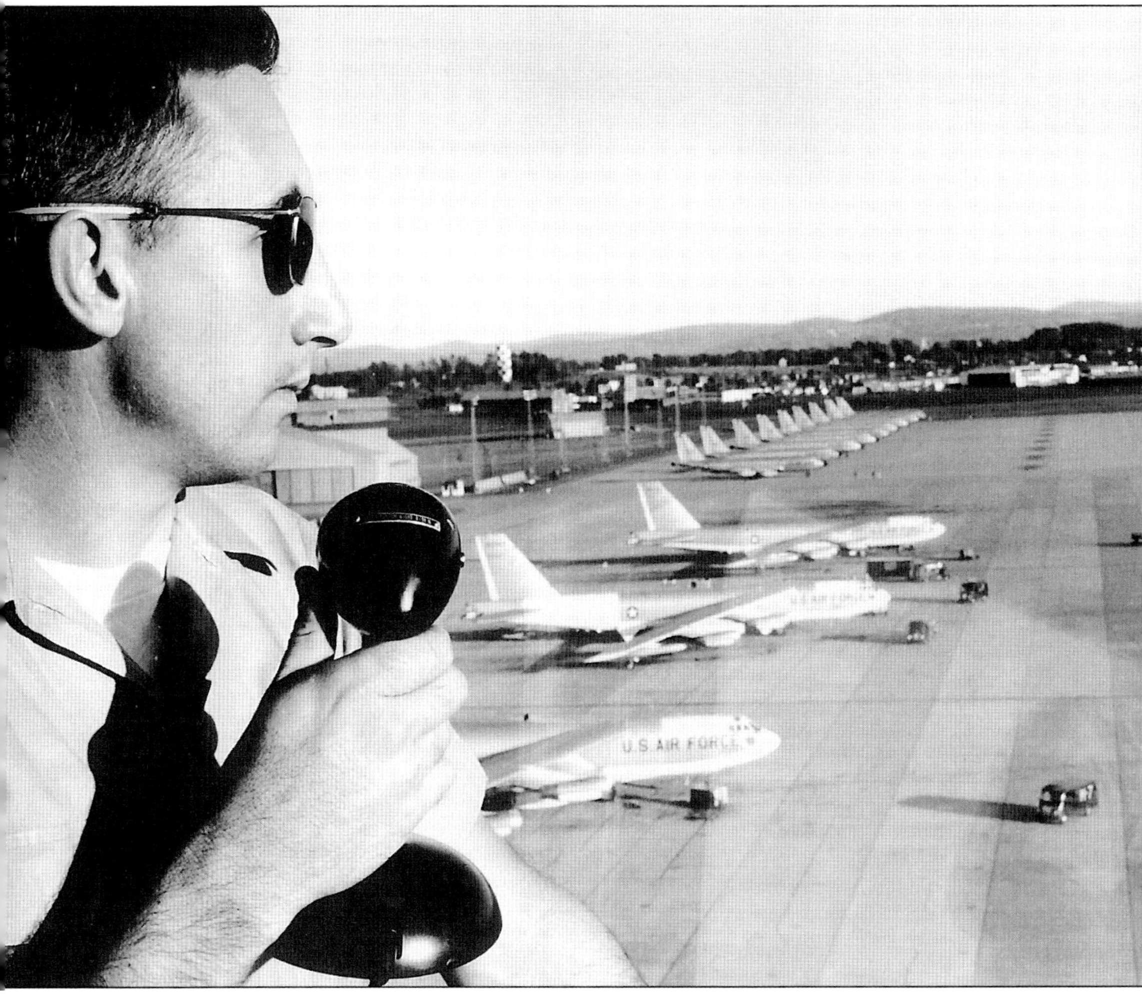

The control tower at Dow Air Force Base affords a fine view of the runway for *Bangor Daily News* photographer Jack Loftus, who snapped this photograph in 1964. The base took over the old Bangor Airfield after the bombing of Pearl Harbor on December 7, 1941. Later its runways were greatly expanded to accommodate the big bombers of the Strategic Air Command. In 1968 the city acquired the base and named it the Bangor International Airport.

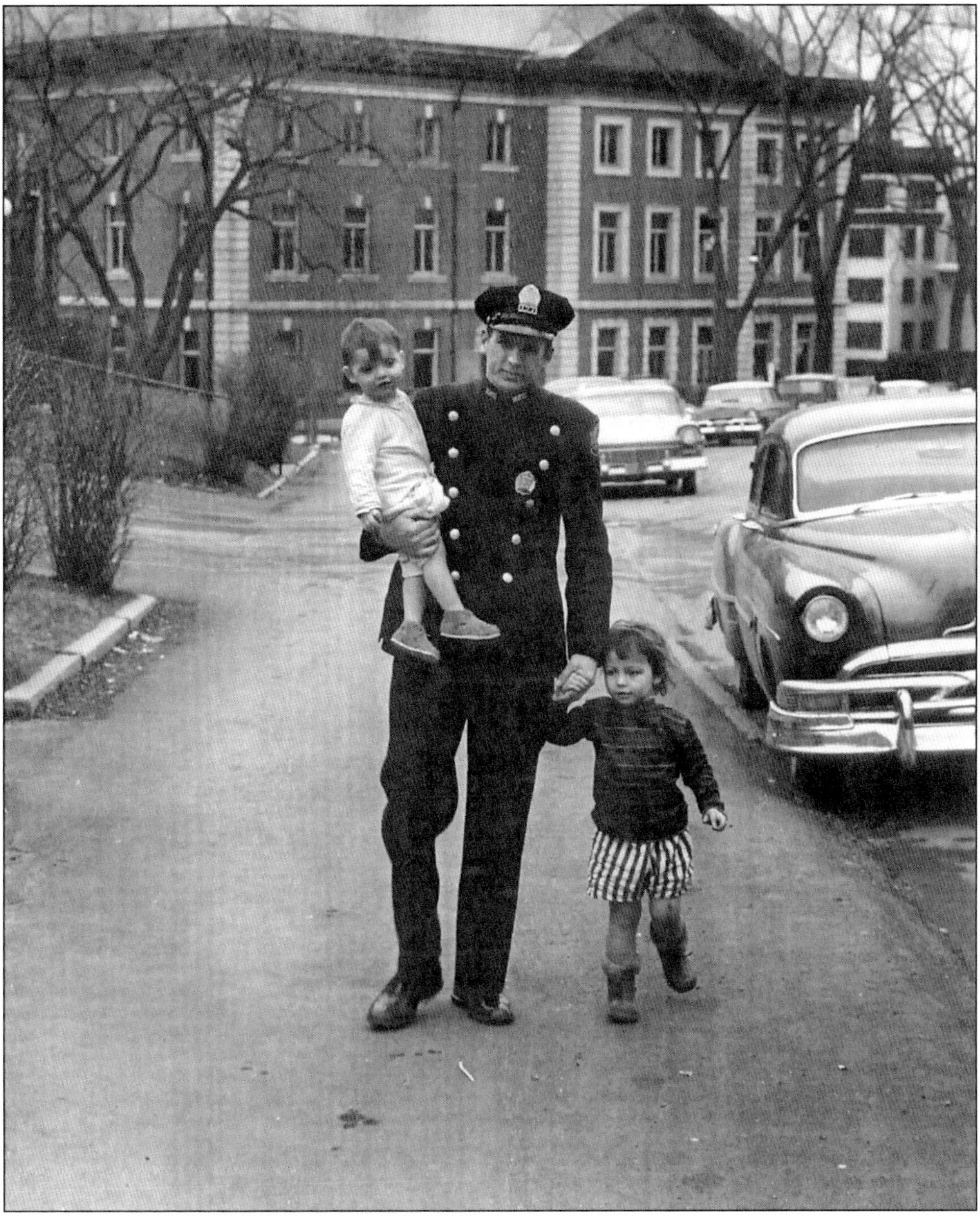

Maurice E. Thurston was a well-liked member of the Bangor Police Department. This typical scene shows him with the children he loved near the police station on Court Street, c. 1960. Patrolman Thurston, a graduate of Old Town High School, joined the police force in 1956.

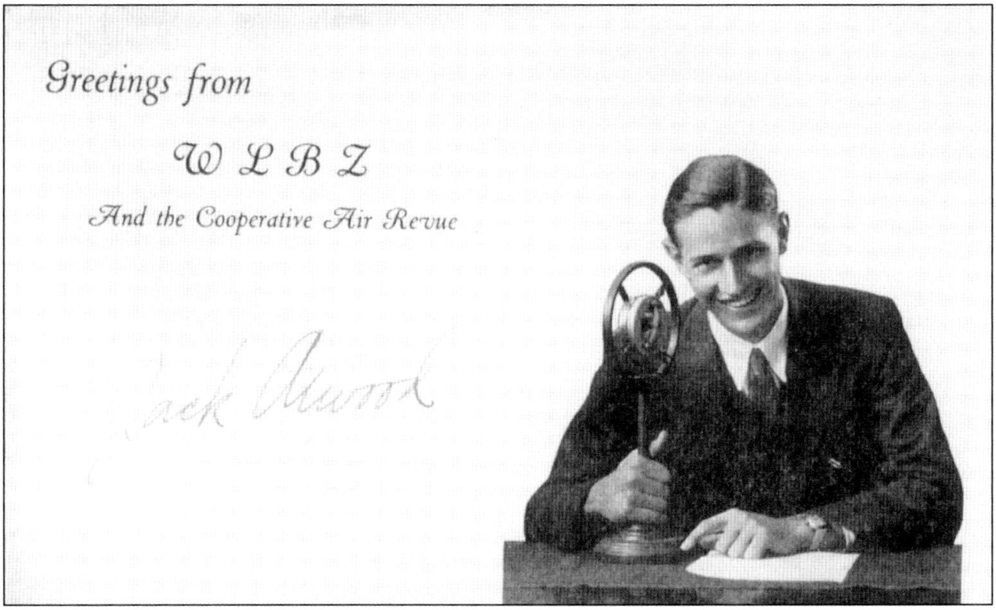

Jack Atwood was a pioneer in broadcasting. This autographed card promotes the "Cooperative Air Revue," a radio program featuring dance hits, favorite melodies and requested songs.

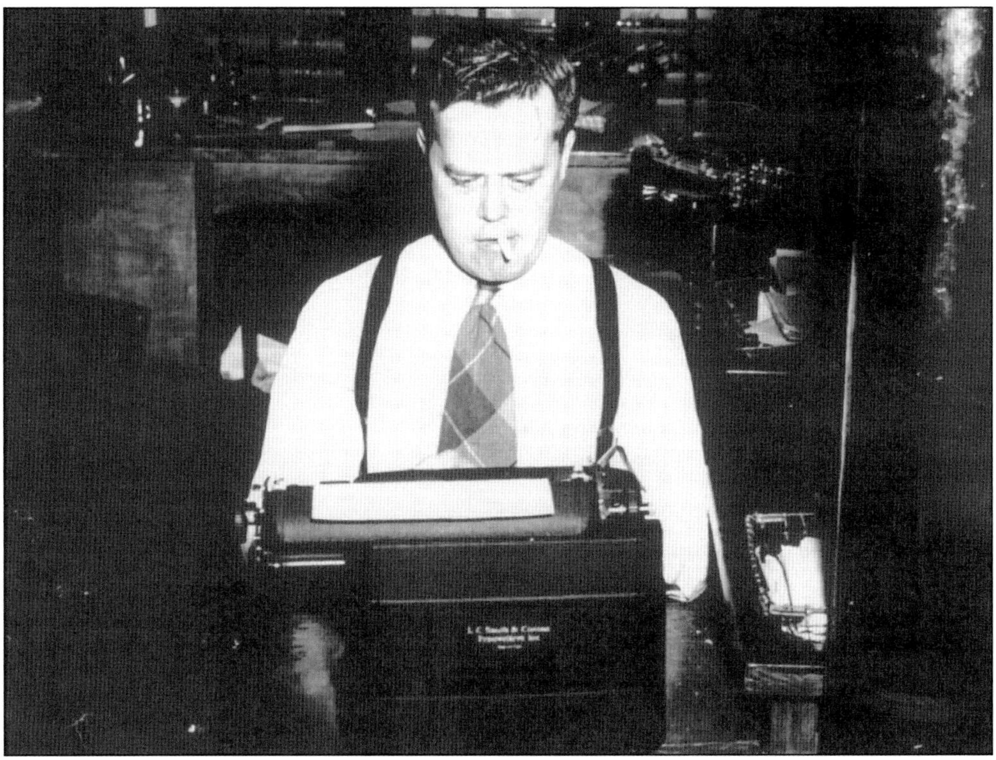
Wayne St. Germain was a brilliant police and court reporter who beat the competition time and again. His greatest scoop came in 1939, when he and photographer Eddie Baker walked miles into the woods to photograph and interview Donn Fendler, a twelve-year-old Boy Scout who was lost and believed dead near Baxter State Park.

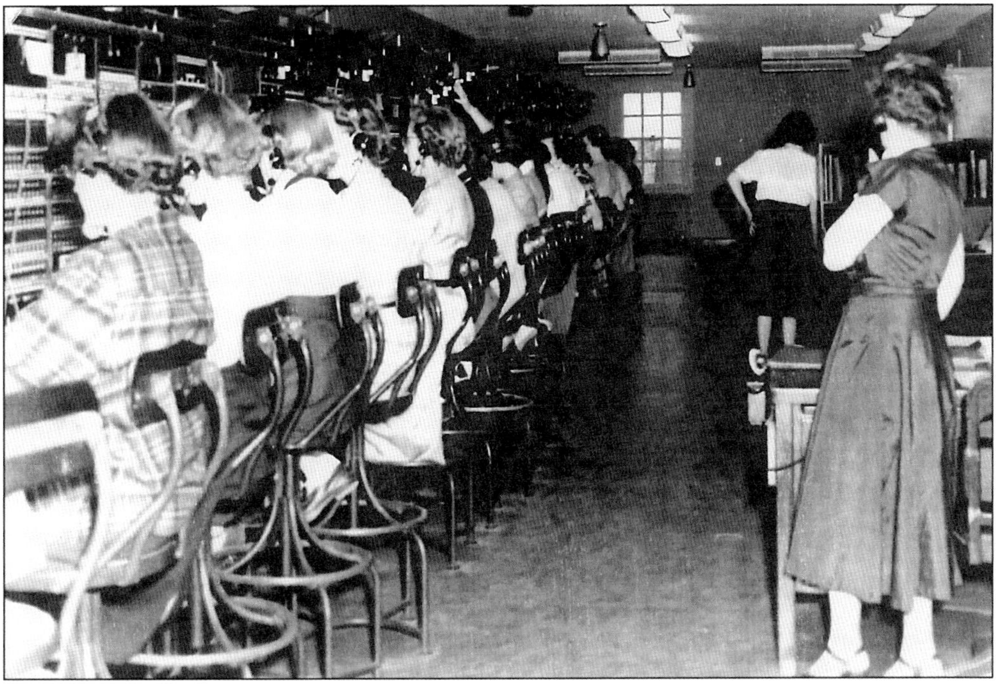

The old switchboard of the Bangor Telephone Exchange, *c*. 1940. When dial telephones were introduced in 1931, newspapers published Bell Telephone Company instructions, as many people needed assistance in their use.

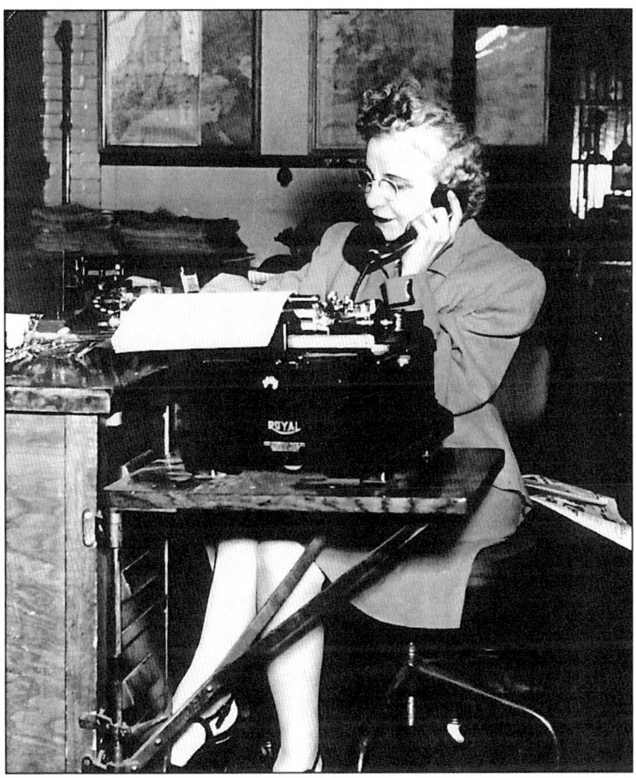

Nelle Penley was a veteran *Bangor Daily News* society editor who held her own in a newsroom full of male reporters and editors. She interviewed Franklin D. Roosevelt during a surprise visit to Campobello, and also spoke with Amelia Earhart and John F. Kennedy in Bangor.

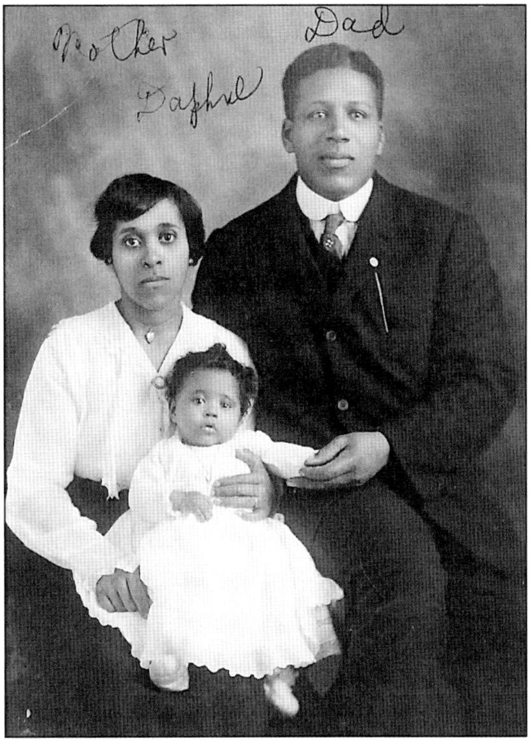

Arthur Wallace Leek and his wife, Mary Tephy, proudly hold baby Daphne for a family portrait, *c.* 1918. Arthur, a laborer for the city, worked hard to provide for Daphne and his other children.

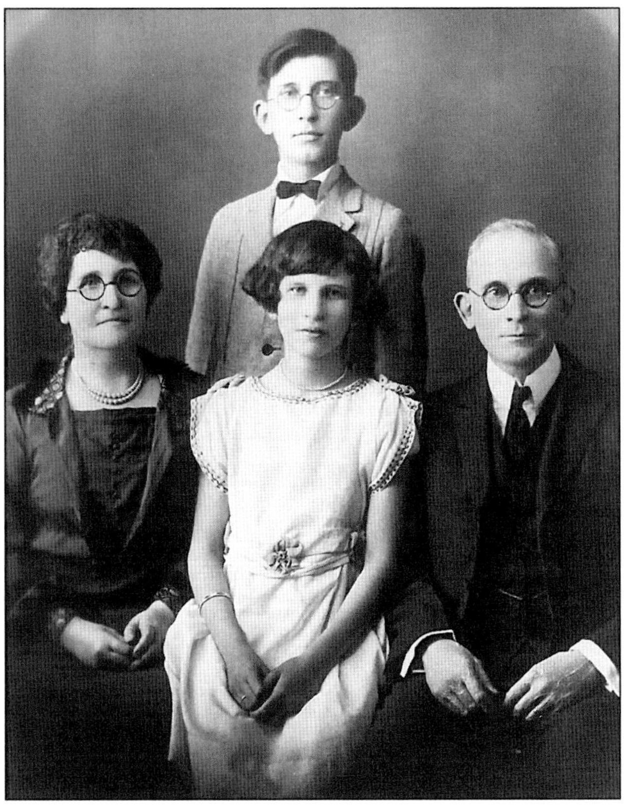

The Duran family, *c.* 1926. Zopher and Hattie Duran lived at 94 Congress Street with their two children, Frances and Eugene. Zopher was a bookkeeper for an insurance company; Frances played the violin in the school orchestra, and Eugene played the cornet in the school band.

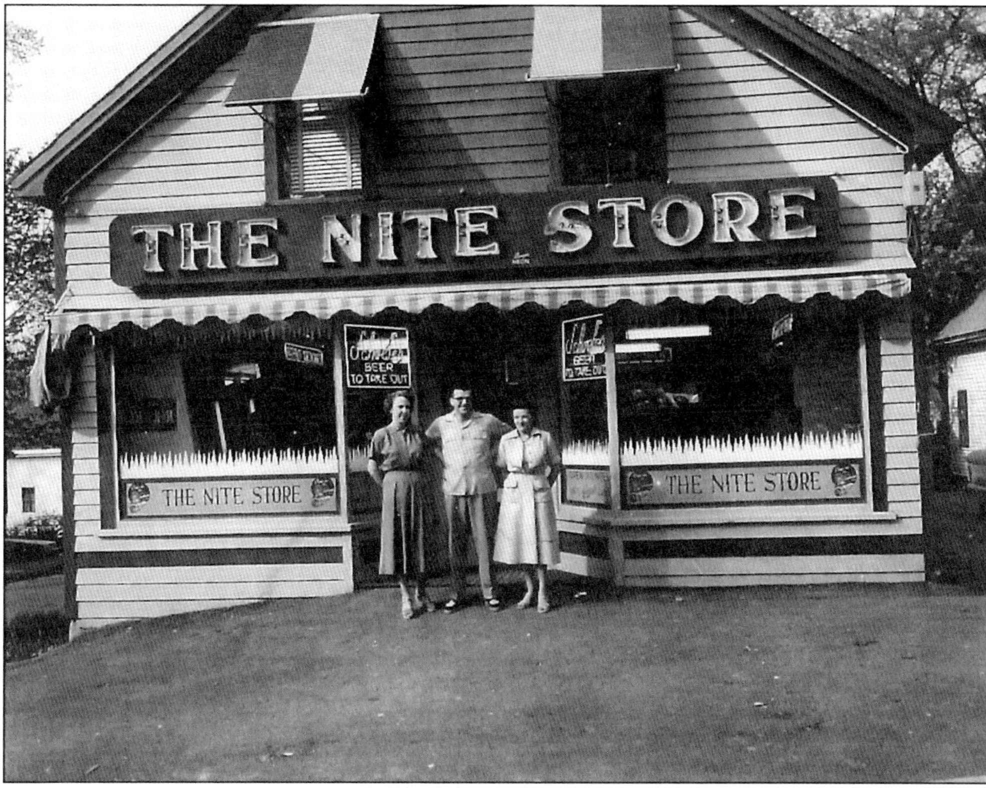

The long, lighted sign of The Nite Store was a landmark at 313 Ohio Street after Patrick Parent (seen here with his wife, Edith, and a family member) bought the business *c.* 1949. Before that the little store with the big inventory was operated by Arthur Lambert and the Cloverdale and First National chains. The Parents sold the market to Stanley Cameron in the 1950s, who ran it for many years. Although no longer owned by the Cameron family, it still goes by the name of Cameron's Market. Many corner markets closed after major supermarkets lured customers with more variety, cheaper prices and Sunday sales.

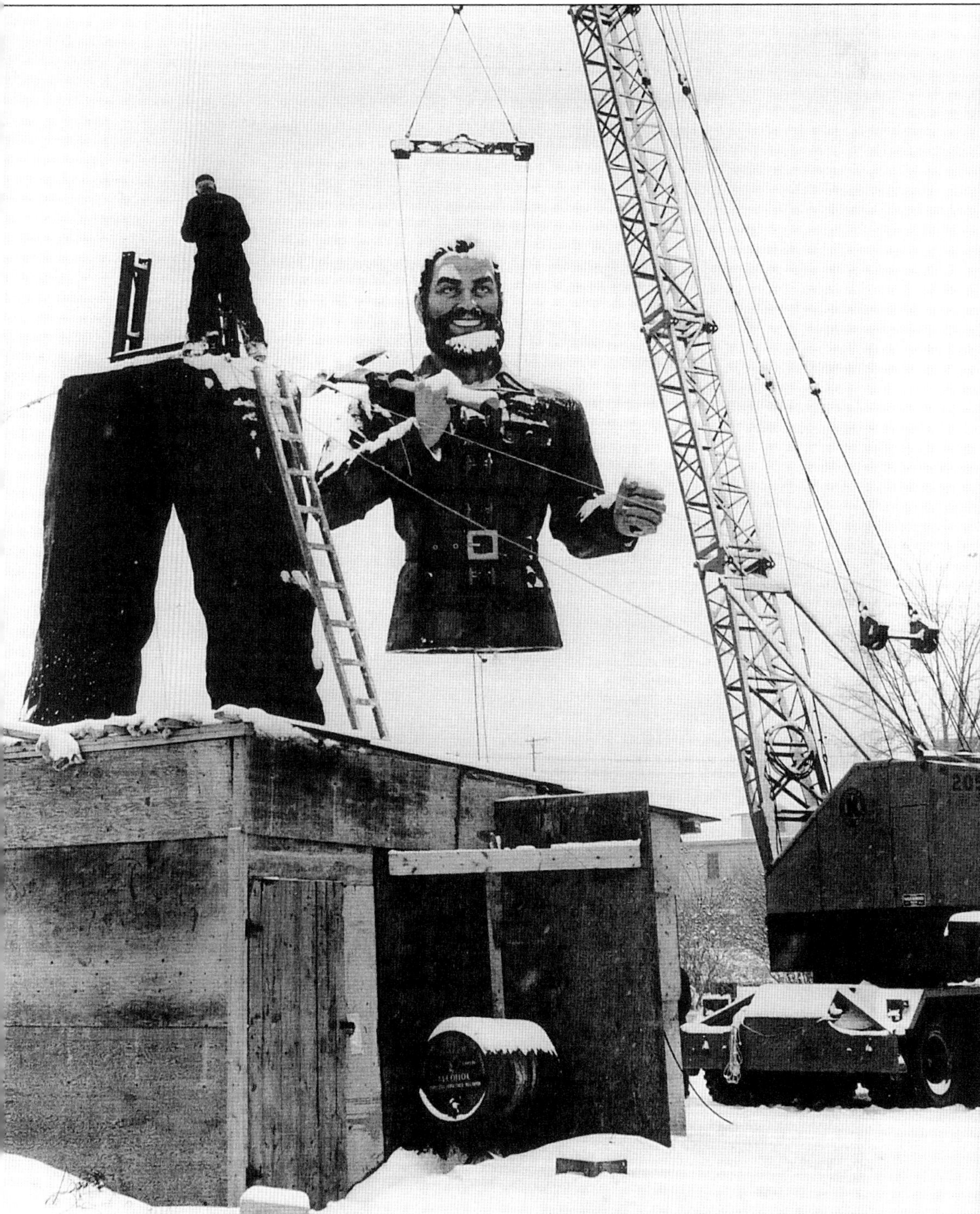

Paul Bunyan's upper torso was hoisted into place at Bass Park in 1959. Normand Martin, a Bangor commercial artist, designed the 37-foot-high statue of the mythical lumberjack as a publicity gimmick for the city's 125th birthday. The statue consists of wooden frames and wire covered with fiberglass.

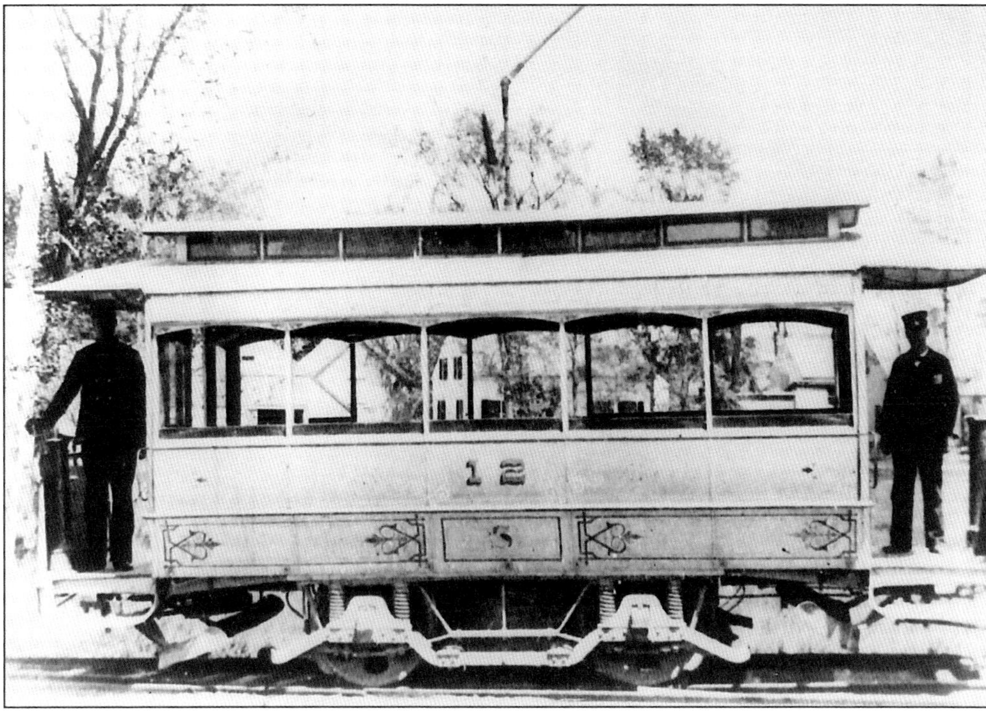

Two conductors add balance to Bangor Street Railway Car No. 12. This was the first electric trolley car in Maine.

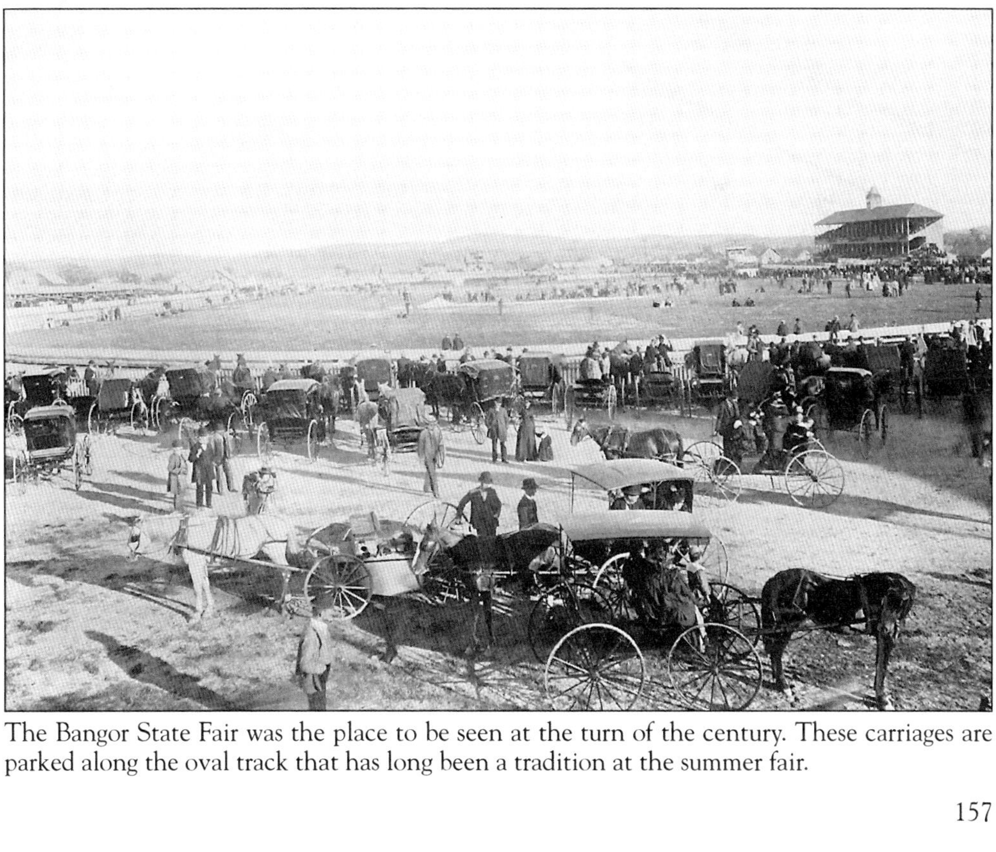

The Bangor State Fair was the place to be seen at the turn of the century. These carriages are parked along the oval track that has long been a tradition at the summer fair.

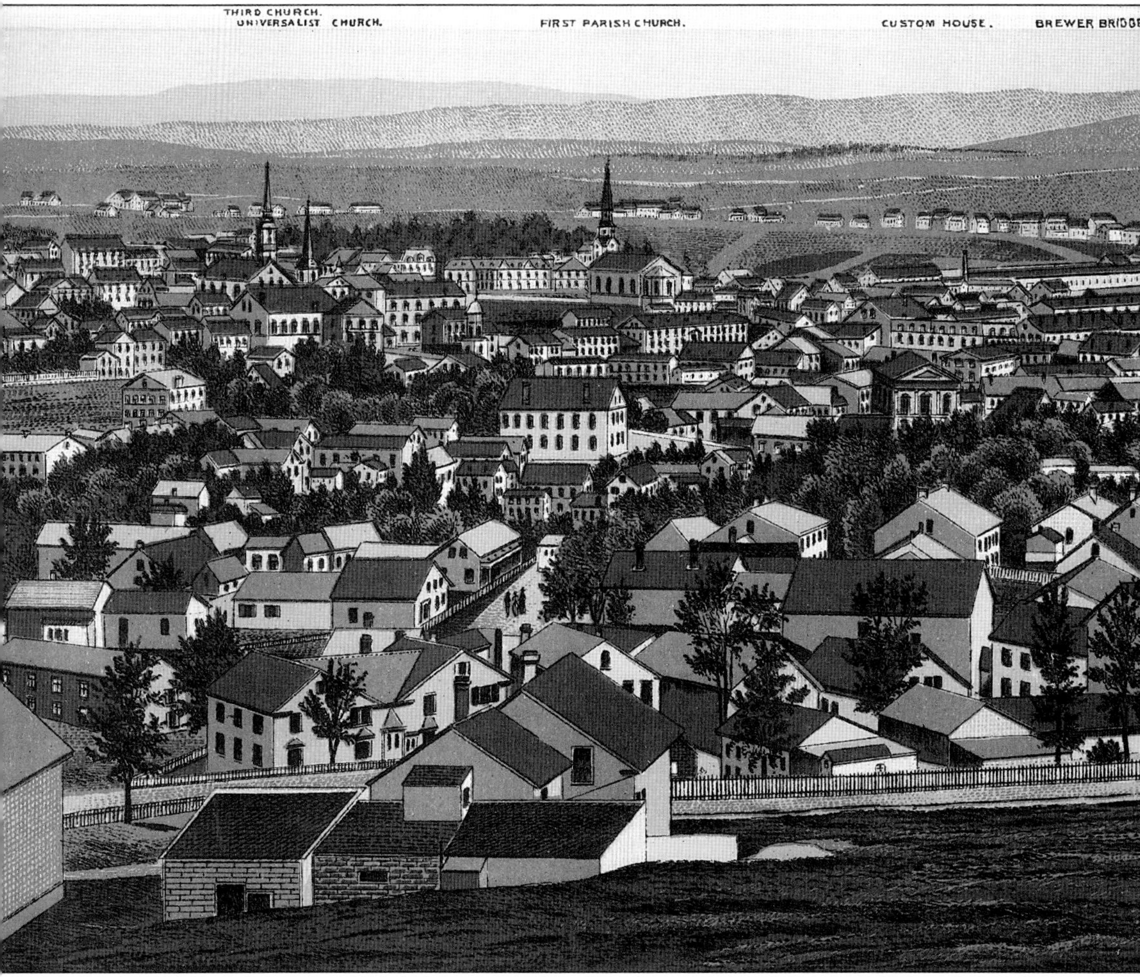

Bangor was a city of tidy white houses, brick homes and church spires in this 1890s panorama sketched from Thomas Hill. Much of the property in the distance was destroyed in the Great Fire of 1911, but some of the buildings in the foreground remain to this day.

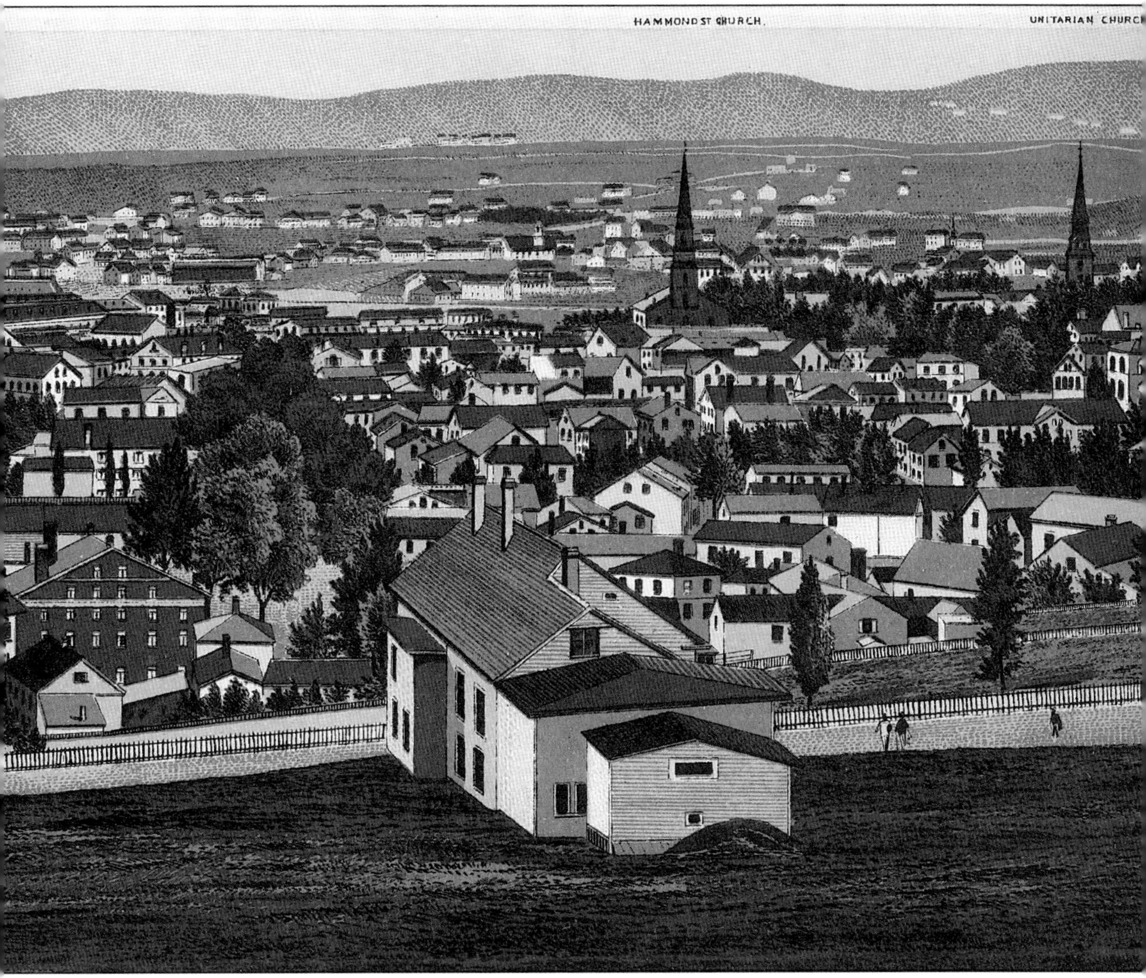

No other city in America looks quite like Bangor, situated in a natural basin surrounded by lovely mountains and bordered by a river and a stream.

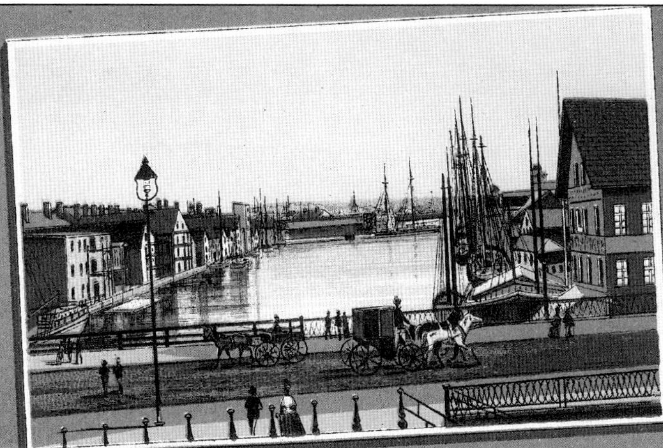

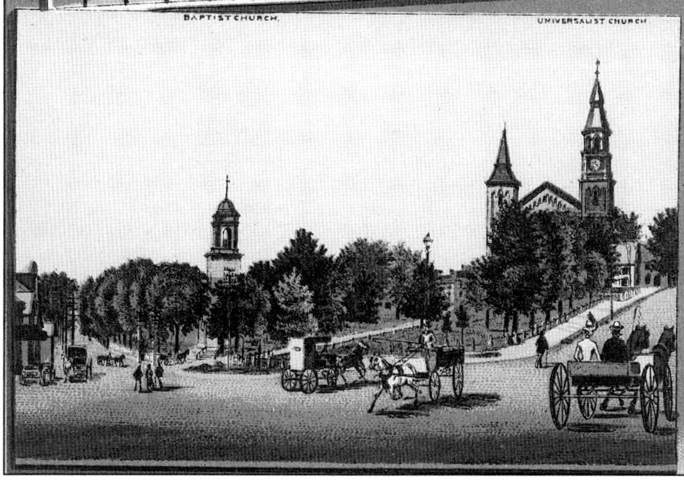

Acknowledgments

This book would not have been possible without the kindness of the following people: Richard J. Warren, editor and publisher of the *Bangor Daily News*, graciously allowed me to examine the Dan Maher collection; James B. Vickery loaned many photographs from his magnificent collection and patiently answered my questions; Blanche Martin turned over her impressive postcard albums and helped write interesting captions; Patricia and Carroll Pickard allowed the use of fine old postcards and photographs; Ki Ayoob loaned old newspaper glossies and named people and dates; and Charles Campo and Jill Marston of the News Library printed up photographs under deadline. Thanks also to: Bud Leavitt, Edward Gross, Sonny Miller, Ken Buckley, Mary Danby, Evarts Leighton, Estelle Habenicht, Earle Shettleworth (Maine Historic Preservation Commission), Lowell Kjenstad (Cole Land Transportation Museum), Pam McTigue (Bangor Historical Society), the Federal Bureau of Investigation, Mary Duran, the reference staff of the Bangor Public Library, and the technicians of Northeast Reprographics. Important references were Vickery's *Illustrated History of Bangor*, three volumes of *Godfrey Journals*, *Woodsmen and Whigs*, edited by Abigail Zelz and Marilyn Zoidis, and Deborah Thompson's *Architectural History of Bangor*.